DEVIANT REALITY
Alternative World Views

Second Edition

Jeremiah Lowney
Spring Hill College

Robert W. Winslow
San Diego State University

Virginia Winslow

ALLYN AND BACON, INC.
Boston · London · Sydney · Toronto

To All Our Students

Library of Congress Cataloging in Publication Data

Lowney, Jeremiah, 1939–
 Deviant reality.

 First ed. by R. W. Winslow and V. Winslow.
 Includes bibliographies.
 1. Deviant behavior. 2. Crime and criminals.
3. Sexual deviation. I. Winslow, Robert Wallace,
1940–   joint author. II. Winslow, Virginia,
joint author. III. Winslow, Robert Wallace,
1940–   Deviant reality. IV. Title.
HM291.W52   1980   302.5   80–20408
ISBN 0–205–07243–7

10 9 8 7 6 5 4 3 2   85 84 83 82 81

Printed in the United States of America.

Contents

4 Heroin Addiction   103

5 Prostitution: From the Street Walker to the Masseuse   137

6 The "Gay" Life: Male Homosexuality and Lesbianism   184

7 Transsexualism   235

8 Organized Crime   262

9 White Collar Crime: Embezzlement; "Street" Crime: Robbery   290

10 Forcible Rape   330

11 Murder   350

12 The Victim   366

13 Deviant Reality and the Study of Deviancy   397

Preface to the Second Edition

It was somewhat of a surprise to me when I was asked by Allyn and Bacon, Inc., at the request of Bob and Ginny Winslow, to revise *Deviant Reality*. When someone has been one's mentor, as Robert Winslow has been mine, it is difficult to consider oneself capable of updating or improving upon his work. It was even more of a readjustment for me to hear that a major portion of the revision was to expand upon the theoretical portions of the text. In the years that I was his student, his teaching assistant, and, later, his colleague, Dr. Winslow and I had always had a similar philosophy of teaching and had shared similar approaches to the study of sociology. Our relationship has always been a complementary one, but it had been my role to be familiar with the "firsthand" experiences in the field, while his was to place these learning experiences within the perspective of existing theories. My admiration for his keen mind and adeptness in conceptualization grew from these interchanges. Thus, it is with humility that I present this revision of a recognized work in the field of deviant behavior.

After leaving San Diego State University, I completed my doctoral studies in the Department of Behavioral Science at the University of Kentucky. The interdisciplinary nature of that department has no doubt influenced the manner in which I approach the study of human behavior. I have carried this approach with me into the classroom along with the Winslow method of bringing speakers and experiential learning opportunities to my students. The additional interviews incorporated within this edition are primarily a result of that method. These interviews were done at the University of Richmond and, later, at Spring Hill College.

The basic purpose of the book remains to "understand" deviant reality through firsthand accounts, and to place the comments of deviants within existing theoretical frameworks. Increased emphasis on and expansion of theories are incorporated within this edition. These have been accomplished by inclusion of social control, subcultural, and alienation theories, and by the addition of a section entitled "Theoretical Implications" within each chapter. In this section, the comments of the deviants are analyzed more fully as to their conceptual implications.

Although the book remains strongly sociological in its approach, consideration is also given to the biological and psychological factors that may interact with sociological ones in explaining deviant behavior and the reality of deviants.

Other changes are in keeping with current directions in the field of sociology and the study of deviant behavior. They include: the addition of a chapter on "The Victim"; combining the examination of male homosexuality and lesbianism within a single chapter, "The 'Gay' Life"; the addition of an interview with a "masseuse-prostitute"; and consideration of the property crimes of robbery and embezzlement within one chapter in order to compare and contrast "street crime" with "white collar crime." Increased emphasis has been given to methods of social control and implications and issues related to it.

Robert and Virginia Winslow, and I, trust that this edition will be of benefit to the understanding of deviant reality and, consequently, human behavior.

Preface to the First Edition

Teaching of the sociology of deviancy, social problems, and related subjects has traditionally followed the familiar format of presenting definitions of major concepts, typologies, theories, and statistical studies, both in the lectures we give in the classroom and in the textbooks and anthologies that have been published for classroom use. This "ideational" or "cognitive" approach to the subject of deviancy has been met in recent years with criticism revolving around the relevance of this approach to the "real world." "Book knowledge is one thing, but there's really no substitute for experience," has been the layman's pledge and the academician's anathema. Long a point of conflict between the academic and nonacademic world, this idea is more and more working its way into the classroom. For example, an instructor who has not used psychedelic drugs will, when attempting to address the subject in the classroom, find contention with quite a few "experts" whose knowledge of the drugs being discussed (such as LSD) has been derived from firsthand experience. Some members of the audience may have gone beyond immediate experience and acquired cognitive "book knowledge" as well.

Ideally, to be fully adequate in our presentation of course materials, we would have not only book knowledge but also firsthand and intensive experience of each social problem we study. However, questions of personal and professional ethics almost inevitably arise when we attempt to study firsthand such problems as drug abuse or homosexuality. It is difficult, if not impossible, to engage in other areas of participant observation—for example, for a white sociologist to act as participant-observer as a black ghetto resident.

Although we support the efforts of our fellow sociologists to gain firsthand experience and therefore knowledge, we also recognize limitations of time and personal capabilities that make it necessary for us to depend on substitute or vicarious experience through the accounts of others.

About three years ago we started to bring into the classroom people who had themselves experienced the various social problems being discussed in class. Not only did this procedure heighten the interest level of the students, but it also validated in a concrete way many of the general points previously made in lectures or in the textbook, points that would probably have passed without their importance being realized by the students.

At the outset we were somewhat skeptical about the prospects of locating appropriate people to serve as speakers. We found that one problem we confronted was perhaps indicative of the situation of the academic sociologist—we did not *know* any homosexuals, drug addicts, embezzlers, etc. We found, however, that speakers on almost any social problem who had been or were currently members of a particular deviant group could be located through various city help agencies. We located a drug addict through the Salvation Army Rehabilitation Center. We located an armed robber through Project JOVE (Jobs, On-the-Job Training, and Vocational Education), an ex-convict rehabilitation organization. We located a nudist through a local nudist camp. We located a homosexual through the Gay Liberation Front. In some cases we went to meetings to establish rapport with particular organizations or groups (for example, CAIG, Community Achievement and Improvement Group, an ex-convict self-help organization) and to locate possible informants. In many cases, informants were located through student acquaintances. We were relieved to find that most respondents were not reluctant to come into class to talk about themselves. In all of the contacts we made, we had only one refusal. When they spoke, our respondents were members of deviant groups. We make no pretenses that these people are typical of all members (nor do they).

The benefit of these speakers, and—we hope—the benefit of this book, is that they provide an additional source of information to the definitions, typologies, theories, and statistics given in class—firsthand experience. What we have presented are the results of over 100 hours of tape recording and hundreds of hours of transcribing. We have selected and edited the best of the transcripts, choosing particularly those which are unique in some way in the questions raised by the speakers in regard to certain theories, concepts, and definitions; in the vividness with which a transcript seems to illustrate a particular existing theory or definition; or in the rareness of the phenomenon or lack of current study.

Introduction

1

DEVIANT REALITY: METHOD OF ANALYSIS

The present volume is an attempt to set forth a book of edited readings and interpretations in the field of social problems—deviant behavior that gives an approach to various forms of deviation based upon *live, firsthand*, "own story" accounts from the point of view of *deviant actors themselves*. The core of this work consists of verbatim transcripts taken from lecture-interviews of people who have been labeled deviant, either officially or informally. The settings for these presentations were upper division sociology classrooms. The usual format was presentation of the person's own story, followed by a question and answer session with the class. The presentations varied in length. In some cases the respondent-lecturer spoke for twenty to thirty minutes and answered questions for another forty-five minutes. In other cases the lecture period was longer. Interviewing was conducted by the editors before and/or after class if the respondent spontaneously began providing information outside of class or where it was felt that the respondent had more to say on a subject, or if it was necessary to get specifics on a particular point that was mentioned in the lecture. We have taken special care to protect the identity of all our respondents by changing their names in the transcript.

The book, then, is built around verbatim transcripts on a variety of subjects. We have divided these deviant activities into "victimless" crimes and "real" crimes, followed by an interview with a victim of crime. Victimless crimes are ranked in rough order from the least to the most "career-oriented." The opposite is true for the real crimes, which are ranked according to decreasing career-orientation but in order of increasing seriousness. The resulting order is: social nudism, problem drinking and alcoholism, drug addiction, homosexuality, transsexualism, prostitution, organized crime, embezzlement and robbery, rape, murder, and the victim. Although we will develop the rationale for this typology later in this chapter, it will probably seem intuitively understandable, except perhaps in the case of organized crime, which in popular and academic literature has been portrayed as extremely sinister, costly, and damaging to society and personally threatening to citizens. However, our placement of organized crime is by no means capricious or arbitrary. It is placed in rank according to its position as having the highest degree of career involvement but a relatively low potential for injurious effects upon individuals or serious consequences for public order. This is, first of all, based upon public opinion data we have uncovered and a thesis developed from recent studies that challenge the assumption that organized crime is a serious threat to society. Additionally, we view organized crime as a possible "link" between some of those deviancies which are engaged in solely for one's own pleasure and those which bring harm to others, conceivably as a means to or as a result of the satisfaction of that pleasure. (Examples include: robbery in order to sustain a drug habit, embezzlement of funds to pay debts incurred from alcohol or gambling compulsions, and murder either while under the influence of drugs or alcohol or to avoid the disclosure of one's sexual deviancy.) This is not meant to imply that all or even a substantial portion of "real" crimes are related to victimless crimes, or that organized crime is involved in a substantial percent of other deviancies. Organized crime is, however, conceived as requiring a strong career commitment and may, at times, play a role in both victimless and real crimes.

Each chapter in this book has a "deviant transcript" toward which we have directed our analysis. In the initial stages of the development of the book, we were attracted to the idea of putting together a reader consisting of such transcripts simply because they make interesting and sociologically relevant reading, in and of themselves. As time passed, however, we began to realize that the significance of these various transcripts goes far beyond their readability. In fact, in a number of areas these interviews proved to be strategic in the sense that they served as an exploratory source of new definitions or hypotheses where previous research or theoretical formulation was lacking or as a focal point for the examination of existing definitions and hypotheses. We then came to broaden our analysis, so that each chapter now contains essentially four parts: 1) a section in which current definitions of or relating to a given form of deviancy are examined (e.g., what is homosexuality?); 2) a section in which major theories or explanations (especially sociological ones) are briefly examined and codified; 3) the verbatim transcript of the informant's classroom presentation; 4) a section in which current information, data, and definitions are examined in the light of comments made by our respondent; and 5) a section in which the theoretical implications of these comments are explored with an eye to the possible reformulation of old definitions and hypotheses and development of new ones.

In presenting the materials in the above format, we feel our work has implications bearing upon a number of methodologies and approaches, some developed recently and some old, but all directed at the refocusing and reformulation of the sociological study of deviancy. This confluence of methodological techniques includes: 1) the use of depth interviews or focused interviews; 2) participant observation; 3) a partial emphasis derived from ethnomethodology; and 4) a basic approach inspired by a method used years ago—analytic induction. Elements of all four of these approaches are present in this book. We are conducting interviews with deviants in class, and we feel that the extensiveness of the questioning and other criteria qualify these interviews as "depth interviews" as well as "focused interviews." The accounts that the deviants give us in class are participant-observer accounts, with an emphasis upon *participant*, but also qualifying at least loosely for the sociological classification of participant observation. We feel our analysis qualifies at least a starting point for ethnomethodological study, sharing in common with that body of studies the objective of deriving the actor's point of view and especially his commonsense view of the world, which we believe should be legitimately considered as a basis for his past, present, and future behavior. We cannot rightfully maintain, however, that we present anything like a full-scale ethnomethodological study in our "one case" approach. While we strive to arrive at the particulars of an actor's commonsense view of the world, we cannot provide more than a truncated analysis, insofar as we are attempting to cover a scan of topics rather than providing extensive analysis of one topic. We maintain, though, that because in so many areas of deviance such study has not even been initiated, we are providing a contribution by opening up such analysis. In other areas, such as in the study of drinking behavior, prostitution, marihuana use, embezzlement, and homosexuality, some pioneering ethnomethodological or quasi-ethnomethodological research has been done, and in those fields our studies may serve either as corroboration of previous research or as a point of comparison.

Finally, this volume has been inspired most of all by a method of analysis developed by Thomas and Znaniecki in their study, *The Polish Peasant in Europe and America*. Analytic induction, the method used with great rigor by Thomas and Znaniecki, yielded findings so significant as to serve as a starting point for the study of social disorganization in America. A more recent version of analytic induction was presented in Cressey's analysis of embezzlement in *Other People's Money*.[1] Cressey's methodology, despite its potency in explaining the phenomenon he studied, has received little attention or favorable treatment in subsequent studies in the sociology of deviant behavior. We feel this an unfortunate omission.

The present volume, because of the unique situs of information gathering, brings together a variety of qualitative methods in the study of deviance. They are all important to us and to this volume, and so they deserve at least brief statement. What are these methodologies and what are the rules laid out for the pursuit of these techniques of analysis? In answering these questions we will be able to specify in some detail "what we are about" in this book.

Depth Interview versus Focused Interview

Depth interviews are not confined to the social sciences but in fact are done continuously by the lay public. For that reason, they are especially valuable as a methodology in our case since our "interviewers" are students of sociology who occupy a quasi-lay status. The commonness of the depth interview is pointed out by Wiseman and Aron:

> One of the major tools of the social scientist—the depth interview—is also a favorite of the average citizen. Everyone at one time or another has used this technique to learn more about a subject of interest. A person will start by asking someone general questions. As he receives answers, he follows up on certain points with increasingly specific questions until he has acquired an "understanding" of the topic.[2]

Thus, depth interviewing can be (and often in field work is) done by the lay public without training in sociology or social science. We should also stress that there are certain theoretical advantages in having members of the lay public or quasi-lay public involved in the interview process. Their intimations and perspectives are often different from those of the professional sociologist and reflect more closely the commonsense world views of the lay public. Of course, we must also note the potential danger of including lay people in an interview. They may lack orientation in the nonnormative approach to deviance and may in certain cases become condemnatory, judgmental, and reactive to the statements made by the informant in such a way as to jeopardize not only rapport but also the informant's tendency to self-revelation. Nevertheless, we did not find this reactiveness to be much of a problem with our college student-interviewers. Students were surprisingly capable of taking a detached, neutral attitude toward the respondents. On the occasions when a speaker was talking about extremely grave offenses, we were often surprised at the reserve and objectivity of the students.

The interviews we conducted, by virtue of our presence in the class-room and participation in the interview process, constitute a close approximation to a particular type of depth interview termed by Merton and Kendall "the focused interview." [3] Merton and Kendall summarize the characteristics of the focused interviews as follows:

1. Persons interviewed are known to have been involved in a *particular concrete situation* ...
2. The hypothetically significant elements, patterns, and total structure of this situation have been previously analyzed by the investigator.
3. On the basis of the analysis, the investigator has fashioned an *interview guide,* setting forth the major areas of inquiry and hypotheses which locate the pertinence of data to be obtained in the interview.
4. The interview is focused on the *subjective experiences* of persons exposed to the preanalyzed situation.[4]

Although Merton and Kendall were talking particularly about studies of social and psychological effects of mass communication, our study is quite similar, even though the topic itself is different. First, our respondents have been involved in a particular concrete situation of participation in a deviant scene or subculture. Second, prior to conducting our interview in class, we had familiarized ourselves (and to some extent so had the students in the class) with the literature on the subject. Third, prior to each presentation in class, an interview schedule was read to the respondent, and he or she was given a copy of the schedule to refer to in giving the presentation before the class. In the case of the victim, several items on the schedule did not apply, but other items, reflecting the literature on victimology, were asked during the interview. A copy of the schedule for all other respondents is presented in Table 1.

The questions in Table 1 were directed at bringing out the nature of deviancy (questions 1 and 2), subtypes (question 3), and locating possible causal factors. In this way we could discern the relevance of particular theories. Questions were also included to evoke statements about various theories of deviancy. To do this we tried to incorporate the major variables or units of analysis considered to be causal factors in various theories of deviancy, including the family (question 5), the peer group (questions 6 and 7), reference groups (question 8), self-concept (question 9), societal reaction (questions 10 and 11), subcultural socialization (question 12), social control (questions 5, 11, and 14), and alienation (question 13). Our strategy then was to follow up with additional questions any statement made by the informant about any of the factors mentioned as important.

Respondents, of course, varied in the extent to which they followed the interview schedule. We purposely did not bind them by it for basically two reasons: 1) we assume that the respondent's divergence from the interview schedule is traced in large part to selective attention to other factors defined as more relevant or germane to presenting one's own story, and 2) it was not difficult to bring out the schedule items during

TABLE 1　*Interview Schedule*

In your presentation, please indicate your responses to the following questions:

1. What offenses or offense did you commit or were you arrested for?
2. Explain how these offenses were committed.
3. What are the different types of related offenses, offenders?
4. What do you think were the precipitating causal factors—those just prior to the offense(s)?
5. What influence did your childhood relations with father, mother, siblings, and friends have upon your subsequent offenses?
6. What was the influence of adolescent peer group relationships in junior high and high school?
7. Were you a member of a gang?
8. Were you "popular" or part of the high school in-group?
9. Did you conceive of yourself as a delinquent or criminal, and did this concept change before and after your offense(s)?
10. What was the reaction of your parents, peers, and siblings to your offenses? What is the reaction of others when they find out about your offenses?
11. If you could change the law or penalties, how would you?
12. Characterize the subculture of such offenders. How is it different from the straight society?
13. How would you characterize your attitudes? Are you or have you been alienated, depressed, or lonely?
14. What accounts for your being rehabilitated (if you are)?

the question session. In fact, very often the items in our schedule were intuitively asked by the students in class. Last, through our line of questioning we have in all cases specifically focused on the actor's own point of view and subjective reactions to various aspects of being labeled a deviant, and a particular kind of deviant, by society.

There are some additional features or rules of both depth interviews in general and focused interviews that should be mentioned. One all-encompassing rule is that of establishing the confidence of the respondent prior to the interview and of maintaining rapport during the interview. We feel that by bringing our deviant informant into class as an "expert authority on the subject," we not only help establish confidence, but also provide an elevated semiprofessional status. By bringing him or her before a college class, we show that we not only respect that person, but we also consider his or her views worthwhile and of higher educational value. This situation contrasts markedly with the field situation where the professional sociologist "comes down" to speak with the deviant informant and as so often noted "looks down" upon the person being interviewed (or is perceived as doing such). Incidentally, we have found it is not at all difficult to locate deviant speakers and get them to come to class. This contrasts with the normal interview situation where respondents either fail to show up at the appointed time or, in the house-to-house situation, slam the door in one's face.

Rapport also seemed almost automatic in the lecture situation, although respondents weren't always as relaxed as they would be in a one-to-one situation and several commented about their "nervousness." However, by having our deviant informant speak for twenty or thirty minutes, we developed a relationship that lasted throughout the hour.

Another guideline for interviewing is to get the respondent's words "as nearly verbatim as possible." [5] This is ordinarily a problem when the interviewer is previously a total stranger to the respondent and the respondent may be suspicious about having personal comments tape recorded. In the situation of informant-speaker, our interviewee had no doubts about the purposes for which we were tape recording. In no case were we refused permission to tape record a respondent's talk and comments, and we think the tape recording added to the feeling of self-importance that the classroom presentation seemed to bring. In one case we were asked for a copy of the tape to be played back to friends, a request we later granted.

Several other requisites for depth interviewing are mentioned by Merton and Kendall:

1. *Nondirection:* In the interview, guidance and direction by the interviewer should be at a minimum.
2. *Specificity:* The subject's definition of the situation should find full and specific expression.
3. *Range:* The interview should maximize the range of evocative stimuli and responses reported by the subject.
4. *Depth and personal context:* The interview should bring out the effective and value-laden implications of the subject's responses, to determine whether the experience had central or peripheral significance.[6]

We feel that our "lecture situation" lends itself well to all of these criteria. By initiating the interview with a "lecture" by the respondent, we are arriving at the criterion of nondirection. By including a classroom full of interviewers each with a different perspective from which to ask questions, the specificity and range criteria are met. The criteria of depth and personal context may appear problematic. To what extent can we maximize self-revelatory comments from respondents and evoke extensive gut-level feelings from a respondent in a classroom situation? Will the respondent tend to clam up under these circumstances? While this can only be assessed from reading the transcripts, we may affirm that a wide range of intimacies were indeed revealed in the classroom, sometimes for rhetorical shock value, but at other times because the informant felt in tune with a sympathetic audience. Often, our informants admitted they had said things in class they had never told anybody before, and that things they had not thought about for many years had been brought out. It may be that this occurred because our students were questioning the informants from a position of relative anonymity and were therefore able to probe deeper than the respondents had previously experienced. We can only say in reference to depth that we believe that because of the extensiveness of the questioning, points were brought out that may not have been mentioned in a one-to-one situation, while admitting at the same time that the one-to-one interview situation would contain its own unique advantages.

Importance of Depth and Focused Interviews in the Study of Deviancy

Depth interviews provide unique information that cannot be gained by other methods. They are useful as exploratory tools, for locating information and getting detailed descriptions, and they serve as a source of hypotheses for further study. Depth interviews can help us in areas of deviancy in which explanations, definitions, and descriptions are either weak or lacking. The unique advantage of the depth interview is its flexibility, enabling an investigator to develop definitions, categorizations, and hypotheses in the course of investigation.

The focused interview, on the other hand, provides an additional layer of unique information because we go into the interview with hypotheses and definitions in mind. In the sociology of deviance, many such operational definitions and hypotheses or theories have been developed, based upon questionnaire studies or inferences made from official statistics. We shall see in our discussion of ethnomethodology that such definitions and hypotheses are often ill-advised because the investigator mistakenly assumes he or she shares a common universe of discourse with the respondent or with the official agencies from whom the records are derived. As a result, measurement error occurs and the data have to be bent to fit the hypotheses. Through focused interviews we can locate the errors of operationalization and critically examine weak and sometimes post hoc formulated hypotheses and theories (i.e., those formulated to fit the data after data have been assembled).

There is a possible area of weakness of hypotheses or explanations derived from depth and focused interviews. It is entirely possible that the respondent is unable to verbalize the "true" reasons for personal decisions and actions and that at best what is related are "rationalizations." We maintain, however, that even rationalization forms a part of an individual's motivational profile in the sense that if a person believes something motivates his or her behavior, it will continue to do so in a kind of self-fulfilling prophecy. The same holds true for "realities" that may have been created or influenced by punishment or treatment modalities such as prison enculturation or psychiatric therapy. We are also inclined to side with those adherents who are convinced that people do know why they act in certain ways, and that their commonsense explanations of their own behavior are indeed the ones that are "real" to them.

Participant Observation

The main characteristic of participant observation is that an investigator becomes a member of the group being observed. Ordinarily this method refers to a field technique used by sociologists who in order to gather data seek out membership in a group they are studying. However, it has been noted that worthwhile participant-observer accounts have been written by nonsociologists. Wiseman and Aron make this point:

> The autobiographies of those who have lived for many years in institutions such as prisons (Black, 1927) or convents (Baldwin, 1959) are particularly insightful studies of these "closed" societies. Though these individuals were not trained sociologists, they were participant observers *par excellence.*[7]

Though our informants vary in this respect, many of the transcripts contained in this volume have the earmarks of a genuine participant-observer account. There are, of course, certain rules for forming a participant-observer account. The observer must gain access to a group to observe and remain long enough to observe recurring patterns of behavior. One should keep a "diary" or journal of observations describing patterns observed, and also try to explain why individuals observed behave as they do. The observer should be involved in such a way that members of the group interact with him or her in a "normal" way so that data can be gathered without arousing fear and hostility. Most of all, one should be deeply enough involved with a group to observe without causing a disturbance, but at the same time should be sufficiently detached so that behavior patterns are observed "objectively" and not missed because they have come to seem "normal."

Few, if any, of our informants have kept a diary of their experiences, though in most other respects they have complied with the participant observation model. They are generally long-time or former long-time members of the groups in which they participated. They certainly observed behavior patterns. They were sufficiently a member to be considered "normal" in social interaction. However, we do not meet the criterion of "objectivity" in our informants as participant-observers. Instead, they have been normatively involved in the groups in which they participated and in relatively few cases detached and objective about what was happening. Of course, this is one of the usual problems and pitfalls of all participant observation research. In their descriptions of their lives as deviants, much is lost no doubt in that memory cannot recount the routine details of everyday life that seem to the respondent to be unimportant. To some extent, however, through our barrage of questions, we can bring out these details so that the respondent relates them to us.

Beyond stating that our respondents' lack of objectivity is a pitfall, we can justifiably maintain that such lack of objectivity is in some respects a great advantage to us. In many participant observation accounts, a real problem to validity of observation is that the sociologist-as-observer does not really become an "insider," and rarely do sociologists actually penetrate the "inner core" of the groups or subcultures they study. With our respondents, on the other hand, such "insiderness" is the rule rather than the exception. Thus, they give us unique perspectives somewhat different from the usual sociological ones.

One basic problem with participant observation and other direct contact field work techniques is that deviants are people who almost by definition are inclined to be deceptive and distrustful and therefore are likely to present a "managed impression" or false image of themselves to people who observe them. For instance, among homosexuals there is the practice of "camping," the phenomenon in which the limp-wristed, ultra-feminine stereotype of the homosexual is portrayed before outsiders, partly for its shock value. Douglas perceptively delineates this problem:

> We must always keep in mind that "deviants" are people who, by their very definition, have many enemies who can often harm them in some way. For this reason, deviants are wary of being observed by outsiders. Some deviant groups have carefully prepared an orchestrated *front* that they use to mislead outsiders, sometimes simply as a put-on, but sometimes to avoid being revealed. For these reasons, any sociologist doing participant-observer studies has to be extremely careful to win his subjects' trust.[9]

Thus, the sociologist as participant-observer may present in the report little more than an account of this front that deviants have presented. By contrast, our informants *are* insiders, and as such their accounts are truly accounts *from the inside*. To what extent is it possible that our informants, though they are insiders, are giving us merely a false-front impression? This we admit is always a danger. However, when deviants are brought into class *in the role of authority on a subject*, it seems likely that they have a vested interest in presenting a true picture, in "telling these college kids about the way things really are in the real world." To the extent that they relate genuine details drawn from their life experiences, they maintain a hold upon their audience of students. Also, our speakers are up against a highly critical and diverse audience of students, "some of whom have been there themselves." The speaker must always be cognizant of the possibility that if he or she lies, there may be somebody out there in the group who knows of the lying and will penetrate the facade and expose it. Most important of all, however, is the different situation of the classroom as opposed to a field interview. If an individual sociologist goes out into the field "slumming it" among deviants, here is one person up against a group of deviants who reinforce each other in playing games with the sociologist. On the other hand, if a deviant comes before a group of students of sociology, here is one individual up against a group. We are nevertheless not so naive as to believe that everything our informants tell us is true of the real world in which they have lived, and we must take precautions to detect spurious information. Again, to cite Douglas:

> It is because of this difficulty of managing the fronts of deviants and of establishing trust that we must constantly be critical of the methods used to study deviance. . . . To a considerable degree we have to rely on our previous knowledge of deviance to give us some clear idea of whether the researcher is being taken in by the fronts or is romanticizing the group.[10]

What we are presenting, bearing in mind the above limitations, are "insider accounts" with many of the elements of participant observation where the emphasis is upon participation. We can categorize participant-observer accounts in terms of polar extremes. In some such accounts the researcher becomes an active participant in the group, while in other such accounts the researcher remains marginal to the group so as to maintain objectivity. Lowney has noted that it is often necessary in the study of deviance to remain a "nonparticipant *of* deviancy" even within the sub-culture in order to avoid many moral, legal, and ethical dilemmas.[11] By our emphasis upon *participant*, we have accrued certain definite advantages. More intensive participation affords the observer a greater exposure to both the routine and unusual activities of the group studied. Such participation makes it more likely that the investigator will uncover the "secret" vernacular of the group studied, the meanings employed by the group when strangers are not around.[12] A good case can be made that the discovery of routine activities and meanings is in fact the emphasis that should take priority in the sociology of deviance in its current stage of development. If this is true, our emphasis seems to be justified.

Ethnomethodology

Although our pursuit in this book cannot qualify as a full-scale ethno-methodological study, it is nevertheless ethnomethodological in its intent, design, and outcome. The *exact meaning* of the term ethnomethodology has not been stated. Instead of referring to any specific technique in social research, it seems to refer to a methodological perspective toward doing research encompassing a variety of ethnographic techniques such as interviewing and participant observation, which we have already discussed. A generalized definition of ethnomethodology as a perspective might be composed as follows: the pursuit of knowledge of everyday activities and members' explanations or accounts of those activities combined with the ways in which actors measure or indicate those activities (make them accountable), meanings surrounding such activities and accompanying basic categories of daily life, expectancies of actors in typical situations, sanctions used by actors for violation of those expectancies, and, last, actors' ways of handling exigencies (demands not covered in prior expectancies) by virtue of their commonsense knowledge of the social structure (or lay sense of sociological reality).[13]

Ethnomethodology contains a critique of much of what goes on in current and former sociological research. Implicit in this approach is a wholesale repudiation of all studies in which findings and conclusions are based upon a naive acceptance of official reports as indicators of social phenomena:

> Most of the data that sociologists honor as "given," ... are largely the product of bureaucratically organized activities, for example, census bureaus, vital statistics bureaus, correctional agencies, welfare agencies, and business agencies. The multitudinous perceptions and interpretations that went into the assembly of such data are invariably lost to the reader or user of such materials. The quantitative features must be accepted by fiat.[14]

The problem with these official sources of statistics is that indicators derived from them may not indicate what we intend to measure. For instance, measures of "delinquency" may not measure "true delinquency" or "real crime" as we conceptualize it but may contain many biases leading in extreme cases to a biased sample of "juveniles labeled delinquent" whose acts of misbehavior are relatively harmless and even noncriminal in nature.

The ethnomethodological approach stresses avoidance of the assumption that the social scientist and the subjects form a common culture, avoidance of the tendency to impute one's own frame of reference to one's subjects, and avoidance of prior preconceptions. This contrasts with survey research and experimental study where concepts are "operationally defined" prior to research being carried out. This could be successfully done only if subject and researcher shared common meanings and culture, and this is exceedingly rare in the study of deviance, where almost by definition the deviant subject is at variance with the middle class sociologist in the deviant's universe of discourse. Ethnomethodological studies, then, favor a critical examination of categories and meanings in terms of the subject's own point of view prior to attempts to test hypotheses in terms of these categories. Cicourel maps out what appears to be a model of an ideal-typical ethnomethodological study as follows:

> One possible solution might be to participate intensively during the first part of the research and map out the necessary details for hypothesis testing, then use later events, presumed here to be in part recurrences of past events, as the basis for testing hypotheses. ... If the observer's role is appropriately structured, he could then conduct formal interviews at some later date.[15]

In a very direct sense, this is exactly what we have done in class with our deviant speakers, and generally the presentation in class followed exactly this format. First, our deviant speaker gave a presentation dealing largely with personal point of view and categories of thought. Then followed a question-and-answer session in which there was additional conceptual development plus extensive hypothesis testing in terms of the categories developed.

Analytic Induction

Though our work bears a close connection to the above methods and techniques, of most influence in its impact upon our thinking is a technique of analysis *reintroduced* by Cressey some twenty years ago, a method that has been termed "analytic induction." [16] Our focus is upon the individual cases—"one person's views about life as a deviant." Skeptics about this approach may complain, "How can one validly generalize from individual cases of the phenomenon at hand?" In anticipation of this query, we answer that we are not attempting to form generalizations. Generalizations, explanations, and theories aplenty are already available in the literature. What we would like to do is examine these existing hypotheses in the light of our individual cases. In a significant number of cases examined in this book, the case is in one respect or another a "negative case" in terms of the generalization derived from the literature. Ordinarily in social research, negative cases are discarded as "measurement error" or through an implicit assumption that "the exception proves the rule." We stringently protest this logic, in accord with Cressey, who succinctly states the importance of negative cases. "Negative cases are the growing point of science, exceptional instances forcing us either to reject or revise generalizations." [17] Cressey states that the focus upon negative cases is not entirely foreign to either sociological or scientific inquiry:

> It has its roots in John Stuart Mill's "method of difference," was elaborated as a method of "analytic induction" by Znaniecki, and was referred to as the "principle of limited inquiry" by Lindesmith.[18]

Sociological study of deviant behavior has rarely probed individual cases with the purpose of formulating universal generalizations. It is our opinion that this is a source of much frustration to students of sociology. Indeed, students often complain that sociological explanations (which often constitute little more than statistical comparison of "average" traits or characteristics of deviants or nebulous post hoc, armchair theories derived from a quasi-commonsense examination of empirical regularities) are nothing more than "meaningless generalizations," "just words," or "not relevant to the real world." The examination of an individual case forces the investigator to define theory terms so that they are acceptable in dealing with the case at hand and so that they correspond with the point of view of the subject. This may entail a total reformulation of a vast array of theories. Such examination may also force the investigator to reformulate his or her theory, to specify the conditions under which the theory is applicable, or even to abandon this theory entirely if indeed this is a case that the theory is meant to apply to but doesn't. The essentials of this "acid test" of theory are formulated in steps by Cressey:

> First, a rough definition of the phenomenon to be explained is formulated. Second, an hypothetical explanation of that phenomenon is formulated. Third, one case is studied in light of the hypothesis with the object of determining whether the hypothesis fits the facts in that case. Fourth, if the hypothesis does not fit the facts, either the hypothesis is re-formulated or the phenomenon to be explained is re-defined, so that the case is excluded. This definition must be more precise than the first one. Fifth, practical certainty may be attained after a small number of cases has been examined, but the discovery by the investigator or any other investigator of a single negative case disproves the explanation and requires a re-formulation. Sixth, this procedure of examining cases, re-defining the phenomenon and re-formulating the hypothesis is continued until a universal relationship is established, each negative case calling for a re-definition or re-formulation. Seventh, for purposes of proof, cases outside the area circumscribed by the definition are examined to determine whether or not the final hypothesis applies to them.[19]

In the above seven steps, steps one through four correspond exactly to the outline of each chapter of this book. In each chapter we first define the phenomenon to be studied, based upon definitions given in the literature. Second, we draw hypotheses (theories) in a similar fashion from the literature. Third, we study an individual case in the light of the hypothesis. Last, in our commentary at the end of each chapter, we discuss our definitions and hypotheses in the light of the case we have examined, with an eye to reformulation. In many areas of deviancy under study, we have a feeling we have pushed inquiry in those areas, and through this method, beyond what is available in the literature. Hopefully, generalizations and definitions that we develop can serve as a starting point for further research that can carry the case analysis on to steps five through seven. At any rate, we hope that what results is a body of readings of heuristic value providing a depth of understanding not achieved through the study of other kinds of texts or readings on deviancy.

THE NATURE OF DEVIANCY

The people whose cases are presented in this book are "deviants." Most of them are also either admitted or convicted "criminals." Both of these are harsh terms, although usually used by sociologists quite glibly, possibly because discussion is kept on an academic and general level without actually confronting individual cases—people we know firsthand.

In this book, however, we deal with real human beings, not statistics. Many of the people in this book have become friends or acquaintances of ours; some have visited our homes on social occasions, or we have gone to theirs. The attachment of these labels to these people, then, is not something done without careful consideration.

We are not saying, however, that *all* of these people are our friends or that we would want them as members of our family or to baby-sit with our daughter. Some of them we would consider "true deviants" and "real criminals," implying we don't *feel* we could trust them and that there is an element of fear involved. Others are "deviants" only because society labels them as such. If we were to ask the people in this second category if they consider themselves "deviant" or "criminal," they would probably say, "That is a label put on me by society because of society's ignorance."

The above considerations are important ones and must have an influence upon the framework of this book. Therefore, it is imperative that in this introduction we clarify our concepts as best we can, first by clearly defining the terms "deviance" and "criminal" and then by developing a system of classification that can be used for organizing the remainder of the text. If biases are involved in our analysis, we can at least be open and clear-cut about them.

There are almost as many ways of looking at deviancy and deciding who is deviant as there are deviants themselves. The same person may be defined as "deviant" using one frame of reference and "normal" using another. It may also be seen that these classification schemes vary widely in the degree to which they correspond to the public definition of deviancy. In our opinion, useful ways of looking at deviancy must make provision for the intuitive consensual feelings people have about the phenomenon.

A common definition of deviance identifies it with departure from statistical norms. This statistical concept of deviance is often employed by counseling psychologists who develop trait profiles on people based upon tests like the Minnesota Multiphasic Personality Inventory. If a person varies one or two standard deviations from the average on a given trait, e.g., dominance-submission, he is said to be deviant. This departs from lay conceptions of deviance in that most people may be deviant in one or another respect without any great importance being attached to it. From the point of view of this text, this definition fails to capture an intuitive, public, commonsense meaning of the word deviance, and such a deviant label would be unacceptable not only to society but also to the alleged deviant himself.

Another approach, quite the opposite of the statistical one, states that deviance does not imply any adjustment to statistical norms, since what is average in society may itself be deviant in absolute terms. Current humanist thinking seems to imply this point of view. Erich Fromm, an exponent of this point of view, holds that, in defining "insanity," people who live in a society that makes unreasonable, exploitative demands upon them may be alienated and on the average "neurotic" in their attempts to adjust to those unreasonable demands. The average person in these circumstances has lost the capacity to love and to transcend self, so that average should not be considered "normal" and that which differs from average should not be considered "deviant." [20] Instead, the reverse is true. Clearly, according to our criterion of intuitiveness of definition, this absolute norm concept of deviance fails to measure up. Most people living in society today would not consider themselves insane, and there is no real proof that they are. Fromm appears to take a "concentration camp" view of contemporary society, and while there are some who adhere to this point of view, it is doubtful that things are all that dismal.

In opposition to the normative-humanist point of view, but still not in accord with the statistical point of view, is another definition, one used frequently by practicing social workers, probation officers, and psychiatrists. This is the view that deviant behavior is pathology or disease which, based upon textbook descriptions of symptoms, can be diagnosed, treated, and sometimes cured. This conception employs the medical model of illness treatment and applies it to social and psychological phenomena. Definite labels such as kleptomaniac, paranoid schizophrenic, and hypochondriac are used in the diagnosis of an ailment, and treatment proceeds in terms of the ailment. A major failing of this approach is that the symptomatology may change from day to day. Also, in dealing with social behavior, the ailment may not lie *within* the individual but instead in the role relationships in which he or she participates. From the point of view of this text, however, the major failing of this definition is lack of intuitiveness. The people to whom these labels are applied often rebel against them or fail to understand what is meant by them and have to be "educated" to understand the whole approach.

A major current approach to deviance used in sociology today is the labeling perspective, which holds that deviance is relative to the group norms and values in which it occurs. To us, a certain person may be a deviant. To that person, we may be deviant. His or her norms are no less valid than ours. Nothing can intrinsically be called deviance. Behavior can be called deviant only if a deviant label has successfully been applied and a "deviant is one to whom that label has successfully been applied." [21] This approach certainly rests upon intuitive and consensual understanding. It is therefore the starting point for our analysis of deviance. By calling deviance "what people say it is" we certainly comply with the requirement that what we term deviance will be agreeable not only to society but perhaps to the deviant who has been socialized to the label society has assigned. However, this is a definition without referent. It really gives us no help with what is generally considered deviance from the point of view of society.

Marshall B. Clinard, a student of labeling theory, recognizes this limitation of its definition of deviance, and offers his own approach. *Only those deviations in which behavior is in a disapproved direction,* and of sufficient degree to exceed the tolerance limit of the community, constitute deviant behavior.[22] This definition is an improvement upon labeling theory and it contains elements of intuitive, commonsense application; but there is a risk in the use of this definition, the risk that in agreeing so thoroughly with the community, we become a party to negative thinking about a behavior that is not against the community interest but in fact may be a contribution. Thus, "encounter groups" may be opposed by the community and participation in them considered deviancy, but their long-run effect may be beneficial. Thus, to Clinard's definition we must attach a qualification that in order to be considered deviant by serious students of deviancy, behavior must be shown to be against the best interest of the community. Here another problem arises. Although there are some behaviors that are pretty clearly against the community's best interest (e.g., forcible rape, murder, assassination), there are other actions in which the effect upon community interest is not clear and therefore the assignment of the deviant label is problematic. The latter is the case with the so-called victimless offenses—drunkenness, homosexual acts, gambling, prostitution, vagrancy, etc. There is no agreement—either within our own society or from society to society—about which of these offenses, if any, should be considered deviant behavior.

Deviance is here defined as *behavior that is beyond the tolerance limits of the community and is contrary to the best interests of the community.* The first part of this definition can be operationalized through assessment of opinion polls. The second part of the definition, however, will necessarily draw upon our own values, values that hopefully reflect current thinking about deviant behavior and society and an "educated guess" as to what the community's best interests are. A prime assumption we shall employ is that victimless offenses are less contrary to community interests than offenses involving a victim. Studies in which college students rated various criminal offenses show a general agreement with this assumption. Based upon the above definition of deviance, this book will be organized on a polar typological continuum. We shall cover, first, behaviors that, from what we can discern, are least damaging to society (and therefore least "deviant" *from our point of view*) and last, behaviors that are most damaging (and most "deviant" from our point of view).

CRIME AND DEVIANCE

A clue to people's perception of how damaging a particular act may be can be found in the laws dealing with certain behaviors. Legislators, criminal courts, and judges have for centuries concerned themselves with this question. Our distinction (tolerance limits versus best interests) is enacted in law in the idea of *mala in se* (bad in itself) versus *mala prohibita* (bad because it is prohibited). Judges and legislators have had to concern themselves with community interest above and beyond what people in the community think is bad or wrong.

The term *crime* is generally defined as a violation of criminal or penal law and *criminal*, a person guilty or convicted of violation of such law. Such a definition makes no distinction between serious and minor crime and fails to capture the popular connotation and intuitive meaning of the term *criminal*—felon, hoodlum, crook, gangster, deviant. In the search for such a distinction, we may arrive at a polar typology of offenses usable as an organizational scheme for this book. We shall cover two basic approaches to rank ordering offenses: the legal and the sociological.

The Legal Approach

The law itself incorporates a distinction between violations of minor laws and violations of serious ones. In English Common Law, the term *felony* long ago came to apply to crimes of a serious or heinous nature—"malicious, wicked, and base"—and a felon was a person who committed such crimes. The term still carries this popular connotation even though today the category felony includes crimes such as illegal drug usage and homosexual behavior, whose seriousness is questioned by many. This problem of criminalization of behavior arises partly because there is no clear definition of the term felony written into current laws. It refers simply to crimes for which one could be incarcerated in a state institution for one year or more, as distinguished from a *misdemeanor* (literally an act of misconduct) or a crime for which one may not be incarcerated for more than one year, usually in a county institution. The latter does not constitute an adequate definition of crime because it fails to indicate the "behaviors or actions involved in" crime. It merely indicates the penalties attached to such behaviors.

Partly because of the vagueness of legal definitions of felony, sociologists engaged in the study of crime have devoted much attention to clearly defining "real crime" or "serious crime."

The Sociological Approach

Three approaches to definition and classification of offenses and offenders in sociology may be specified: 1) serious crime as participation in a crime *contraculture*; 2) serious crime as involvement in a *career* in crime; and 3) serious crime as *victimization* of a person in terms of bodily harm, theft, or property damage. These definitions are not mutually exclusive, but may be combined to provide a general typology.

CRIME CONTRACULTURE   Cavan provides a useful typology of criminal behavior that includes contracultural criminality as its most serious form.[23] In contracultural crime, as opposed to less serious forms, the offender identifies with a criminal way of life, rejecting society's values and in turn being rejected by society through ostracism, imprisonment, or other punitive sanction. A major virtue of this approach is its focus upon values of society and the contradiction between the offenses of major criminals and the values of society. This gives us at least a starting point in defining "real crime"—a focus upon society's values. But which crimes contradict society's values? What logical or empirical basis do we have for considering some crimes more offensive to community values than others? This isn't really made clear in Cavan's classification, although she does not indicate what crimes *she thinks* should be placed in the category of contracultural crime, as well as other less serious categories. Under criminal contraculture she includes "professional crime, e.g., robbery, burglary, swindling; organized crime, e.g., armed robbery, kidnapping for ransom by gangs; illegal business such as gambling; racketeering, e.g., extortion; corrupt politics; addiction to alcohol, drugs." [24] Cavan, however, produces no empirical or logical basis for her placement of these deviant acts in the contracultural crime category. Are alcoholics and corrupt politicians viewed with such condemnation in actual public opinion? Cavan's ranking may not bear a direct relation to public ranking of deviant acts and may fall into the trap of "classification by fiat," failing to incorporate commonsense, everyday, public views of what is dangerous or serious crime.

CAREER CRIME   The second sociological approach to defining serious or real crime is to determine what crimes or types of criminal offenders imply a reliance upon crime as a means of livelihood or career in crime. Clinard summarizes this approach:

> A criminal career as distinguished from a noncriminal career involves a life organization of roles built about criminal activities, such as identification with crime, a conception of self as a criminal, extensive association with criminal activities, including other criminals, and, finally, progression in crime. Progression in crime means the acquisition of more complex techniques, more frequent offenses, and, ultimately, dependence on crime as a frequent or sole means of livelihood.[25]

Based upon these explicit criteria, Clinard generated a detailed typology of offenders ranging on a polar continuum of noncareer to career offenders. On the noncareer side are violent personal offenders, followed by occasional property offenders, political offenders, prostitutes, homosexuals, and habitual petty offenders. On the career side as we proceed along the continuum are occupational offenders, conventional criminals, organized criminals, and professional criminals (the most career-oriented of offenders).

Donald Cressey has developed a set of criteria for degree of "professionalism" in a career of crime. These are similar to those laid down by Clinard, except that Cressey excludes organized crime as a profession and includes the criterion of "status" among other criminals.[26] Thus, a typology based on degree of professionalism would place sex offenders as well as murderers within the noncareer category.

The paradox and limitation of these typologies is that if we were to use career crime as a criterion of seriousness or operationalization of the term *felony*, we would be giving shoplifters and pickpockets extreme penalties—even capital punishment—and would be releasing forcible rapists and murderers with a warning, fine, or probation. Thus, these typologies carry us far afield from everyday commonsense views of offense seriousness.

It further appears that both Cressey and Clinard were concerned with "crime" rather than deviancy in general, whether illegal or not. For our purposes, we wish to include the criterion of degree of "commitment" to a deviant lifestyle. For instance, the homosexual is usually more "career oriented" than the nudist. Neither of these individuals may earn a living in an occupation related to the deviancy. The same is true of the transsexual who also makes a strong commitment to a way of life. Still, career orientation alone, even including commitment, does not satisfy our needs entirely.

VICTIMIZATION AS A CRITERION OF SERIOUS CRIME   Sellin and Wolfgang have developed an empirical classification of offenses upon the extent and seriousness of victimization, the most serious crimes involving victimization in the sense of bodily injury, property theft, or property damage, in descending order of seriousness. Less serious offenses involve intimidation, threat, and diffuse victimization, such as victimization of large businesses or vague "public order." [27] This typology helps us to overcome the limitations of both Cressey's and Clinard's typologies and provides a compromise of Cressey's, Clinard's, and Cavan's typologies.

In addition to providing a logical criterion of classification, Sellin and Wolfgang have provided empirically derived scale scores for individual offenses based upon public opinion rankings of these offenses. The agreement on these rankings is said to be very high, based upon ranking by different samples of respondents in different parts of the United States and other countries. Based on the rankings produced by the raters used by Sellin and Wolfgang (and translating Sellin and Wolfgang's offense descriptions into the terms used in this text), the rank ordering of offenders presented in this text is given in Table 2.

The typology presented in Table 2 serves somewhat as a partial basis of organization of the readings to follow. Its virtue is that it combines Clinard's emphasis upon career crime with Cavan's emphasis upon contracultural crime. At the most serious end of the continuum are career offenders and/or violent personal offenders. One major discrepancy with the Cavan and Clinard typology is the placement of organized crime, assuming illegal gambling enterprise is the major component of

TABLE 2 *Offenders Ranked by Sellin and Wolfgang Scale Scores**

Most serious	1. Murderers
	2. Forcible rapists
	3. Armed robbers
	4. Embezzlers
	5. Prostitutes
	6. Homosexuals
	7. Nudists (exposure of genitals in public)
	8. Heroin addicts
	9. Drunkenness offenders
	10. Organized crime offenders (running illegal gambling establishment)
Least serious	11. Juvenile delinquency (truancy)

* Note: Sellin and Wolfgang provide ratings in this order only for *single offenses* while we are generalizing these ratings to categories of *offenders* for purposes of our typology.

organized crime. We prefer to accept Cressey's distinction of organized crime constituting a separate career from that of other crimes. We suggest it as a potential link between the career-oriented victimless crimes and the career-oriented more serious crimes. In some instances, organized crime may be extremely high in seriousness and victimization (an example might be a "murder-for-hire"), and in other circumstances it would rank rather low in victimization (such as involvement in gambling and prostitution). The link may be only indirect to some forms of deviance (such as a link from pornography to the homosexual subculture).

Using our criterion of "commitment" to a deviant lifestyle, we would place nudism as the least career-oriented victimless deviancy. In order to classify transsexualism, we would rate its lack of potential for victimization as equal to that of homosexuality but, due to the commitment involved, we would rank it somewhat higher than homosexuality in degree of career-orientation. If we were to graph our typology, it would appear as shown in Table 3.

═══ OUTLINE OF THE BOOK

The operational definition of serious versus minor offenders produced in Table 2 is in accord with our definition of deviance as "behavior that is beyond the tolerance limits of the community and is contrary to the best interests of the community." Even the last part of the definition (best interests of the community) appears to be met, possibly because the Sellin and Wolfgang ratings were done by students who are less influenced by popular stereotypes and prejudices toward deviants—but also because respondents are rating isolated acts rather than deviant labels—e.g., "drug addict"—which are fraught with nega-

TABLE 3   *Typology of Deviance by Degree of Career-Orientation and Degree of Seriousness (Victimization)*

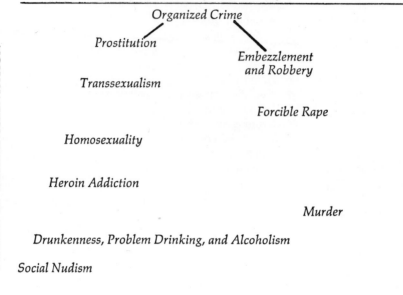

DEGREE OF CAREER-ORIENTATION

Organized Crime

Prostitution

Embezzlement and Robbery

Transsexualism

Forcible Rape

Homosexuality

Heroin Addiction

Murder

Drunkenness, Problem Drinking, and Alcoholism

Social Nudism

DEGREE OF SERIOUSNESS (VICTIMIZATION)

tive connotations. Nevertheless, we are somewhat satisfied with the typology and, with the modifications mentioned above, we will use it, in part, as the basis for the following readings. We will begin with victimless deviants—or categories of deviants generally not involving victims. These offenders have in common a sense of unjust treatment by society. They may even present a *minority group plight* and plea for public tolerance. They may be termed "deviant minorities," and have been shown to be the target of public stereotyping and prejudice.[28] With these offenders there is a strong appeal given for legalization or decriminalization of their offenses. We will examine them according to their increasing order of career-orientation. Thus, the first part of this book will focus on deviant minorities as follows:

1. Social nudism.
2. Drunkenness, problem drinking, and alcoholism.
3. Heroin addiction.
4. Prostitution.
5. Homosexuality and lesbianism.
6. Transsexualism.

By contrast with the first part of the book, Chapters 8 through 12 focus upon serious crime and "true" deviancy. Such offenders may have begun their criminal careers as deviant minorities, but as a cumulative result of society's stigmatic labeling of them and/or association with other offenders, they may have progressed to more serious offenses.

As noted above, organized crime will serve as the link between the two forms of deviance. We will discuss the more serious crimes in order of their increasing seriousness but their decreasing degree of career-orientation. Bearing these considerations in mind, Chapters 8 through 12 will include a cross section of violent offenses including:

1. Organized crime.
2. Embezzlement and robbery.
3. Forcible rape.
4. Murder.

Finally, we will consider the victim, particularly the rape victim. It may surprise some that the victim is frequently considered a deviant. The victim should be considered apart from any typology that is based on career-orientation and victimization. Considering the victim as the object of "true" crimes, we shall discuss this individual after dealing with crimes themselves.

GENERAL THEORIES OF DEVIANCY

In this book we will examine a wide variety of forms of deviancy. These range from skipping school to criminal homicide, and, while our typology gives some ordering or sequence to the chapters, up to now we lack any explanatory framework for viewing deviancy. We will see that for almost every form of deviancy there are related theories that have been developed to explain it. Some of these are theories arising from empirical study (post hoc explanations), but many are microtheories or hypotheses drawing from larger general theories of deviancy. Since the general theories will be constantly referred to in chapters to follow, not only in editorial comments but also in the deviants' own self-analyses, a brief summation is appropriate at this point.

Here, and in subsequent chapters where applicable, we discuss the general theories within three major classifications: 1) biological, 2) psychological, and 3) sociological. Some theories will later be classified as either "social-psychological" or "psychosocial" because of their combined and relative emphases of the two disciplines in explaining a particular form of deviant behavior. The theories summarized here differ from the numerous theories we will review in chapters to follow in that they purport to explain deviancy in general rather than a limited number of forms of deviancy. Frequently, we will mention the general theory under which a more limited explanation best appears to fall. In those instances in which specific deviancies have not been the object of one or the other discipline or theory, the lack of applicability is either mentioned briefly or considered obvious to the reader.

The major emphasis of this book is sociological. Nevertheless, we incorporate biological and psychological explanations in order to allow us to consider their contribution to the understanding of human behavior in general and deviant behavior specifically. The authors' backgrounds and expertise are essentially sociological, with considerable exposure to psychology and, we admit, somewhat less to biology. We endorse a "holistic" approach to the study of human behavior. In doing so, we wish to avoid the fallacy of some recent attempts of "sociobiology" that appear to explain all human behavior in biological terms under the guise of an interdisciplinary approach. However, we recognize that the division of science today is the result of historical accidents and the relative strength of competing academicians as the structure of universities developed. Thus, *homo sapiens* is not usually studied as a whole. Biochemists analyze effects upon and result of changes in body chemicals; geneticists study the impact of genes, chromosomes, and DNA structure; psychologists center upon the functioning of the human mind and individual personality; sociologists examine the interaction of individuals in groups; and anthropologists trace the impact and development of culture. It is our contention that consideration must be given to all these factors and that a holistic, interdisciplinary approach could break through many of the existing barriers to the advancement of an understanding of humankind. These issues have been addressed elsewhere[29] and progress has been made in some areas. There has been little advancement in the area of deviant behavior; the contribution herein is extremely modest. Still, while remaining primarily sociological in our focus, we will examine theories from other disciplines in the hope of establishing a precipitous beginning to a holistic approach in this field.

We will not attempt to criticize theories here or examine the empirical evidence relating to these theories. Our purpose is merely to present these theories, to see if they are applicable in individual cases, and, incidentally, to see whether deviants themselves accept or reject these theories.

The approaches we will summarize are not the only general theories available for consideration. We exclude, or only mention in passing, a number of older approaches that have been discarded because of evidence to the contrary (e.g., the theory of born criminal, phrenology, feeble-mindedness) or replacement by more recent theories (e.g., economic determinism and imitation-suggestion). The approaches we present are those most widely employed by practitioners and academicians.

Before presenting the summations, it would be well to point out certain issues of philosophy and logic that pervade the study of deviant behavior. Philosophically, one should always bear in mind the assumptions inherent in any theory and the resultant effects of those assumptions upon the theory and its application. The most important assumption in theories about deviance rests in the unresolved issue of "free will" versus "determinism." If one assumes humans have free will, it is logical to conclude that they are, in some degree, responsible for their behavior. As a result, they are able to perceive the consequences of their actions, and to take them into account before acting. Thus, efforts of deterrence or punishment might be effective as means of social control. On the other hand, if one's behavior is the result of determined characteristics, either inborn or resulting from predictable reactions to one's environment, whether early childhood psychological factors or those stemming from one's economic or social position, then the individual is not responsible for resulting behavior. Effective means of social control might include "treatments" such as psychoanalysis, changes in diet, lobotomy, hormone injections, and the like, or direct dealing with the "social pathologies" of racism, capitalism, economic inequalities, broken homes, and so on. The former, *free will assumption*, is inherent in the social control mechanisms of the "legal" or "criminal" models. The latter, *deterministic assumption*, is inherent in social control mechanisms of the "medical model."

The philosophical debate regarding the two assumptions has existed since the time of Aristotle and Plato. Perhaps the only statement that a substantial majority of behavioral scientists would support is one to the effect that, at least, the choices available to humans are limited according to the individual's biological, psychological, social, and economic potential and, thus, patterns of behavior will emerge. One may recognize that the free will assumption, in addition to being an underlying factor in theories, is inherent to the different methodologies discussed earlier. Thus, whether one seeks to measure, predict, and, thus, control human behavior, or to discover patterns of action that one may understand is largely based on one's resolution of this philosophical issue.

As mentioned above, we will not attempt to point out the empirical evidence supporting each theory. Nevertheless, one point in analyzing data regarding deviance is particularly important. This is the avoidance of the "dualistic fallacy" to which many early theorists fell prey. The fallacy is based upon an assumption that there exist two (or dual) separate, distinct, and homogeneous groups in society, *"deviants"* and *"nondeviants."* Additionally, it is assumed that official records or other groupings accurately reflect a sample of "deviants" who may then be compared with another homogeneous group made up of those not recorded officially, therefore classified as "nondeviants." Given these assumptions, one then looks for traits or characteristics that distinguish one group from the other and uses these as the basis to explain deviance. In addition to the fact that nearly everyone deviates to some degree at some time, erroneous conclusions may result in that the differences between the two groups may actually reflect factors that either: 1) created the greater likelihood that one would be apprehended, arrested, adjudicated, imprisoned, treated, or otherwise labeled as a deviant; or 2) caused differences to come about *as a result* of one's arrest, incarceration, treatment, or labeling, but did *not* contribute to the original deviant act.

To illustrate by example, let us present the hypothetical cases of Ted and Chris. Let us say that both are males, sixteen years of age, who engaged in some minor homosexual activity, each with his best friend. At the time of this initial act, the youths were similar except that Ted was black, of lower socioeconomic status, from a broken home, and lived within the inner-city of a large metropolitan area; Chris, on the other hand, was white, from an upper-middle class, intact family and resided in a small suburban community. Ted did not have the privacy of a separate bedroom and, as a result, he and his friend engaged in their activity in an abandoned tenement. Police, who had been on the lookout for vandalism and arson in that area of the city, caught the youths and placed them under arrest for "acts against nature." Ted was unable to afford an attorney, and the juvenile judge, taking into account the fact that Ted did not have a father present in his home to serve as an adequate role model and to exercise discipline, found him guilty and sent him to a home for juveniles where he would receive psychiatric treatment for his sexual "problems." At the home, Ted participated in continuing homosexual activity, a rather common occurrence within the single-sex institution. He was caught again on several occasions and remains in treatment receiving psychoanalytic counseling.

Turning our attention back to Chris, we find that he and his friend were never caught in their activity, which took place when the youths were "sleeping-over." (We might ask ourselves how, or if, Chris might have been treated differently by the police or court had he been caught.) Nevertheless, Chris outgrew this "phase" of his adolescence and is today a college graduate, working for a large corporation, married, and the father of two children. He has never received any form of psychological counseling, nor has he been institutionalized.

Now let us imagine that the cases of Ted and Chris are not unique. If, for instance, such fictitious cases each represent a typical set of patterns, we might speculate as to what "causes" of homosexuality might be erroneously discovered by a researcher comparing an official, institutionalized group of "Ted's" with a separate sample of "Chris's." Race, social class, family status, father-absence, and area of residence are all characteristics that would separate the two groups and might then be considered as "causes" of the initial deviance. Further, one might expect Ted's group to respond to a survey or interview with answers fitting a psychoanalytic explanation of their behavior, with less likelihood such explanation would be offered by Chris's group. Indeed, the example could be carried *ad infinitum* if one considers the subcultural interaction and development of attitudes that might result within an institutionalized population. The illustration is sufficient at this point, however, to demonstrate the logical error inherent within the dualistic fallacy.

This issue is most important in studying deviant behavior because of the relative ease with which "official" data may be obtained as compared to gathering "unofficial" data. Official data include information obtained from arrest reports, court and prison files, medical reports, and, most frequently, the FBI Uniform Crime Reports. The dualistic fallacy is less likely if research is based upon unofficial data, such as self-reports of deviancy, victimization surveys, observation, and so on. Frequently, however, obtaining such data is virtually impossible. One must then be aware of the methodological problems and issues surrounding the assessment of theories and avoid the fallacy. We will point to the methodological issues where particularly appropriate in our discussion of the theories regarding specific forms of deviancy, such as alcoholism, homosexuality, forcible rape, and so on. Indeed, much of our discussion will be cautioned in terms of whether the "reality" of our informants was prior to initial deviance, or the result of treatment and/or incarceration. The student is cautioned to bear in mind the determinism versus free will question and the dualistic fallacy as the summations of theories are presented—both here and in succeeding chapters.

Biological Theories

Biological theories are variously referred to as "physiological," "genetic," "constitutional," and so on, depending upon the orientation of the author or the particular emphasis of a theory. All of them have in common a belief that human behavior can be explained by, or at least heavily influenced by, biological traits. Indeed, the earliest studies of deviance and even the beginning of criminology tended to rely almost solely on physiological explanations.[30] Findings were often based upon studies of incarcerated inmates. The dualistic fallacies involved, and perhaps their potential for abuse by racists, chauvinists, nationalists, and others, have contributed to a lack of enthusiasm for consideration of biological factors by sociologists. Recently, however, an increased resurgence of interest has developed in the consideration of biological factors as they may interact with psychological and sociological factors in influencing human behavior.[31]

EARLY THEORIES OF THE BORN CRIMINAL Cesare Lombroso, often called "the father of criminology," was a physician who examined thousands of inmates within the Italian penal system in the late 1800s. Lombroso classified the prisoners according to their physical traits and types of crime. He defined the "born criminal" as having prehuman characteristics, such as large ears, a retreating forehead, and low cranial capacity. Lombroso termed this phenomenon "atavism," a throwback to prehuman man. A more developed type, the "criminaloid," differed in degree and committed crimes only occasionally. A third type, "criminals by passion," were not born criminals, but acted in the heat of various passions or emotions.[32] Thus, unlike some of his successors and critics, namely Garofalo and Ferri, Lombroso took environmental factors into account in explaining crime.[33]

Early in this century, Hooten described habitual criminals as "hopeless constitutional inferiors" who should not be allowed to breed.[34] Hooten compared inmates of the Massachusetts penal system with "noncriminals," made up largely of firemen and outpatients of a hospital. Among many other statistical differences, Hooten found the inmates were more likely to have sloping foreheads, dark hair, long necks, high nasal bridges, overbites, and thin lips.[35] Hooten's work was not well received in general, but it did appear to keep alive the search for biological components to deviant behavior.[36]

LATER MODELS OF BIOLOGICAL TRAITS AND "BODY TYPES"   Other theories developed to explain crime and deviance through various physiological characteristics. These included: *phrenology*, the study of human cranial cavities and shapes of human skulls; *endocrinology*, the study of the endocrine or glandular system, which attributes deviant behavior to an imbalance in this system, particularly in the imbalance of testosterone, the male sex hormone;[37] *heredity*, including the study of institutionalized and noninstitutionalized twins;[38] and body types. Early attention was given to body types. This may be due to the fact that the major proponents of the inclusion of body types, termed "somatotypes," as a criterion in deviant behavior have not isolated them from other factors. Sheldon classified three body types: the *ectomorph*, or tall and skinny; the *endomorph*, or short and fat; and the *mesomorph*, or athletic type. These body types correlate with three general types of temperament.[39] The Gluecks expanded upon Sheldon's body types and added a fourth, "balanced." In measuring various social, psychological, and physiological factors of 500 delinquents and comparing these with 500 nondelinquents, the Gluecks concluded that ". . . physique alone does not adequately explain delinquent behavior, it is nevertheless clear that, in conjunction with other forces, it does bear a relationship to delinquency." [40]

LATEST THEORIES: GENES AND THE XYY MODEL   Recent advances in genetics have spurred an interest in how genetic and chromosomal abnormalities may affect human behavior. The *XYY theory of deviant behavior* has received a substantial amount of notoriety. This theory is based upon studies that indicate a disproportionate number of inmates have an extra Y, or male, chromosome,[41] compared with the general population. Thus, it is hypothesized such individuals have a predisposition toward violent behavior.[42] Because chromosomes are not visible to others, outside of laboratory studies, this model would preclude an interaction of others' expectations in producing a behavioral pattern.[43] On the other hand, in addition to aggressive behavior, those with an XYY chromosome pattern appear to be more introverted and more frequently homosexual—behaviors not usually associated with violence. Other difficulties include the lack of criminality among the population of XYY males outside of prisons and the aggressiveness of inmates within prisons who do not have an extra male chromosome.[44] In short, no causal link or interacting pattern has been established in this relatively new field of inquiry into deviant behavior.

Our methodology and schedule items are not adequate to fully test for biological traits. Nevertheless, we shall find that some physiological factors do play a part in our informants' cases.

Psychological Theories

A wide variety of psychological explanations have been offered in the study of deviance. We shall summarize the psychiatric, or psychoanalytic, model and some personality theories, particularly that of the "criminal" or "sociopathic" personality.

PSYCHIATRIC THEORY OF DEVIANT BEHAVIOR   Psychiatric theory, with its emphasis that deviant behavior is a result of early childhood experiences, is popular in public opinion. This view is also the dominant one in use by social workers, probation officers, psychologists, and psychiatrists dealing directly as therapists with criminals, mentally ill, and other deviants. This view corresponds roughly with the "sickness" view of deviancy. We will find in our transcripts that when the deviants analyze themselves, they will often refer to the psychiatric view as the one to which they have been exposed in prison as explanatory of their behavior. Their satisfaction or dissatisfaction with the psychiatric explanation and other explanations provides major data for the evaluation of those theories.

Among psychiatric theories the psychoanalytic explanation, developed notably by Sigmund Freud, is the most widely used approach and the one we shall examine here. Briefly, deviant behavior is viewed as "antisocial conduct" that is a result of the dynamics of the unconscious mind rather than the conscious activities of mental life. Personality is considered to consist of three parts: the *id*, or underlying instinctual forces; the *superego*, or internalized prohibitions or standards; and the *ego*, or conscious self, largely concerned with mediating between the id and superego when they come into conflict. In this framework, the origin of all crime is the activation of the primitive id, which is considered to be instinctively savage, sensual, and destructive. Two basic instincts are said to be love or life instinct and death or hate instinct. Crime generally arises out of inadequate social restrictions or superego controls upon the id. The id may manifest itself in different ways through life—in externalized or internalized aggression, in infantile sexuality or polymorphous perversion—and in various stages of psychosexual development. Thus, individual forms of deviancy such as homosexuality, murder, and alcoholism are merely different manifestations of id impulses to be found in common in all people.

For our purposes, let us examine some common psychoanalytic theories of various forms of deviancy.

Murder   Murder is explained simply as a momentary release of the id impulses concerned with attack or defense. Or it may be due to a distorted or concealed erotic drive.[45]

Forcible rape   Infantile sexuality and polymorphous perversion are the sources of rape. In psychoanalytic theory, infants are bisexual at birth. Thus, there are masculine and feminine components in all of us, and these components may conflict with each other. The rapist may feel a strong conflict based upon an awareness of infantile bisexuality, and this conflict results in a feeling of inferiority and fear of sexual inadequacy that not only prevents normal sexual alliances and sexual intercourse but also causes the rapist to overcompensate by stressing the aggressive masculine component as a way of convincing himself that he is indeed male.

Theft   Psychosexual development of personality involves changes in the nature of sexual pleasure from the oral and anal preoccupation of infant life, to narcissism or love of self, to love of the parent of the opposite sex, culminating finally in love of a person of the opposite sex other than one's parents. According to one theory, various forms of theft are explained by regression to the early oral stage. Automobile theft is based upon regression to this stage. Burglary, forgery, and embezzlement are due to regression to the late oral stage. Armed robbery is due to regression to the late anal stage.[46]

Prostitution and homosexuality   These are generally explained in terms of overattachment to father or mother. Homosexuality in a man has been explained as resulting from overattachment to the mother (Oedipus complex), causing him to reject sex relations with other women.[47] Female prostitution and also lesbianism are due to overattachment of a girl to her father (Electra complex), resulting in her inability to receive

TABLE 4   *Forms of Deviance along a Continuum from Id to Superego*

Id			Superego
Infantile sexuality	Oral stage	Anal stage	Genital stage
Murder	Alcoholism	Embezzlement*	Prostitution
Forcible rape	Drug addiction	Armed robbery	Homosexuality

* Authors' interpretation.

sexual gratification from other men. Sexual immaturity, however, may also result in prostitution, so that a girl who has been denied sufficient parental love, affection, and security in childhood establishes liaisons because she wants to feel that she is wanted and needed.

Drug addiction and alcoholism   The general explanation for both of these disorders in psychoanalytic thinking is infantile regression, particularly to the oral stage, so that "oral personalities" (passive, insecure, dependent) are characteristic. Drinking may serve other functions, however, including overcoming feelings of sexual impotency.

Overview   The psychoanalytic view, from the above analysis, seems to imply a kind of paradigm of deviancy based upon the psychosexual stage that seems to be implied by the form of deviancy. The paradigm is roughly portrayed in Table 4, based upon a psychosexual sequence of development from id-dominant self to superego-dominant self. The particular form of deviance that would occur depends upon either fixation at a particular psychosexual stage or regression to that stage due to sudden suspension of superego controls.

PERSONALITY EXPLANATIONS: THE SOCIOPATH   Freudian influence has pervaded the field of psychology. Thus, many other explanations contain an emphasis upon early childhood factors in personality development. Some are more Freudian than others, but personality explanations of deviance tend to emphasize the result of childhood influences rather than the process of development. A large body of information has been written regarding that personality type alternately designed as "criminal," "psychopathic," or, more commonly, "sociopathic." There appears to be no specific delineation as to the totality of characteristics of this personality. However, a list of generally accepted traits would include:

1. Inability to form close, interpersonal relationships.[48]
2. Lack of feelings of guilt.[49]
3. Impulsiveness, lack of self-control.[50]
4. Hedonistic; seeks immediate rather than deferred gratification.[51]
5. Egocentric.[52]
6. Sexual immaturity and a lack of satisfactory sexual performance.[53]
7. Emotional immaturity.[54]
8. A lack of time perspective.[55]
9. A general lack of regard for community standards and chronic antisocial behavior.[56]

Yochelson and Samenow note that the "criminal personality" is also characterized by boredom, lying, dependency, irresponsibility, and a tendency to have difficulties in school in spite of a higher than average I.Q.[57] Many psychologists trace the development of the sociopath to maternal deprivation during early years (birth to three).[58] Yochelson and Samenow disagree with those who emphasize early and later childhood factors as "shaping" the criminal. They claim that many such individuals have adequate home lives, marked by a balance of discipline and affection, yet from the onset are "different" from siblings and others.[59] The criminal-to-be, they contend, shows initial traits of ambivalent emotions and morality, shies away from affection, and lies to ("cons") and exploits his or her parents.[60]

Other psychologists have attributed deviant behavior to mental retardation, subnormal I.Q., and feelings of fear and of being unloved.[61] Currently, a frequent personality characteristic cited is that of a "low self-esteem," or "negative self-concept." [62] The difficulty in establishing a causal relationship lies in the fact that the low self-esteem may follow or result from the deviant behavior rather than lead to it.[63]

A team of behavioral scientists, headed by Jessor, has developed a theory that is, in effect, a "psychosocial" model of deviant behavior. The model includes what is termed a "personality system." [64] The components of the system include various sociological concepts that will be discussed below. Factors related to social control, alienation, and anomie theories are said to be internalized within the personality system through the process of socialization.[65] The main components of the personality system leading to deviant behavior are: 1) *the perceived opportunity structure*, including "personal disjunctions" and "increased pressure toward use of illegitimate means"; 2) *the personal belief structure*, including alienation, belief in external control, and "attenuated control against use of illegitimate means"; and 3) *the personal control structure*, including tolerance of deviance, tendency toward immediate gratification, short-time perspective and "attenuated control against use of illegitimate means." [66] In many ways, the model proposed by Jessor and his colleagues could be classified as a "social control" explanation. Social control theories will constitute the initial set of sociological explanations that will next be summarized.

Sociological Theories

As mentioned at the beginning of this section, some theories herein described as sociological have varying degrees of psychological emphases. They are at times termed "social-psychological," or "psychosocial." We shall begin with summations of those theories with the greatest degree of psychological, or individual, orientation (i.e., at the "micro" level) and progress toward those with a societal (or "macro") level of emphasis. In subsequent chapters, this order will vary according to whatever format better suits the form of deviance under explanation. The order of our summaries is: social control theories, labeling, differential association, subcultural, anomie and opportunity theories, and alienation or conflict theories.

SOCIAL CONTROL THEORIES   The focus of social control theories is not only why some individuals deviate from the norms of society, but also why other individuals act according to those norms, that is, the effectiveness of group "controls." They seek to explain, for instance, why some juveniles in areas of high rates of delinquency do not participate in delinquent behavior, or why some persons living in neighborhoods marked by access to and consumption of drugs do not become drug addicts. These theories range from those with a high degree of psychoanalytic emphasis, called "psychodynamic" or "psychosocial" models, to those which have as their emphasis the social sanctions or deterrent effects of the legal system. They have in common a consideration of the interacting nature of the individual and society, the manner in which the group, or society, is able to exert its power over the individual's actions, and the manner in which the individual accepts or rejects that authority.

PSYCHOSOCIAL MODELS   Eysenck and Trasler explain deviant behavior in terms of "defective social training." Behavior and "conscience" are the result of rewards and punishments. Conforming, or deviant behavior, thus, are acquired through "conditioning," by stimuli being administered associated simultaneously, or nearly simultaneously, with a desired behavior. The administration of stimuli prior to desired behavior is termed "classical" or "respondent" conditioning. A more effective form is "operant" or "instrumental" conditioning, in which a reward or punishment follows one's acts. Timing, intensity, and consistency are important components of effective social training. Defective training or lack of adequate punishment for antisocial behavior will reinforce that behavior and adult deviance will result.[67] Bandura and Walters have expanded upon the model of Eysenck and Trasler through the inclusion of "modeling" as a training technique in addition to conditioning. By imitating role models, and viewing what rewards and punishments the model receive for behavior, children will acquire behavior patterns. Thus, for instance, if a prominent citizen is given probation for embezzling thousands of dollars and a poor person is sent to prison for stealing twenty-five dollars, a child will learn "it is acceptable to steal if you have influential friends and steal large amounts." Likewise, what happens to the "good guys" on television as opposed to violent or aggressive "bad buys" may influence behavior more than the amount of televised violence.[68]

RECKLESS' CONTAINMENT MODEL   Walker Reckless approaches social control in a broader context and places greater emphasis upon the interaction of social and psychological factors. Reckless terms his model "containment theory." According to Reckless, containment, or social control, has two major aspects: "external" containment and "internal" containment. These have also been referred to as "outer" and "inner" controls or control mechanisms. External components of containment reside primarily in the family and other "supportive groups." They include:

1. A *role structure* that provides scope for the individual.
2. A set of reasonable *limits and responsibilities* for members.
3. An *opportunity* for the individual to achieve a status.
4. *Cohesion* among members, including joint activity and togetherness.
5. Sense of *belongingness* (identification with the group).
6. *Identification* with one or more persons within the group.
7. Provision for supplying *alternative ways* and means of satisfaction (when one or more ways are closed).[69]

Internal containment consists of "self" components (perhaps similar to "conscience"). They are:

1. A *favorable image of self* in relation to other persons, groups, and institutions.
2. An awareness of being an *inner-directed, goal-oriented* person.
3. A high level of *frustration tolerance*.
4. Strongly *internalized morals* and ethics.
5. A *well developed ego and superego*.[70]

Reckless views the two components of control as interacting and corollary to each other. Internal containment is a "microcosm" that reflects the larger, external "macrocosm." [71] The two systems of containment are seen as "buffers" or "insulations" against "pressures, pulls, and pushes" to deviate. When both components are weak, an individual is "vulnerable" to deviant behavior. Greater strength in either or both components reduces this vulnerability correspondingly.[72] Reckless proposes that his model may be of use to probation officers, governmental agencies, and institutions in both the treatment of offenders and the "prevention of crime and delinquency." [73] Thus, the components of outer or external control may be seen to include mechanism of control such as police, the judicial system, psychiatry, and so on. Reckless pointed out initially that in modern, mobile, industrialized societies "inner" containment is the more important and "outer" mechanism is less effective. In tribal societies, the opposite holds true.[74] In later works with Dinitz, Reckless emphasizes the importance of internal control and elaborates upon the "self-concept" component as the primary factor in vulnerability.[75]

OTHER SOCIAL CONTROL THEORIES   There have been several other attempts to further delineate components of social control. Hirschi proposes a model that accentuates the link or *"bond"* between the individual and society. The elements of this bond appear to embrace components of both internal and external mechanisms of control. Hirschi views these elements as the control factors that prevent deviancy and, rather than operating separately, interact and are interrelated. They include attachment, commitment, involvement, and belief. *Attachment* is the sense of moral obligation to the opinions of others (such as parents and peers). This attachment to conventional others is related to *commitment* toward conventional activities and resultant investment of time and energy in these activities (hence, one is reluctant to risk time in prison and the resultant loss of this investment). *Involvement* in conventional activities places one apart in time and place from deviant activities. *Belief* in conventional activities goes hand-in-hand with one's actions and one's attachment to conventional others. In sum, these elements explain *not* why some individuals deviate, but why others conform.[76]

Albert Cohen develops certain concepts that may be considered, in effect, an expansion of Reckless' "external" containment. Cohen notes that social control includes not only the "manifest control structure," such as police, probation officers, judges, and programs of prevention, but also anything "that people do that is *socially defined* as 'doing something about deviance,' whatever that 'something' is: prevention, deterrence, reform, vengeance, justice, reparation, compensation of the victim." [77] He notes the increasing role of youth organizations, correctional institutions, treatment facilities, regulators, and the like, as agents of social control in modern societies. As a result, he suggests, their role *in* deviance must be considered as well as their potential *for* deviance, through corruption, favoritism, and negligence.[78]

LABELING   Labeling is sometimes called a theory, at other times, a "perspective." The reason for the discussion is that labeling theory differs from psychoanalytic theory, social control, and others in that it does not include any revelation of underlying "causes." Howard Becker suggests that the idea that all causes of deviancy operate simultaneously is not true, and that what is needed is a "sequential model of deviance" that takes into account the fact that patterns of behavior develop in an orderly sequence. Each step along the way requires explanation, and what may operate as a cause at one step may be of negligible importance at another step.[79]

In another way, too, there is an omission of causal analysis in labeling theory. That is, the starting point for labeling theory is *primary deviance*—deviance that has not been reacted to or labeled. There is little concern in labeling theory with what went before the primary deviance. Instead, there is a shift in interest from how deviant behavior originates to the problem of societal reaction. If causes exist, they are to be found in the societal reaction to primary deviance rather than in what went before. Thus, if labeling theory explains anything, it explains *secondary deviance*—deviance that has been in some way reacted to by society, has resulted in stigmatic labeling and other punishment, and in turn is a result of the deviant's reaction to society's treatment through greater participation in deviant subcultures and perhaps commission of more serious or sophisticated acts of deviance. Lemert traces the labeling theory approach to the development of a deviant career through several stages:

> 1) primary deviation; 2) social penalties; 3) further primary deviation; 4) stronger penalties and rejection; 5) further deviation, perhaps with hostilities and resentment beginning to focus upon those doing the penalizing; 6) crisis reached in the tolerance quotient, expressed in formal action by the community stigmatizing of the deviant; 7) strengthening of the deviant conduct as a negative reaction to the stigmatizing and penalties; 8) ultimate acceptance of deviant social status and efforts at adjustment on the basis of the associated role.[80]

The final step in the labeling process thus is an acceptance of the stigmatizing label, the adoption of this stigma as a "self-concept." It should be noted that a realization of "self-concept" is seen as a beginning rather than an end, as in the psychological and social control theories described above.

The same or similar process of societal reaction and progression is postulated for all forms of deviancy. This differs from other approaches, which yielded paradigms for different forms of deviancy with associated underlying causes or personal dynamics. Instead, labeling theory yields a constantly increasing literature of ethnographies and case studies that trace in detail the process and development of one or another form of deviancy. The explanations given in these accounts are often eclectic, drawing upon explanations that seem to apply in the individual cases. But there also seems to be an underlying assumption that primary deviancy is distributed almost randomly throughout the society, and the subsequent development of more serious forms of secondary deviation is a result of differential labeling of behavior by society.

The labeling theory approach and related methodologies have opened up whole new vistas in the study of deviancy. For once, those who study labeling accounts can come to feel they understand deviants from the point of view of deviants. If we can approach the subject from this angle, an approach of striving for what Weber called *verstehen* or intuitive understanding, not only do we develop a better feel for the real world, but we can, through our understanding, strengthen our knowledge of underlying causes and explanations of behavior. This, then, is one task of this text. We hope to show the supportive rather than antagonistic relationship between the ethnographic-labeling approach, which stresses intuitive understanding, and other approaches, which focus upon explanation of behavior.

DIFFERENTIAL ASSOCIATION THEORY   Sutherland developed a theory of differential association, later expanded upon by Cressey. This theory emphasizes the factors of learning and primary groups. It has been stated axiomatically as a list of propositions, each of which is testable:

1) deviant behavior is learned rather than inherited; 2) it is learned in interaction with other persons in a process of communication; 3) the principal part of the learning occurs within intimate personal groups rather than through impersonal agencies such as movies and newspapers; 4) the learning includes a) techniques of committing delinquent acts, and b) the specific direction of motives, drives, rationalizations, and attitudes; 5) the specific direction of motives and drives is learned from definitions of the legal codes as favorable or unfavorable; 6) a person becomes deviant because of an excess of definitions favorable to violation of law over definitions unfavorable to violation of law; 7) differential associations may vary in frequency, duration, priority, and intensity; 8) this process involves all the mechanisms involved in other learning; and 9) deviant behavior is not explained by needs and values, since nondeviant behavior is an expression of the same needs and values.[81]

The basic process envisioned, then, is one of *learning* rationalizations and techniques *within primary* groups. The *definitions* learned are those both *favorable and unfavorable* to deviance.

This theory is somewhat fundamental and essentially involves a process of socialization and/or resocialization. It has received considerable attention in the field of deviance. Because it is explicit and direct, it does not require a great deal of additional explanation. The amount of space that is given herein thus reflects this explicitness rather than its relative importance in sociological thought. At the same time, the theory has been criticized as too basic and broad, thus explaining everything without shedding new enlightenment. It will be found in succeeding chapters that differential association has wide application to a variety of deviant patterns. Whether this is a strength or a weakness will not be decided at this point.

ALIENATION OR CONFLICT THEORIES   Just as the concept of anomie was brought to sociology by Durkheim, the concept of alienation entered American sociology through the theories of Karl Marx. The concept, basically, means "to be separate or estranged from" (hence, "alien to"). Alienation is a key concept, if not the basic concept, in Marx's grand theory. The basis of alienation, to Marx, was the appropriation of private property by humans. Thereafter, humans became alienated from themselves, from each other, and from nature, because such appropriation and resulting economic structures were against human nature. History is a series of alienating experiences between succeeding social classes, each marked by the exploitation of the "have-nots," or workers, by the "haves" who control the means of production. Alienation will cease when private property no longer exists and humankind lives in its true state of nature, as beings working for the good of the entire species. Until such a state is reached, however, humankind will live in a state of "false consciousness" accepting the ideology of the dominant class.[82]

The successors to Marxian theory in American studies of deviance today are the "conflict theorists." At times, their theories are termed "alienation theories," and some non-Marxians have utilized a concept of alienation to explain such aspects of deviance as "the youth subculture," and so on. We will briefly summarize these approaches.

Richard Quinney is the foremost proponent of conflict theory within criminology today. He claims that "justice" has as its objective the promotion of social order, and that "in capitalist society the healthy order is the one that benefits the capitalist class." [83] Thus, "equal justice," as we see it, is a product of our false consciousness and capitalist ideology.[84] The dominant, capitalist class defines certain behavior as "criminal," along with defining those who are "criminals." [85] Many of the crimes in capitalist society are crimes of "accommodation" (e.g., to conditions of unemployment) or "resistance" to the exploitation of the workers.[86] Quinney has cited the background of those in the major governmental regulatory agencies and the Department of Justice as evidence of their ruling class roots as not inclined to question the established social order.[87] Other conflict theorists cite the differential enforcement of laws that uphold the interests of the dominant class as opposed to the lower socioeconomic groups as evidence of Marxian concepts.[88]

To a considerable degree, these conflict approaches are similar to labeling approaches and are a critique of the manner in which deviance is defined and reacted to rather than a set of explanatory hypotheses as to the "causes" of deviance.

SUBCULTURAL THEORIES   A great deal of research and theories regarding deviance in the United States during the first half of this century dealt with subcultures. Relying to a great extent upon patterns of official data, they had in common attempts to explain deviance as: 1) primarily related to, part of, or stemming from delinquency; 2) associated with lower-class strata, thus made up of racial, ethnic, religious, immigrant, and other minorities; and, 3) a part of "gangs" that appeared to form in the inner-city, large metropolitan areas. Availability of unofficial data, new methods of research, the upward mobility of many of the "lower-class" groups, and other factors have called into question many of the assumptions regarding the existence and nature of such "gangs," the norms and values of lower socioeconomic groups, and the distribution of crime, delinquency, and deviancy across social class boundaries.

Nevertheless, these theories are important for their contribution to the development of sociological thought and they contain concepts and factors related to other theoretical explanations. The major theories, as they relate to delinquency, follow.

Status deprivation theory   According to this theory, delinquency is traced to the inability of lower class boys to compete in school with middle class youngsters, based upon the limited abilities of lower class youngsters. While lower class youngsters may partially internalize middle class success values, they find they have limited opportunities to achieve them. The delinquent gang offers an alternative status system with alternative values antithetical to middle class values, emphasizing actions that are malicious, negativistic, and nonutilitarian, and thus delinquent in middle class terms.[89]

Drift theory   This theory was developed as an alternative to theories of delinquency that view the delinquent as somehow constrained by gangs in which he participates to commit delinquent acts.[90] Actually, the theory states, delinquency is only a fraction of total behavior of "delinquents" and it is generally accompanied by feelings of guilt. Delinquency will take place on a continuous basis only if an adolescent can successfully neutralize his guilt; the delinquent, instead of living in a monolithic subculture of delinquency, vacillates in limbo, drifting from conforming to delinquent patterns of behavior—a state characterized as *anomie*. Drift theory is thus linked to social control theories already presented as well as to anomie/opportunity theories that will follow.

The theory of cultural transmission   This theory states that delinquency is a product not just of lower class peer group affiliation per se, but of the entire lower class community, which conflicts in its values with the middle class. Such lower class values include autonomy, fate, excitement, smartness, toughness, and trouble, and they are passed on largely through the agency of the peer group, which serves the emotional function of the middle class family. Thus, gang activities, such as assault and theft, are self-consciously law-violating and motivated by a strict alternative code of moral standards.[91] This theory may also be seen as incorporating the learning aspects of differential association theory. The "definitions" passed on by the peer group are those favorable to delinquency.

Certain "gang" or youthful "subculture" theories are closely related to anomie and alienation theories and will be explained shortly. It should be noted, however, that other subcultural factors, such as the existence of a "subculture of violence" and the Mafia, are related to those explanations given above. Finally, various deviant groups form subcultures as a protection from the larger society and as a means of engaging in their deviant activities. These are not necessarily related to social class or minority status.

Opportunity theory   This theory is based directly upon Merton's anomie approach. Merton views delinquency as an attempt by lower class youngsters to adapt to a situation of limited opportunity by using illegitimate means such as theft to attain the goal of pecuniary success. Differential opportunity theory, developed by Cloward and Ohlin, is an extension of Merton's anomie approach. To Merton's discussion of differential access to legitimate means, Cloward and Ohlin add a discussion of differential access to *illegitimate means*. While legitimate means are more available in the middle class, illegitimate means are more available in the lower class. Delinquency results when, failing access to legitimate means, a youngster seeks and gains access to membership in a delinquent subculture. However, if the individual fails to gain access to a delinquent subculture, he becomes a "double failure" and falls into the less organized and less demanding "retreatist subculture." [92]

ANOMIE/OPPORTUNITY THEORIES   The concept of *anomie* in sociology was originally defined by the famous French sociologist Emile Durkheim. It has been reconceptualized in American sociology by Robert Merton. To Durkheim, society was a "moral force" exerting the "collective conscience" upon individuals. Through its norms and value system, society restrains "individual passions" in a process of regulation. However, when society is "disturbed" by "abrupt transitions" (whether "painful" or "beneficent") it "is momentarily incapable of exercising this influence." This condition, a period in which the former norms do not fit the new situation, Durkheim saw as a state of *"anomie."* [93]

Merton's theory of anomie   The anomie theory of deviancy, developed in this country by Merton, is the present-day successor to the theory of social disorganization and is the predecessor to numerous microtheories.[94] Widespread deviant behavior will occur, in Merton's terms, under a condition of *anomie,* which he defines as:

> ...a breakdown in the cultural structure, occurring particularly when there is an acute dysjunction between the cultural norms and goals and the socially structured capacities of members of the group to act in accord with them.[95]

Anomie in these terms occurs in American society because there is a strong emphasis upon the value of the specific goal of pecuniary success, but a relatively slight concern with the institutionally appropriate modes of attaining this goal, combined with a differential allocation of access to institutional means to success. This situation leads to a strain toward deviancy in the lower class. Lower class people lack access to legitimate means to success (education, money, capital, know-how) but at the same time are encouraged to achieve the goal of pecuniary success. Lacking legitimate means, lower class people may turn to crime as an alternate or "technically most feasible procedure" for rising socially. Some lower class people fail even in crime, so that they may come to reject not only conventional means to success, but also the success goal. These people may become alcoholics, drug addicts, vagrants, and psychotics. Another reaction might be total rebellion against the system of means and goals, and the setting up of an alternative society or subculture within society.

With the exception of a few examples of deviancy, Merton does not discuss in detail individual forms of deviancy, but he provides a general paradigm of deviancy that could be applied to various forms of deviancy. Since the two major elements in Merton's theory are cultural goals and institutionalized means, he is able to develop a paradigm of

TABLE 5   *Merton's Paradigm of Deviant Behavior: A Typology of Modes of Individual Adaptation**

Modes of adaptation	Cultural goals	Institutionalized Means
I. Conformity	+	+
II. Innovation	+	−
III. Ritualism	−	+
IV. Retreatism	−	−
V. Rebellion	±	±

(+) = Acceptance
(−) = Rejection
(±) = Rebellion

* From Robert K. Merton, *Social Theory and Social Structure*, Revised and Enlarged Edition, p. 140. Copyright 1957 by The Free Press, a Corporation.

deviancy based simply upon acceptance or rejection of these goals or means. Merton's paradigm is shown in Table 5. Though references to specific forms of deviancy are vague in Merton's essay, we can infer from it a connection between these general types and some of the specific forms of deviancy covered in this book. "Innovation," utilization of illegitimate means to attain success goals, appears to encompass most official forms of crime and delinquency, particularly pecuniary crimes. Thus, it includes violent crimes and robbery, but as a route to success Merton also includes embezzlement and perhaps organized crime within this category. Since vice is often a means of pecuniary support, Merton would also include prostitution within this category. Most other major forms of deviancy are covered under "retreatism," which entails rejection of both legitimate means and success goals, including "psychotics, autists, outcasts, vagrants, tramps, chronic drunkards, and drug addicts." [96] The other two categories, ritualism and rebellion, are largely residual.

It should be noted that the major focus of Merton's theory is the social class basis of deviancy and that most forms of major deviancy are located in the lower class, although the general state of anomie in our society may yield a strain toward middle forms of deviancy among middle and upper class people as well. This assumption of lower class link will be of interest in the transcripts to follow. We shall also be interested to see if the development of a deviant career follows the logical path of carefully calculated acceptance or rejection of means or ends presupposed by anomie theory.

We should keep in mind that although Merton's theory has largely been utilized in explaining the discrepancy between pecuniary goals and means, it is possible to internalize other goals, such as sexual prowess, or to internalize a pecuniary goal beyond the legitimate means available to that individual in spite of his relative wealth. Thus, "*overemphasis*" of goals, of whatever nature, is important to Merton's theory and our inquiry.

═══ A CONCLUDING NOTE

Students frequently complain of the multiplicity of theories and concepts in the study of sociology and of deviant behavior in particular. It is hoped that the above classifications and summarizations have helped eliminate some of this confusion. The reader may have noted that certain factors, and even concepts, seem to overlap and converge between theories. In the succeeding chapters, this will become even more evident. We will note the "interaction" of various factors from biology, psychology, and sociology. The application to concrete life histories and cases will, hopefully, enhance one's grasp of abstract concepts and theories, as well as allow us to better understand the reality of deviants as that reality is placed within theoretical frameworks.

═══ NOTES

1. Donald Cressy, *Other People's Money* (Glencoe, Ill.: The Free Press, 1953).
2. Jacqueline Wiseman and Marcia Aron, *Field Projects for Sociology Students* (Cambridge, Mass.: Schenkman Publishing Co., 1970), p. 27.
3. Robert Merton and Patricia Kendall, "The Focused Interview," *American Journal of Sociology*, 51 (1946), pp. 541–557.
4. Ibid., p. 541.
5. Wiseman and Aron, *Field Projects*, p. 34.
6. Merton and Kendall, "The Focused Interview," p. 546.
7. Wiseman and Aron, *Field Projects*, p. 50.
8. Ibid., pp. 51–53.
9. Jack Douglas, *Observations of Deviance* (New York: Random House, 1970), p. 8.
10. Ibid.
11. Jeremiah Lowney, "The Role of a Non-Participant Observer in Drug Abuse Field Research," unpublished paper presented to the Society for the Study of Social Problems, Annual Meeting, San Francisco, August, 1975.
12. Aaron V. Cicourel, *Method and Measurement in Sociology* (New York: The Free Press, 1964), p. 45.
13. Harold Garfinkel, *Studies in Ethnomethodology* (Englewood Cliffs, N.J.: Prentice-Hall, Inc., 1967).
14. Cicourel, *Method and Measurement*, p. 36.
15. Ibid., p. 47.
16. Cressey, *Other People's Money*.
17. Ibid., p. 14.
18. Ibid.
19. Ibid., p. 16.
20. Erich Fromm, *The Sane Society* (New York: Rinehart & Co., 1958).
21. Howard Becker, *Outsiders* (New York: The Free Press, 1963), p. 9.
22. Marshall B. Clinard, *Sociology of Deviant Behavior* (New York: Holt, Rinehart and Winston, 1968), p. 28.

23. Ruth S. Cavan, *Criminology* (New York: Thomas Y. Crowell, 1962), chap. 3.

24. Ibid., p. 46.

25. Clinard, *Deviant Behavior*, p. 256.

26. Edwin H. Sutherland and Donald R. Cressey, *Criminology*, 10th ed. (Philadelphia: J. B. Lippincott, 1978), pp. 277–279.

27. Thorsten Sellin and Marvin E. Wolfgang, *The Measurement of Delinquency* (New York: John Wiley & Sons, 1964).

28. Robert W. Winslow, *The Emergence of Deviant Minorities* (San Ramon, Calif.: Consensus Publishing Co., 1972).

29. Pierre L. van den Berghe, *Man in Society: A Biosocial View* (New York: Elsevier, 1975).

30. Sue Titus Reid, *Crime and Criminology*, 2nd ed. (New York: Holt, Rinehart and Winston, 1979), pp. 136–161.

31. Ibid., p. 161; Edward Sagarin, *Deviants and Deviance* (New York: Praeger, 1975), p. 88; van den Berghe, *Man in Society*.

32. Reid, *Crime and Criminology*, 2nd ed., pp. 137–138.

33. Ibid., pp. 142–146.

34. Sue Titus Reid, *Crime and Criminology*, 1st ed. (Hinsdale, Ill.: The Dryden Press, 1976), p. 136.

35. Ibid., pp. 134–135.

36. Ibid., p. 131.

37. Reid, *Crime and Criminology*, 2nd ed. (1979), pp. 148–149.

38. Ibid., pp. 152–153.

39. W. H. Sheldon, *The Varieties of Human Physique: An Introduction to Constitutional Psychology* (New York: Harper & Row, 1940), pp. 8–9.

40. Sheldon Glueck and Eleanor Glueck, *Physique and Delinquency* (New York: Harper & Row, 1956), pp. 2, 249.

41. Sagarin, *Deviants and Deviance*, p. 86.

42. Ibid.

43. Ibid., p. 87.

44. Ibid., pp. 86–87; Reid, *Crime and Criminology*, pp. 138–139.

45. David Abrahamson, *Crime and the Human Mind* (New York: Harcourt, Brace & World, 1943).

46. Arthur N. Foxe, "Classification of the Criminotic Indivdual," in Robert Lindner and Robert Seliger, eds., *Handbook of Correctional Psychology* (New York: Philosophical Library, 1947).

47. Aron Krich, ed., *The Homosexuals* (New York: The Citadel Press, 1954).

48. Reid, *Crime and Criminology*, 1st ed (1976), p. 162.

49. Samuel Yochelson and Stanton E. Samenow, *The Criminal Personality, Vol. I: A Profile for Change* (New York: Jason Aronson, 1976), p. 90.

50. Ibid.

51. Reid, *Crime and Criminology*, 1st ed. (1976), p. 162.

52. Ibid., p. 162; Yochelson and Samenow, *The Criminal Personality*, p. 90.

53. Yochelson and Samenow, *The Criminal Personality*, pp. 90, 93.

54. Ibid., p. 90; Reid, *Crime and Criminology*, 1st ed. (1976), p. 162.

55. Yochelson and Samenow, *The Criminal Personality*, p. 97.

56. Ibid., p. 90.

57. Ibid., pp. 90, 92–93, 144–156.

58. Reid, *Crime and Criminology*, 1st ed. (1976), p. 163.

59. Yochelson and Samenow, *The Criminal Personality*, pp. 119–128.

60. Ibid., pp. 127–134.

61. Sagarin, *Deviants and Deviance*, pp. 89–90.

62. Ibid., p. 90.

63. Ibid.

64. Richard Jessor, Theodore D. Graves, Robert C. Hanson, and Shirley L. Jessor, *Society, Personality and Deviant Behavior* (New York: Holt, Rinehart and Winston, 1968), pp. 83–112.

65. Ibid., pp. 116–133.

66. Ibid., p. 111.

67. Gwynn Nettler, *Explaining Crime*, 2nd ed. (New York: McGraw-Hill, 1978), pp. 314–318.

68. Ibid., pp. 315–320.

69. Walter C. Reckless, "Containment Theory," in Barry Krisberg and James Austin (eds.), *The Children of Ishmael: Critical Perspectives on Juvenile Justice* (Palo Alto, Calif.: Mayfield Publishing, 1978), pp. 187–189.

70. Ibid., p. 189.

71. Ibid., pp. 191–192.

72. Ibid., pp. 189–191.

73. Ibid., pp. 191–192.

74. Ibid., p. 190.

75. Walter C. Reckless and Simon Dinitz, "Pioneering with Self-Concept as a Vulnerability Factor in Delinquency," *Journal of Criminal Law, Criminology, and Police Science* (Chicago: Northwestern University School of Law, 1967), Vol. 58, No. 4.

76. Travis Hirschi, *Causes of Delinquency* (Berkeley: University of California Press, 1969).

77. Albert K. Cohen, *Devance and Control* (Englewood Cliffs, N.J.: Prentice-Hall, Inc., 1966), p. 39.

78. Ibid., pp. 39–40.

79. Becker, *Outsiders*.

80. Edwin M. Lemert, *Human Deviance, Social Problems, and Social Control* (Englewood Cliffs, N.J.: Prentice-Hall, Inc., 1962), p. 17.

81. Edwin Sutherland, *Principles of Criminology* (Philadelphia: J.B. Lippincott, 1960), chap. 4.

82. Karl Marx, "Economic and Philosophical Manuscripts," as in Erich Fromm, *Marx's Concept of Man* (New York: Frederick Ungar Publishing, 1961), pp. 90–191.

83. Richard Quinney, *Class, State and Crime: On the Theory and Practice of Criminal Justice* (New York: David McKay, 1977), p. 3.

84. Ibid., pp. 2–4.

85. Ibid., pp. 33–62.

86. Ibid., pp. 52–61.

87. Richard Quinney, *Critique of Legal Order: Crime Control in a Capitalist Society* (Boston: Little, Brown, 1974).

88. William J. Chambliss, *Functional and Conflict Theories of Crime* (New York: MSS Modular Publications, 1974), pp. 16–23.

89. Albert Cohen, *Delinquent Boys: The Culture of the Gang* (Glencoe, Ill.: The Free Press, 1955).

90. David Matza, *Delinquency and Drift* (New York: John Wiley & Sons, 1964).

91. William Kvaraceus et al., *Delinquent Behavior: Culture and the Individual* (Washington, D.C.: Juvenile Delinquency Project, N.E.A., 1201 Sixteenth St., N. W., 1959); Walter Miller, "Lower Class Culture as a Generating Milieu of Gang Delinquency," *Journal of Social Issues*, 14 (April, 1958), pp. 5–19.

92. R. A. Cloward and L. E. Ohlin, *Delinquency and Opportunity* (Glencoe, Ill.: The Free Press, 1960).

93. Emile Durkheim, *Suicide*, trans. by John A. Spaulding and George Simpson (New York: The Free Press, 1951), pp. 251–252.

94. Robert K. Merton, *Social Theory and Social Structure* (Glencoe, Ill.: The Free Press, 1957), chap. 4, "Social Structure and Anomie."

95. Ibid., p. 162.

96. Ibid., p. 187.

Social Nudism

2

Nudism is a topic rarely studied by sociologists. This may be due to the sensitive nature of nudity, or to the fact that nudism is one of the extreme forms of "victimless" deviance. Both views will be examined within this chapter. Most reports by sociologists have been written for the lay reader. They contain little theoretical framework that would be useful for our purposes.[1] The major work on the subject of social nudism has been done by Martin Weinberg. His work is oriented to the phenomenological and interactionist approaches. We will rely heavily upon Weinberg's analysis within this chapter.

THE NATURE OF NUDISM

In traditional public opinion, nudism is probably linked with voyeurism and/or exhibitionism. These, in turn, are linked with other forms of sexual deviance in the public mind and, thus, nudism may be indirectly perceived as a threat to sexual mores and family life. On the other hand, increasing sociological research has been geared to other forms of "victimless" crimes in recent years with little attention paid to nudism. Likewise, public behavior in recent years has sanctioned formally or informally such phenomena as a "streaking" craze on college campuses and an apparent increase in the number and use of nude beaches.

To the more traditional "social nudist," one who has joined a nudist association and frequented nudist camps, nudism has a special meaning distinct from the forms of psychopathology, voyeurism, and exhibitionism to which it is linked in more traditional public opinion. Apparently nudists go to great efforts to distinguish between themselves and what the public thinks they are. Nudists also take steps to screen sexual deviants from their midst. The distinction between nudism, on the one hand, and exhibitionism and voyeurism, on the other, is not merely terminological but actively employed in admission of people to nudist camps and in excluding and ejecting those who fail to comply.

Voyeurism

Voyeurism, or scopophilia, has been defined as "the act of window peeping, generally for the purpose of viewing a female disrobing." [2] Window peeping has been studied primarily by psychiatrists, and there are conflicting perspectives in that field. One perspective is that voyeurs are men who are acting out thwarted impulses to view female nudity and heterosexual activity, while another is that voyeurism is derived from elements in our social structure that make the viewing of private behaviors such as nudity and coital activities highly attractive to virtually all males. Etiologically, it is agreed among authorities that voyeurs are passive individuals who desire no further contact with the persons they observe, in contrast to the public fear that they are potentially violent menaces.[3] In addition, they are generally young men (average age 23.8 years), generally unmarried, and show a continuous pattern of peeping.[4]

There is, of course, a conceptual difference between voyeurs and social nudists in that voyeurs are not generally visible to the people they observe, while social nudists are mutually visible. While the voyeur may wish to hide from the person being observed, the social nudist wishes to be seen or at least consents to be seen nude by the person or persons being observed in their nude state.

Exhibitionism

Exhibitionism, or indecent exposure, is defined as "public genital exhibitionism on the part of the male" in this country.[5] Few if any females are arrested for this offense. It is believed that anticipation of sexual interest on the part of the female is the motivating force in exhibitionism.

Like voyeurism, exhibitionism has been studied principally by psychiatrists, who generally hold that exhibitionism is undertaken to reassure the male of his own masculinity by way of the shocked reactions of observing females; that exhibitionism is generated by a faulty mother-son relationship and that the act is an attempt to overcome dominance of the male by his mother; that exhibitionists generally come from families in which the father is passive; the exhibitionists are generally between the ages of twenty-three and thirty-nine, with a median age of thirty years; and that the majority are unusually timid, retiring, and often highly conscientious individuals.[6] According to one definition, *nudism* is a "sanctioned form of exhibitionism" that takes place within American society.[7]

Nudism

Nudism is conceptually distinct from both voyeurism and exhibitionism. Conceivably, however, a nudist could be both a voyeur and an exhibitionist simultaneously. Thus, the foregoing psychiatric studies may give us clues to "nudist personality."

Social Nudism from the Nudist's Point of View

Weinberg's thoroughgoing analysis of nudists and nudism sheds some light on the relationship between nudism, voyeurism, and exhibitionism. Weinberg used ethnomethodological techniques of participant observation and interview. He conducted 101 interviews with nudists in the Chicago area, spent two successive summers of participant observation in nudist camps, and analyzed results from 617 mailed questionnaires completed by nudists located throughout the United States and Canada. The location of Weinberg's research should be given serious thought in terms of his findings. Nudist attitudes in Chicago may be quite different from those on the West Coast and in other parts of the world.

Nudists do not, according to Weinberg's results, see themselves as exhibitionists or voyeurs. In fact, they see themselves as sexually modest and even "prudish." The norms of nudist camps explicitly preclude all forms of sexual conduct and distinguish between nudity and sexuality. Thus, organizational precautions include such norms as "no staring," no sex talk, a taboo on body contact, no alcoholic beverages, a taboo on accentuation of the body, a taboo on suggestive dancing, and a taboo on photography except by legitimate nudist photographers.[8] Nudist camps exclude people who become erotically aroused at the sight of the nude body. Nudist camps, in addition to employing post hoc mechanisms of excluding "erotic deviants," employ several preventive mechanisms. Most camps, Weinberg finds, do not allow unmarried individuals, especially single men, or allow only a small quota of singles, sometimes charging them up to 35 percent more for a single's membership than is charged for an entire family.[9] Also, in nudist camps, single and married members are generally segregated. Another preventive mechanism is certification by the camp owner, a requirement sometimes complemented by the necessity of three letters of recommendation regarding the character of the applicant.[10] A limit is sometimes set on the number of trial visits that can be made to the camp without membership in the camp organization and a limit is usually set on the length of time one is allowed to remain clothed.

Thus, nudist camps attempt to exclude exhibitionists and voyeurs, there are norms that help to anesthetize any sexual meaning of nudity (e.g., no staring), and people caught violating the rules are excluded from the camps.

Nudism as Deviance

If nudism is publicly linked with voyeurism and exhibitionism and thus publicly labeled deviancy, seen from the point of view of our analytical framework, the nudist is a member of a "deviant minority group." First, the person is subject to stereotyping and categorical discrimination and perceives such a reaction from the general public:

> They anticipate that if their nudist participation were "known about" they would be socially typed in the following ways: 1) as sexually available or "promiscuous," 2) as "nuts." ... Nudists anticipate sanctions in both social and economic arenas; social ostracism is anticipated, as well as deleterious consequences for one's occupational career. Fifty-nine percent of the interviewees mentioned social consequences if their nudist identity were revealed; 22 percent mentioned economic-occupational consequences.[11]

In the face of this threat of social ostracism, nudists attempt to "pass" for nonnudists publicly by maintaining secrecy of their nudist participation, and this even extends to a "first name only" ruling of social interaction in the nudist camp. We have seen the nudists maintain a pristine code of sexual modesty (excepting nudity) perhaps as part of a minority group concern for self-purification. But despite their efforts toward self-purification, they must live in two worlds, and thus face the problem of marginal ambivalence between the conflicting perspectives on nudity found in those two worlds. In the nudist camp, nonnudity is seen as deviancy and emotions such as shame, guilt, or sexual jealousy lose any relation to heterosexual nudity. By contrast, in the outside world, the nudist perceives nudity to be deviant and associated with all of the above emotions. Also, when in certain situations in the outside world, e.g., in church, one retrospectively may associate these emotions with camp nudity, and even define camp nudity as "deviance."

BECOMING A NUDIST

Weinberg seems to maintain that participation in nudism does not result from prior personality or attitude insofar as nudists generally do not give nudism much thought prior to their initial visit to a nudist camp. Thus, there are certain *situational factors* that seem to combine to lead to the first camp experience. Initial interest in nudism for men is generally incited by nudist magazines (47 percent) or another person (31 percent), while for women initial interest is through spouses (47 percent) or another person (23 percent). The initial motivation is usually "curiosity" for males (33 percent) and desire to satisfy spouse (38 percent) or curiosity (25 percent) for females. There is much anxiety prior to a first visit perhaps because the person has no past similar situations to serve as "rehearsal." Nevertheless, most visitors adjust rapidly to the nudist way of life.

DARRELL: A Social Nudist

Darrell is a nudist from a nudist camp located in California. He contradicts somewhat the psychiatric image of "nudist." A tall, handsome, tanned person, he seems to be highly self-assured, persuasive, outgoing, and gregarious. Darrell also gives us an account of nudism in California that contrasts somewhat with Weinberg's account of Chicago-area nudism. There are certain departures from the strict nudist code in the West Coast nudist scene as Darrell sees it.

DARRELL: I did not prepare any kind of speech for today. I belong to a club which is affiliated with the national association, and I don't have anything to do with that association. I am just a member of the club. So what I have to say is about nudism in general, drawing from my own particular experiences. When you say nudism, what it means is social nudism because obviously you can take your clothes off in your house if you want to, but social nudism means you go naked in front of a group of people in a social setting and outside. Nudists believe that if you can consider the human body to be wholesome, then the naked body also is wholesome and it profits when exposed to the air and also in the company of other people. Of course, this concept isn't exactly too prevalent in our culture. The Winslows asked me the other night how I became interested in nudism, and I had to sit back and think back about four years and I forgot exactly how I really became interested in it. But thinking about it, I remember I guess I was in high school and one of the local drive-ins had a nudist picture on their billing and it was a kind of flashy thing, X-rated, under twenty-one you can't get in but I sneaked in and was only seventeen. It turned out to be a rotten movie. It didn't have much of a plot but it showed a nudist camp in Florida, which turned out to be the biggest one in the country with about forty or fifty acres. Anyway, I saw the movie and I thought, well, it looks like a lot of fun is going on there. After that movie I didn't think too much about it but noticed that from then on I was kind of aware of anything to do with nudism. I cut papers out of books. For instance, one of my favorite books is *Summerhill* by an English educator and he makes comments on nudism in there and I picked that up and I picked up comments from Bertrand Russell. So after I saw this film, as I recall, it was a period of four years lapse, but within that time I thought about it and considered it and it scared me a bit, it's a bit frightening to think about not wearing clothes in a social situation because for myself and for most of the people I know quite a bit of self-identity is wrapped up in their clothes and they dress the way they picture themselves, so it's kind of frightening if somebody isn't particularly strong in identity or isn't sufficiently matured yet to go without their clothes. It's a frightening situation, something new and strange, something you have never done before. In most cases, a person's mother and father see each other naked and they see their kids until the age of about seven or eight but after that they have the tendency not to see each other naked particularly in a middle class family when they could afford to give their kids their own bathroom.

QUESTION: *Does being a nudist in a nudist camp deflate your status to that of a child?*

DARRELL: I don't think so in general, though I suppose it would depend on the state of the individual. Of course, there's a lot of people who truly identify themselves with a particular set of clothes, and to that person nudity would have a tendency to reduce him to a child state. But I think that would be momentary. I don't think that would hold because that's a social situation where everyone who's there is of their own free will, not like a mental hospital where they take your clothes off you and you have no choice. In a nudist camp, people are there voluntarily, so they are able to maintain the status they would have in the outside world.

QUESTION: *Is there any kind of status system in the nudist camp?*

DARRELL: Obviously you don't get status with your clothes because you don't have any clothes. Of course, there are other ways: for instance, the people who live out there all the time can get involved in other functions. The president of the club, vice-president, they could be involved in activity with a festival two or three times a year. So if they're looking for status or something to rate themselves above the others, then all they have to do is become involved in the club and the activity. I could raise myself in the pecking order out there by coming out here and giving a speech.

QUESTION: *So in other words what you're saying is there's no organization and it's just simply doing your own thing and that there is no leadership and there is no other basis for ranking people other than their physical attractiveness by society's standards.*

DARRELL: Let me take time to say something about the organization of the club. All nudist camps are run by private individuals and are held to general standards set down by the national organization. They're really resorts. They are resorts and health clubs, places where you could go out naked legally and mingle with other people who have the same ideas that you have. Since they are clubs, there are two types of membership. There is a permanent, the one that lives on the grounds, and there is a transient member who just comes out on the weekends and enjoys the facilities such as the club's swimming pool, tennis courts, volleyball courts, and sunny lawns, plus any kind of sport you can think about, plus a few social organizations. So if there is any kind of status involved, it would be for the people who live on the grounds, not the people who come on weekends. On weekends, any kind of status tends to break down, except for the managers of course, but anyone else would be reduced to equal with everyone else there. During the week you have your permanent people who live there, a group of about a hundred, and within that group you have status then.

QUESTION: *Since this is a kind of deviant behavior, when people are initially going into it do you have a process to ease them into it so that they feel more comfortable or do you just leave them alone? I could see where maybe people first coming in are leery and modest.*

DARRELL: Yes, they usually are, but then again, when you come into any institution they strip you of the beliefs of the outside world. You're naked and everyone else is naked, too, so you don't feel deviant. You don't joke around because you find everyone else is the same as you are.

QUESTION: *But do you have a process of easing people in?*

DARRELL: No, not really. Most people I take out there and most people I see come out usually are quite nervous, say up to the point where they take their clothes off, and then they're nervous ten to twenty minutes after that and then the nervousness goes. The biggest thing is going out there and taking your clothes off, and once you're beyond that you've established that everyone else is naked and you find it pretty easy to talk to everyone. I don't think I've ever seen anyone have a hard time talking because everyone is quite sociable and they'll come up and talk to you.

QUESTION: *Is sex connected with nudist camps?*

DARRELL: Well, the most common fear among men coming out is getting an erection and girls I know are afraid of coming out too 'cause they're afraid of becoming sexually aroused and they won't be able to do anything about it. But it usually doesn't turn out to be that way. I've never seen a man come out and get an erection. If he comes out again say two or three times, then he's interested enough to return and he'll get an erection once he's relaxed. If you want to make love, you go off and seek your own privacy. You don't do it in front of everybody. I saw one fellow get an erection and he had just come out there for the first time. His mother works there as a cook. She was divorced, and the son came out to spend the summer with her, and he found it sort of hard to control himself at first. But after he had been there two or three days, he pretty well picked up the rules of how people acted and he was able to control himself. Actually, people think it's sexually stimulating to see everyone in the nude. It might be if people aren't used to it, but you don't get sexually aroused because you're in a situation where it wouldn't be allowed, and it's not the proper thing to do. If you're outside socializing, you're outside playing around, you're not going to make love.

QUESTION: *How many people live out there? Where do they live?*

DARRELL: There are 100 people who live out there. It is a trailer park with fifty spaces and there is house and motel.

QUESTION: *Do people have jobs?*

DARRELL: Yes, it is pretty much like a trailer park. A few people live and work there but some work in town and commute back and forth. I suppose I could say something about the group of people who belong out there. It goes all the way up to doctors and lawyers and dentists.

QUESTION: *What do you think about the articles saying sun is extremely bad for you and when you go into the sun you should be all covered up?*

DARRELL: Well, when you go out there it's pretty hot and if you're playing a game or you're swimming or sometimes you just want to get a tan, then you're out in the sun, but most of the time you're sitting under a tree. They're not going to get out there and get burned alive. But I think it is healthy to get out into the sun to expose your whole body.

QUESTION: *Does being a nudist affect the social relationship?*

DARRELL: The standards pretty much depend on the managers in the individual camps, but when people first come out to the club, I get a kick out of watching them. Most people have never seen naked bodies. I suppose the girls have seen other girls in gym class, but they've never seen a guy unless it was their boyfriend. It was probably one man. So it's a strange thing to be able to look around and there's a hundred naked men and naked women and there's a tendency to look. New people have a tendency to look and stare. I remember one couple came out and I got a big kick out of them. They wore sun glasses when they came out. They sat down on the lawn and they sat back to back and they didn't say a word. They just looked. They stayed in one place for about fifteen to twenty minutes and looked at everyone and then they moved to another part of the canyon. All during the day they moved to different parts of the canyon. There's nothing wrong about this and nobody gets uptight about it. Obviously, why should you get uptight? If I'm naked and someone stares at me, I'm not going to get uptight about it. If they are really staring point blank with force of contact, then I'll get uptight about it. There is also a rule that says no bodily contact. No excessive bodily contact. They don't go into the definition of what excessive means, but it depends. If you're in the swimming pool and you get in there and horse around, you play like you're in a regular swimming pool, like if you put a chick on your back, there's a lot of physical contact.

QUESTION: *If people do want to make love, then, are they inhibited by the rules?*

DARRELL: If they want to make love out on the lawn, then they are inhibited by the rules. I wouldn't want to make love all the time. It's tiring. Most of the time you just want to relax, but if you do want to make love, then you could go into your trailer or hide behind some bushes that are well hidden.

QUESTION: *It seems to me that the role of nudity in the nude society and clothes in the greater society are similar. People find self-identity in clothing, the same type of self-identity served by nudity in camp and one is as identifying as the other.*

DARRELL: Yes, I agree with you. I think you are right. That's why most people are nervous when they first go out there 'cause there's a completely new type of behavior, something that they find completely strange to them. But pretty much everything else is the same and people are more friendly. My girlfriend had her girlfriend out a couple of weeks ago and we had a party and she stayed the night. The next morning she had to take her clothes off and she was pretty nervous about it, but she went ahead and did it. At the end of the day, she thought it was really great. She didn't have any trouble at all. We treated her so natural. She found out everything else was pretty much the same. When she finally left, she put on a dress or a short skirt and she decided not to wear any underwear and she was getting into her car and then she decided to wear her underwear so she put them on and it sort of blew her mind that she could do it in front of other people.

QUESTION: *Do you have to conceal that you are a nudist to your friends or family or work associates, and does this lead to paranoia and make it sort of uncomfortable?*

DARRELL: Well, that depends on the individual. Some people feel that there are some things that they have to conceal and then they become embarrassed if these people find out. There are quite a few teachers at the club. It's been my experience that when people find out about it they usually get a reaction like, "Jesus Christ! You run around naked?" But then after that there isn't much reaction. Now, whether or not it would be difficult for a teacher would depend on the principal and the parent of the student. I think that nowadays there would be much less reason to fear than ten years ago when nudity was pretty much a popular subject. It's much less a big deal now.

QUESTION: *Do people go to nudist camps for exhibitionist purposes in the sense that they get a sexual thrill from it?*

DARRELL: Almost everybody simply because of the fact that our society hooks up nudity to sex. But I don't think it persists.

QUESTION: *Do people come back from time to time for that motive?*

DARRELL: I would tend to think not, but then some people do. I think it's a pretty natural tendency and maybe it is.

QUESTION: *To what extent do you have any harassment by the legal authorities?*

There has been harassment, but there is less now because the climate is accepted with tolerance. Social nudism is supposed to have started in 1903 in Germany. A fellow wrote a book on it and two years later the Germans started organized tribes of clubs. These were allowed in Germany before Hitler, and then he outlawed them in 1929. The Germans came over to America and opened a camp in New York State. They got quite a bit of publicity in the papers and it was allowed. Generally they have spread out since 1929. The largest camp is in Florida. This city has two camps. Right after the opening of our camp, the law tried to close it down and they made a raid of the place. It was a cool day and everyone had their clothes on, so they wanted them to take their clothes off so they could arrest them. There are still a few states that do not allow them.

QUESTION: *Do you have to be licensed?*

DARRELL: Our club is licensed, but I don't know what the procedure is. Every so often the cops come in. But it turns out that the guy that runs the camp spent twenty-seven years in the navy but retired and went on the police force. He is a sergeant at this time on the police force. He's very much associated with the community.

QUESTION: *One of the things Norman Mailer has been quoted as saying is he likes sex dirty and you shouldn't take the filth out of nudity. What is your view on that?*

DARRELL: I get pleasure out of sex, so my sexual pleasures are derived from sex and I haven't found this unpleasant. Matter of fact, I have found it has been increased because I am much more relaxed. Me and my girl both live together as man and wife though we're not married. So the club is not a puritanical organization as long as you're adults and not bothering anyone else. My personal philosophy, and my girl's too, is the more simply you can live, the better. I like the country. I like to be able to go free with no clothes and be as simple as I can and eat organic foods, and I find it restful and recreational. I think that nudism could have a positive effect within certain areas. People can be one with life, and I think you could clear up a lot of sexual problems.

QUESTION: *Is there much pot at the club?*

DARRELL: When you get to the problem of drugs, drugs could be a real problem 'cause they are legally not permitted. The managers out there get rather uptight about drugs when someone is using them. They're afraid that if a narcotic agent came in it would hit the front page news and it would be bad publicity. My personal opinion is to stay away from it 'cause it is too hot now. For the most part the membership is overwhelmingly families, although there are quite a few single people. Incidentally, if you come out to see me at the club, you have to be twenty-one or over to use the grounds or if under twenty-one be accompanied by a parent.

QUESTION: *A person could go nude in his own backyard. If a person could do that, why would he want to go to a place like a nudist colony?*

DARRELL: Well, there is a difference between nudism and social nudism. If you're doing it in your backyard, you're just doing it with yourself and your family. To be with other people is social nudism.

QUESTION: *How do you break down the membership?*

DARRELL: The club has 400 memberships. There are pregnant women, babies, children, teen-agers, people in their thirties, forties, and I know people there as old as eighty. It seems like a pretty even breakdown. The club covers just about seventy acres.

QUESTION: *How much does it cost?*

DARRELL: Its cost vary. A couple per year is $135. Single guys $125 and single girls $115. Sometimes it's easier to get single guys out there than it is to get single girls. I think the reason is women seem to be more caught up in beauty and women's liberation.

QUESTION: *I've heard from some people that in the nudist colonies, there is a disproportion of old people, and people's bodies aren't all that good. Maybe that's why they go, because it really doesn't matter. I'm vaguely wondering if participation in that kind of setting doesn't make you somewhat disdainful of the human nude body.*

DARRELL: Well, that would depend on the individual philosophy. I have known a person at the club for three or four months, a woman personally who I think has a very pleasant body with a nice personality, but she is flat chested. She has some chest, but it's flat 'cause it's not very much. She considers herself a bean pole. She came out there and she saw all the people. She thought, "Wow, there are all kinds of ugly people." Now, that's her attitude. But I personally like to see people who aren't fat 'cause it's very bad physically. I never think of them as ugly. I just think of them as people.

QUESTION: *I understand that if you're married, you can't come unless your spouse comes.*

DARRELL: Yes, they have that rule, but that rule actually ties up more of legality. Say, for instance, a married man comes without his spouse and then any kind of divorce action, the club is dragged into the papers. If you are divorced or separated but not divorced, you need a release from your spouse.

QUESTION: *If they come out, doesn't it happen that a woman comes out more or less unwillingly and there may be a big fight from that?*

DARRELL: Maybe, but there is no legal hassle here. If one didn't like it that is a personal problem.

QUESTION: *Are they afraid of civil suit?*

DARRELL: Yes, they're afraid of civil suit. Afraid of, well, some people are uptight about nudism, afraid to admit that they are nudists.

QUESTION: *Would you say there is more sexual activity with clothes or without?*

DARRELL: My opinion is that there is no more sex inside or outside. I think that nudism promotes a feeling of intimacy between people.

QUESTION: *So there isn't that great a difference?*

DARRELL: No, because if you take your clothes off you're not going to make love to every girl around. You're going to have pretty much the same distinction. Some girls you like, others you don't.

QUESTION: *Would you say that intimacy is intensified?*

DARRELL: The people I know use clothes for hiding. You identify with your clothes, I with my beard. People just use clothes for self-identity.

QUESTION: *Would you say that the dominant cultural pattern which says that nudity is erotic is actually changed by the socialization that takes place within the nudist camp, or do people still harbor such attitudes?*

DARRELL: It is something you have to experience yourself. The longer your exposure to the nudist camp, the more affirmative this change.

QUESTION: *Darrell, have you ever seen your mother naked?*

DARRELL: By accident, maybe a little.

QUESTION: *I have a friend who, having nudity at home and in fact having been nude in front of his parents with no particular reaction, having this liberal atmosphere in the home, he doesn't have the need to go to a nudist camp.*

DARRELL: He doesn't have the freedom to go outside. Nudism to him should be very natural. If it is a very hot day, it should be very natural for him to go to a store to pick up a newspaper and walk back in the nude. He should be able to do this if he doesn't have any hangups.

QUESTION: *What about alcohol in camp?*

DARRELL: Alcohol has somewhat changed. When nudism first came in in 1929 it was illegal. But you can't get so drunk you're disturbing someone.

QUESTION: *How much pressure do you get from the dominant group?*

DARRELL: There is quite a bit of pressure from groups. I don't have any pressure because I'm a student right now. I do have a lot of freedom.

COMMENTARY

The interview with Darrell reveals a number of points similar to the portrait of social nudism drawn by Weinberg, and a number that differ.

Darrell does not talk at great length about his early childhood or adolescent development, perhaps indicating that to him this is not significant in explaining his interest in nudism. He traces his interest back to the age of seventeen, having viewed a movie filmed in a nudist colony and later reading about nudist camps. As a person, we have seen, as we have already commented, that Darrell does not appear at all to resemble the timid, retiring, passive, overly conscientious young man described as either the voyeur or exhibitionist character type. On the contrary, he is outgoing, direct, actively involved, and even somewhat lacking in ambition, insofar as nudism might bar future employment opportunities.

Like Weinberg's typical nudist, Darrell experienced considerable anxiety upon his first visit to a nudist camp and became socialized to the ideology that the "human body is wholesome—and the naked body is wholesome." He experienced the typical perception that *in that situation* being nude was not "deviant" because everybody else was. Darrell observes the lack of status differentiation among nudists (other than a functional differentiation of "permanent" versus "transient"), and he contends typically that nudism promotes a feeling of intimacy among people.

Points of difference with Weinberg's analysis indicated by Darrell's comments are perhaps of greater significance.

1. Darrell indicates that the camp is not entirely devoid of sexual activity: "you go off by yourself if you want to make love and seek your own privacy." He implies that eroticism does take place without immediate ostracism, as in the case of the boy who was in the camp two or three days before he learned to control his eroticism.

2. Darrell suggests that there is deviation from the formal "no staring" rule: "... new people have a tendency to look and stare.... There's nothing wrong about that and nobody gets uptight about it."

3. The rule of "no excessive body contact" too is not always strictly enforced: "They don't go into the definition of what excessive means, but it depends. If you're in the swimming pool and you get in there and horse around ... if you put a chick on your back, there's a lot of physical contact."

4. As to the alleged puritanical rule of some camps regarding singles, Darrell maintains he is unmarried and living with his girl friend at the camp.

5. Most striking is the violation of the "no alcohol rule": "Alcohol has somewhat changed.... But you can't get so drunk you're disturbing someone."

Thus, the formal rules laid down by the National Nudist Association are like formal rules of other formal organizations—occasionally bent or violated in the ongoing everyday operations of the organization.

Darrell's comments may be indicative of a different social atmosphere from the setting Weinberg studied in Chicago, possibly reflecting in some way a different social climate emerging specifically on the West Coast, a part of the United States less bound by traditional concepts of morality.

It could be that our more in-depth interview format had pierced some of the "pat responses" of the nudist subculture that Weinberg's survey did not. This explanation is likely in that Jack Douglas found a similar dual ethic in his participant observation study of a nude beach. According to Douglas, the nude bathers initially expressed a "naturalistic ethos" devoid of sexual reasons for coming to the nude beach. As Douglas's acceptance and trust relationships developed, however, he found that to some degree persons were hiding behind the "naturalistic front" to hide their "sexual feelings, motives, thoughts, and actions." [12] It should be pointed out, however, that Douglas's research was also conducted within the social climate of the West Coast. Nevertheless, it may be true that the ethic or the protective front established by social nudists disguises a degree of voyeurism, exhibitionism, or other sexual activity not immediately apparent in Weinberg's study.

THEORETICAL IMPLICATIONS

While we stated earlier that most of the studies of nudism have been made outside of a theoretical framework, we see from Darrell's appearance and interview that several theories may be examined to explain social nudism.

PSYCHIATRIC THEORIES   While our knowledge of Darrell and his family background is limited, it has been pointed out that his self-esteem and outgoing manner did not appear to be in keeping with the psychiatric research at least as it pertains to voyeurs and exhibitionists.

Sociological Theories

ANOMIE   There appears to be little in anomie theory that would appear to explain social nudism. Certainly the conventional goals of obtaining material wealth would not seem to find expression by means provided in a nudist colony. Neither does it appear, for the most part, that social nudism provides an outlet for sexual activity that is not provided for through inequitable distribution of any legitimate outlets. While there is a deemphasis of conventional recognition of social status through clothing, this does not appear to be a motivating factor for Darrell or others to become nudists.

LABELING THEORY   Labeling theory in its purest form does not appear to be explanatory in nature. That is, we do not find the reactions of others to the primary deviant act and the acquisition of a new self-concept that leads to secondary deviance. However, Darrell does speak of a new "self-identity" as people "voluntarily" remove their clothing and he states that because "everyone else is naked, so you don't feel deviant." At the same time, in addition to this interactional process, Darrell discusses what might be termed "anticipated" societal reactions in his statement:

> Some people feel that there are some things that they have to conceal and then they become embarrassed if these people find out. There are quite a few teachers at the club. It's been my experience that when people find out about it they usually get a reaction like, "Jesus Christ! You run around naked?"

Thus, it is conceivable that the interactional nature of the labeling process involved may be one of self-labeling due to anticipated reaction and acquisition of a new self-concept, that of "nudist," in interaction with other nudists.

DIFFERENTIAL ASSOCIATION   Perhaps of considerable explanatory power, if taken in conjunction with the interaction process, is differential association. The process of the development of continuous participation in nudism appears to be related to several factors: 1) adoption of the nudist code that camp nudity is not shameful or intrinsically sexual but instead brings such rewards as freedom and natural pleasure, physical, mental, and spiritual well-being, family-centered recreation and cohesion, and a social context of friendliness and sociability; 2) a decline in or low amount of participation in nonnudist informal associations; and 3) a reduction in social contact with relatives. The factors suggest differential association with nudists as explanatory of a continuing participation in nudism as a way of life.[13]

SOCIAL CONTROL THEORY   Perhaps the most interesting analysis of social nudism may be made in studying the applicability of social control theory. In the process we have already examined, it could be said that the original internal control mechanisms are transformed through differential association so that a new self-identity emerges. Moreover, upon accepting this new identity the nudist is required to submit to the external controls of his new reference group. We also have shown that Darrell's interview and other evidence indicate that these formal rules of the National Nudist Association are not always fully observed. Thus, perhaps due to a lack of internal controls, the external mechanisms break down partially among the members of the group.

On a higher, societal level of external control we see mixed results. We see that formal or legal external controls appear to be ineffective.

Darrell describes how the "law tried to close it (the nudist camp) down" and was unable to do so initially and that currently "the guy that runs the camp" is "a sergeant at this time on the police force." Douglas described a portion of the inability of the police to enforce nudity regulations on a secluded beach whether such activity was legal or illegal.[14] This may be because secluded social nudism, entirely out of view from those who might be offended by it, could be the most victimless form of crime or deviance in our culture. It is of little threat to the overall society under such circumstances; even those sociologists who have called for decriminalization or legalization of victimless crimes in general have overlooked nudism in their works.[15] Thus, it would appear that enforcement of such laws in such circumstances becomes a "non-issue." On the other hand, direct contacts with nudity appear to be a threat to a substantial portion of the American public. Indeed, Darrell indicates the shocked reaction received from nonnudists who discover they are in contact with someone who goes about "naked." He specifically points to the need for teachers who are nudists to protect themselves depending on "the principal and the parent of the student." This indicates that nudism is perceived as a threat to basic sexual mores of our society, and, as a result, the Nudist Association protects itself from such sexual connotation through external, formal rules.

In total, it appears that external controls are less than effective when they run counter to the individual's internal control mechanisms. Additionally, formal external controls are less effective than informal sanctions from which the nudists protect themselves.

QUESTIONS FOR DISCUSSION

1. Do you think that Darrell is typical of nudists in his personality and attitudes?
2. Do you think nudists are sincere in their beliefs regarding the wholesomeness of the human body, its need for exposure to air, etc.? Is nudism, in your opinion, entirely nonsexual in motivation as implied by Darrell?
3. If nudity were not illegal, do you think it would be more or less popular? Why?
4. Weinberg found that women usually are inducted into nudism to satisfy their spouses rather than through intrinsic motivation. Why do you think nudism seems to be more appealing to men than to women?
5. Do you think children in nudist families practice nudism when they themselves are adults? Why or why not?
6. Do you believe there is a greater acceptance of social nudism today as nudity becomes more acceptable to the public in the movies, magazines, and other media? Is this new acceptance, if any, an indication of lessened sexual connotation to nudity itself?

▅▅▅▅▅ RELATED READINGS

American Sunbathing Association, "Sunbathers, Ahoy!" in Charles H. McCagny et al., *In Their Own Behalf: Voices from the Margin* (New York: Appleton-Century-Crofts, 1968), pp. 5–9.

Douglas, Jack D., "Major Tactics of Investigative Research," reprinted in *Focus: Unexplored Deviance*, Charles H. Swanson, ed. (Sluice Dock, Guilford, Ct.: The Dushkin Publishing Group, 1978), pp. 206–220.

Hartman, William, et al., *Nudist Society: An Authoritative Complete Study of Nudism in America* (New York: Crown Publishers, 1970).

Kirk, Ruth, "A Mother Speaks of Nudism," in Charles H. McCagny et al., *In Their Own Behalf: Voices from the Margin* (New York: Appleton-Century-Crofts, 1968), pp. 129–134.

Weinberg, Martin, "Becoming a Nudist," in Earl Rubington and Martin Weinberg, *Deviance: The Interactionist Perspective* (New York: Macmillan, 1968).

——, "Sexual Modesty and the Nudist Camp," *Social Problems*, 12 (Winter, 1965), pp. 311–318.

——, "The Nudist Management of Respectability: Strategy for, and Consequences of, the Construction of Situated Morality," pp. 375–403, in Jack D. Douglas, ed., *Deviance and Respectability* (New York: Basic Books, 1970), pp. 375–403.

▅▅▅▅▅ NOTES

1. William Hartman et al., *Nudist Society: An Authoritative Complete Study of Nudism in America* (New York: Crown Publishers, 1970).

2. Herbert Bloch and Gilbert Geis, *Man, Crime, and Society* (New York: Random House, 1962), p. 257.

3. Paul Gebhard et al., *Sex Offenders* (New York: Harper & Row, 1965), p. 374.

4. Bloch and Geis, *Man, Crime, and Society*, p. 259.

5. Ibid.

6. Ibid., pp. 259–260.

7. Ibid., p. 261.

8. Martin Weinberg, "Sexual Modesty and the Nudist Camp," *Social Problems*, 12 (Winter, 1965), pp. 311–318.

9. Martin Weinberg, "The Nudist Management of Respectability: Strategy for, and Consequences of, the Construction of a Situated Morality," pp. 375–403 in Jack D. Douglas, ed., *Deviance and Respectability* (New York: Basic Books, 1970), p. 376.

10. Ibid., p. 377.

11. Ibid., pp. 394–395.

12. Jack D. Douglas, "Major Tactics of Investigative Research," reprinted in Charles H. Swanson, *Focus: Unexplored Deviance* (Sluice Dock, Guilford, Ct.: The Dushkin Publishing Group, 1978), pp. 216–217.

13. Martin Weinberg, "Becoming a Nudist," in Earl Rubington and Martin Weinberg, *Deviance: The Interactionist Perspective* (New York: Macmillan, 1968), pp. 240–251.

14. Jack D. Douglas, "Major Tactics of Investigative Research," pp. 217–218.

15. Morris and Hawkins, *The Honest Politician's Guide to Crime Control* (Chicago: University of Chicago Press, 1960); Gilbert Geis, *Not the Law's Business? An Examination of Homosexuality, Abortion, Prostitution, Narcotics, and Gambling in the United States* (Rockville, Md.: National Institute of Mental Health, Center for the Study of Crime and Delinquency, 1972); and Edwin M. Schur, *Crimes Without Victims: Deviant Behavior and Public Policy, Abortion, Homosexuality, Drug Addiction* (Englewood Cliffs, N.J.: Prentice-Hall, Inc., 1965).

Drunkenness, Problem Drinking, and Alcoholism

3

If the subject of social nudism covered in the preceding chapter has been neglected by sociologists, writings about drunkenness, problem drinking, and alcoholism in and outside of sociology are abundant and give evidence of the degree with which they have been defined as "social problems" within academia. Yet these problems are often given short shrift by the public and felt to be minor when compared with more serious areas such as murder, robbery, and rape, or with more sensational problems such as transsexualism, homosexuality, and drug addiction. What appears to be lost is the fact that alcohol is involved directly or indirectly in a substantial number of crimes and that alcohol itself is an addictive drug. Alcoholism differs from many of the forms of deviancy we are studying in the degree to which it touches many, if not most, of us. While we may not usually come into contact with drug addicts or transsexuals, we are often in the company of drinkers and may participate in drinking activity to a greater or lesser degree. Perhaps, for that reason, we are tempted to feel we know enough about that problem, and we should therefore turn our attention to other areas. We shall see, however, that drinking behavior and subcultures connected with drinking are much more significant and are farther from "normal consciousness" or commonsense middle class perspectives than meets the eye. For that reason, recent studies of drinking behavior have proved to be among the most significant in sociology.

THE NATURE OF DRUNKENNESS, PROBLEM DRINKING, AND ALCOHOLISM

The lay conception of alcoholism, largely influenced by the popularized perspectives of Alcoholics Anonymous, links it with chronic drunkenness. The drunk is an alcoholic and an alcoholic is one who cannot stop drinking. He drinks all he can during all or most of his waking hours. Alcoholism is progressive drunkenness marked by secret or solitary drinking, guilt feelings, and physical disorders such as blackouts, tremors, and cirrhosis of the liver. A drinker progresses over the years from a "social drinker" to an "alcoholic drinker." Further, the alcoholic may be one who has an idiosyncratic susceptibility or "allergy" to alcohol that makes him more prone to addiction.[1]

Recent studies of drunkenness and alcoholism have yielded findings in contrast to this view of drinking behavior. It has been pointed out that there is a distinction between drunkenness and alcoholism. Reckless distinguishes between the drunk and the alcoholic as follows:

> One can become drunk without being an alcoholic, but one can also become drunk and be a chronic alcoholic. . . . The alcoholic, however, is an uncontrolled drinker who has developed a dependence on alcohol and usually consumes large amounts daily. . . . More and more the accepted criterion of alcoholism is uncontrolled drinking. . . . A man may be a heavy drinker for twenty years without becoming an alcoholic.[2]

Another recent study has sharpened the distinction between alcoholism and drunkenness even more. Wallace finds that excessive and daily drinking on skid row does not coincide with alcoholism:

> The drunk . . . is not to be confused with the alcoholic, although both drink to excess. Excessive drinking on skid row does not equal alcoholism, nor do theories of alcoholism necessarily apply to the behavior patterns of the skid rower. . . . Heavy drinking on skid row is a product of group norms rather than a result of individual, addictive craving for alcohol.[3]

Currently an emphasis has been placed upon the distinction, not only between drunkenness and alcoholism, but also between problem drinking and alcoholism. All alcoholics are classified as problem drinkers but not all problem drinkers are alcoholics. Robert Straus distinguishes the two in the following definitions:

... "problem drinker" will be defined as encompassing all individuals who *repeatedly* use alcohol to an extent that exceeds customary dietary use or prevailing socially accepted customs or in amounts that, for them, cause problems of physical health, interfere with interpersonal relations, or disrupt the fulfillment of family, economic, or community expectations. This definition recognizes both social and individual dimensions. Problem drinking exists if either social customs or the individual's capacity to handle alcohol are repeatedly violated.

Among problem drinkers, *alcoholics* can be defined as those whose persistent abuse of alcohol is associated with a state of physical or psychological dependence involving often unbearable stress or discomfort or tension. The origin of the discomfort may be physiological, psychological, or social, or a blending of all three. The factors that distinguish alcoholics from other problem drinkers are their degree of dependence and their inability to control their drinking.[4]

Thus, both Reckless and Straus emphasize the alcoholic as having the qualities of *dependence* and *inability to control one's drinking*. While it is quite conceivable that a drunk could be both an alcoholic and thus a problem drinker or a problem drinker without being an alcoholic, it would still appear that a drunk could be neither a problem drinker nor an alcoholic. Straus elaborates on the term "dependence" as "comparable to the concept of addiction."[5] He further emphasizes that the dependence can be physical, psychological, or social, or a combination of the three. Physical dependence is characterized by increased tolerance and/or physical distress when alcohol is abruptly withdrawn. Psychological dependence is characterized by "loss of control" either in the inability to stop once drinking has started or to refrain from drinking under inappropriate circumstances, most commonly those circumstances deemed stressful. Social dependence is characterized by satisfying needs within specific social situations, such as the salesperson who feels compelled to drink to make a sale or college students who feel compelled to drink to be accepted by their peers.[6]

Extent of Alcohol Use and Alcohol Problems in the United States

Recent studies have pointed to the increased prevalence of alcohol use and problem drinking within the United States. The use of alcohol has increased in the U.S. so that from the end of prohibition to 1975 the per capita consumption of each kind (beer, distilled spirits, and wine) has more than doubled.[7] In 1974, 68% of Americans classified themselves as users of alcohol.[8] Rates vary so that men drink more frequently and in greater amounts than women (although the rate of female drinkers has been increasing), and frequency of alcohol use increases with education and income. The "wet" East and Midwest areas have higher

rates of drinking than the "dryer" South.[9] Higher rates of use of alcohol
have been noted among those at earlier ages. A 1975 study conducted
by the Research Triangle Institute indicated that 73.8% of high school
students drink, including 31% of the males and 18% of the females
who were classified as "heavy" drinkers.[10] A 1976 study by a team of
researchers headed by O'Donnell found that alcohol was the most widely
and frequently used drug among their sample of men aged twenty to
thirty with 97% having ever used alcohol and 93% using alcohol
currently.[11]

However, amount of alcohol consumed on a national basis is no
more an indication of alcohol problems within the U.S. than is the
amount consumed individually an indication of that individual's alcoholism. Other studies have addressed this issue. The National Commission
on Marijuana and Drug Use concluded, in 1973, that alcohol was "the
number one drug problem" in the U.S.[12] Another recent study, by
Cahalan and Room, addressed the specifics of problem drinking among
American men. It revealed that 72% of American men had at some
time experienced such a problem, including 55% who reported that one
or more of those problems had reached a "high" level of severity. Drinking problems (as opposed to consumption levels) were more common
in the "dry" regions of the country, among those of lower socioeconomic status, and among the more conservative Protestants. Problem
drinking was also associated with residence within a metropolitan urban
area and with the experience of childhood deprivation.[13]

Skid Row Residency

A continuous thrust of these recent studies has been that the alcoholic
is far from confined to skid row. Additionally, the alcoholic is certainly
not the only social type to be found on skid row.

Wallace recognizes not only drunks as separate from alcoholics
among participants in skid row subculture, but also several other types.
There are hobos, beggars, tour directors (con artists who specialize in
showing outsiders around), mission stiffs (who depend on missions for
support), and reliefers (who depend on public agencies for support).
Wallace indicates there is a status hierarchy among these various types
based on degree of integration into skid row subculture. The alcoholic in
this ranking actually proves to be somewhat of an "outsider" on skid
row:

> The alcoholic is somewhat suspect because of his superior social back-
> ground as well as his previous more extensive attachments in the com-
> munity. . . . The hobo who works sullies his skid row status by his con-
> tact with employers; and because he does not retain his place within the
> confines of skid row, he is presumed to have more to do with outsiders
> than skid row society approves of. . . . A beggar must approach out-

siders and . . . even though he does so just to get money, nevertheless deference implies denigration of skid row norms and values. . . . The tour director may be a con artist, but he actually talks to outsiders, and often betrays group standards and goals. Finally, the mission stiff is the most contemptible of all as he actively collaborates with members of the outside world, threatens group boundaries, and is disloyal.[14]

If there is a basis for status ranking in skid row, it is not degree of drinking but degree of integration into the web of affiliations on skid row.

Probably the most detailed taxonomy of skid row drinkers has been constructed by Spradley, an anthropologist who used ethnographic methods, interviews, and participant observation to derive a typology constructed from the language actually used by skid row residents.[15] Spradley finds that while outsiders think of skid row residents as bums, alcoholics, drunks, vagrants, and homeless men, few residents of skid row identify with these terms as self-conceptions. Skid row residents most frequently consider themselves "tramps," and there are various types of tramps, including: working stiffs (construction tramps, sea tramps, tramp miners, harvest tramps, and fruit tramps), mission stiffs (nose divers and professional nose divers), and various other types including bindle stiffs, airedales, rubber tramps, home guard tramps, box car tramps, and "dings." The proliferation of such types indicates even more that drinking behavior is subcultural and that the amount of drinking may be peripheral if not even sometimes irrelevant to what actually is going on.

There are several explanations of "how people come to live on skid row" in the literature, and they can be summarized briefly as follows:

1. They fail to maintain their economic resources, suffering either swift vertical descent or relative descent of migratory workers.[16]
2. Undersocialized, highly mobile workingmen lose contact with their homes and drift into the area in search of specialized services offered by the area and become assimilated into the life-style that exists there.[17]
3. Individuals who for a long period of time lack social affiliation drift into skid row in search of social affiliation.[18]

These "drift" explanations stress factors that push a person into skid row. Other explanations focus upon factors that pull a person to skid row, or trap him and hold him there.

Wiseman emphasizes the pull of skid row subculture and categorizes the drift view as the "professional's view of skid row." There are by contrast positive attractions of skid row life as shown in the "skid row resident's view." Alcohol itself shapes this perspective, "creating a warm glow of optimism and dulling feelings of unhappiness, loneliness, social inadequacy, and awareness of unattractive surroundings or persons." Once a person has experienced life on skid row, one learns and is lured by its strategies of survival, enabling one to maintain a way of life "independent" of the rest of society. Wiseman shows how through cunning and creativity, the skid row person *redefines* "facilities, objects, and general public practices for [his or her] own purposes, thus creating a hospitable instead of a hostile world."[19]

Spradley views the police, the courts, and the jail as a *trap* for any who should be unfortunate enough to come near. Once labeled a drunk, a person is stripped of his identity, and in fact in jail taught the identity, style of life, and survival skills of a tramp. With his criminal record, he will be unable to return to a nondeviant identity.

For twenty-five years Straus followed the life of "Frank Moore," who had been a subject of an earlier study of "homeless men" in a skid row. Straus notes the manner in which early undersocialization, dependency needs, and lack of familial ties intertwine with alcoholism and "institutional dependency" provided for on skid row:

> Like most of the hundreds of thousands of other men who have filled the live-in jobs and inhabited the skid rows, jails, mental hospitals, and public infirmaries of our country, Frank Moore had a background of early parental deprivation, disruption of normal family and community living, and undersocialization. He escaped into institutional living in the formative years of adolescence and, from that point on, had difficulty living outside of settings where his basic needs would be met. Frank Moore spent some forty years in the Navy, the Army, and the Maritime Service, the Civilian Conservation Corps, lumber camps, railroad labor camps, agriculture camps, resort-area live-in jobs, religious retreats, and numerous other institutions where he was able to find live-in employment. He frequented skid-row flophouses and work shelters, prisons and jails, and mental hospitals and public infirmaries. Between episodes of institutional living when his dependency needs were not being met, alcohol permitted him to escape from desperate feelings of despair, loneliness, and anxiety, and, at the same time, served to assure access to institutional care and to provide a rationale for his way of life.[20]

It should, therefore, be reemphasized that skid row residency is separate from alcoholism and alcoholism most frequently occurs without skid row residency. It would be best to view simultaneously only those traits with conceptual similarity, such as dependency or escapism, lest we be misled into stereotypes or false explanations of either factor.

METHODOLOGICAL CONSIDERATIONS

Straus noted his concern for ascertaining information regarding alcohol use and skid row residency in an "objective" manner as opposed to a more in-depth response:

Experience revealed that the majority of homeless alcoholics had developed a set of pat responses which they were accustomed to giving in
the countless situations when they were interviewed at various jails, missions, shelters, and employment agencies. Most also had fantasy life
histories which they exchanged with each other as a way of putting some
spice into their dull, routine existence. Somewhere between the safe pat
responses and the fantasy life lay the true histories and experiences of
these men.[21]

Recently, there has been an increasing concern in the study of alcohol use with arriving at the insider's "subjective" view as a means of
deriving knowledge not ascertained by previous "objective" studies (formal questionnaires and interview schedules used to derive demographic,
attitudinal, and other characteristics of alcohol users and/or skid row
residents).[22] As regards the use of alcohol and alcoholism, the "objective" studies have been criticized in that: 1) they may be measuring the
results of psychological "treatment" or other efforts at rehabilitation;[23]
2) they have often assumed that attitudes or intentions reflect behavior;[24]
3) there appears to be a somewhat consistent underreporting of degree
of use by the heavier drinkers.[25] As they have applied to skid row, such
studies have been called to task on various grounds: 1) because they
alienate the informant through implicitly assuming the respondent is a
failure;[26] 2) because the people interviewed are often "tour directors"
who are not representative of the inner core of skid row life;[27] 3) because such studies employ preconceptions (e.g., the concept "alcoholic")
that are not those used by residents on skid row,[28] and 4) because the
approach in such studies is to treat the skid row population as "problem population" from the point of view of middle class values—work,
sobriety, individual responsibility, cleanliness, health, and stability.[29]

Aside from the negative critique of questionnaire or structured
interview studies, there is a positive assertion of alternative methodology
and epistemology in the subjectivist studies. Jacqueline Wiseman takes
the subjectivist phenomenological stance that the world of skid row represents an alternative and genuinely valid world view in a world of
pluralistic world views. She distinguishes between the "professional
view of skid row" and "skid row as residents see it," as two distinctly
different world views. She considers problems of validity to be moot,
insofar as such plural perspectives exist and "one man's reality could
be another man's gross distortion."[30] Her objective was to reconstruct
the social reality (through participant observation and unstructured interview techniques) such that a person could live fairly well in the world
described, knowing its major features of action.[31] In a similar fashion,
Spradley, the anthropologist, studied the culture of the people of skid
row in Seattle in order to derive the insider's point of view.

By viewing the deviant subculture as an alternative world view,
these recent subjective studies have yielded conclusions of much importance in reshaping current and traditional explanations or theories of

drunkenness, problem drinking and alcoholism relative to "how they got that way."

<hr>

EXPLANATIONS OF DRINKING BEHAVIOR

We have already examined some of the explanations of skid row residency. We shall now review some of the major theories that deal with the specifics of drinking behavior. Most of these explanations have been utilized in reference to the more "severe" form of problem drinking, that of alcoholism. As we have seen, this "dependency" is of a physical, psychological, and/or social nature. Thus, explanations have been offered that emphasize one or the other aspect of uncontrolled drinking or a combination of such factors.

Jellinek's Progression: From Drinking to Alcoholism

For the last several years, there has been rather widespread acceptance of a model initiated by E. M. Jellinek in 1946. The Jellinek Model is heavily laden with physiological and psychological factors and, thus, has lent itself to a "disease" concept of alcoholism, separate from other forms of "nonaddictive alcoholism." Alcoholism seems to lend itself well to the sequential role model of stepwise progression. Jellinek charts the development of "addictive alcoholism" (which we term merely alcoholism) through some forty-three stages that begin when a person associates alcohol use with relief of tension and acquires a tolerance for alcohol.[32] During the "prodromal phase," the prospective alcoholic goes through seven stages: 1) alcoholic "blackouts," 2) surreptitious drinking, 3) preoccupation with alcohol, 4) avid drinking, 5) guilt feelings about drinking behavior, 6) avoidance of reference to alcohol in conversation, and 7) increasing frequency of alcoholic blackouts. This is followed by the "crucial phase" of many steps, beginning with 8) loss of control over alcohol consumption and "chain reaction" of cumulative physical demand for alcohol, and culminating in 30) regular morning drinking. This is followed by the "chronic phase" characterized by 31) periods of prolonged intoxication or "benders" and progressing to a final stage 43) in which the person admits defeat and the rationalization system fails, making one spontaneously accessible to treatment.

Jellinek clearly distinguishes between the nonaddictive alcoholic and the addictive alcoholic (our distinction between heavy drinker and alcoholic). The nonaddictive drinker may progress through the prodromal stage up to stage six, though usually with fewer blackouts, but if after ten or twelve years he has not lost control (stage seven), it is safe to diagnose him as nonaddictive. However, even nonaddictive drinkers may experience the physiological effects of prolonged heavy drinking, including delirium tremens.

Recently, the Jellinek model and the "disease" concept of alcoholism have been under increasing criticism. These criticisms point to the fact that Jellinek's research was based upon a questionnaire administered through an Alcoholics Anonymous publication and fits the "reality" that may result from A.A. influence and interaction rather than perceptions from the individuals' earlier life experiences. Additionally, the medical profession and political organizations have had an interest in promoting this concept for ideological reasons.[33]

Whether or not one accepts the progressive phases model of Jellinek, it is apparent that the model of "addictive alcoholism" requires further theoretical development. Such development would likely warrant additional refinement of the physiological, psychological, and social factors involved. Keeping this in mind, we shall examine various theories that deal with explanations involving these factors.

Physiological or Genetic Theories

While there is little debate that alcohol is "addictive" in the physiological sense (that an increased tolerance develops with use and that some individuals experience physical withdrawal symptoms), there is considerable controversy as to the manner in which such physical effects interact with other factors. It is also unclear whether such physiological effects have a basis in genetic or physical differences that distinguish or predispose alcoholics. Some studies have pointed to the incidence of alcoholism among children raised apart from their alcoholic parents.[34] There have also been reports of some persons who are said to have an alcoholic "allergy." It is said that such individuals experience severe headaches or other physical symptoms when they initially use alcohol; if they continue to use alcohol in spite of these "warnings," the symptoms disappear but alcoholism frequently follows soon thereafter. The exact nature of all such physical factors is unknown, as is the manner in which they may interact with psychological, ethnic, and social factors. In addition, such physical factors are, at best, found in only a small percent of all reported alcoholics.

Psychological and Psychiatric Theories

A good deal of theory has been developed as to the existence of psychological predispositions to alcoholism or of an "addictive personality." Some explanations, as stated in Chapter One, emphasize personality factors traceable to childhood, such as neurosis, homosexuality, sexual fears, low frustration tolerance, unresolved Oedipal problems, or more general factors such as extreme feelings of inadequacy, excessively high internal standards, chronic anxiety, excessive dependence on emotional support

from others, and feelings of emotional insecurity. Such psychopathological factors, however, are found among nonalcoholic neurotics, persons addicted to food, drug addicts, and even "normals," and thus cannot be considered true causal explanations or universal generalizations.
At best, these factors interact with other factors to provide a causal sequence.

An attempt has been made by two sociologists, William and Joan
McCord, to provide such a sequence between psychoanalytic and sociological variables. Their model could be interpreted as a specific application of social control theory to alcoholism. It is often referred to as a
"psychodynamic" model referring to the interaction of personality and
social factors. The model resulted from personal histories of a delinquency study conducted in the 1930s and 1940s followed up for alcoholism by the McCords in 1948 and 1956. Their model envisions a "dependency conflict" resulting from erratic satisfaction of early dependency
needs and lack of adequate male role definition. The inadequately prepared male, with a weak masculine self-image, is faced with an exaggerated definition of the adult male role through the media and other
social factors. The increased pressure for masculinity and independence
brings about tension that is alleviated by the use of alcohol. Alcohol
relieves the tension in its physical effects as well as in its social-psychological definition as a symbol of aggressiveness, achievement, and manliness.[35]

Another group of researchers, headed by McClelland, has interpreted the McCord data and their own as indicating alcohol as satisfying
"power needs" of the male rather then unsatisfied "dependency needs." [36]
It would appear that, to some degree, the models are similar and differences are somewhat semantic in degree of emphasis of psychological
versus sociological factors. The data and their interpretation are not incompatible with the Jellinek model. They leave room, however, for little
explanation of the female alcoholic. They also lack proper delineation of sociological and cultural variables that interact with personality
factors.

Sociological and Cultural Theories

A possible explanatory variable that has been explored is "adherence to
a culture conducive to alcoholism." Bales, commenting on the high rates
of alcoholism among Irish as compared with Jews and Italians, despite
similarities in amounts of alcohol consumed, developed a culture theory.
Alcoholism is highest under four conditions (present in the case of the
Irish): 1) one's group or culture generates high levels of inner tension
(e.g., anxiety, repressed sex, and aggression); 2) there is a lack of anti-
alcohol attitudes; 3) drinking serves individual rather than group functions, and 4) there are few alternatives to the use of alcohol for relieving
anxiety and expressing masculinity.[37]

Such an explanation is applicable to American society, since it could probably be shown that all four conditions are present here, especially in certain social circles. How do we account for differentials in alcoholism within the United States? The major theory that has been advanced for this is anomie theory. Merton has a place for alcoholism within his category "retreatism." Retreatism comprises some of the adaptive activities of "psychotics, autists, pariahs, outcasts, vagrants, tramps, chronic drunkards, and drug addicts.[38] In Merton's theory a person fails to succeed and resigns from the competition, rejecting the goal of success as well as the means to attaining success. Cloward and Ohlin would add a person fails also to attain access to criminal means to success, and thus becomes a "double failure."[39] Downward social mobility may, in combination with a few other delimiting factors, prove to be the mark of alcoholism in contrast to heavy drinking per se. One such delimiting factor may be the presence of "normative isolation," as discussed by Wallace.[40] Individuals may come to engage in steady though nonaddictive drinking through coincidence of having moved into drinking circles such as those found on skid row. But in alcoholism, the heavy use of alcohol is *reactive* to previous failure, rejection, and lowering of self-concept. Typically this would be the adaptation of a middle class person who, either through inability, lack of motivation, problems resulting from the use of alcohol itself, or the interaction of these factors, had suffered economic loss or loss of job and had come to use alcohol for escapist or retreatist purposes. Thus, one's motivation is to withdraw, to reduce tension or strain caused by prior deviancy or failure. It is apparent that this theme of downward mobility is manifest in members of Alcoholics Anonymous; also, lower class persons typically fail in their attempts to affiliate with Alcoholics Anonymous.[41]

HAZEL AND GEORGE:
An Alcoholic and a Drunk

In the transcripts that follow, we will have a chance to compare the perspective of a person who became an alcoholic though not a resident of skid row with that of a person who lived on skid row. Hazel, the alcoholic, is now a middle class businesswoman: although she is not necessarily typical of members of Alcoholics Anonymous, her statements are indicative of some of the themes described above.

Hazel

HAZEL: My name is Hazel and I am an alcoholic, but I am not unique. I am not unique in my circumstances and I am not unique in what happened to me. Alcoholism a few years ago was considered a problem

of a person with no morals, no guts, with no intestinal fortitude. Someone whom the doctors and whom their families talked to and said, "Why
don't you quit drinking? For heaven's sake, you are ruining yourself,
ruining your family—quit it, knock it off, use your willpower." It wasn't
until about ten years ago that the American Medical Association, after
quite a long time at studying alcoholics, defined alcoholism as a disease
for the first time in man's history. The disease is twofold—the allergy
of the body coupled with an obsession of the mind. The allergy of the
body is a strange thing. In alcoholics a drink, and I don't mean every
single drink but a drink, can trigger a great demand. This is physical.
The body sets up a round-robin type of thing where one drink demands
another and another drink and so on. The alcoholic has no control over
this and the medical profession feels that there is some difference in the
body of the alcoholic, the so-called social drinker, and even the hard
drinker. Between the hard drinker, the heavy drinker, and the alcoholic
there is a very fine line. There is one difference. The alcoholic, once he
has taken a drink, cannot always tell when he is going to stop. He may
think he can, but he is unable to. The heavy drinker and the so-called
social drinker can stop whenever they make up their minds to do so.
The compulsion in my mind is twofold. There is the mental compulsion
to drink. The other compulsion is the desire, the wish, and all of them
false, that he may someday drink like a normal social drinker.

Alcoholism can affect any person. It is just like any other disease—
like diabetes, like TB, like the common cold. It can affect everyone. In
Alcoholics Anonymous today we have people who are professors. We
have bank presidents. We have one man who at present is a senator
and at one time was the governor of this state. We have people who are
millionaires and we have people who have never had a dime to line their
pockets with, unless they stole. Only 3 percent of alcoholics come from
skid row originally. Those who are on skid row usually have a large
number of problems that are interrelated, but only about 3 percent are
really alcoholics.

The alcoholic is usually a person of great inner feeling. He has
great empathy for those around him for a while. He is a person who is
sensitive, overly sensitive. Usually he is a person who is somewhat im-
mature in many ways. He is very often of above-average intelligence.
Quite frequently he is a person who has emotional or mental disabilities,
however. The alcoholic is often voted the most likely to succeed and has
often attained success.

My husband and I didn't drink when we were first married, and I
very seldom drank as a young woman and I didn't drink until I was
graduated from college because I had promised my parents I wouldn't.
They didn't disapprove of drinking, but they didn't drink themselves
and they felt anybody who was away at school should behave themselves and know what they were doing at all times. I was graduated at
twenty and became twenty-one shortly thereafter and I was very proud

of myself and had a few drinks, but not very much because it didn't interest me or do anything for me. When I was married, I had gone back to school and gotten my master's degree and I had taught in the meantime. Then when we were married my husband and I couldn't afford to drink and so we didn't. We weren't interested and we didn't start to drink until quite some time after we had been married. This was after my husband had gone to an island in the Pacific during World War II. After he came back we were stationed near Washington, D.C., and it was a custom at that time in Washington, D.C., and I presume in other places, to have a predinner cocktail. We did have the predinner cocktail and it was quite pleasant. By that time we had three children, and he'd come home and we would sit down and relax and we would send the children outside to play for a while and we'd have a cocktail and we would talk. This went on for quite a while. Then finally it go to the point where one cocktail wasn't sufficient to finish our talking so we would have a second cocktail and you know it wasn't too long before the talking time was extended and I don't know how much talking we did, but the talking time extended and the eating time grew shorter. I finally got to the point where I would feed the children before we were ready to eat, and this was the beginning of a rite. Everything was done around the bottle. We would have dinner parties and the cocktail hour would last two hours. So this is the sort of thing that is likely to make people want to drink more. However, let me say this: my husband and I, and I think this is the point I was heading for, my husband and I both drank approximately the same, and if anything, he drank more than I did, and neither one of us got drunk very often. But with him, when the doctor told him he should stop drinking, he was able to do so. With me, when the doctor told me I should stop drinking, I couldn't stop. I didn't know how, and believe me, I tried.

There are many reasons why people drink. Some drink because they are psychotic or neurotic and have personality problems. Many start drinking because they feel inadequate because the people around them don't want to admit them to the group unless they have more personality or are more adequate. They find that alcohol makes them so, at least in their own mind. We find the five-foot man has grown to six feet ten. Alcohol will do that to people and therefore they will drink. They have their problems and the alcohol settles their problems because naturally it's a sedative. It soothes over and smooths over the feelings that people have that come underneath. Now these are the people who have problems to begin with. Then there are people who have no problems—and I had no problems. I had a good husband. I had three kids who weren't old enough to cause me any problems yet except when they got lost. I was adequately housed and clothed. My husband was an officer in the Navy, and while we weren't rich, we had plenty of money to do with what we wanted. And when we didn't, I had Mama and Daddy to fall back upon. I was one of the privileged people of my generation, who are few. I was able to go to school. I was able to get my master's degree, and I got three-quarters of the way through my Ph.D. degree, fell in love, and decided that it wasn't worth it, that love was more important and truly it was. I had no reason to drink other than the social reason. It isn't important to me that I became an alcoholic because I drank socially. The thing that is important to me today is to know that I am an alcoholic and that I am able to stop drinking through Alcoholics Anonymous. I was not able to in any other way. Let me quickly go through several things that I think are important for people to know about alcoholism. There are actually three stages, three stairsteps of alcoholism. The first one we call controlled drinking, and this is the very beginning. From the beginning of the disease there is no cure. Once an alcoholic, always an alcoholic. It has been ten years. Actually I received what we call a birthday cake last night at an A.A. meeting downtown. Each one, or five, or ten years an alcoholic is rewarded or we celebrate our anniversary of coming into A.A. I have not had a drink in ten years and some days. But if I were to start drinking today, according to the doctors and those who have already tried it, I would be in worse shape within a very, very short time than I was when I stopped drinking because it is progressive and no matter whether I had been drinking or not, the disease has become worse. I didn't have problems before I started to drink but I sure developed them afterwards. Now there are people who had the problems originally. Alcoholics are as different as there are alcoholics. Each alcoholic has his own problem and his own method of behavior and his own reactions. So in the first stage the person may have been drinking for years and years or he may have just started drinking. But when you reach a certain point, there is a body change and along comes the mental compulsion. At the beginning of the second stage we begin to need more alcohol than we did before. It isn't important enough to the person to overstep at all times although he does overstep frequently. During this period, people begin to develop blackouts, and this is one of the extreme symptoms of alcoholism. The alcoholic will function as though he were sometimes drunk, sometimes sober. He will be in a state of amnesia. This is not passing out, just a state of blackout and many of these people do not know what has happened to them for over a period of time. The blackout may last for an hour, an evening, a week. I know one woman who had a blackout for three months. She started drinking in New York City and she came to herself out of an amnesic state here in San Diego and she had no idea how she'd gotten here, what she'd done to pay her way. She was in a hotel room three months later and she had no knowledge and never has found out what happened. This can be very scary and especially if it happens very often. I personally never had a blackout. You don't have to have all the symptoms to be an alcoholic. But I did find that my intake was increasing, as I told you a while ago—one cocktail wasn't enough, and two cocktails weren't enough. I cannot think of alcohol in any way except by the quart. I never drank a quart a day but I think if I had continued to drink very long I would have ended up with a quart a day or more— and I know people who drank as much as two or three. There are three things that happen to an alcoholic. You stop drinking. You become a vegetable, or you go insane or die, or, of course, all three. You stop drinking when you die. It happens to many of us. We have, first, the increased desire for alcohol, and we begin to drink more. We begin to sneak a few drinks because nobody is drinking enough to keep us satisfied, and we may sneak into the kitchen to get a little extra. Fifty percent of the alcoholics are women nowadays. Women have become, as you know, more emancipated, and are able to go out and people aren't hiding it any more. We aren't trying to hide old mom in the closet because she is drinking too much. We are trying to do something for her. In the second stage our hangovers become intense. We have nausea in the morning and nausea all the time, and we are beginning to want to drink and we are starting to fight it. We are beginning to think, "Well, wait a minute, it is not normal for me to start out my breakfast with five Bloody Marys. It isn't normal for me to want to go over to the liquor closet in the morning and get a big double or a shot of bourbon. Mothers just don't do this, and fathers who are going to work just don't do this because if we do we are going to do something that is not quite right about our home life."

So we begin to drink more and more, and by now our tolerance has built up and we are pretty proud of the fact that we are able to drink everyone else under the table. We are also beginning to hide our alcohol because for a while we are beginning to fear that someone will find out, our husbands, our wives, our parents, our children, or whoever we are living with, our associates. We don't want them to know how much we are drinking so we begin to hide our bottles. I never did really hide bottles except I would buy a bottle and hide it so I would have sufficient to replace the family supply. When I would be drinking during the day and my husband would come home and I would not want him to see I had been drinking and had taken the bottle down so much, so I would hide the bottle and then would come out and fill up the bottle because we always had liquor in the house. I don't know what he thought. I don't know why he thought I had alcohol on my breath when the bottle was exactly the same. This is alcoholic thinking. You are not always logical.

Now, there are people who go off and get drunk and this is a different thing. But these people I'm talking about, and I am one of them, we can't control it. We don't know when we are going to go, and we are working hard against it. So we have the fear. We have the heavy hangovers, the constant nausea. We have self-pity, the most defeating thing that can happen to a person because then he becomes defensive and nobody understands him; he hates everybody. So we have hate and this begins to build up and build up until finally we go into the third stage.

In the third stage, we are interested in nothing but the bottle. We have lost everything but we don't give a damn. It doesn't make any difference because the bottle is the thing we are crawling into because this is our aim. This is taking us away from all of these problems that have developed. We are blaming everyone but ourselves for our own situation. In this third stage, if we don't stop drinking we face insanity or death. At this point, we don't care what crimes we commit. Fifty-two percent of the crimes in San Diego and a much larger percentage in the general population are committed due to alcohol and many are committed in order to get the funds to sustain their habit. In the third stage, too, we develop many diseases which may have been developing all along, like cirrhosis of the liver, tuberculosis, or diabetes and things like that. We become very sanguine about our drinking. We don't want to do it. We hate it. We fight it. We want to crawl into a hole, but we don't seem to be able to do anything about it so we go on. Now I personally never had these problems to a great extent. My habit we call "bottom" in A.A. It was pretty much what we call a "high bottom" because I wasn't arrested. I didn't lose my husband or my children, and incidentally, by the time I actually became an alcoholic, I had five children, which is enough to drive anyone to alcohol. But my husband knew I had a problem, and although he didn't want to stop drinking, he wanted me to. He didn't know I was an alcoholic and couldn't stop drinking when I wanted like he could, and he didn't understand this. And my husband is a medical man—a dentist. Some psychiatrists say that the alcohol is a symptom of an underlying cause, and in many cases this is true, but not always. And in my case, definitely not. I would say in about 85 percent of the people, not. Alcohol is the cause; the others are the symptoms in my mind.

QUESTION: *You mentioned that your husband had used alcohol as much if not more than you and yet you feel alcohol is the cause. How is that?*

HAZEL: Only to me. Something within my body made it different, made it change, so after a while I was unable to stop drinking when I wanted to. This was a terrible blow to me, because I didn't think women ought to get drunk, and I still don't, but at that time I was even more adamant about it than I am now. I didn't think a lady got drunk, and I was getting drunk. Now, I wasn't getting falling-down drunk. I kept my alcohol level about 80 proof and that's going pretty good.

QUESTION: *You didn't feel there was any difference in your husband's background and your family background that might be the reason for your becoming an alcoholic?*

HAZEL: Sure, there were differences in background. My background was one of French extraction and we all know the French are great drinkers. His background was a combination of German and English.

QUESTION: *Does the taste of alcohol attract you to it?*

HAZEL: Not always. I loved bourbon. I hated scotch though after a while I liked it, but it got so expensive I couldn't get it. I liked wine. I liked beer. I hated vodka and I hated gin. But when it came to being choosy in the last stages, I'd say I was only in the true alcoholic stages for five years, but I went downhill fast and I think only another two or three months and I would have been in an institution. By the time I went to A.A., I didn't care. I would drink anything. Fortunately for me, I've lost the interest in alcohol even to my smelling senses. I don't like the smell of it anymore, which is good.

QUESTION: *Did you ever have withdrawal?*

HAZEL: Fortunately not. I did for a little while, naturally, and something happened to me. I had a spiritual experience.

QUESTION: *Did your husband continue drinking?*

HAZEL: Yes, and it was very difficult for the first year because of that particular point. I thought he was an alcoholic too and he would not quit drinking. In fact, he got drunker than he had ever gotten before that first year I was in A.A. And he really got staggering drunk every night for weeks and months. It was very difficult for me. Then something happened to him, and I don't know what. All of a sudden, bingo, he had control over it and he's had control ever since. So he is not an alcoholic. He's a heavy drinker but he's not an alcoholic.

QUESTION: *Do you still have alcohol in your house?*

HAZEL: Definitely. My husband and my daughter have cocktails before dinner every night. We have beer around all the time and we try always to give a large cocktail party at Christmastime. I always have a bowl of what my husband calls kiddie punch. I have friends who don't drink—both in A.A. and I have many friends who are Mormons, and when they come they drink kiddie punch. Everybody else gets smashed and we have fun. Let's say we feel great and they feel lousy.

QUESTION: *Because there is a drinker in your family, do you feel pressure to drink?*

HAZEL: There is social pressure only if you allow it. I don't care. What I do is my business. One evening we were out at a party, and a friend of mine whom I've known for years and attended parties for years before and after and still didn't know I wasn't drinking said, "What dear, are you drinking?" I said, "I'm drinking tonic with a twist of lemon." She said, "Don't you drink alcohol? Why don't you have a real drink?" I said, "I don't drink alcohol." Now I am not ashamed of the fact that I am in A.A. With other people it's all right for them to get smashed, to get drunk, to get stoned, but if I say I sobered up in A.A., then this means that I have admitted that I have a problem and they attach a social stigma. There shouldn't be one any more than the guy who has cancer. At any rate, she said, "Well, why don't you drink?" I said, "I'm allergic to alcohol." She said, "Oh?" I'm not quite sure if this is a woman who has a college education, but anyway she said, "What does it do, does it make you break out?" I said, "No, it makes me drunk." That stopped the questions. There's never been any reference to it again. Even if there is pressure, I don't feel it, and if they get too pressured, too pushy, I say, "Look, I'm an alcoholic, I can't drink." Boy, that does stop them!

QUESTION: *What led you to join A.A.?*

HAZEL: Well, the thing that led me to join A.A. was that I had hit bottom with my self-respect. This was a psychological thing with me, I think. It was a thing within myself. I hated me and I had to change me somehow, and that triggered my interest in A.A. For six months, I read every article I could get on alcoholism and then rebutted it and went out and drank some more because I wasn't like those people. For a year I did this. For six months I did it more intensely. I tried to prove that I wasn't an alcoholic by drinking more alcohol. There isn't too much you can do for the alcoholic except you can be understanding, and this is important. The alcoholic who is nagged is going to react by drinking more. The person who is the alcoholic needs understanding and needs love. The person who lives with the alcoholic must never make a threat which he or she is unwilling to carry out. Alcoholics are great liars and they think everyone else lies.

COMMENTARY

How can we account for Hazel's alcoholism? Does it result from a physiological "allergic" reaction to alcohol, as she would lead us to believe? She also gives the impression that there were no prior causes or predisposing psychological factors, although admitting she knows of such cases. Her feeling was that her amount of alcohol consumption was no greater than her husband's, and yet her husband did not become a compulsive drinker, an alcoholic. Thus, to her, the allergy factor is the only logical differentiating factor. However, can we assume her situation and her biography were identical to her husband's? Certainly during the time that she and he both developed heavy drinking patterns while stationed in Washington, D.C., their situations were not identical. He was required to perform his daily duties as an officer in the Navy, while she was in a different situation as a housewife. There was certainly a drinking culture to which they were both exposed, but while he would have to sober up for his daily responsibilities, she was left alone to engage in solitary drinking. We don't know much of her husband's biography (except that he was of German and English descent), but in Hazel's background there are some indications of dependence on parents. She commented about this:

> I was adequately housed and clothed.... We had plenty of money to do with what we wanted. And when we didn't, I had Mama and Daddy to fall back upon.

Such a statement would appear to fit the concept of dependence of Straus and the overall model of the McCords. However, how do we explain that the McCord model is geared to masculinity while Hazel is a female? Perhaps it would be best to note that the elements of masculinity to which the McCords refer are those of "independence" and "achievement." We find that Hazel may be influenced by the modern, "liberated" concept of feminism in that she was struggling for greater independence in academia:

> I was able to get my master's degree, and I got three-quarters of the way through my Ph.D. degree, ...

And, we find that Hazel may have been in a conflict of independence-dependence, in that she gave up her Ph.D. studies because she "fell in love." Her more traditional, dependent female role pull is given in the words:

> ...and, incidentally, by the time I actually became an alcoholic, I had five children, *which is enough to drive anyone to alcohol.*

Such an interpretation would not only fit a "dependent" or "power" conflict model, but also could provide clues to the increasing rate of female alcoholics (although not as great as the "fifty percent" Hazel claims).

The cultural element is also present in Hazel's testimony:

> My background was one of French extraction and we all know the French are great drinkers.

This is combined with an ambivalence toward alcohol by Hazel's parents:

> ... I very seldom drank as a young woman and I didn't drink until I was graduated from college because I had promised my parents I wouldn't. They didn't disapprove of drinking, but they didn't drink themselves and they felt anybody who was away at school should behave themselves and know what they were doing at all times.

Perhaps this ambivalence combined with a lack of complete independence (not knowing what one is doing at all times) contributed to the pronounced guilt she felt about her alcohol consumption through her years of drinking. Various comments indicate this:

> In the second stage our hangovers become intense. We have nausea in the morning and nausea all of the time. . . . We are beginning to think, "Well, wait a minute, it is not normal for me to start out my breakfast with five Bloody Marys. It isn't normal for me to want to go over to the liquor closet in the morning and get a big double or a shot of bourbon. *Mothers just don't do this, and fathers who are going to work just don't do this because if we do we are going to do something that is not quite right about our home life.* . . . [Italics added] I didn't think women ought to get drunk, and I still don't, but at that time I was even more adamant about it than I am now. I didn't think a lady got drunk, and I was getting drunk.

It is conceivable from the above statements that many of the "symptoms of alcoholism" are manifestations of guilt; secret drinking, morning drinking, amnesic blackouts, and hangovers, for instance, all may be linked with guilt. This would not only fit the Jellinek model but also expand upon it.

We may hypothesize that although heavy drinking may result from a conditioned use of alcohol to relieve stress or tension, *addictive drinking or alcoholism results from the use of alcohol to neutralize guilt about one's own prior use of alcohol or problems that resulted from this deviancy.* When drinking functions to cover guilt that results from prior drinking, each drink or drinking bout brings more future guilt, which then is conditioned to relief by more drinking, creating a compulsive chain reaction. This guilt-neutralizing chain reaction eventually gives way to the escapist or retreatist syndrome that characterizes the chronic alcoholic. In Hazel's words:

> In the third stage, we are interested in nothing but the bottle. We have lost everything, but we don't give a damn. It doesn't make any difference because the bottle is the thing we are crawling into because this is our aim. This is taking us away from *all of these problems that have developed.*

We are interested here not in explaining heavy drinking, but in explaining alcoholism. One does not imply the other. In alcoholism, based on Hazel's case, we posit four basic conditions: 1) excessive use of alcohol (and what for Hazel may have been excessive in her perspective may not be for another person); 2) problems resulting from the use of alcohol (and Hazel did not experience many problems experienced by alcoholics, but she perceived the existence of problems); 3) guilt over the use of alcohol or related problems; and 4) use of alcohol to neutralize this guilt.

This explanation seems to "fit the facts," especially those pertaining to members of Alcoholics Anonymous. We know that members of Alcoholics Anonymous are generally from a middle class background and have "fallen." Hazel indicates this:

> Alcoholics are people voted most likely to succeed. . . . We have people who are professors. We have bank presidents. We have one man who at present is a senator. . . . We have people who are millionaires. . . . Only 3 percent of alcoholics come from skid row originally.

This point is also made by Trice and Roman, who, we saw, find a common theme in A.A. talks of people fallen from positions of relative success.[42]

Thus, the members of A.A. are people who 1) are heavy or excessive users of alcohol, 2) have had problems resulting from alcohol precipitating their membership, and 3) have been socialized to believe that excessive use of alcohol is "deviancy" as a norm of middle class society. Conceivably, all may have the fourth situational factor in common, so that, like Hazel, they were in a situation whereby alcohol could be used, without restraint, to cover or neutralize guilt resulting from its previous use.

Our universal generalization also seems to fit the emphasis in A.A. upon the allergy concept. Alcoholics Anonymous ideology seems to account for the guilt-laden, self-deprecating tendencies of alcoholics. Hazel comments on her own self-hatred prior to membership:

> I hated me and I had to change me somehow. . . . We become very sanguine about our drinking. We know we don't want to do it. We hate it. We fight it. We want to crawl into a hole, but we don't seem to be able to do anything about it so we go on.

Prior to joining A.A., most alcoholics accede to a cultural tendency to blame themselves and feel guilty for alcohol problems, as Hazel says:

> Alcoholism a few years ago was considered a problem of a person with no morals, no guts, and no intestinal fortitude.

But this guilt about alcohol use is, according to our analysis, at the heart of alcoholism. Alcoholics Anonymous ideology neutralized this guilt by way of the "allergy concept." There is no defect of will, because the body is infested with a "disease." This allergy concept serves the function of a delabeling process, helping the individual to shed not only public stigma (as Hazel is able to do at cocktail parties) but also self-recrimination.[43] When the individual stops feeling guilty about past indiscretions regarding alcohol use, the chain reaction of drinking is broken.

We can also see in our explanation where "normative isolation" fits into the career of an alcoholic. Chiding by family members may only aggravate the guilt feelings and hasten the chain reaction. "The alcoholic who is nagged is going to react by drinking more."

We should also posit that some people in society are in a position to engage in heavy drinking without becoming alcoholics. These would be people whose duties or responsibilities can be carried out despite their heavy drinking, such as some career military jobs or unskilled civilian jobs. Perhaps this accounts for the absence of lower class persons in Alcoholics Anonymous. Also included would be people whose heavy drinking does not evoke feelings of guilt, including perhaps people born and raised on skid row. But if guilt is a result of heavy drinking, alcoholism can still be circumvented if the individual is restrained from utilizing alcohol as a means of assuaging guilt (by circumstances of employment, family controls, or self-controls).

George

Unlike Hazel, George, our next informant, was not a "lone drinker" but almost always drank in peer company. Most important, he became a resident of skid row and later "recovered" from alcoholism by his contact not with A.A. but with the Salvation Army. George is now fifty-nine years old and a counselor with the Salvation Army.

GEORGE: I am really happy to be here today. About nine years ago I wouldn't have been able to crawl through that door, much less walk. I can sure thank God that I found out alcohol was a terrible thing. To go back into my background, my name is George. I was born in San Francisco in 1913. I first started to drink when I was eighteen, but of course in those days it was all bootleg—we made our own beer and gin, etc. By the age of twenty I feel that I was a confirmed alcoholic. I had all the bad signs, the blackouts, but I was to the point where I was actually doing daily drinking, and that is really bad—serious trouble. At twenty-one I got married. Two years later I lost my job because of drinking. I then proceeded to keep up the drinking, wandering from job to job. I had a rough time supporting my family, was on relief. Half the time I was never home, and in 1940 when the war had started, I joined the Navy. During my Navy career, which lasted fourteen years, I was a terrific drunk. How I stayed in the Navy, I don't know. But I made Navy chief and came out Navy third class. In my last station, half the time I couldn't report for duty. Finally, the commanding officer came to see me one day and told me that it was either going to be a misconduct discharge or I could get out while I could still get my honorables. I guess you know, I got out while I could get my honorables. That was in 1954. From 1954 to 1963 I lived nothin' but a life of Hell. Anyone who thinks that this alcohol drinking is an easy thing and you can't get hooked on it, had better think. I would go to the clubs—that's when the trouble started. I lost my family. After getting out of the Navy, I went to sea. I didn't last there either. I had a good job, but just got progressively worse with my drinking. Frequent blackouts. In 1960 I landed in State Hospital. I had the DT's and they picked me up on Los Angeles Street and they strapped me down. I stayed there for ninety days, but that didn't help because I didn't want it. If you don't want something, then you're not going to get it. I got another job, but just like my other employment—first payday, first drunk. My drinking at that time was at the stage like some of these people who are addicted to drugs. I didn't care about my family, my friends, my job. I was just going to get booze, and I got it. In the meantime I was broke, I was walking the streets. I had landed in Los Angeles on 5th and Wall—skid row—just living a life of bummin'. Askin' people for money till I'd get enough for a bottle of wine. It's a terrible, terrible life. Finally, I heard about the Salvation Army program and I went there and asked for help. They took me in, but I didn't want it right away. I rebelled against it. I couldn't see going to psychologists. I couldn't see being in at 11 o'clock. I couldn't see not being able to take a drink. Why I went there I don't know. In the foggy state of mind that I was in, I took the easiest way out—shelter. Temporary shelter. After thirty days there, I was back out on the streets again, back to the same pattern of living. Living in a dingy apartment. My dear mother was sending money to the landlord so that I could at least have a room. She never would send me the money, though. I again landed back down on skid row of Los Angeles getting picked up. Skid row life is every man for himself. If you don't work with them and share a bottle when you have one, you are just excluded from the crowd. They have their own codes. It was hard to cope with. I wasn't used to that kind of life. If you had a bottle, you had to watch yourself. They'd kill for a drink. Many a time I was injured from beatings and landed in Central or Emergency Hospital. So, in December of 1962, I was lying in a cheap room and I happened to get a letter from home about this captain from the Salvation Army who had helped me and telling me that he was back in town and was interested in how I was doing. So I bought a bottle of wine to calm my shakes so that I could write a letter back, and within two days that captain was up there to pick me up. That started me on the way back because I figured that someone cared. I had decided that I was either going to kill myself or I could come back to where I had started. I think that if you were raised in a good home that training is going to show up even if you stray off a good path. I came back to the center here in San Diego and in January of 1963 I decided that with the help of prayer and cooperation from myself I was going to stop it, and I did. I graduated from the center in June of 1963. I remarried, got a job managing apartments, but then again I got cocky. I was going around collecting rents and everyone was calling me "Mister" and it sounded pretty good. Then they'd invite me in for a beer and at first I'd shun it, then I'd think, "Well, you've been doing pretty good. You're married, got a job." So I went and took the first one, and thank God, I saw the light, and I've never had a drink since. I realize today that we have a way of life that everywhere you go there's a drink involved. But I thank God that I can say no, and it really doesn't bother me any more. All I have to do is think about where I came from. I've dedicated my life to helping these men that are in the same boat that I am.

There are a lot of them that like that way of life, but I've also seen a lot of them die. I've seen a lot of my own friends die. My only message is that this alcoholism thing is getting worse. Your family can be your worst enemy when you're trying to make a comeback. We sometimes recommend to our boys in that predicament that they make a geographical change and get away from their family and start over and make a new life. Get sober and then come back. I have a son that I met in 1968. He's thirty-four now; I hadn't seen him for fifteen years. But through the grapevine he knew that I'd made it, that I'd made a comeback. He phoned. I wouldn't phone him because I was too ashamed and I didn't want to butt in on him and his family. Now we're real good friends. I got four grand-kids and I just met 'em. They don't call me Granddad. They call me George. I'm just so happy that I know them and that we're friends that I don't care what they call me. It just shows you what this social drinking can do, and I'm not the only one it happened to. There's thousands and thousands of them, and there are thousands that are recovered and making a good life. But I wouldn't want anybody to go that route. It sure is a shameful way to live, going around so dirty and nasty, never taking a bath. Half the time you don't even have shoes that are right for you. You're bummin' all the time. People give you a dime to get rid of you. It's not a good life. It is a death sentence. It is a killer.

QUESTION: *When you were on skid row, did you see very many women?*

GEORGE: Oh, yes. Sometimes you'd go to one just to get a bottle. Misery loves company, and that is one of the most miserable states.

QUESTION: *Is there a fine line between a heavy social drinker and an alcoholic?*

GEORGE: Sure, but the main difference is that a heavy social drinker will come in with the executive or someone, drink, and then leave, while an alcoholic will close that bar and then have something either in the car or at home.

QUESTION: *Would you say that the Navy way of life facilitates drinking as part of that life?*

GEORGE: Well, the guys that I hung around with when I was in the Navy were pretty much in the same boat I was; we were all drunks. We would just wait for liberty to come and that was our life. I think, though, that we went in with the idea that a sailor has to drink. That's a false way of thinking. The Navy didn't do anything to me. I did it to myself. Now, the Navy frowns on drinking. They frown on me, too, but they stood it for fourteen years. I was just fortunate I didn't get kicked out.

QUESTION: *You said that you started drinking during Prohibition. Do you think that your problem was a result of the fact that drinking was illegal, or because of the crowd you were in, it wouldn't have made any difference?*

GEORGE: Well, at first it was a kick to go around to these bootleg places and be only sixteen and have the guys look at you. But pretty soon we'd learned how to make the stuff ourselves and it started becoming a way of life. It's really hard to blame any one thing for drinking.

QUESTION: *Two questions. First, what do you think made you start drinking excessively? Second, do you think that if you had stayed in L.A. instead of coming down here with the captain you could have been rehabilitated?*

GEORGE: No, to the second question. If I had stayed, I don't think that I would be alive today. I was so deteriorated from drinking that I don't think I would have made it. When he came and got me, he put me in a hospital because I was so dehydrated, because I hadn't eaten, and because I couldn't move. On the first question, I just gradually, well, I call it just getting hooked on it. It just got to where I wanted it all the time. At first I would just have to go to the bar as soon as it opened, then I had to have a morning drink even before the bar opened, then I had to have some with me all the time.

QUESTION: *You don't think that there is anything that you could put your finger on as being a cause for you to continue drinking in the first place?*

GEORGE: No. I hated the taste of whiskey or scotch, but I sure drank a lot of it. But that's just my cause. Some drink to drown things, some just for the kick. I drank because I had a craving for it.

QUESTION: *I read that one of the reasons that a person drinks is a lack of power; they don't feel capable of doing things. Do you think this is true?*

GEORGE: Well, it did give me a little more nerve. If I didn't have the guts to do something, well, a couple of jolts and I was on my way.

QUESTION: *Do you think that there's a certain type of person or personality that is more susceptible to being an alcoholic?*

GEORGE: No, I don't think so. I think that anyone can be an alcoholic. Alcohol has no respect for anyone. It all depends on how much you drink and how your system handles it.

QUESTION: *What about motivation? In your case was it escapism? And if it was, what from?*

GEORGE: I guess because I wasn't wanted. I was picked on. I started out by liking those places because at first it was fun. I had a lot of fun for a few years.

QUESTION: *Could you describe what it's like to go to a bar and become part of the group there?*

GEORGE: You just start going to the bar and become a good paying customer and you start meeting the people who also frequent the place—which is usually a beer joint.

QUESTION: *Do you develop any close friendships?*

GEORGE: Sure, until you run out of money. You kind of lean on each other. Most of the time only a couple of fellows would be working and you try to get close friends with them to kind of get you through your low spell. That's the pattern. They're all just a bunch of leeches. When you're in a bind or want some help, they don't know you.

QUESTION: *It seems to me that when you walk inside a bar you see a bunch of cronies and they look like friends. They call each other by nicknames.*

GEORGE: I wouldn't want to tell you some of the nicknames they call me. I wouldn't call them friendly, either.

QUESTION: *Do you think some people drink because they have problems meeting people?*

GEORGE: I think so. I was one of those people. What do you call them? Introverts? One who was always by himself—well, that was me. But I didn't have the funds, when my jobs dwindled and my earning power dwindled, to keep up with the upper bars. I was down there with the beer and wine. And those people there to me are just a bunch of room drinkers. They take their bottle and sit in there and hibernate until it's empty and then go make a run or have someone make a run for them. They live in some flophouse where it's all winos and never have to worry about a drink.

QUESTION: *What would be a typical day on skid row?*

GEORGE: A typical day for me would be if I didn't have a drink in the room or couldn't find a buddy by five, well, I'd start walking the streets because the bars usually open at six in the morning. If you knew someone who was swabbing a bar, you'd go and bang on the door till they'd let you in. The majority of times if you have a good friend, which I did, you would get in and then grab a broom and try to help him if you could stand up to get a drink. Then you'd make the first touch, get yourself a bottle, and then hibernate in a room and then you'd gradually wake up. Then it would be day, and it would be who would be the first guy who could walk out without getting in trouble with the cops, and you'd go to the grocery store and get the wine. You'd usually try to get the cheapest you could. Sometimes it would be ninety-seven cents a gallon.

QUESTION: *Any preferences? Muscatel?*

GEORGE: When you get to that point you drink anything you can get your hands on. It's really horrible. It's a horrible sickness. Sometimes when the fellows come in I take a bottle away from them. I can't stand the smell of the stuff and yet I used to think I loved it. Skid row is terrible. Just like I said. I think if you're raised right, though—I come from a very good family—I don't think you forget that raising, and I think you get to the bottom and you start taking inventory. You can't cope with 'em. The fellows that really go with that drinking for a living and prefer skid row life. They spot you and you just don't belong in their league. It's a rough life. They'll toss you out, and I don't mean easy.

QUESTION: *At what point did you finally admit to yourself that you were an alcoholic? Was it when you finally called for help?*

GEORGE: Oh no, I knew I was an alcoholic, but I didn't want to admit it to myself. But I wouldn't come out and tell probably you or anybody but then I would. I was an alcoholic. There are no *if, and,* or *maybes,* but to everybody else I was just a social drinker. I relied upon this illness deal too. I got the sympathy of many people. He's an alcoholic. He's ill. You'd be surprised how that works. I think too many rely on that.

QUESTION: *When you were on skid row, did you run across many kids that were in their very early teens or younger than most alcoholics?*

GEORGE: I couldn't really tell you. I associated with ones about my own age. You'd see some young people down there, but they were down there just making a tour. I don't see how they could cope with that type. It's just very rough living.

QUESTION: *Some people might like that way of life. Could you explain this?*

GEORGE: Well, it's an easy way to go for them, in their stupid thinking. You've got so much. You've got your big city where you have your missions. Fella's don't have to worry about sleeping. They've got schedules where they can rotate and they've got their beds for every night in the year. And maybe they can eat, as long as they're sober. As long as they can stand up to take a tray, then they can eat. They can always flop. A lot of missions are very strict about taking them in if they're drunk. We won't take them in at our center if they're drunk. They'll have to go and straighten out somewhere and come in sober.

QUESTION: *Did you ever ride the rails or anything like that?*

GEORGE: No, I haven't. I would have got killed doing that. I have seen many a fellow hurt.

QUESTION: *You said there were certain "codes" on skid row. Could you explain about those? Do you know about "bottle gangs"?*

GEORGE: A bottle group is when you come out in the morning and come out on the street and they'll ask you how much you got for a run. You might have a dime. Four or five will go in together. You'll go down main street and see what you can rustle up.

QUESTION: *Mostly panhandling?*

GEORGE: Panhandling? I'd have to have a drink before I'd even come out and talk. You panhandle practically all morning. These professionals, they get enough for the day. If you're having a rough time the word will get around and they'll say there's such and such a gang down on the next corner, and try to break in on that one. Usually they all share. Thus, you never go dry. It's easy.

QUESTION: *Are they really generous people?*

GEORGE: Yes, they are. They'll come up to you if you are in a flophouse, ask you if you need a drink. Tell you a little story about where they've been.

QUESTION: *If they have strong group solidarity, why is it they don't develop abiding friendships?*

GEORGE: Because they each mistrust each other, see. If a drunk can get away with it, you pass a bottle to him and he'll take the whole thing. So they watch. They don't trust you. They'll help you at the same time. But, boy, you got to stay off that bottle.

QUESTION: *How do they regulate that?*

GEORGE: You don't have all of your teeth if you don't do it. That's the way they do it. And if you don't share, you're out. You could walk down the street and you could be dying and they couldn't care less. I didn't actually spend that much time on skid row, off and on about a year. I couldn't cope. I couldn't get in with a gang. I did my part but then I didn't have the guts. If I sober up, I feel changed, and so on.

COMMENTARY

George presents a case study that seems to call into question a number of points of definition and explanation discussed in the introduction to this chapter and to verify others. According to his own account, George was an alcoholic from the age of twenty. He became an uncontrolled drinker with the familiar alcoholic symptoms of daily drinking, blackouts, and DT's. We would expect, according to Wallace's distinction between drunks and alcoholics, that George would have readily become a solitary drinker. However, he became a peer-oriented drinker throughout his years of drinking. He drank in the company of peers in his late teens, in the Navy, in the bars, and later as a room drinker on skid row.

George's life pattern is somewhat reminiscent of Straus' account of Frank Moore. After George became an alcoholic, he did not descend rapidly to life on skid row. Rather, although he lost jobs while he was an alcoholic prior to entering the Navy, once in the Navy his dependency needs appear to have been satisfied. Although he "was a terrific drunk" all during his fourteen years of service, he actually rose to the rank of Navy chief and came out "Navy third class." There are other signs of a dependency conflict and institutional dependency meeting such needs. These include his statements regarding his family (although we have almost none of his childhood biography):

My dear mother was sending money to the landlord so that I could at least have a room.
Your family can be your worst enemy when you're trying to make a comeback.
We sometimes recommend to our boys ... that they ... get away from their family ...

In addition, there are statements attesting that various aspects of skid row satisfied George's dependency needs:

You kind of lean on each other.
I landed in State Hospital.
You've got so much. You've got your big city where you have your missions. Fella's don't have to worry about sleeping ... they've got their beds ... They can eat ... They can always flop.

Such statements are not only consistent with the McCord model and Straus' findings, but they verify much of the deviant perspectives found by Wiseman as well. In addition, George made several statements that would fit McClelland's interpretation of the use of alcohol to meet "power" rather than dependency needs:

> Well, it did give me a little more nerve. If I didn't have guts to do something, well, a couple of jolts and I was on my way.
>
> I was one of those people . . . Introverts? One who was always by himself—well, that was me. But I didn't have the funds . . . and my earning power dwindled, to keep up with the upper bars. I was down there with the beer and wine.
>
> . . . I got cocky . . . everyone was calling me "Mister" and it sounded pretty good. . . .

Further, George makes several references to the fact that his recovery was due to the help of "prayer" and "God." McClelland refers to this as one means of solving one's power needs by "borrowing strength." A.A. is noted as one form of borrowing strength, including their emphasis on a "higher power." [44] It is possible, of course, that much of this perspective is the result of George's interactions within A.A. membership.

Consistent with a "dependency" model, after his discharge from the Navy, the distinction between drunk and alcoholic, which Wallace makes, was not so clear, and as time passed, George became more an alcoholic or compulsive drinker, and less a drunk, despite his peer-oriented drinking. He drifted from job to job, and lost contact with his wife and family. He eventually drifted into skid row, but his retreatism was not quite that posited in anomie theory. He did not drink because of economic failure, but rather he failed because of drinking. Also, he did not come to skid row to escape from a socially or economically frustrating situation. Such factors may have influenced his earlier drinking, but the immediate cause of the drift to skid row was his demand for alcohol. He did not, as Bogue and Dunham theorize, come to skid row in search of specialized services or to satisfy economic need. He didn't avail himself of the missions and other services until late in his year on skid row. Nor did he come in search of affiliation, as Bahr postulated, since his prior drinking had always been done in the context of peer affiliation in bars.

It is doubtful that Spradley's labeling approach applies in George's case. According to his own account, he spent only a weekend in jail and this had no effect upon his subsequent drinking or adjustment to life on skid row. (George's discussion of his jail experience does not appear on the tape transcript.)

The theoretical model that seems to fit George's case well is a Jellinek sequential role model elaborated with "dependency" or "power" needs. The "causes" varied at different stages of his career as a drinker.

His early drinking was apparently a route to social affiliation. The early "social drinking" was followed by a later stage of "heavy social drinking" that possibly accompanied his job failures and isolation from family ties. Eventually, the alcohol came to be used to neutralize problems that it created in the guilt chain reaction described above. Whereas drinking had been a means to making friends, it became an "end in itself" when George became an alcoholic. Friends became instrumental to drink. George then moved to skid row in search of a lower-cost supply of alcohol.

While alcoholism led George to skid row, and, by his own admission, it was easy for him to get all the alcohol he wanted there, what accounts for his eventual recovery from alcoholism? George's recovery was probably heavily influenced by the fact that he could not get in with a skid row gang on any stable basis. He was actually an outsider on skid row. There are various reasons why he became an outsider: 1) he was an alcoholic and so he tended to be predatory in a situation where sharing was a norm. Various statements indicate his prior conflicts over alcohol:

> Skid row is every man for himself. If you don't work with them and share a bottle when you have one, you are just excluded from the crowd. . . . They'd kill for a drink. Many a time I was injured from beatings and landed in Central or Emergency Hospital.

It is highly possible that the spoken norm of "sharing" is not truly practiced in the skid row subculture. This has been found in other subcultures in which there is a discrepancy between the spoken and the behavioral norms. Likewise, "sharing" and other words are parts of the "fronts" or "pat responses" that George no longer requires.

Quite possibly, as Wallace suggests and Hazel indicates, skid row gang drinkers are not by and large alcoholics, and so an alcoholic in their midst is a normative deviate. Another reason George may have been ostracized was 2) his tendency toward moralizing, reflecting the guilt syndrome we have described as basic to alcoholism. When he sobered up, he would probably convey his shame, guilt, and basic self-hate to his peers, a tendency not likely to endear him to them. His current statements reflect his former attitudes that he might have conveyed when sober.

> It's sure a shameful way to live, going around so dirty and nasty, never taking a bath. . . . It's really horrible. It's a horrible sickness. . . . I can't stand the smell of the stuff.

The last reason George was an outsider on skid row was 3) that he came from a middle class background, and he did not know how to handle himself or understand the value system of lower class peers.

I come from a very good family. I don't think you forget that raising, and I think you get to the bottom and you start taking inventory. You can't cope with 'em. The fellows that really go with that drinking for a living and prefer skid row life. They spot you and you just don't belong in their league. It's a rough life. They'll toss you out and I don't mean easy.... I couldn't cope. I couldn't get in with a gang. I did my part but then I didn't have the guts. If I sober up I feel changed, and so on.

George became a "mission stiff" and perhaps a "nose diver," social types we have seen that would be contemptible to his skid row peers. But his return to sobriety may not have resulted so much from strength of will, as from a desire to escape from his unpleasant peer situation. It proved to be his only option other than suicide. Thus the need to survive may have overshadowed any dependency or power needs.

THEORETICAL IMPLICATIONS

Having examined our interviews within some of the specific theories regarding alcoholism, let us now review them within our larger theoretical frameworks.

Physiological Theories

There appears to be some evidence of genetic predisposition or an "allergy" to alcohol as Hazel contends. The manner in which this operates—if indeed it exists—is unknown, as is how it might interact with other factors. Also unclear is the degree to which statements such as Hazel's are the results of group interaction within A.A. and elsewhere that fit a medical or "disease" model of alcoholism.

Psychiatric Theories

While simple personality traits or unfulfilled "needs" do not in themselves distinguish alcoholics or problem drinkers from others, it does appear that, considering them within larger frameworks with other factors, they do have a degree of explanatory power. Thus, when elaborating on the Jellinek model along with that of the McCords, we see that both Hazel and George displayed dependency (or power) conflict due to other social and cultural factors. Elaboration, we hypothesize, is necessary to further develop such theories especially as they may pertain to females. They are, perhaps, of strongest potential when considered within a "social control" framework, if taken as lack of internal control mechanisms. This will be further examined below.

Sociological Theories

SUBCULTURAL THEORIES   The subcultural theories in themselves appear to have little to offer in explaining the etiology of problem drinking and alcoholism. Several of these are geared to "lower class" values and socialization. Both Hazel and George indicate that they come from middle class or above. Skid row itself is a subculture that George joined. We have gained some insights into this subculture that tend to verify the early findings of "insider" accounts by Straus, Wallace, Spradley, and Wiseman.

DIFFERENTIAL ASSOCIATION   There appear to be values, purposes, styles, and types of drinking that are learned by individuals. Such learning is accomplished in interaction with parents and peers. As we see, particularly in the case of Hazel whose parents had differing values and drinking habits than her husband, variation in the definitions regarding alcohol use does exist. Similarly, George learned drinking patterns primarily among his peers. More important for this theoretical framework, however, may be the later associations formed within Alcoholics Anonymous by both Hazel and George. Both adopted new definitions of themselves and of alcohol that led them to abstinence patterns.

LABELING THEORY   Perhaps the best illustration of labeling theory also applies to A.A. membership. The process whereby one comes to accept the stigma of "alcoholic," then redefines alcoholism as a disease that one has a predisposition toward, would appear to fit both interviewees. This process is the thesis of Trice and Roman's article "De-labeling, Relabeling, and Alcoholics Anonymous." They maintain that the new definitions (or labels) acquired within A.A. allow the person to accept the less stigmatized "disease" self-concept and that one should then refrain totally from the consumption of alcohol.[45]

ANOMIE   As stated earlier, Merton's "retreatist" adaptation to anomie postulating that alcoholics were "double failures" does not apply to either Hazel or George. Both individuals were economically successful before becoming alcoholics. Only a revamping of the theory stressing the overemphasis of the cultural goals of "independence" and "power" might serve as explanatory of their behavior.

SOCIAL CONTROL THEORY   The Reckless' Containment Model of social control may provide the most complete framework in which to view drunkenness, problem drinking, and alcoholism.

The compulsive nature of alcohol abuse may easily be explained as a breakdown of inner control mechanisms. The manner in which this internal control is weakened or does not properly develop has been traced above, within the Jellinek and McCord models, as the psychiatric component of such a "psychodynamic" interpretation. It should be emphasized again that the psychological factors interact with and are influenced by social and cultural factors within the family and the larger society. Media influence must be considered as one such cultural factor.

The two forms of external controls, formal or legal controls, and informal controls, should be considered separately, at the same time taking into account the manner in which they interact. The degree of tolerance of the use of alcohol (informal control) has been reflected in variation in legal controls. Thus, early in George's drinking career (at one point he says he was eighteen, at another sixteen) he was violating legal sanctions imposed by Prohibition. These formal controls were ineffective even to the point that, as he states, "we made own own." The failure of legal sanctions in curbing problem drinking and alcoholism may be viewed today in those studies cited earlier that indicate an increased rate of problems among teen-agers and in the "dryer" areas of the country. George's immediate group had informal norms that supported drinking behavior. The same can be said of Hazel at the point where she began drinking heavily, in D.C. However, in both cases we see ambivalences in the external controls. Hazel's early socialization and controls were somewhat prohibitive of alcohol use. The legal sanctions were prohibitive when George began to drink. The degree to which such external controls may have been partially internalized may explain the guilt both experienced. We earlier hypothesized that alcoholism results from the use of alcohol to neutralize guilt about one's own prior use of alcohol or problems resulting from this deviancy. Such a hypothesis would fit the above application of a social control explanation.

All such social control must be placed within the cultural context of the United States today and the manner in which alcohol is viewed. The ambivalence toward alcohol has already been mentioned. We should further elaborate upon the trend within the United States to attempt to exert control through the medical model rather than the legal model. Thus, alcoholism has become a "disease" rather than a "crime" in an attempt to remove the stigma connected with "treatment" for alcoholism. Schneider has traced the history and politics involved in this transformation and the manner in which Alcoholics Anonymous, Jellinek's study, and the medical profession were involved in creating a new reality.[46] If such criticisms are valid and the "addiction" of alcoholism is a reality created by the interaction of these groups, society, and the heavy drinker, a recent Rand Corporation report that some alcoholics have been able to return to controlled social drinking[47] may have increased validity. In addition, it might be pointed out that the medical control of alcoholism may show some success in "rehabilitating" alcoholics, but it has apparently not shown any stronger deterrent effect than its predecessor had. (Consider reports of prevalence of problem drinking such as

Cahalan's.) With these criticisms in mind, we must again question the source of the disease concept of alcoholism upon which both informants rely.

The question and nature of addiction will be further examined in the following chapter.

QUESTIONS FOR DISCUSSION

1. Hazel states that alcoholism combines "the allergy of the body coupled with an obsession of the mind." She also claims that "alcoholism can affect any person." Are these two statements incompatible? If they are not, how can they be reconciled? If they are incompatible, what function do you think the "allergy concept" serves in her thinking or in the ideology of Alcoholics Anonymous?

2. Hazel maintains that very few members of Alcoholics Anonymous come from skid row. Why do you think this is so?

3. Hazel pointed out that very few residents of skid row are alcoholics. After reading George's story, do you believe this is true? What social pressures on skid row might serve to deter alcoholics from living there? Do you think that almost all residents of skid row eventually become alcoholics?

4. Both Hazel and George are reformed drinkers. How do you think their perspectives might differ from those of people who are currently living on skid row or are currently active alcoholics?

5. Like George, many alcoholics started drinking during Prohibition. Do you see any similarities between their situation and that of addictive drug users in today's drug scene?

RELATED READINGS

Alcoholics Anonymous, A Co-Founder, *Alcoholics Anonymous Comes of Age* (New York: Harper and Brothers, 1957).

American Medical Association, *Manual on Alcoholism* (Chicago: American Medical Association, 1968).

Bahr, Howard, *Homelessness and Disaffiliation* (New York: Columbia University, Bureau of Applied Social Research, 1968).

———, *Skid Row: An Introduction to Disaffiliation* (London: Oxford University Press, 1973).

Blumberg, Leonard, et al., *The Men on Skid Row* (Philadelphia: Temple University, Department of Psychiatry, 1960).

Bogue, Donald, *Skid Row in American Cities* (Chicago: University of Chicago Press, 1963).

Cahalan, Don, and Room, Robin, *Problem Drinking among American Men* (New Brunswick, N.J.: Rutgers Center of Alcohol Studies, 1974).

Dunham, H. Warren, *Homeless Men and Their Habitats* (Detroit: Wayne State University, Department of Sociology, 1954).

Fort, Joel, *Alcohol: Our Biggest Drug Problem* (New York: McGraw-Hill, 1973).

McClelland, David C.; Davis, William N.; Kalin, Rudolf, and Wanner, Eric, *The Drinking Man* (New York: The Free Press, 1972).

McCord, William, and McCord, Joan, with Gudeman, Jon, *Origins of Alcoholism* (Stanford, Calif.: Stanford University Press, 1960).

Oakley, Ray, *Drugs, Society, and Human Behavior* (St. Louis: C. V. Mosby Company, 1978), pp. 124–161.

Pittman, David, ed., *Alcoholism* (New York: Harper & Row, 1967).

Plaut, Thomas, *Alcohol Problems: A Report to the Nation by the Cooperative Commission on the Study of Alcoholism* (New York: Oxford University Press, 1967).

President's Commission on Law Enforcement and Administration of Justice, *Task Force Report: Drunkenness* (Washington, D.C.: U.S. Government Printing Office, 1967).

Robinson, David, *From Drinking to Alcoholism: A Sociological Commentary* (London: John Wiley and Sons, 1976).

Spradley, James, *You Owe Yourself a Drunk* (Boston: Little, Brown, 1970).

Straus, Robert, "Alcoholism and Problem Drinking," in Merton, Robert K., and Nisbet, Robert, eds., *Contemporary Social Problems*, 4th ed. (New York: Harcourt Brace Jovanovich, Inc., 1976), pp. 181–217.

————, *Escape from Custody* (New York: Harper & Row, 1974).

Trice, Harrison, *Alcoholism in America* (New York: McGraw-Hill, 1966).

Wallace, Samuel, *Skid Row As a Way of Life* (Totowa, N.J.: The Bedminister Press, 1965).

Wiseman, Jacqueline, *Stations of the Lost* (Englewood Cliffs, N.J.: Prentice-Hall, Inc., 1970).

NOTES

1. Harrison Trice and Paul Roman, "Delabeling, Relabeling, and Alcoholics Anonymous," *Social Problems*, 17 (Spring, 1970), pp. 538–546.

2. Walter Reckless, *The Crime Problem* (New York: Appleton-Century-Crofts, 1967), p. 186.

3. Samuel Wallace, "The Road to Skid Row," *Social Problems*, 16 (Summer, 1968), p. 102.

4. Robert Straus, "Alcoholism and Problem Drinking," in Robert K. Merton and Robert Nisbet, eds., *Contemporary Social Problems*, 4th ed. (New York: Harcourt Brace Jovanovich, Inc., 1976), p. 193.

5. Ibid., pp. 193–194.

6. Ibid., p. 194.

7. Ray Oakley, *Drugs, Society, and Human Behavior* (St. Louis: C. V. Mosby Company, 1978), pp. 133–137.

8. Robert Straus, "Alcoholism and Problem Drinking," p. 189.

9. Ibid.

10. Research Triangle Institute, *Hypotenuse* (Research Triangle, N.C.: Research Triangle Institute, February, 1976), pp. 1–3.

11. John A. O'Donnell et al., *Young Men and Drugs: A Nationwide Survey* (Rockville, Md.: National Institute on Drug Abuse, February, 1976), pp. 13–17.

12. National Commission on Marijuana and Drug Abuse, *Drug Use in America: Problem in Perspective* (2nd report) (Washington, D.C.: U.S. Government Printing Office, 1973).

13. Don Cahalan and Robin Room, *Problem Drinking among American Men* (New Brunswick, N.J.: Rutgers Center of Alcohol Studies, 1974).

14. Wallace, "The Road to Skid Row," p. 104.

15. James Spradley, *You Owe Yourself a Drunk* (Boston: Little, Brown, 1970).

16. Donald Bogue, *Skid Row in American Cities* (Chicago: University of Chicago Press, 1963).

17. H. Warren Dunham, *Homeless Men and Their Habitats* (Detroit: Wayne State University, Department of Sociology, 1954).

18. Howard Bahr, *Homelessness and Disaffiliation* (New York: Columbia University, Bureau of Applied Social Research, 1968).

19. Jacqueline Wiseman, *Stations of the Lost* (Englewood Cliffs, N.J.: Prentice-Hall, Inc., 1970), p. 16.

20. Robert Straus, *Escape from Custody* (New York: Harper and Row, 1974), p. 335.

21. Ibid., p. 19.

22. Bahr, *Homelessness and Disaffiliation*; Leonard Blumberg et al., *The Men on Skid Row* (Philadelphia: Temple University, Department of Psychiatry, 1960); Bogue, *Skid Row in American Cities*.

23. Jeremiah Lowney, *Drug Use among Young Males*, unpublished doctoral dissertation (Lexington, Ky.: The University of Kentucky, 1976), p. 12.

24. ———, "Correspondence Between Attitudes and Drinking and Drug Behavior: Youth Subculture Over Time," unpublished paper presented to the Society for the Study of Social Problems, Chicago, September, 1977.

25. David Robinson, *From Drinking to Alcoholism: A Sociological Commentary* (London: John Wiley and Sons, 1976), pp. 23–25.

26. Samuel Wallace, *Skid Row as a Way of Life* (Totowa, N.J.: The Bedminister Press, 1965), p. 159.

27. Wallace, "The Road to Skid Row," p. 104.

28. Spradley, *You Owe Yourself a Drunk*, p. 68.

29. Wiseman, *Stations of the Lost*.

30. Ibid., p. 280.

31. Ibid., p. 12.

32. Wallace, "The Road to Skid Row," p. 97.

33. Joseph W. Schneider, "Deviant Drinking As Disease: Alcoholism As a Social Accomplishment," *Social Problems*, Vol. 25, No. 4 (April, 1978), pp. 361–372.

34. D. W. Goodwin et al., "Alcohol Problems in Adoptees Raised Apart from Alcoholic Biological Parents," *Archives of General Psychiatry*, 28 (1973), pp. 238–243.

35. William McCord and Joan McCord, with Jon Gudeman, *Origins of Alcoholism* (Stanford, Calif.: Stanford University Press, 1960).

36. David C. McClelland et al., *The Drinking Man* (New York: The Free Press, 1972), pp. 301–309.

37. Robert Bales, "Cultural Differences in Rates of Alcoholism," *Quarterly Journal of Studies on Alcohol*, 6 (1949), pp. 480–499.

38. Robert K. Merton, *Social Theory and Social Structure* (Glencoe, Ill.: The Free Press, 1957), chap. 4, "Social Structure and Anomie," pp. 131–160.

39. Richard Cloward and Lloyd Ohlin, *Delinquency and Opportunity* (Glencoe, Ill.: The Free Press, 1960).

40. Wallace, "The Road to Skid Row."

41. Trice and Roman, "Delabeling, Relabeling, and Alcoholics Anonymous."

42. Ibid.

43. Ibid.

44. McClelland et al., *The Drinking Man*, p. 310.

45. Trice and Roman, "Delabeling, Relabeling, and Alcoholics Anonymous."

46. Joseph W. Schneider, "Deviant Drinking As Disease: Alcoholism As a Social Accomplishment."

47. "Social Drinking and the Alcoholic," *The Washington Post*, January 16, 1977, p. B2.

Heroin Addiction

4

We have seen that nudism has been neglected somewhat among scientists and that alcohol abuse may be frequently overlooked by the public as a form of deviance. In contrast, heroin addiction has been given ample attention by both. In public opinion heroin addiction is probably considered the most extreme and serious form of nonmedical drug use. As a drug, heroin is most frequently linked with the term "addiction." In actuality, many other substances are probably more addicting and more dangerous than heroin. However, heroin has become the classic drug of addiction in the United States. Recent studies, as we shall see, have cast new light on the nature of this addiction and there appears to be increased pressure for medical rather than criminal controls of its use.

THE NATURE OF HEROIN AND ADDICTION

Heroin is a semisynthetic derivative of morphine. It generally is a white, odorless, crystalline powder with a bitter taste, although Mexican heroin is brown. Heroin was developed in Germany in 1898. When first produced, it was touted as a cure for morphine addiction and was considered to be nonaddictive (somewhat analogous to claims made for methadone recently). The effects of heroin are essentially the same as those of morphine: analgesia, drowsiness, euphoria, constipation, vomiting, sedation, and respiratory depression. Heroin, like morphine, produces a "high" feeling of being above all cares and hurts, sexual and food hungers, and fears. In short, it produces a state of euphoria. In some users, heroin produces a kind of sexual pleasure akin to orgasm centering in the stomach. However, all of these effects are dulled after continuous use and for most users the drug may be continued primarily to relieve withdrawal symptoms.[1]

Addiction, though often linked with heroin, is a separate topic. Addiction is a complex rather than a simple or an automatic process, and, as we have seen in the case of alcohol addiction, is not fully understood. Generally, however, addiction has been traditionally defined as an overwhelming involvement with, and craving for, a substance, often accompanied by increased tolerance and physical dependence, resulting in a syndrome of identifiable symptoms when the drug is withdrawn.[2] Addiction involves more than mere physical dependence and increased tolerance, however. It also entails a kind of psychic dependence (sometimes termed "habituation"), involving psychological compulsive feelings in the user that he or she cannot live without the drug, conceiving of self as an addict, and a high tendency to increase dosage beyond bodily need. A strong tendency to relapse after having been withdrawn from the substance is also the mark of addiction. Lindesmith gives a composite definition of addiction that traces the development of addiction through several stages: 1) the individual takes the drug; 2) he or she experiences withdrawal; 3) the individual understands the withdrawal distress as being due to the absence of the drug; 4) he or she takes more of the drug; 5) he or she experiences relief, and 6) one comes to think of oneself as "hooked" or "a dope fiend." [3]

The critical steps in the Lindesmith model are the use of heroin to relieve the withdrawal and the realization that the heroin accomplishes this. In the Lindesmith model, once this connection is made and the person accepts the self-identity of an addict, one is always an addict.

The Lindesmith model has been criticized in the "always an addict" concept. Lindesmith argued, from his interviews with addicts, that even though an addict might abstain from heroin for a lengthy period of time the person would eventually return to the use of heroin. The relapse was most likely to occur during a period of stress. Critics point to the tautology of such an eventuality, since Lindesmith specifies no time limit as to the number of years the "addict" lived without using while viewing all those who died without a relapse as though they would have relapsed had they lived. Thus, all persons who had become addicts were either: 1) currently using heroin, 2) not using heroin but will eventually again use it, or 3) dead before the relapse occurred.[4] Such criticism of this portion of Lindesmith's model is bolstered by data that indicate many persons were addicted to heroin and other opiates prior to such drugs being made unavailable or illegal and these "addicts" did not continue to use them. Other data indicate that more liberal interpretation of abstinence from use would show a somewhat substantial number of addicts respond to "treatment" [5] or "mature out" of addiction.[6] Recent data regarding Vietnam veterans indicate that heroin users who used substantial daily amounts of heroin overseas ceased using it upon discharge in the United States and an anticipated "heroin epidemic" did not materialize.[7]

Stanton Peele and others have noted there has been an overemphasis upon the pharmacological and physical aspects of "addiction." They point to the "addiction" of gambling and "addictive" emotional relationships. Peele's concept of addiction is similar to Straus' psychological "dependence" regarding alcoholism. Peele, like Lindesmith, points to the meaning (or realization) of the person involved:

> Addiction is not a chemical reaction. Addiction is an *experience*—one which grows out of an individual's routinized subjective response to something that has special meaning for him—something, anything, that he finds so safe and reassuring that he cannot be without it. If we want to come to terms with addiction, we have to stop blaming drugs and start looking at people, at ourselves, and at what makes us dependent.[8]

Peele also emphasizes the social or cultural aspects involved in addiction:

> We will find that we learn habits of dependence by growing up in a culture which teaches a sense of personal inadequacy, a reliance on external bulwarks, and a preoccupation with the negative or painful rather than the positive or joyous.
>   Addiction is not an abnormality in our society. It is not an aberration from the norm; it is itself the norm ... Those young people ... who seek solace in drugs ... are only expressing tendencies that were always present in acceptable guises in their home and school lives.[9]

Thus, we see similarities between alcoholism and heroin addiction. But we also see differences. Alcoholism and heroin addiction appear to have physiological, psychological, and social components. Alcohol, however, is viewed as the norm in everyday lives of Americans while heroin use is illegal under all circumstances (even the physician is not allowed to prescribe its medical use).

The Extent of Heroin Addiction

While hard figures are difficult to come by, it is estimated that there are approximately 500,000 heroin addicts in the United States today, but twice as many or more who are "chippers" or occasional users.[10] Ray

Oakley notes the recent trends among users and the manner in which they may not fit the stereotype of the ghetto black male addict:

> Every year, in drug use as in other behaviors, the differences between males and females, blacks and whites become less distinct. In the 1969–70 period four males entered drug treatment programs for every female. By 1975 the ratio was 3 to 1. Over this same period the proportion of those admitted to treatment programs who were black decreased from 55% to 35%. The proportion who were white increased from 30% to 53%. There are similar trends in age at entry into treatment programs. Three age groupings were used: under 18, 18 to 25, and over 25. The respective percentages in 1969 were 6%, 37%, 57%. In 1975 they were 15%, 44%, 40%.[11]

There are indications that the socioeconomic status of addicts has been moving upward since the days of "Haight-Ashbury" in the late 1960s. It should be noted that for many years physicians have ranked as the number one profession subject to narcotic addiction and such addiction has been termed "an occupational hazard among physicians." [12]

METHODOLOGICAL CONSIDERATIONS

Both the stereotypes and sound scientific research are affected by the difficulty of researching heroin addicts. Any of the ordinary "pretest" and "posttest" experiments administered for medical drugs must be precluded on ethical grounds. Thus, much is unknown as to the manner in which physiological effects interact with psychological and social factors. As is evident from the above quote by Oakley, most of our data are limited to what is gathered from treatment programs. Many such programs are largely serving court referrals or court alternatives from those who are caught and arrested. How such samples differ from the total population is a matter of speculation. Such samples are further contaminated by the treatment and arrest processes that may particularly affect the psychological factors involved. Many of the early theories and misconceptions regarding heroin addiction were undoubtedly influenced by the fact that most research was conducted among those sent by the courts to the Addiction Research Centers in Lexington, Kentucky, and, later, Fort Worth, Texas. Stephens has pointed to the problems in dealing with the truthfulness of such respondents in research projects.[13]

Recently, increasing attention has been paid to the "everyday life" of the addict. Preble and Casey, Agar, and others have conducted street ethnographies that reveal a more subjective depth than did many of the earlier studies based on "objective" questionnaires.[14] Such ethnographies, however, tend to be selective in the manner in which locations are chosen and entree is gained. The selectivity appears to lend itself toward lower socioeconomic groupings. Areas selected are those in which heroin use is substantial based solely upon official data. There is a paucity of data, for instance, on physician-addicts and other higher socioeconomic heroin users who have not come to the attention of enforcement authorities. Such data are important, for instance, in examining the relationship between heroin addiction and crime. An extensve national survey by O'Donnell and his colleagues questions a one-way relationship:

> This preliminary examination of the data suggests that neither the hypothesis that drug use leads to criminal activity nor the one that criminal behavior leads to drug use is unambiguously supported.[15]

These difficulties in methodology should be kept in mind as we examine various theoretical explanations of heroin addiction.

EXPLANATIONS OF HEROIN ADDICTION

Popular belief and the views of many law enforcement agencies portray heroin addiction as an outgrowth of the use of minor illegal drugs, especially marijuana. (A review of the history of the literature indicates that this belief may have resulted from the statistical correlation among addicts at Lexington, Ky.) Evidence generally cited for this view is the relatively high incidence of marijuana use in the background of most heroin addicts, and thus a causal link is often imputed. The stepping-stone view has often been used as an argument in favor of strict controls over marijuana, and adherents to this view also link marijuana to crime, immorality, ruination of careers, insanity, and complete breakdown of inhibitions. It should be noted here, however, that the causal link made is between marijuana and heroin addiction (as well as other evils), with no assumption made about the impact of peer associations in this relationship. Instead, it is argued that marijuana is the *direct cause* of heroin addiction.[16] The *indirect* links may be explained by differential association theory within the drug subculture that will be examined shortly.

Psychological views of addiction that link it with personality traits such as passivity, insecurity, and dependence have largely been discarded by sociologists for reasons similar to those discussed for alcoholism. However, a major study by Chein and his colleagues points to a psychodynamic model for heroin addiction similar to that advanced by the McCords for alcoholism. Among groups of addicts and controls from areas of high availability of heroin, Chein found family factors—particularly the absence of an adequate father-figure—the most distinguishing set of characteristics between the two groups.[17] Chein sees the resulting offspring as weak in masculine identity and without "inner restraints."

He hypothesizes that if such a youth is placed in an environment that is conducive to "antisocial" behavior, he or she is vulnerable to heroin addiction and other delinquencies.[18] This psychodynamic model should be considered in assessing an ongoing dialogue among sociologists concerning psychological motivation involved in becoming a heroin addict, and sociological theories can be viewed as taking one or another stand on that issue.

The sociological dialogue started with Merton's *anomie theorie*, in which drug addiction is viewed as an escapist or retreatist reaction of a person who finds the path to success blocked and who is inhibited from using illegitimate or criminal means of seeking success. Thus, in Merton's theory, the motivation in drug addiction is to *escape* from the frustrating situation. The euphoria of the heroin "high" enables the user to forget about personal problems and to feel good even though the objective socioeconomic situation is bad. Merton's approach is supported by Finestone's study of fifty black male users of heroin in Chicago.[19] Finestone found that drug addicts reject conventional values like success in favor of the "kick" and reject conventional means to these values, preferring the "hustle." Finestone argues that this alternative value scheme is basically a rationalization of failure and that drug addicts are following an "Uncle Tom" pattern of accommodation to dominant white society, and thus a pattern of retreatism.

A modification of anomie theory was made by Cloward and Ohlin in what came to be termed the *double failure hypothesis*.[20] Addicts do engage in crime, as shown by their criminal records prior to addiction. But those most likely to become addicts have failed in their use of both legitimate and illegitimate means. That is, they have been unable to maintain lucrative empolyment in a regular job and they have been unsuccessful in gaining access to criminal gangs or subcultures. They are willing to use legitimate or illegitimate means but have failed in their efforts at both, so they become "double failures." Thus, they retreat from the competitive struggle in both conventional and criminal worlds, with the drug addict subculture the only one available to them. (This explanation bears a striking similarity to the drift hypothesis discussed in Chapter Three.)

Although for some time the opportunity theory approach was probably the most influential one, probably because it was for some time clear that most addicts were from lower socioeconomic backgrounds, another approach, which we might term *availability theory*, has risen to challenge opportunity theory. Availability theory is closely allied with labeling theory in the sense that as public policy changes, introducing a penal stigma or label for heroin or other drug use, so does the pattern of availability. Lindesmith argues that lower class black males are high in rates of drug addiction today, not because of a desire for escape or retreatment, but because our harsh penalization of heroin sales has restricted its use by other groups in the population. As evidence, Linde-

smith shows that drug addiction was highest among "respectable females" during the nineteenth century prior to enactment of strict regulatory laws (starting with the Harrison Act of 1914). Currently, however,
they have very limited access because of strict regulatory laws, while
access to drugs is high among urban blacks, who now have a high rate
of drug use. Interestingly, the incidence of drug addiction among physicians has remained high in both the last century and currently, and
the pattern of drug availability has remained high.[21] Under the condition
of prohibition and punishment for addicts, Lindesmith says, the main
channel of recruitment of new addicts is through association between
addicts and nonaddicts, whereas when penal control is not used (as in
the nineteetnh century), the main channel of recruitment is via therapeutic use of the drug through a doctor's prescription or from folk
medicine. Thus, under current conditions in this country, the main
"cause" of addiction is differential association with addicts rather than
escapism. Also, the usual pattern is prior association for other reasons,
rather than one person seeking another simply because the person is an
addict or wants to become one.[22] Lindesmith challenges the view that
escapism is the major motivation for such group association, and argues
that other motivations are important at all stages of the "career" of
an addict. Beginning addicts may never experience euphoria from the
drug. Some persons become addicts without ever taking the drug voluntarily. In later stages, the euphoria disappears and the addict must resort to highly innovative, criminal means to maintain the habit.[23] Last,
in the case of the physician addicts and other employed people, a productive "conformist" life may be maintained over a long period of time
while the person is, in fact, an addict.

Lindesmith's explanation would appear to fit the data cited earlier
and to be compatible with Chein and other findings as well. It should be
pointed out that the differences between Lindesmith and Chein are
primarily a matter of emphasis. Lindesmith, the sociologist, points to
the process of differential association within the group. Chein, a psychiatrist, views as primary the "vulnerable" personality placed within
this social environment. The peer process involved is further supported
by the findings of O'Donnell and Jones who trace the development of
an "intravenous subculture" among opiate users.[24] Finally, Feldman
views the social process in which "ideological supports" aid one in
becoming and remaining a heroin addict.[25]

Various writers have described a process of alienation that leads
to drug abuse including heroin. They point to the recent "youth rebellion" as evidence of alienation among young people who reject the
values, particularly materialistic values, of the dominant society.[26] This
might also apply to minorities and others who reject societal values.
However, Lowney found in a longitudinal project that such expressions
of alienation were more a product of a particular historical moment
(the late 1960s) and not a strong predictor of increasing drug involve-

ment.[27] One might also question whether or not the expressions of alienation follow increasing drug involvement as "ideological supports" or whether the alienation precedes drug use.

≡≡≡≡ RICK:
A Drug Addict

With these theories in mind, we can now turn our attention to an individual who has been a drug addict. The transcript was taken in class from an "ex-addict" who was a resident of the Salvation Army Rehabilitation Center. He had been drug-free for eighteen months prior to his talk. However, we now regret having had him speak and be interviewed, because this could have been a factor in his subsequent relapse. Several weeks after his presentation he began taking heroin again. His parole officer felt that apparently Rick was inspired by his presentation before a college class to seek employment in his former position as an electronics engineer. Rick had had four years of college-equivalent courses in electronics and had worked, while an addict, in the field of electronics. However, Rick's prior record of drug offenses made subsequent employment prohibitive in the field of electronics. After the talk from which this tape was taken, Rick went to several aircraft electronics firms seeking employment and was turned down rather harshly. Apparently he was overwhelmed by this rejection and this precipitated a relapse. Rick was picked up by his parole officer, detained at the county jail for a week, and then sent to a state mental hospital. The last we heard, he is still there.

RICK: I come from an upper middle class family. I started having what you call problems, or what I call symptoms at about seven or eight years old. I went on into grade school, and about eighth grade, I think it was, I started experimenting with drugs. Cough syrup, pills, well, what they were were diet pills out of the medicine cabinet. I went on into high school and my freshman year of high school started smoking weed, and the first time I had a lid, and after that was gone a group of us started making runs across this border down here bringing back kilos so it started being an everyday sort of thing.

QUESTION: *Was this in San Diego?*

RICK: No, this was in the San Francisco Bay area, Redwood City, and ended in San Francisco. So we were bringing this weed back and were trafficking in weed, and were doing a lot of things, there's fighting, a lot of truancy, drinking, minor scrapes with the law. The last day of my junior year I was expelled from high school for fighting with a couple of my teachers because I didn't like their ideas and they didn't like mine, I guess. So, at this time I was about seventeen years old, and I did get a job laying carpets though I didn't stay at it very long.

When I was in my late seventeens I took my first shot of heroin. This is the time I had seen your educational films they were using at this time about how bad these drugs and things are. At this particular time I wasn't going to get hooked because all these films were showing it was your mainliners who were getting hooked, so I just took a skin pop, which everybody knows is not dangerous. So, it took me about twenty minutes to get hooked for life instead of about three seconds if I'd have put it right in the sewer. This went on for quite some time, a number of years actually, with a number of dry-out periods. I probably should have been in jail, but coming from a middle class family, that helped me stay out. We had the county health director living right down the street. At this time when you checked into the hospital they didn't have to call the police so it was quite some time before I did end up in some kind of a jail. I think the first time was here in San Diego on a smuggling charge that I bought my way out of. So this went on until about 1959 until after my second or third arrest for addiction under the old drug addict laws that they don't have any more. I was finally going to have to do some time, so in order to beat this time I went to the U.S. Federal Narcotic Hospital in Fort Worth, Texas. I was hooked pretty bad at this time and probably would have been real sick but they took about eleven or twelve days and they brought me down with this methadone and I came out of there and I stayed clean for about thirty days, which was about the longest period I had stayed clean during this time. Started right back using it again and I used it again for about a year and checked in to the county hospital and did another three-week dry-out. Came out of the county hospital and I don't think I was clean and I didn't stay clean and I started getting loaded agian. This went on for another year, I guess, and in 1962 I was picked up again, only this time it was under the new humane laws, and instead of giving us ninety days in the county jail they give us ten years in the hospital over here at the California Rehabilitation Center. I was in there for about eighteen months and got a parole. And this time I think I stayed clean until about 2:00 in the afternoon of the day I got out. The reason it took so long was because I had to get from Riverside back to San Francisco. I was out for a period of about forty days, and I had it figured out how to beat the naline tests, which really aren't too hard to beat if you know them, but I had it figured out they weren't going to find the marks because I was fixing them in my legs. But they weren't quite as dumb as I thought they were because on one of these tests they made me drop my strags and they found something like 105 marks all up and down my legs, so I had violated again, so they sent me back to C.R.C. At this time I went back and started legal action because I didn't like the place. And after a year of fighting my case, fighting it myself without funds, I was finally released from the Ninth Circuit Court of Appeals here in

San Diego on a writ of habeas corpus, so I went back. This was in about 1964, I guess, and was out about forty days when I was picked up in a flophouse with from what they say was an overdose of narcotics. There are things in this apartment that I am in from a drug store burglary. So I was convicted of these. Actually, I wasn't convicted—I actually pled guilty, which was a bad mistake and nobody should ever do it in my opinion, to the drug store burglary and was sentenced to state prison for six months to fifteen years. I ended up doing three and a half years. I came out seventeen months ago with a five-year parole with narcotics testing, using urine analysis, and I could probably think of some way to beat the urine analysis, but I'm so tired and sick of being in jail and things like that, I think I'm about ready to quit. Right now, I think my attitude has changed quite a bit and I've stopped trying to fight these people, though actually the motives for a lot of the things I do are revenge, but if I go about it in ways that are acceptable by society I can get my little taste of revenge on society. I think I'm running out of things to say and this would be a good place to start the questions.

QUESTON: *What factors originally led you to take drugs? Did you have a brother or sister or some contact like this who encouraged you to take drugs or was it a gang you ran around with, and what were your feelings when you started taking heroin?*

RICK: These things in my opinion are all just symptoms. I can give you what I feel a few of the reasons are. I don't really think it was because my mother put me on the pot crooked when I was two, but this family situation I grew up in was a bad situation. This father of mine, and I'm still a little sorry I didn't kill him, said that none of my friends were good enough for my family type setting, and none were good enough for me. I think as these friends were being eliminated that I kept looking for a worse and worse type of friend, if you want to call it that, but people who are more out of society or dropping out of society.

QUESTION: *You got out of prison two or three times and each time immediately had a relapse. What factors led to you returning immediately to drugs, knowing that you might go back to prison?*

RICK: I think one thing is that drugs are so good. The feelings that I get out of drugs are so good and I would do it in a minute if they legalized narcotics; I would start shooting heroin right now today.

QUESTION: *Do you think you rely on this physical pleasure so much because you have nothing else to occupy your time? Do you have a job?*

RICK: Let me get into this a little bit. I think I understand your question. I think at a certain time this might be true as why you might go back to narcotics, but once you've taken the first fix of heroin I believe the reasons why in this type of thing are really not as important as a lot of people today are trying to make it out to be. Thing is, you've got an actual problem, you've got an addict who would rather take narcotics than have sex or get into bed with somebody. And it's the most pleasurable thing in his life so the reason why—I hate that word *why*, especially from psychologists and psychiatrists—I don't feel it's really important any more.

QUESTION: *What is a "skin pop"?*

RICK: Well, I think this is something I haven't spent as much time getting involved in in the education in schools and I don't know what they're teaching, but the difference between a skin pop is that it is an intramuscular shot or a shot in the vein. I think this is very important using the big scare factor of this mainliner and scare a guy, and actually I think I was scared of this picture that I had of a mainline hyp. The only difference, as I said, is that it will take twenty minutes to reach your brain through your muscles and it's going to take three or four seconds if you stick it in your vein. I did miss part of a question. I would like to add I am just barely functioning in society today. As to what I do, I'm down at the Salvation Army in a rehabilitation program and this is where Dr. Winslow picked me up. Actually, he had heard me someplace else, but he looked for a speaker down there. I've been there five months in the rehabilitation program and I feel these five months have been a better five months than any five months in the past ten years. If anyone wants to ask me a question about the Salvation Army, I think it's just a terrific place.

QUESTION: *What in their program has helped you the most?*

RICK: In the first place, I think, which is a big problem with most of these guys coming out, we are emotionally dependent on the people we're living with. It's a tight situation. We may not like the people that we're living with, in fact I hate most of them, but we do understand each other; there is no lack of communication. You know who is going to take a knife and kill somebody, and who is capable of doing what type of thing. Down there at the Salvation Army, I'm with people I do understand. We have murderers down there, we have sex offenders down there, we have just plain alcoholic drunks down there, we have juvenile delinquents down there, and a lot of people just aren't aware of just what is going on down there. I know the picture I had of the Salvation Army . . . a bunch of these idiots ringing bells on the sidewalk. But they're working with the derelict alcoholic and they see a bunch of drunks stacked up in a dark men's dormitory throwing up all over each other and things like this. The fact is, I live in one of the cleanest, nicest hotels in San Diego and I eat three times a day. It takes a lot of social pressure off of me, I don't have to worry about washers and dryers, television, or telephones. Actually, if you're talking about success, I would give a successful treatment program to the Salvation Army in my case.

QUESTION: *Was there much drug use within the institutions you have been in?*

RICK: It is now probably worse because all these addicts are looking for some kind of salvation; they'll go for anything because they're hooked. At the time I was there, it was a new type program in which our salvation was we're going to get cured this time and stay out and straigthen out our lives and become normal citizens or whatever you want to call it. So there wasn't much drug activity in C.R.C. when I was there. Now my guess, and I don't know this, is that it is now another program and there is no hope for those addicts; there isn't any place else really at the present time. They've been back four or five times on violations which right now they are operating a swinging door type policy—they are letting these guys out in a short period of time while, when I was there, they needed bodies to fill the beds to start the program, but now they have so many bodies they've just got to kick them out, so now with these wonderful new ideas they're carrying them seven months instead of eighteen and things like when I was in there.

QUESTION: *When you referred to your "drying-out" periods, were these of your own choice?*

RICK: I never went in on my own choice. It was always something else—police pressure, family pressure—police pressure really is the only thing that has ever made me dry out. I think I did once or twice for lack of drugs, but I just didn't have the money, didn't have somebody that was clean enough to make the border run down here; their arms are looking so bad they can't cross any border.

QUESTION: *What is your opinion on drug use and drug abuse? Have you ever used psychedelics?*

RICK: I think a lot of these drugs people can't handle and a lot of them are bad, but from a moral issue I don't have anything against these drugs and I actually think weed should be legalized whether it is harmful or not, which I don't actually think has been determined yet, but I'm going on the assumption that it can't be any worse than this booze that these fools are out there drinking. Costs millions of dollars, kills thousands of people, and breaks up homes.

QUESTION: *Did you think you could handle drugs?*

RICK: Yes, because you see, I was smart. I didn't mainline it. I would like to talk about some of the other drugs, like speed and amphetamines. Really, you know, the physical effects aren't that good. Many people, I think, are forced to use it and will try to use it like for a substitute for heroin, maybe they can't get any, but I feel it's really a harmful drug. These idiots up in the legislature making your laws take a drug like speed which is really a harmful thing and causes aggressive crimes and involves other people besides the addict himself and make it a misdemeanor, while weed, which just can't be as bad, even say it is bad, it just can't be as bad as this methedrine and methedrine is a misdemeanor, and I don't think you can end up in prison for it except for sale.

QUESTION: *Do you believe in the stepping-stone theory, which states marijuana use leads to further experimentation with more dangerous drugs?*

RICK: I think you're placing your young people in a situation where ... no, I don't think this is true, but you're placing your young people in a position where they're traveling in circles where these things are available. Your curiosity, it might just be curiosity, or actually, I think that a kid smoking weed—that it is a symptom and he's trying to tell you something. He may not like society, he may not like his family, but he might not be so messed up that he can't go on and become one of you people here in the State University and function in society, which most of them will. We're talking about a really small percentage of them who will be jammed up and in bad trouble that they can't get out of.

QUESTION: *What kinds of attitudes did the police have toward you and other addicts?*

RICK: Well, you know, there are good cops and bad cops and today I'm getting to the point where I can even accept the bad ones. There are some I have a lot of respect for and have had all through my life even when I was hating these cops, and I did hate cops because I was beaten by cops four or five times, three of these times I asked for it. But it still isn't one of these things your legislators stand up and say these police officers must do. They are always talking about their duty and this type of thing; the legislators don't want them using corporal punishment. I actually got slapped around the first time when I was innocent of the charge, and I got roughed up for it. I was about eight years old and was roughed up by a detail of the county sheriff's office.

QUESTION: *Do you think an effective program of drug education in the city schools would aid in lowering the use of these drugs?*

RICK: Let me go into this this way, as far as the understanding knowledge of the people that you get in the city schools teaching narcotics abuse, or whatever you want to call it—I was down the other day, first, let me tell you the city schools are looking for an addict to get involved in a narcotics prevention program, education through the health services. So I have to watch my motives when I get involved in a thing like this because I go into somewhere and get these feelings about trying to save the world and do all this good type thing, but I was curious. I went out there, set up an appointment, and—this is just my opinion—there was two fairly aggressive thirty-year-old, I guess, psychologists with teaching credentials who are actually presenting this program to the youngsters on the eighth grade or junior high school level. There in the room was a fifty-year-old psychiatrist that thinks I'm crazy and wants to save me and give me some help and all this type of thing, but I really can't stand any more help. The business administrator of the program was also in the room and I find they have no concept . . . they haven't even thought the problem out. Somebody gets the bright idea—let's save those kids that are smoking that weed and dope, yet they don't even know what an addict is. I started asking, after I told them pretty much the same history, what kind of an addict are you looking for, and what kind of an addict are you going to present to this age group of people. I definitely don't feel I'm the addict for this kind of thing; these kids don't need a radical, bitter, hostile type person at this age, anyway.

QUESTION: *Aren't all addicts hostile and bitter?*

RICK: Well, I don't think so. I think you could find a mild type addict that didn't have a long history of use, but is an addict and probably going down the drain. While some addicts find their salvation, very few—we're talking about 1 percent to 3 percent depending upon whose figures you are using—find their salvation after about one or two trips to C.R.C., I imagine they could come up with a winner if you put them on the spot. Those who have gone through some good counseling sessions and had some good psychiatric treatment along with a little insight, I don't know where you find them, but I'm sure you could dig one up somewhere. I think I've thrown a monkey wrench into this thing down there. In the first place, I'm flooding them with addicts. I tell everyone I see, I tell them they're looking for an addict in the city schools and I won't tell them any more about it. Most addicts would like to help somebody, of course, they can't even help themselves, and they want to go out and save the world or do something good or something like that. I feel I did pretty much throw a monkey wrench into it. I did tell them that I didn't feel I was the type of an addict they were looking for, and they should be looking for an addict with a minimum of three years clean on the streets. Especially in a program like this where you haven't got any programs with addicts that are successful, you might even be able to find one of those. The things they are trying in Los Angeles are not successful.

QUESTON: *Do sociological theories of drug addiction seem realistic to you?*

RICK: I don't believe it and like I've gone for these, like I say an addict is looking for help, looking for salvation, and I have actually gone for what you people are probably presenting, which is the psychological approach—like I came out of C.R.C. with this bag of psychological tricks I wanted to play because I had to learn to play to get out of there. I come out with this bag of tricks here, and you get out on the streets and you find they are not any real answers to your problems. You can't look in your bag to cure loneliness or find someone you can communicate with and understand, and there is not one there or an answer to emotional dependency that you've acquired being in with this type of people that are doing the same thing. I think a lot of these counseling sessions actually help to make the people more emotionally dependent on the psychological part of this thing. You're dependent in a dozen different ways, but when you get out here on the streets and these things won't be any good. Another thing, these addicts in there, they might be getting loaded once in a while inside, but for the most part they are living pretty much as you are out here; they are functioning in an environment. It's not the street but it is an environment. They're keeping regular hours, they are sleeping, they are eating, they are involved in physical activity, they are playing basketball, baseball, and you know that should satisfy a lot of people and will satisfy these addicts while they have them in this type of environment. He feels he's really cured, but when he gets out here and sees he hasn't got it anymore.

QUESTION: *Have you ever checked out Synanon?*

RICK: I have checked out Synanon, and actually I could probably tell you about any type of program that is available. Synanon I don't knock; I think they do help a lot of people, but some addicts can find their way like through Synanon while another finds it through A.A., and another might see the light and have Jesus Christ come into his life and be saved by a religious trip. To this day I haven't found my particular bag for what is going to cure me. There are a lot of us like me, hostile, bitter people who just can't go for any of these other programs.

QUESTION: *Do you feel professors and other members of various institutions lead such narrow lives they can't possibly deal realistically with addicts? Is this why you prefer the people you are living with?*

RICK: I have respect for these people in institutions, too, and some of the things they are doing. I've gained respect in this new relationship with cops, if they'll accept me like I am when I tell them I love to shoot narcotics and I'm sorry I didn't kill my father and this type of thing—

just accepting me like I am as long as I'm not doing anything to bother anybody else in society. Whether they like my ideas at all doesn't matter. I would like to say one thing: people tend to go for whatever they hear. Right now there are people who are probably going for what I am saying, and I am very much against this. I am one person and I haven't got any answers, though I think I do. One is legalizing narcotics—heavy narcotics—and take the profit out of the fifty cents worth of pot that those addicts are paying $200 a day for. These existing addicts that you have right now, that you don't have anything to do with and nobody has an answer for, they may tell you they do but in my opinion they don't, let them shoot themselves to death. These guys are gone anyway for all practical purposes, they are just walking death. Let them shoot themselves to death if this is what the addict wants to do, and I'm sure it is what he wants to do.

QUESTION: *Do you feel you want to shoot yourself to death?*

RICK: Yes, as long as I don't bother anybody else in society, I don't feel anyone should impress their morals on me.

QUESTION: *In your case the law seems to be a deterrent against your using drugs.*

RICK: Yes, and that is the only deterrent.

QUESTION: *Isn't that an argument against legalizing drugs? If it wasn't for these laws, wouldn't more people become drug addicts?*

RICK: This is something I did leave out. This thing would be set up so you aren't going to be starting new addicts. Like any narcotics you are giving—say, to me, you are putting it right in the sewer in my arm and you're setting it up so you can't start new addicts by taking the profit out of it. When we die off you may not have any addicts left.

QUESTION: *The governor is trying to do that right now with Operation Intercept. Do you think that is effective, do you think it can be done?*

RICK: They are not going to stop that—they have no program. Another thing, this thing in the city schools, the education type thing— they are not going to help most of these kids; most of the kids are going to turn out fine, you know; they are beautiful kids and they are going to make it by themselves. They'll smoke a little weed, and . . .

QUESTION: *Are you high right now?*

RICK: No, just scared.

QUESTION: *Could you elaborate on your plan to legalize narcotics?*

RICK: Oh, yes, I lost my train of thought. First of all, you'd have to establish who your addicts are.

QUESTION: *Would this be similar to the plan in England?*

RICK: Well, England, I think it did work out. It's not working out now because they have lost control. They did start with something like about 3,000 addicts and had it down at one time to, I think, 280 people. They let it get out of control by giving doctors the power to put these narcotics out. You know my figures . . . well, don't take anything I say serious; find out for yourself.

QUESTION: *How did you support your habit? You mentioned figures as high as $200 a day.*

RICK: Well, another thing I'm talking about a habit, and when you are talking about the cost of an addict's habit it's really hard to judge what . . . even if you know how much an addict is shooting a day. One spoon of narcotics may be as strong as three spoons of narcotics you are getting somewhere else. I'm a narcotics dealer; it's my basic bag. But I've committed about every crime there is, armed robbery, burglary . . .

QUESTION: *Who introduced you to drugs? Was it a gang in your neighborhood?*

RICK: I think that I grew up in what you call suburbia, but it was an exclusive section of town, but in this particular town it just depends on what area you're in. You're all going to the same school. So I had access to everybody around and I'm kind of incorrigible and I'm making the scene from San Jose to San Francisco and everything in between. You know the addict is doing something to support his habit. I was fortunate by being a dealer and a smuggler, that this $200-a-day habit I'm talking about is costing me $15 a day.

QUESTION: *Have you ever been married?*

RICK: Yes, another thing I'm . . . a girl I really fell for, and two children, but that's all gone now too.

QUESTION: *Do you think everybody needs some kind of crutch, starting from coffee and Pepsi to heroin?*

RICK: Definitely, even right down to your television sets and moving pictures, football games, are actually all crutches.

QUESTION: *Do you see any program working effectively to re-duce the rate of drug use?*

RICK: No, I don't feel you have any programs in progress right now that are going to change your figures. I don't think they are going to go; I don't think they are at it now, but these schools downtown are going to go to 60 percent of the people experimenting with drugs. I don't think they are there now, but they are going to go there. There is no question in my mind that they are going to go there. Whether they start utilizing the addicts and ex-offenders like they are talking in this new brainstorm they've got about putting some in the city schools, it's not going to stop them. Might help a couple of addicts by taking them in there. If you don't help anyone else you may help the two addicts, or three, or how many they are going to have in there.

QUESTION: *You mentioned because of your upper middle class background you were able to buy your way out of some scrapes with the law. Has this made you resent the authority for not doing a good enough job in stopping you?*

RICK: I think so. A kid is not born prejudiced, for one thing, though kids can have feelings about other people. You know how one kid is always getting away with it, and say like this gentleman here who is always coming into the picture, he's getting a raw deal somewhere else; you're going to have feelings about it. You may not like it; this may be one of the things that enters later on as he continues to dislike society. These kids will tell you, these kids, you know—people should listen to these kids.

QUESTION: *Do you think if you had been given more support as a child, things would have been better for you? I've read where children taken out of their homes and placed in foster homes seem to make a better adjustment in a more loving atmosphere.*

RICK: Well, I think your environment has a lot to do with it, but if it wasn't me in this environment it would be somebody else. And some people can probably live in the same environment and come out all right.

QUESTION: *Earlier you said using narcotics can cause some good. What do you mean by this, and is there anything bad about heroin?*

RICK: For society my opinion would be yes, but for the individual addict I would say no. The body and physical effects of this type of thing, that actually it is a narcotic, it produces narcosis or whatever some of these fancy words are and actually makes a passive type person; he is not usually involved in aggressive type crimes. There is no sexual drive, so I say I doubt they can dig up an addict with a history of sexual offense.

QUESTION: *Did you have guilt feelings about deviating from your parents' wishes when you first started taking drugs?*

RICK: I'm sure there were, but they are nothing compared to the guilt feelings I have now, where actually I'm sure that I am responsible for at least six people who aren't alive today. These are people who were never really born because of an abortion type situation. I lost my train of thought.

QUESTION: *Do you take drugs to get away from these guilt feelings?*

RICK: I'd like to get away from a lot of things. Yes, I think guilt feelings have a lot to do with it. I think these kids today are having a lot of guilt feelings about what their parents are doing and the way they are handling things. You take, well, like these small town politicians who are running this country, and you take a city, basically, a city, I feel your city is run more from your Lions Club type thing that is actually from your city officials and they are scratching each other's backs. Most of the things they do are illegal as far as how morally right they are and whether kids are going to think what they are doing is morally right . . .

QUESTION: *You said that you would like to kill your father. How do you feel about your mother?*

RICK: She's something else. This is probably the only broad I'll love again, is my mother and she's alive today.

QUESTION: *Do you have any brothers and sisters?*

RICK: Yes. An older sister and an older brother, and a younger sister.

QUESTION: *What was your relationship with them when you first started using drugs at the age of eight?*

RICK: That is a pretty long way back.

QUESTION: *Did they know you were involved with drugs?*

RICK: Yes. Of course, another thing coming from a middle class family, when you get involved in something like this, instead of the parent finding out that the kid is involved in drug traffic and stuff like that by some uniformed police officer bringing him home, it's usually told to your father by the county sheriff or the chief of police in the town you live in.

QUESTION: *What kinds of relationships have you had with the Mafia, Cosa Nostra, and other organized crime?*

RICK: I have had some, but they are smart enough not to get involved with an addict. I have some pretty good relations with several people and this is something I would like to bring out. You know, these people that you have in prison today, in my opinion, are sick people. If they were plain dishonest people, like, say, somebody who is working for the Mafia type situation, he's not going to get caught. He goes about a trade learning to be dishonest and he is a dishonest person and is not playing an adult form of hide and go seek or cops and robbers or whatever you want to call it. He's just a plain dishonest person; he is very seldom in jail. This one particular person I'm thinking about is a safe-cracker; he does nothing but go around the country opening safes. These things are usually set up before he does it. He wouldn't open a safe unless he knew what was in it first. He knows how to do it and he does the same way that, say, if you had a safe and you called up one of your local locksmiths to open it because you had lost your combination. Safes are built with soft spots in them and are made to be opened by people that know how in case locks jam or things like this. But I have tried to get him to take me with him on several occasions and he says, "I like you but I just don't need you." This is another situation you can judge, a crime, take a burglar, a burglary is a one-man job. Now, if there are two people going out on a burglary, in my opinion the guy has got a psychological hang-up because he has to take the guy along for psychological reasons or something like this.

QUESTION: *Is legalization the answer for the drug problem?*

RICK: Well, I don't know, but I do know nobody has the answer right now, and this is my opinion. A lot of people don't like my opinion, but there are a lot of people that I don't like theirs, too.

QUESTION: *What is the structure of the Salvation Army?*

RICK: Like you can't go there if you've taken a drink in twenty-four hours, a little petty rule. But it works well for some people.

QUESTION: *You don't like this tight coercive structure for yourself?*

RICK: No, I don't feel it is the answer for me, but they do have a lot of answers out there.

QUESTION: *You mentioned that life in a prison is the only way a drug addict can stay clean. Do you think this coercive structure is needed by most drug addicts to keep them away from drugs?*

RICK: If this is what you are going to do, and this is what society is doing. Although the addict realizes he is through, he is going to stop using them. The police department is not going to let him use it out here on the street, and they are good enough at their game and the addict is not good enough at his, so for all practical purposes the addict is cured; he's going to stop using drugs but the thing is where he's going to take it.

QUESTION: *What is it that appeals to you about the Salvation Army?*

RICK: I don't know. It's just that they put their money where their mouth is. They work with people that nobody else will touch or talk to.

QUESTION: *Are they older people who run the Salvation Army?*

RICK: Well, they've got a couple of doctors here at the university that are on the board of directors. It is actually a religious-based organization, but there are a lot of other things. They have group counseling, outside activities, but people down there are not too motivated to do anything, even if you set it up so they can.

QUESTION: *Did you ever go through an involvement with crime? If you did, were you a success at it, or did you have difficulties procuring money?*

RICK: This is something I'd like to say is, don't ever believe in anything I say when it comes to how successful or unsuccessful somebody is. My Mafia contacts were on a personal level and they wouldn't even talk to me but I happened to know an old-time addict that came up—he was fifty years old. He had been in that type of environment; they wouldn't talk to him either, but I met the guy through him and, you know, there are very few people who will talk about it, and I hate to mention names because I don't want anyone in the Mafia mad at me either. But I have friends that I met on the inside. You don't meet very many of these guys, but you do get one or two.

QUESTION: *What about ordinary hustling? Did you have any trouble making contacts through illegal means because you were an addict, or was it primarily the Mafia you were excluded from?*

RICK: Well, the Mafia and organized crime, I consider myself a sick person and not a dishonest person and the things I have done I've been forced to do to support my addiction. How I made my money and how successful I was was something that wasn't brought up. When I got out of high school I was using, I was supporting a family. I did start a state-sponsored, four-year apprenticeship as an electrician. I took four years of night school plus eight hours a week of on-the-job training. These are college accepted courses in a state-sponsored apprenticeship program. And I was functioning so I had a working income that was pretty good. I wasn't maintaining my habit with that, I was maintaining my living expenses and none of my addict expenses, or money I needed to support my habit was coming out. I was using this money to support my family, pay my bills.

QUESTION: *Was your wife aware that you were an addict?*

RICK: Yes, she was a little grasshopper herself. But she didn't go on to become an addict. I never really tried to turn anybody on, and I don't think I've ever sold to anyone that wasn't already an addict, or had started to anyway or was working on it. I sold to someone who did sell to a new addict or maybe a teenager. But I was selling narcotics and I wasn't greedy and this was one reason I got away with it for so long, was I was selling about $200 a week worth of narcotics and supporting my habit and keeping my entertainment running at a pretty good level, and I always had plenty of money and this sort of thing.

QUESTION: *Did you find your health declining?*

RICK: Actually, an addict that is living in a family type setting like I was, working, keeping reasonable hours, eating three times a day, is not going to get in too bad of physical shape. But take an addict that is unmarried, living in a hotel someplace, and eating is not that important that he's going to go a block to get something to eat—it's not that important to him. Why they get run down is because they don't eat and they don't sleep, but I don't think the drug itself, if you are using it in the family type setting, would necessarily get you run down physically.

QUESTION: *You mentioned you were beaten by sheriffs when you were eight years old. Do you think this contributed to your alienation?*

RICK: Yes, I think so. I still have some pretty strong feelings about it. There was a church when I was in the third grade somewhere around there, and they had what I think they called pilgrim fellowship meeting. It was a small town and they never locked any doors or anything; this was Woodside, California, an exclusive, almost rural area. This church was broken into by kids. I had been hanging around the church on the night it was broken into by kids, and we had been in the church, but we left without hurting anything. After we left, somebody, who actually was a friend of mine, broke in and set the altar flags on fire. It was one of these places that has a kitchen and recreation room type thing and they took boxes of kitchen matches and threw these all over the hardwood dancing floor, I guess, striking them before throwing them and burning marks on the floor. They broke the drinking fountain, burnt up the flags, and scarred up some walls and things like this. We had been seen going in the church and in the churchyard and things like that. This group of four or five people I was with that didn't do anything wrong, but you know how it is, they get the sheriff's department out there the next day, which was Halloween. This is why I have such a vivid picture of this because Halloween has just gone by. The first day of interrogation by the sheriff's department, they excluded, well, I guess, I had a bad attitude at the time anyway and I liked cops and robbers and didn't like cops at the time, though I hadn't been in much trouble.

QUESTION: *You were only eight or nine?*

RICK: Yes, I guess it was just before fifth grade. So they picked on me; they pretty well let the other kids go. I guess I must have started having problems with grades and things at school and I suppose they had some reason to pick me out. I was too young to be truant. The first day of interrogation was conducted at the firehouse and was conducted by two inspectors of the sheriff's department. I didn't have anything to admit so it didn't work to say, "Come on kid, tell the truth." Of course, I'm innocent so it is pretty easy to stay with a story, but this interrogation went on for four or five hours a day for about five days in the sheriff's office.

QUESTION: *Were you held over?*

RICK: No, I was released to my family to go home every day, and I was to report back to the firehouse the next day. I would be there, and this is one thing that I think a parent, instead of being willing to let the police department raise their kids, I feel a parent should get behind me in this situation, where I think they were behind the police department and actually believed the police department because they were so sure that I had done this. They tried tactics like bringing both of them in and one would be nice and one would use scare tactics, and things like this.

QUESTION: *Did they ever force you to admit to something you hadn't done?*

RICK: No. I got caught and grabbed out of a chair; I didn't get hurt. I got slapped a couple of times.

QUESTION: *Did you feel betrayed by your parents?*

RICK: Yes, I'm sure I did. I still feel . . .

QUESTION: *Did their attitude change as a result of that?*

RICK: I think yes, probably, I can't remember but I'm sure there was a certain amount of prestige with the other kids in the neighborhood.

QUESTION: *What kind of association did you have in junior high school?*

RICK: Well, I think I started with one of the best of friends. I think one of them is right now a professor at U.C., Berkeley. One is a school teacher in a school district down around San Jose. Another is a member of the 1960 Olympic Team as a wrestler and played football at Cal Poly. Actually, I was kind of active in high school myself. I participated in sports.

QUESTION: *Then something happened to change this?*

RICK: You're right. It's a pattern, really, and all these things are symptoms, really. I keep dropping further and further out of society. Oh, these two people I was talking about are two of the people who weren't good enough for me at the time.

QUESTION: *When did you start using heroin?*

RICK: Late seventeens.

QUESTION: *Does heroin give you a delirious feeling?*

RICK: I don't think so. Heroin is really pretty close to reality.

QUESTION: *Is it pretty close to the way you feel now?*

RICK: No, I feel bad now. It is a relaxing type of drug; it's not like a stimulant that speeds everything up. It's along the lines of a strong tranquilizer, only more extreme.

QUESTION: *So with heroin you get to a point where you cannot stop yourself, it is almost out of your hands, all you want to do is have a shot of heroin?*

RICK: That is actually all I'd like to do right now, except maybe get a little revenge on society. My desires and needs now . . .

QUESTION: *Why don't you strike back with violence?*

RICK: I have done this, and I think it comes right down to I'm a lot smarter. I have approached a guy, which is a pretty good way to approach a guy who is really a loser, a long history, a four or five time loser, is to approach him on a smart and stupid pitch. You can either be a damn fool and go and do this or you can go do something else. They have no moral values, like I haven't got any right now, and I don't feel any moral obligation to society.

QUESTION: *From all that you have said, it seems honesty is pretty important to you.*

RICK: Yes, I think it is. I don't lie to me, myself. Sometimes I lie by omission, the things I'm just not ready to talk about right now. I enjoy making people uncomfortable and I do make a lot of people . . . when I get my chances I can make a lot of people feel uncomfortable. Everybody has hangs-ups—even what are normally called well-adjusted people, if you get these people in a room and start talking about sex, homosexuality, lesbians, and things like that, and kind of look around the room at these people and say there is someone in this room and just don't say any more, people, whether they are guilty or not, have feelings because they are all guilty.

QUESTION: *When you first became involved in drugs, did everyone in the group take them, just a few, or were you the only one?*

RICK: It depends on where you start. I think like when I'm talking about these two friends of mine, who I still consider pretty good friends, I don't think, though I think one has had some experience with some drug, but I don't think either one of them has ever smoked weed to my knowledge.

QUESTION: *Were the people you were associating with at the time you started shooting heroin the same people you started smoking marijuana with?*

RICK: Yes, it's a group of people, and there aren't too many of us left alive, and I don't know how many are out on the streets now. Maybe one or two and I know of three at least that are dead.

QUESTION: *Was this the norm of the group, to take drugs?*

RICK: Yes, we were loaded all the time.

QUESTION: *Was there a lot of experimentation?*

RICK: When I got to experimenting with a lot of types of drugs was when I couldn't find my stuff and was unable to maintain myself. I would have rather like stayed with weed and I did for years stay with weed and Benzedrine before I went on to heroin and even dropped the Benzedrine and stayed with heroin. But when I couldn't maintain myself any longer I stopped functioning as well. Where in 1959 I paid taxes on $9,500 at about twenty-two or twenty-three years old is a lot of money even today, and was a lot more then, and probably sold another $10,000 worth of narcotics along with it. So I'm twenty-two years old and making approximately $20,000 a year.

QUESTION: *When you first started taking heroin did you feel like you were resigning from society?*

RICK: I don't think I really had any feelings at the time, except I knew I wasn't going to get hooked because I wasn't mainlining it.

QUESTION: *Did you feel it was something to try for kicks?*

RICK: I don't know, I feel I was coached into it by . . . I did turn it down at first, but was coached into it by being called chicken, don't be chicken.

QUESTION: *How were the first people in your group introduced to heroin?*

RICK: It was on a trip a couple of the people had made to Mexico. A vacation type thing.

QUESTION: *Were you hooked from the first time?*

RICK: The first time I did fix I got pretty sick and I didn't fix for approximately another week and maybe I only fixed one time this week, but got a better feeling out of it than the first time when I got pretty sick.

COMMENTARY

In assessing Rick's interview, we should keep in mind that the precautions mentioned under "Methodological Considerations" apply here. For instance, Rick is vague as to his connections with "syndicated crime." Many of his responses may have been influenced by the extensive psychological treatment he underwent at Ft. Worth and California Rehabilitation Center. Other attitudes appear to be reflective of inmate and drug subcultures (hostility toward society), who resent either or both the fact that they have been arrested or that substances they desire to use are outlawed.

Nevertheless, Rick's self-analysis sheds some new light on the nature of addiction. Contrary to opportunity theory, socioeconomic deprivation was not a major factor in Rick's background. He came from an "upper middle class" family. Even after he became an addict and had spent time in juvenile and adult correctional institutions, he managed to "function" in a middle class capacity, working in "electronics." During his four years of steady employment in electronics he was an addict, selling drugs to maintain his habit. Apparently there was no deterioration of his performance or health during this period. This finding certainly runs contrary to the dismal picture of the addict drawn in official publications like those of the Bureau of Narcotics.

Rick's return to heroin use and his statements that heroin was good and that he would use it "in a minute" if it were legalized tend to support Lindesmith's "always an addict" concept. He appears to have the self-identity of an addict and a rather negative reflection of such ("the sewer in my arm").

Perhaps, reacting to the forced nature of his psychological "treatment," Rick appears to resist application of psychiatric theory to his situation. He states that he acquired a "psychological bag of tricks" at

C.R.C. and he hates "why." Thus, Rick does not think early childhood factors (whether his mother "put him on the pot crooked") had much to do with his addiction. He admits he hated his father, but asserts he loved his mother. Parents entered in as a factor in their ridiculing of his friends, in driving him to "less worthy companions," and in not supporting him when he faced difficulties (like the incident with the sheriff). However, Rick seems to think another person given the same childhood environment might have turned out differently.

If Rick's denial of family factors were to be interpreted as a case of Freudian repression, and other statements interpreted as an indication of a weak masculine identification, the Chein model might prove explanatory. For instance, Rick is elusive regarding his relationship with females, both about his marriage and about "six people who aren't alive today . . . because of an abortion type situation." At the latter point, Rick admits guilt and states that he "lost" his "train of thought." He also connects "lies by omission," "making people feel uncomfortable" by talking "about sex, homosexuality, lesbians," and guilt. He admits that he first used heroin so as not to be called a "chicken." Finally, he states that addicts "would rather take narcotics than have sex or get into bed with somebody."

In addition to the father-figure and masculine identity links, we find evidence of dependency (similar to George in the preceding chapter). Rick speaks of "emotional dependency" and the manner in which the Salvation Army institutional life "takes a lot of social pressure off of me." Rick appears to be capable of remaining off of heroin when his emotional and other dependency needs are being met by institutional living as provided by the C.R.C., mental hospitals, the Ft. Worth Norcotic Center, and the Salvation Army. One senses that Rick feels a lack of internal power or control and tends to deny responsibility or blame external forces for much of his behavior:

> So I have to watch my motives . . .
> Well, I think your environment has a lot to do with it . . .
> I consider myself a sick person, and not a dishonest person and the things I have done I've been forced to do to support my addiction.
> I never went on my own choice. It was always something else—police pressure, family pressure—police pressure is the only thing that ever made me dry out.

Rick disputes the stepping-stone theory, asserting that, in his case, associations were the determining factor rather than the use of marijuana per se.

> You're placing young people in a position where they're traveling in circles where these things are available.

What is also indicated is that the *availability* of or *opportunity* to use heroin came through Rick's increased involvement in the delinquent and drug subculture. With this involvement, moreover, came increased negative labeling as Rick was caught in delinquent acts or, at least, charged when he claims he was innocent.

However, Rick does not think that association with marijuana users usually leads to heroin use or addiction:

> I think a kid smoking weed—that is a symptom he's trying to tell you something. He may not like society, he may not like his family, but he might not be so messed up that he can't go on and become one of you people here in the State University and function in society, which most of them will. We're talking about a really small percentage of them who will be addicts.

We would ask if anomie theory, as amplified by Cloward and Ohlin, applies in Rick's case. Is Rick a double failure? Did he fail to get into criminal groups? If we're talking about getting into syndicated crime, maybe yes. But that is not the only criminal means available in this country, and certainly few criminals ever become syndicate members. If we're talking about regular participation in a criminal way of life, Rick was certainly capable of using or getting access to illegitimate means. He sold narcotics successfully for some years. He also participated in "about every crime there is—armed robbery, burglary." Also, it may be added, he was successful in carrying on a steady and respectable job while he was an addict.

Above all, Rick's case seems to attest to statements made by Lindesmith and the labeling theorists about the law and its application as actually of "causal" significance. Rick may be described as an alienated personality, and alienated in the sense of "seeking revenge" (his own term), or getting back. His hostility may stem from his early brutal treatment in the hands of a sheriff at the age of eight, charged with a delinquent act he did not commit. His parents failed to support him through days of interrogation and abuse, he felt. What followed was years of experience in the juvenile justice system for minor juvenile offenses (truancy, fighting, incorrigibility). Juvenile institutionalization led him to delinquent contacts who used drugs, and it gave him status among delinquents outside of institutions. These associations led him to marijuana and other minor drugs, and when he was eighteen, he took heroin on a trip to Mexico, so that he wouldn't be called "chicken." He rationalized he wouldn't get hooked because he wasn't mainlining, just "skin popping" (injecting heroin subcutaneously or intramuscularly rather than intravenously). He became hooked very rapidly (showing us that in actual practice the six steps Lindesmith describes occur in rapid succession).

We will return to some of the specific explanations of heroin addiction as we examine them and Rick's case within our larger theoretical network.

THEORETICAL IMPLICATIONS

There are several implications for more general explanations of deviant behavior and we should keep in mind the possible overlap with explanations of alcoholism and "compulsive" behavior in general. We have not found evidence that some persons are genetically or physically "predisposed" to addiction. However, we should mention that the pharmacological effects of the use of heroin are a decrease in pain and an increased tolerance with continued use. These factors should also be borne in mind as we evaluate psychiatric and sociological theories.

Psychiatric Theories

As with alcoholism, psychiatric explanations, taken on their own, do not have great explanatory power in Rick's case or apparently among other addicts. We must again, however, point out that if such personality defects as a dependent personality, low frustration-tolerance, and a weak masculine identity are taken as signs of a lack of internal control (Chein terms them "inner restraints"), they are of greater value when viewed with their interaction with external or social factors.

Sociological Theories

ANOMIE We find little support for anomie theory, either as originally proposed by Merton or as implied by Cloward and Ohlin within the "double failure" hypothesis.

SUBCULTURAL THEORIES We again find that those subcultural explanations that emphasize lower socioeconomic or minority status have little power when considering white middle class (or above) deviancy. We have gained some insight into the deviant subculture of heroin addicts. Rick does not have a high opinion of addicts and "hates most" of the skid row types who live at the Salvation Army with him. This is similar to the feelings of George, the alcoholic. We do find that a youthful delinquent and/or drug subculture provided the initial contact with heroin for Rick. He claims continued contact with the deviant subculture of "the Mafia" as an adult. The status of an addict, however, is low even within this group.

LABELING THEORY We have found that labeling theory is applicable to our case history in more than one instance. Initially, we discovered that Rick was labeled as "bad" or "delinquent" at the age of eight when he claimed innocence. Societal reaction was both formal and informal, including parental rejection. We also find that Rick has adopted the self-identity of "heroin addict" as well as the "sick" or medical frame of reference. The disease identity may well have resulted from Rick's treatment in various facilities. As has been pointed out, the labeling model of Lindesmith appears to have strong explanatory power in assessing Rick's case.

DIFFERENTIAL ASSOCIATION   There also appears to be very strong support for differential association explanation of Rick's addiction. His familial ties to his father were weak and his peer associations led him to be "coached into" heroin use even though he initially declined to do so. Other associations provided Rick with adult criminal contacts. There is a direct application of a process of learning techniques and rationalizations favorable to drug use and other deviant activities within primary groups.

SOCIAL CONTROL THEORY   As with alcoholism, social control models appear to provide the broadest total framework within which to consider Rick's heroin addiction. As stated earlier, the Chein framework and lack of internal mechanisms of control provide a basis for understanding the "compulsive" nature of addiction and susceptibility. These factors must be considered, however, within the external controls with which they interact. Again, we must consider formal and informal controls and view the formal mechanisms within both the legal and medical models.

Rick's alienation seems to have made him resistant to internalization of external controls, both from his father and from society in general. He has little respect for drug education programs in inculcating controls. What is striking is that Rick expresses ambivalence toward both the medical and the criminal models of external controls. He hates psychiatrists and psychologists asking, "Why?" and, at the same time, speaks of himself as being cured and as a "sick" person. He states the legal deterrent is the only deterrent for addicts, yet he has continued to relapse in spite of numerous arrests and took only forty days to find "a way to beat the naline tests." What is perhaps coming through is a desire *to be controlled* from a person who senses his own lack of self-control. It is evident, however, that external controls are not fully effective.

Much of Rick's ambivalence may be reflective of American society today. The history of opiates and their control has been one of swinging back and forth between one model or the other. Today, it appears that we regard the possession or use of heroin as a crime but the user as ill. Some argument could be made that the strong informal sanctions combined with harsh legal penalties have served as a deterrent and prevented far greater numbers of addicts. Nevertheless, since the 1940s and particularly since 1962, there have been rather steady and somewhat dramatic increases in the estimated number of heroin addicts in the United States.[28] Others argue for a "heroin maintenance" program similar to that in Great Britain, which stems the profit from illegal heroin and the necessity for the heroin addict to lead a criminal or other deviant lifestyle in order to support the habit.[29] While methadone maintenance programs have proven less than successful for a variety of reasons,[30] recent studies, such as that of Silverman and Levine, indicate law enforcement successes may actually increase the crime rate by driving the price of heroin upward (a $100-a-day habit becomes a $200-a-day habit).[31]

Rick advocates legalization as his solution to the country's problem of heroin addiction (as do Lindesmith and Chein):

> ... heroin would reduce crime if it were legalized because it induces narcosis, reduces aggression, and sexual drive, which are the basis of major crimes. . . . Let them shoot themselves to death if this is what the addict wants to do, and I'm sure it is what he wants to do.

Then, Rick proposes, there wouldn't be any addicts around to recruit new addicts.

If external control measures do not work, what mechanisms would serve to strengthen internal controls? For those addicted to heroin, "therapeutic communities" such as Phoenix House, Synanon, and Dayton Village appear to be the most effective. Such communities seem to be effective by utilizing primary group techniques and application of differential association in a therapeutic setting.[32] They have been criticized as substituting a dependency on the group for a drug dependency.[33] In the longer run and as means of prevention, perhaps we must begin by strengthening the family system in order that parents may adequately prepare their offspring to tolerate the stresses and pains of life. Perhaps, too, we should alleviate pressures at the societal level and examine cultural forces that predispose individuals to seek solutions through drugs or alcohol. Fort and Cory sum up this view as follows:

> ... Many individuals who use drugs do these things (other costly outlets) too, but it is possible that some drug use may provide escape valves for pent-up social and personal pressures that might otherwise have more dangerous consequences than the consequences of drug use itself ...
>
> In the final analysis, sensible drug prevention requires profound changes in U.S. life. The reputed magical properties of drugs must be demythologized. The use of psychoactive drugs must be made less acceptable and less attractive than participation in the real world ... We know that no chemical can provide a quick or permanent answer to all problems and questions; we know that problems with multiple causes require multiple solutions applied together over a long period. Honest dealing with drugs and drug abuse can be fruitful, but perhaps total solutions will come only with a civilization and morality we can barely conceptualize let alone practice.[34]

═══════ QUESTIONS FOR DISCUSSION

1. What role, if any, did marijuana play in Rick's subsequent development as a heroin user?
2. Do you believe as Rick does that if you take heroin once, you're "hooked for life"?
3. Rick seemed to relapse very quickly after being released from institutional care. If he had withdrawn from heroin while in institutional custody, why do you think he relapsed so quickly? Why do you think he managed to stay free of heroin for eighteen months his last time out?
4. Rick admits he would sometimes "dry out" because of police pressure. If heroin were legalized, so that he could obtain it legally through a medical doctor, how would Rick's life have been affected?
5. Do you see any evidence for labeling theory in Rick's case history?

═══════ RELATED READINGS

Blum, Richard H., and Associates, *Society and Drugs* (San Francisco: Jossey-Bass, Inc., 1970).

Chein, Isidor, et al., *The Road to H: Narcotics, Delinquency, and Social Policy* (New York: Basic Books, 1964).

Fort, Joel, and Cory, Christopher T., *American Drugstore: A (Alcohol) to V (Valium)* (Boston: Little, Brown, 1975).

Judson, Horace Freeland, *Heroin Addiction: What Americans Can Learn from the English Experience* (New York: Vintage Books, 1975).

Kaplan, John, *Marijuana: The New Prohibition* (New York: Pocket Books, 1971).

Lindesmith, Alfred, *The Addict and the Law* (New York: Vintage Books, 1967).

———, *Opiate Addiction* (Bloomington: Indiana University Press, 1947).

Lindesmith, Alfred, and Gagnon, John, "Anomie and Drug Addiction," in Marshall C. Clinard, ed., *Anomie and Deviant Behavior* (New York: The Free Press, 1964).

Musto, David F., *The American Disease: Origins of Narcotic Control* (New Haven: Yale University Press, 1973).

O'Donnell, John, and Ball, John, eds., *Narcotic Addiction* (New York: Harper & Row, 1966).

O'Donnell, John A., et al., *Young Men and Drugs: A Nationwide Survey* (Rockville, Md.: National Institute on Drug Abuse, 1976).

Peele, Stanton, with Brodsky, Archie, *Love and Addiction* (New York: Taplinger, 1975).

President's Commission on Law Enforcement and Administration of Justice, *Task Force Report: Narcotics and Drug Abuse* (Washington, D.C.: U.S. Government Printing Office, 1967).

Ray, Marsh, "The Cycle of Abstinence and Relapse among Heroin Addicts," *Social Problems*, 9 (1961), pp. 132–140.

Ray, Oakley, *Drugs, Society and Human Behavior* (St. Louis: C. V. Mosby Co., 1978).

Report to the Ford Foundation, *Dealing with Drug Abuse* (New York: Praeger, 1972).

Rettig, Richard P.; Torres, Manual J.; and Garrett, Gerald P., *Manny: A Criminal-Addicts Story* (Boston: Houghton Mifflin Co., 1977).

Schur, Edwin, *Narcotics Addiction in Britain and America* (Bloomington: Indiana University Press, 1962).

Smith, David E., and Gay, George R., eds., *"It's So Good, Don't Even Try It Once": Heroin in Perspective* (Englewood Cliffs, N.J.: Prentice-Hall, Inc., 1972).

Szasz, Thomas, *Ceremonial Chemistry* (Garden City, N.Y.: Anchor Books, 1975).

NOTES

1. Ray Oakley, *Drugs, Society, and Human Behavior*, 2nd ed. (St. Louis: C. V. Mosby Co., 1978), p. 322.

2. Richard R. Lingeman, *Drugs from A to Z: A Dictionary* (New York: McGraw-Hill, 1969), p. 2.

3. Alfred Lindesmith and Anselm Strauss, *Social Psychology* (New York: Henry Holt, 1956), pp. 352–354.

4. J. A. O'Donnell, "A Follow-up of Narcotic Addicts: Mortality, Relapse and Abstinence," *American Journal of Orthopsychiatry*, 34 (1964), pp. 948–954.

5. Ibid.

6. C. Winick, "Maturing out of Narcotic Addiction," *Bulletin on Narcotics*, 14, No. 1 (1962), pp. 1–8.

7. L. N. Robins, *The Vietnam Drug User Returns*, Special Action Office for Drug Abuse Prevention Monograph, Series A, No. 2, May, 1974.

8. Stanton Peele with Archie Brodsky, *Love and Addiction* (New York: Taplinger, 1975), p. 19.

9. Ibid., p. 18.

10. Oakley, *Drugs, Society, and Human Behavior*, p. 323.

11. Ibid., pp. 331–332.

12. Michael J. Pescor, "Physician Drug Addicts," in John A. O'Donnell and John C. Ball, eds., *Narcotic Addiction* (New York: Harper & Row, 1966), pp. 164–167.

13. Richard Stephens, "The Truthfulness of Addict Respondents in Research Projects," *International Journal of the Addictions*, 7, No. 3 (1972).

14. Edward Preble and J. J. Casey, Jr., "Taking Care of Business: the Heroin User's Life on the Street," *International Journal of the Addictions*, 4 (March, 1969), pp. 1–4; Michael H. Agar, *Ripping and Running: A Formal Ethnography of Urban Heroin Addicts* (New York: Seminar, 1973); Robert S. Weppner, ed., *Street Ethnography: Selected Studies of Crime and Drug Use in Natural Settings* (Beverly Hills, Calif.: Sage, 1977).

15. John A. O'Donnell et al., *Young Men and Drugs: A Nationwide Survey* (Rockville, Md.: National Institute on Drug Abuse, 1976), p. 95.

16. Harry Anslinger and William Tompkins, *The Traffic in Narcotics* (New York: Funk and Wagnalls, 1953); Earl Rowell and Robert Rowell, *On the Trail of Marijuana, the Weed of Madness* (Mountain View, Calif.: Pacific Press Publishing Association, 1939).

17. Isidor Chein et al., *The Road to H: Narcotics, Delinquency, and Social Policy* (New York: Basic Books, 1964).

18. Isidor Chein, "Narcotic Use Among Juveniles," in John A. O'Donnell and John C. Ball, eds., *Narcotic Addiction*, p. 135.

19. Harold Finestone, "Cats, Kicks, and Color," *Social Problems*, 5 (Summer, 1957), pp. 3–13.

20. Richard Cloward and Lloyd Ohlin, *Delinquency and Opportunity* (Glencoe, Ill.: The Free Press, 1960).

21. Alfred R. Lindesmith, *The Addict and the Law* (New York: Vintage Books, 1967), pp. 128–129.

22. Alfred Lindesmith and John Gagnon, "Anomie and Drug Addiction," in Marshall B. Clinard, ed., *Anomie and Deviant Behavior* (New York: The Free Press, 1964), pp. 318–319.

23. Ibid., p. 176.

24. John A. O'Donnell and Judith P. Jones, "Diffusion of the Intravenous Technique Among Narcotic Addicts in the United States," *Journal of Health and Social Behavior*, 9, No. 2 (June, 1968).

25. Harvey W. Feldman, "Ideological Supports to Becoming and Remaining a Heroin Addict," *Journal of Health and Social Behavior*, 9, No. 2 (June, 1968), pp. 131–139.

26. Edgar Z. Fridenberg, *The Vanishing Adolescent* (New York: Dell, 1959); Paul Goodman, *Growing Up Absurd* (New York: Vintage Books, 1960); Richard C. Schroeder, *The Politics of Drugs: Marijuana to Mainline* (Washington, D.C.: Congressional Quarterly, Inc., 1975).

27. Jeremiah Lowney, "Correspondence Between Attitudes and Drinking and Drug Behavior: Youth Subculture Over Time," Unpublished Paper Presented to the Society for the Study of Social Problems, Chicago, September, 1977.

28. David E. Smith and George R. Gay, eds., *It's So Good Don't Even Try It Once: Heroin in Perspective* (Englewood Cliffs, N.J.: Prentice-Hall, Inc., 1972); Weldon L. Witters and Patricia Jones-Witters, *Drugs and Sex* (New York: Macmillan, 1975), pp. 246–249.

29. Horace Freeland Judson, *Heroin Addiction: What Americans Can Learn from the English Experience* (New York: Vintage Books, 1975); Paul E. Rock, ed., *Drugs and Politics* (New Brunswick, N.J.: Transaction, Inc., 1977); Gilbert Geis, *Not the Law's Business? An Examination of Homosexuality, Abortion, Prostitution, Narcotics and Gambling in the United States* (Rockville, Md.: National Institute of Mental Health, Center for Studies of Crime and Delinquency, 1972, Publication No. 72-9132).

30. Oakley, *Drugs, Society, and Human Behavior*, pp. 335–336.

31. Lester Silverman, Nancy Spruill, and Daniel Levine, "Urban Crime and Heroin Availability," PRI 75-1 (Arlington, Va.: Public Research Institute, 1975).

32. Rita Volkman and Donald R. Cressey, "Differential Association and the Rehabilitation of Drug Addicts," *The American Journal of Sociology*, 69, No. 2 (September, 1963), pp. 129–142; Barry Sugarman, *Dayton Village: A Therapeutic Community* (New York: Holt, Rinehart and Winston, Inc., 1974).

33. Oakley, *Drugs, Society, and Human Behavior*, pp. 334–335.

34. Joel Fort and Christopher T. Cory, *American Drugstore A (Alcohol) To V (Valium)* (Boston: Little, Brown, 1975).

Prostitution: From the Street Walker to the Masseuse

5

Prostitution usually refers to the indiscriminate offer by a female of her body for sexual intercourse or other "lewdness" for the purpose of financial gain. In recent years, some attention has been given to male prostitution whether it be the "gigolo" variety or the male "hustler" of homosexuals. The latter will be dealt with in Chapter Six. In this chapter we shall examine female prostitution and employ the term in its traditional, often legalistic, sense.

Prostitution is characterized by barter, promiscuity, and emotional indifference. In actuality, however, there are many instances of such behavior not ordinarily considered prostitution. For example, when a customer "dates" a shop girl for an evening dinner and show and later engages in sex relations with her, the relationship may be mercenary, promiscuous, and even emotionally indifferent; however, the girl may not be considered, nor consider herself, a prostitute. Thus, there are certain delimited social situations that are probably a necessary part of the definition of prostitution, including sexual bartering on the street or through a second party in the case of call girls or house prostitutes. It is commonly recognized that there are essentially four types of prostitutes—street walkers, house prostitutes, massage parlour prostitutes, and call girls, in direct order of status within the subculture of prostitutes and those they serve. Thus, call girls are highest in status and more often serve upper class men, while street walkers are lowest in status, more often serving lower class clientele.

The persons we have interviewed for this chapter fall into the categories of street prostitute and massage parlor prostitute.

EXPLANATION OF THE AGE-OLD QUESTION: "What's a Nice Girl Like You . . . ?"

What leads to a decision of a young lady or girl to become a prostitute? Or, what "makes" a person become a prostitute? Various theoretical explanations have been offered. There has been a strong bent for certain areas of psychology and sociology to provide causal frameworks. Freudian psychology and anomie or "opportunity" theories in sociology have recently been supplemented by interactionist and labeling explanations. Perhaps the development has been necessitated by lack of data to support the earlier theories. Perhaps, too, those who choose prostitution are less apt to come from lower socioeconomic groups and "poorer" homes. Let us briefly examine some of the major explanations that have been put forth.

Psychological or Psychiatric Theory

We have already seen that Freudian psychoanalysis views prostitution as an outcome of either hatred for the father or excessive love leading to the Electra complex. The prostitute has also been described by Freudians as masochistic, of infantile mentality, and emotionally dangerous to males. Some psychological theories emphasize seduction at an early age, and the pervasive impact of broken homes and/or parental rejection in leading to prostitution. There is an emphasis in many of these explanations upon early childhood relationships with the person's father and a resulting "hatred" of men. In sum, an all-encompassing stress upon early childhood factors characterizes the highly influential psychoanalytic approach, although recent studies have evinced little or no evidence of any difference in the incidence of neurosis or psychological abnormality among prostitutes as compared with housewives.[1]

Sociological Theories

ANOMIE EXPLANATIONS   This emphasis upon dire and unfortunate prior background is carried in some sociological theories of prostitution.

Lemert suggests a kind of opportunity theory of prostitution. There may be a strong tendency for women in our culture to resort to sex as a means of redressing their status differential. The press of situational factors making for prostitution falls more heavily upon women of low socioeconomic status, who are at an even greater disadvantage.[2] Collateral to this is the theory that addicted or alcoholic women resort to prostitution as a means of securing drugs or alcohol.[3] Lemert also develops a kind of "occupational affinity theory" that is related to the opportunity theory approach but also borders on another approach to be discussed shortly—the career and socialization model. Some female occupations, such as waitress, domestic servant, show girl, manicurist, model, and the like, imply a dependency upon masculine largess in the form of tips. From this position of quasi-prostitution, it is an easy step to actual prostitution, since opportunities may constantly present themselves. This theory has another aspect, however. It may be that there is an affinity also between the organizational structure of these utilitarian occupations and that of prostitute groups, making participation in such groups either interchangeable in some cases or logically progressive from one to another.[4]

OTHER SOCIOLOGICAL EXPLANATIONS: SOCIAL CONTROL, INTERACTIONISM, AND DIFFERENTIAL ASSOCIATION WITHIN THE SUBCULTURE   All of the above approaches stress that women are "driven" into prostitution or "pushed" into it by background or environmental factors, whether it be poverty, upbringing, or broken homes. These may be viewed, perhaps, as a lack of either internal or external controls. Recently, broader frameworks have developed that take into account a variety of these and other factors in an interactionist model. Some research sponsored by the British Social Biology Council has indicated that in most cases the prostitute way of life is chosen because it offers greater ease, freedom, and profit than conventional occupations.[5] In fact, there has not yet been enough field study of prostitutes to prove that they all come from blighted backgrounds. This belief is derived either from official records of prostitutes who have been jailed or from preconceptions of what we expect prostitutes to be like.

Recent studies stressing the "pull" of women into the prostitute subculture open up the possibility that prostitutes may come from various socioeconomic strata and backgrounds. Whoever walks into the field of influences may be pulled in by them. The induction of a girl into prostitution has been discussed in terms of the idea of "career," particularly in the case of the call girl. The developmental career of a call girl is said to follow three stages: entrance into the career, apprenticeship, and the development of contacts.[6] Thus, prostitution may involve processes of differential association and socialization discussed in other areas of deviancy.

≡≡≡≡≡≡≡➤ SANDY:
A Street Prostitute

The informant in the following transcript is a for-
mer prostitute. At the time of taping, she was around thirty years of
age and working on an assembly line at a local aircraft plant. A tall
blonde, Sandy worked as a street prostitute for ten years, from age
eighteen through twenty-eight.

SANDY [TO EDITORS]: I don't want to say anything to people
about me, share anything with anybody until I find out what their reaction is to me. I don't want to give anything to anybody. I don't want
you to say anything to the class beforehand about what I want them
to ask me. I'm concerned about what their reaction to me will be.

SANDY [TO AUDIENCE]: Well, I'm about ready to pass out, I'm
so nervous. Offenses: several narcotic offenses. Cops picked me up on
several suspicions of grand theft arrests. They do this in order to nail
prostitutes. Couple of burglaries; everything but murder. Of course I
didn't do any of these things. I turned tricks for years at 5th and Market.
I made a lot of money and I made little money. I've been hungry. I think
when people take to talking about prostitutes, they think about Cadillacs
and the handsome men who they dine out with. They forget about the
times when they have two black eyes and walk the streets hungry. You
look so bad that nobody wants to turn a trick with you. It's really a
bummer. I know girls out on the street who are prostitutes because they
like to gamble or take dope or whatever. There's no urgent reason for
them being out there, but yet they're there. Hustling all day and all night.
Some have pimps, some don't. I guess there's just as many different
reasons for being a prostitute as there is for being anything else. It took
me years and years of therapy at CRC, a place for narcotics addicts, to
realize that my reason was linked to attention-getting. I dug the attention from men, the easy money. You can't beat the hours. The actual
sex part took about thirty seconds.

QUESTION: *How do you go about making contacts?*

SANDY: When you're working with an organization of prostitution, naturally, you just go into the house and she tells you what her
percentage is and what your percentage is, and you leave when you get
ready or when the customers get tired of you. In organized prostitution
where you have your call girls, your $100 tricks, $50, $75, $200 tricks,
the organization contacts you so that the customer has usually already
been screened. Hustling off 5th and Market, you don't really walk two
steps. Everyone who wants a whore goes to 5th and Market, it's that
simple. We call it whoring; you guys call it prostitution.

QUESTION: *Do people come by in their cars?*

SANDY: I find that mostly in L.A. I worked there for a while too. And there you just stand on a corner and they holler, "How much?" and you holler back your price and that was it. That doesn't happen too often down here.

QUESTION: *Did you say that they usually got you for being loaded?*

SANDY: Yeah, well, they usually could get a possession rap on me cuz I was so strung-out that I carried narcotics on me all the time. So, until I got three possessions on me and wised up, I usually didn't have a case. I couldn't holler too loud, you know, cuz when you're doing wrong you can't holler too loud.

QUESTION: *I'm interested in how you got started in prostitution. I've read several books and most of them say that prostitutes usually hate men.*

SANDY: Oh, I don't. I really don't; I don't know if I'm an oddity or what, but uh. It was funny. I was very moralistic as a kid. I kept my cherry until I was seventeen; I was not going to lose it until I got married. And when I did lose it, it was out of curiosity and because all my friends had. You know, I felt like a big dodo. And I had been with this man for three months who is my son's father. And so, anyway, I went ahead, had sex, got pregnant, and had the baby, and then he went to the joint for the fifth time. I was just lost, I was eighteen. I just went crazy. I started getting high, getting it on with anyone and everyone, and just giving it away, when and if I felt like it. It was really a bummer. And I went on like this for about a year, and one night this dude came up to me and offered me some money to sleep with him. I thought, well, I'm broke, so I just jumped into the car and didn't even think. The idea of hustling had never 'til that time crossed my mind. People have a tendency to rationalize what they are doing. When I did not hustle, when I was giving it away, I thought that it was all right as long as I wasn't a dirty prostitute. Now that I'm a dirty prostitute, anyone who gives it away is crazy! So I went and turned that first trick and, well, hell, I think I was gone maybe ten minutes and I got $15. This was in 1960. I had to teach myself everything. I don't think there was anything in my childhood; I think it was just an accident. It looked good to me; I didn't have any money, I was on welfare, trying to raise a baby, getting high, running the streets.

QUESTION: *Would you say that a majority of prostitutes are on drugs?*

SANDY: I'd say 75 percent of all prostitutes are either on drugs or are alcoholics. I don't know anything about the other 25 percent, I really don't.

QUESTION: *Are the other 25 percent in it just for the money?*

SANDY: No, some are exhibitionists, some just crave attention—like I did—I think some are actually hooked on prostitution. It's really strange! It's not that they like to get laid and get paid for it, because they'll lie, cut you up, and steal. They're just cold, cold people. They get to be forty-five or fifty years old and they aren't that pretty, but they're out there making the money just snap, snap, snap. And I don't know what they do with the money.

QUESTION: *Is this the reason they prostitute? To support their habit? Booze? Whatever?*

SANDY: Well, like I said, the hours are good, the pay is great. You really can't beat it. If you have a family, then it means something to you. I have a family that doesn't mean too much to me, my morals were already shot, I was getting high, there was just no reason for me to not be making money.

QUESTION: *Do most girls get suckered into the profession, or do they go in with their eyes wide open?*

SANDY: The women I met were not suckered into it. I suppose there are some that do get suckered into it, but I knew exactly what I was getting into. You do hear about girls being kidnapped and being put in houses and forced to be prostitutes, but it just doesn't happen around here. . . . I got kidnapped once and taken to L.A. You might say, I took off with a girl to L.A.—I get on my kicks where I think I hate men—and it turned out that she was working for these seven men in this organization. And each of them had anywhere from five to twenty girls and half of them were prostitutes and half of them were boosters. And it turned out that she was some kind of a recruiter. So they kept me in a pad for a few days and I turned a few tricks and as soon as they learned to trust me they cut me loose and I took off and came back down here. You can't keep anyone prisoner, not if they don't want to be.

QUESTION: *Those girls called call girls, are they just a small organized group, or are they syndicate? Do they have Mafia connections?*

SANDY: I don't know, and if I did I wouldn't talk about it! This organization that I was talking about, I think, was just a group of businessmen who got together, got some girls together—and some of them are just plain housewives—introduce them to their business associates and collect a cut.

QUESTION: *Do you have steady customers?*

SANDY: Not now. I haven't turned a trick for, well, I was going to say two years, but one of those was spent in honor camp. I've been out for six months.

QUESTION: *Did you have steady customers?*

SANDY: Oh, yeah. We have a code among us just like cocktail waitresses—"If you leave my tricks alone, I'll leave your tricks alone." So, that way, it's safe for any of my tricks to go out and on the street and ask, "Is Sandy here?" and they'll say, "Oh, she went to so-and-so place" or to have him call me or that I'll be right back.

QUESTION: *How did you get involved or why did you get involved with a pimp? And, what kind of situation was it?*

SANDY: That was very strange because I was the girl who laughed at all the other girls giving their money to their pimps. All the pimps hated me, and I got to keep all my money. It was great. And all the queens down on the street took care of me so that I didn't get hurt. He just caught me at the right time. Things were going bad. I was working for only $1.65 an hour, getting strung-out, living at home—my mother and I cannot get along when we live together—my parole officer was putting pressure on me. He just said, "Come on, baby." And I said, "Right on." And I was gone. And I didn't get away for three months. I had to turn myself in to get away from him.

QUESTION: *What sort of a percentage do they take?*

SANDY: He took all of mine. He left me money to eat on. Never enough to get anywhere far. When I was working, he was with me. When the trick and I were in the hotel room, he was right outside the door.

QUESTION: *What kind of protection did he give?*

SANDY: You've got to remember, you're there, with no clothes on, with a man that could be anything. He could be a sex maniac, a murderer, he could be anything. You don't know who you're with. Some of them want to pay you, screw you, then take back the money they gave you and the rest you've made if you've got any. One time I had a guy pull a gun on me. Boy, did I give him his money back—FAST! But with Ed outside the door, all I had to do was raise my voice and he was right there. He'd knock on the door and that was usually enough to frustrate the trick and make him want to get out of there quick. Good protection.

QUESTION: *I'd think that the fear of never knowing whom you were with would be so great that you'd want to quit.*

SANDY: I wasn't scared of anybody. You've got to remember that I was strung-out most of the time and I didn't have sense enough to be scared. I was superwoman!

QUESTION: *Why did you do your second trick? Why did you decide to repeat your actions?*

SANDY: My girlfriend and I were talking about that. She was always telling about how she could turn tricks and all the money she was making, and blah, blah, blah. And I just listened to her. And then I pulled that first one and we talked about it. And she said, "Well, tomorrow night we'll go out and see how much money we can make." And I just said, "Right on." We got loaded and got dressed up and went out and made some money. We each made about $100 that evening and I thought, oooh, that's great. I'm not even tired!

QUESTION: *What are you doing now?*

SANDY: I am an assembler. Once again I'm just starting out, and there have been plenty of weeks when I've been hungry and wanted to turn a trick. And one night I went out and got one, and when we got home I found that my house had been burglarized, that everything I owned and had worked so hard for was either strewn all over the house or gone. And I was so mad that I threw him out. I went crazy and called the police, raving. If someone came up to me and offered me $100 for a trick, $100 can do a lot and I am not above sleeping with a strange man, I don't know if I would or not. I probably would, for $100, after I was pretty sure that he wasn't going to cheat me.

QUESTION: *With so much venereal disease going around, how can you avoid getting infected?*

SANDY: If you're making big money, if you're turning the $50's on up, you don't usually have to worry about it. I contracted syphilis in about my fourth year. When I worked down on 5th and Market, the sailors and screwballs are not too clean. You catch clap pretty often. As a matter of fact, I hustled for nine years with nothing but a douche bag and I never got pregnant. I think that somehow I had gotten things infected once to the point that it made me sterile. When I went to honor camp for a year recently, they unsterilized me. The first thing I did when I got out was get pregnant. No, you don't avoid disease.

QUESTION: *Did you take it upon yourself to get a check periodically?*

SANDY: No, I was one of the lucky ones. I can damn near always tell if I have something. Within twenty-four hours, my discharge starts.

And until my discharge starts, no one else can get it. So very seldom did I purposely go out and trick when I knew I had a disease. It's a bummer. It's also a bummer having to tell the people you trick with that they might have the disease because you do. I remember one time when I had syphilis, and I guess I'd had it, oh, about six months before I found out, by accident. And I was dating this one dude who I was planning to marry at the time, I had a steady job and had stopped tricking and was doing real good, and then I had to tell my boyfriend about my disease. That was a bummer too.

QUESTION: *What is the abortion rate among prostitutes?*

SANDY: I have no idea.

QUESTION: *How difficult is it for a prostitute to obtain an abortion?*

SANDY: Then, you had to go to Tijuana to get one. Now, you can just go to County Hospital. It's very easy to get one now. That's where I got mine when I got pregnant. And they treat it quite lightly, quite lightly. You know, they just say, "Well, this is just something that I have to do, blah, blah, blah . . . O.K., now you can leave."

QUESTION: *How expensive was it?*

SANDY: Medical took care of it. Now, if I had been working on the job I'm working on now, they probably wouldn't have paid for it.

QUESTION: *Can you just walk into the hospital and say that you want an abortion or do you have to talk to a psychiatrist or what?*

SANDY: Yeah, I talked to a psychiatrist. We talked about drugs. I liked him too. But I think that's good, you know, because if a person doesn't want a kid, they aren't going to treat it right and if they do want it, they wouldn't be looking for an abortion.

QUESTION: *Do you have a variety of rates for various techniques or whatever you want to call 'em?*

SANDY: Yeah, there's a variety. You always try to get as much as you can. Depending on the appearance of your trick, the way he carries himself, whatever. You can usually get for a straight lay $10 and then from there you just go on up. I've had men pay as much as $50 or $60 for a straight lay. These were men who, well, there was just something about me they wanted. Or sometimes it's just something that strikes you. Hell, I'd pay [names actor] $5000 for a lay, I swear to God! If I had it! Now, if they ask, if they say, "How much?" Then you say something like $15. Then if they say something like, "Well, what if I want a little head?" Then you say whatever you think they can afford, like $5, $10, whatever. You just work it out somehow, but you always get as much as you can. I didn't steal from my tricks. Not because I don't steal, but because, well, working the same area daily, they're going to be seeing you again. I don't like to be whipped on. I am not a masochist in any manner. I might be hurting myself in other ways, but I don't like anyone hurting me or making me hurt—not physically. Not mentally either, but I'd prefer it mentally rather than physically. I just don't like it. So I didn't steal, I didn't con or whatever. So I didn't have some of the problems some of the other broads had.

QUESTION: *I'd like to know something about your childhood. Did you have brothers and sisters? What was your relationship to your father?*

SANDY: I never saw my father to this day. My mother and I get along just fine when we live separately. While I was a child and growing up, she worked all day. When I was in kindergarten I used to dress myself, fix my own breakfast, and go to school downtown. I've always taken care of myself. I have one brother who is six years younger than me. My baby brother, 6 feet 4 inches, all 200 and some pounds of him. We get along fine. Maybe I picked on him a little too much when we were kids, I don't know. He picked on me a lot too, though.

QUESTION: *What was your mother's attitude toward men?*

SANDY: My mother has not been out with a man since my brother was born that I know of, and that was when I was old enough to realize what Mama was doing at night. My mother just gets up in the morning and goes to work. . . . This last year she finally joined some group at work so that she has some social life, some outside activity. For fifteen to twenty years, my mother got up and went to work, came home, looked after the kids, martyred herself the whole time she stayed in the house until we couldn't stand it anymore and would run the streets. And that was her whole existence. Both my brother and I did get in trouble; I'm still having trouble with the law. My brother's been clean now for, gosh, I guess he still pops a few pills once in a while and smokes a little weed, but other than that, no trouble with the law for almost two or three years. He's a big foreman in Los Angeles, doing great.

QUESTION: *What did he think about your occupation? What was his reaction?*

SANDY: He doesn't like it at all now. Two or three years ago, when he was in with the law, he thought I was what was happening. I was big Sis. He enjoyed telling his girlfriends, "My sister's been to the joint three times." It made him look big cuz his scene was looking big and bad. He loved it. But now I'm a dirty rotten so-and-so. Cuz he's straightened out. A complete switch about.

QUESTION: *Have you ever thought about being one man's mistress?*

SANDY: Yeah, but if you're going to be one man's mistress, why not get a man you really dig and let him be your for-real man? Because, I would rather be with twenty-five men for ten seconds than a man I cannot stand for twenty-four hours. I cannot handle it. Someone touching and kissing on me that I do not want touching and kissing on me.

QUESTION: *Have you ever thought about getting married since this last time?*

SANDY: Yeah, as a matter of fact I'm looking for one right now, but it's pretty difficult under the circumstances. And right now the kind of man that excites me and the kind I want are not really the kind I need. Unless if I'm going to change my life at all. If I'm going to stay in the subculture, and stay getting high.

QUESTION: *Suppose that your child had been a girl instead of a boy. Would that have had any effect on your way of life?*

SANDY: Gee, I don't know. That's a good question, I really don't know.

QUESTION: *Are you caring for your son now or is he in a foster home or what?*

SANDY: My mother has custody of my son as of 1967 when I went to the joint for the second time. He either had to go to a foster home or my mother. I see him almost every weekend. She keeps screaming, "Come and get your boy." But if I ever do, it'll kill her because that's all she lives for now, is my son. So I don't really have anything.

QUESTION: *Did you have any romantic relationships in your profession as a prostitute?*

SANDY: I've met some real close friends. I mean, the kind you keep for years and years and years, that I've met first when they were my trick. But when you're trying to stay clean, when you're trying to do right, and you need them, you hesitate to call, because it's really a bummer to have to cop to you're doing badly again. Romance and prostitution don't go together too well. You kid yourself. Uh, that pimp I had, I tried to believe desperately that I loved him—I couldn't think of any other reason why I was there. But how can you love somebody who puts scars on your body and tells you, "Bitch, if you don't make a certain amount of money you don't live anymore," and then takes all of your money? And that's the way they do it. He used to whip on me. He took me off the streets because we fell in love, so here I am living in a hotel and he's still hanging around with all his pimp friends and evidently, well, they like to talk about what big men they are, how much money their whores make, and who made the most, who did the biggest boost that night, or whatever their thing is. And evidently, somebody said something to him about him taking me off the street and the fact that he only had me, when he usually keeps three or four of them. And so he came home and whipped me. He couldn't tell his friends, "So what?" or whatever. He had to take it out on me. Oh, he whipped good on women. It was somethin' else.

QUESTION: *What's a boost?*

SANDY: It's stealing, theft.

QUESTION: *When you first started prostitution, was that a hang-up at all? The romantic aspects?*

SANDY: No, I never hustled when I had a man. Ever. I'm so aggressive it's going to be my way or no way at all, so that things never lasted very long. I'd either get mad and throw him out or he'd just get to where he couldn't take it anymore. It just gets to a point where it won't work. And my relationships usually last anywhere from two weeks to three months. Three months, that's definitely love! I've only had a couple of those three monthers! But, I do not hustle when I have a man. I expect him to take care of me or I will work too. I really had a thing going about pimps and giving my money to them.

QUESTION: *When you went before the courts for your legal processing, did you find that when they knew you were a prostitute they resented you for this and punished you for being a prostitute rather than the charge you were there for, or both?*

SANDY: I think they punished me because I told them to go screw themselves. See, in 1960, they weren't too many white girls going with black men. You know that. And I was sixteen, and I used to give the traffic department something like $10,000 a year. They used to just get ridiculous messing with me and talk about me so bad that I'd just want to crawl away and hide. Any way they could, they used to mess with me, that's the only way I can say it, they used to screw with me and insist that I went with black men for this reason, not because I wanted to. And they couldn't get it through their heads that I preferred them. And I think that's why they started messing with me. And then with my little smart mouth, big smart mouth—I was a terror when I was that age—I mean, here I was hustling for years and years and years and they never had a case on me—and that pissed them off—the vice were just too uptight. They couldn't get a burglary cuz I didn't steal. The narcotics they did—I think, in 1961 I got my first narcotics beef—then they started slapping them to me hot and heavy. I have eighteen of them, not convicted of all of them, but Jesus Christ. And when they started catching me, I mean 1) attitude hostile, 2) cursed me out all the way to the station, 3) tried to kick me in the left knee, etc., you know, whether I did or didn't. So by the time I get in front of the judge, they sock it to me anyway. Right now if you picked up my rap sheet, it looks horrible, I swear. I was so embarrassed when I took it to my new boss. It really looked like he was hiring Bonnie or something. And I'm not Bonnie; I'm a person. And I feel just like you guys do. Maybe a little cynical, I've had a little bit more experience than some of you at some things. Most of it's been bad.

QUESTION: *Did prostitution ever afford you to live really high?*

SANDY: Yeah.

QUESTION: *How much money do you estimate that you've made?*

SANDY: I never really stopped to figure it out. Now, remember, I'm a dope addict at the same time. Oh, wow! A lot of money. Maybe one year $30,000 to $40,000 and maybe the next I would only work maybe six months and make about $10,000 or $15,000. That's a lot of money.

QUESTION: *What kind of feelings or relationships did you have regarding other prostitutes? And how did you feel about your tricks? Do you feel closer to other tricks or to other prostitutes, that is, when you're on the street?*

SANDY: Being a prostitute is kinda like being a dope addict, you don't become close with your connection, not really close. It's gotta be business, he's gotta have your money. You don't make friends with other dope addicts because they want your dope. And you don't make close friends with people who don't do dope because you're on a different keel. Prostitution, you'd think that we were blood sisters, that we were raised together, that we never left one another except to go turn tricks, but that's just the act, the facade we put on. Respect, yes, I have a lot of respect for those girls out there. Some of them work hard, some are dirty dogs. But, to really like or communicate with them. . . . I would never go to one of them and say, "Boy, I feel really blue, depressed," or "So-and-so happened today." You could tell them that, but what they would say would be so superficial you might as well, you just wasted breath. "Oh, yeah. Well, that's too bad. Excuse me, I've gotta go." With the tricks, I managed to develop some real good relationships. I like those men out there—these poor misled husbands. They're honest and generally very, very nice. Only about 25 percent come on bad.

QUESTION: *What kind of man are you attracted to and what kind of man do you think you need?*

SANDY: The kind of man I'm attracted to, well, number one, if they don't get high now, they've got to have gotten high sometime in their life. I'll not have a thing to do with some dude who's going to preach to me about dope who hasn't tried it and doesn't know a thing he's talking about. I just can't be bothered. I hate people who talk about something that they don't know anything about. If he has been involved with dope, 99 times of 100 he still is. So that's the kind of man. If he's got something going with dope you can bet he's hustlin' somewhere. Cuz, once a hustler, always a hustler of some kind or another. Always with my boss out at work, I flirt and kid and get my way. I haven't plugged in my gun [air gun] at work yet. All the other ladies do. I did rotten in the training period, but I passed. It's just that once you've been in the line, it's a way of life. I don't care if your hustle is just having learned people on the streets. You see all these people hitting these organizations now, ex-offenders. They've learned people in the joint and outside of the joint. Now they can sit down and write a proposition in about $25,000 or $30,000 a year. They're in home. And it's a hustle. It might be what they do best, but it's a hustle. It's easy. They're doing what they would do for free. What I'm saying is that it's hard to not do what you know you're good at. It depends on your code. You have to live with yourself, not anybody else.

QUESTION: *Is your mother very moralistic?*

SANDY: She doesn't smoke or drink, or curse or, well, I got her to say "damn" a couple of times.

QUESTION: *Did she preach to you a lot when you were young?*

SANDY: Yeah. My mother, she martyred herself—"Look what I've done for you kids and look how you do me." At first we fell for it. She used to have fits every time she didn't get her own way. And after she saw that we weren't going for them anymore, after we realized that fits only came when Mama wanted them to come, it was just that martyr bit all the time. I've had a little bit of the therapy with my mom, too, but if you're pointing out something bad to them, they are going to get defensive. I couldn't get through to her; she'd just clam up.

QUESTION: *Have you ever read anything about prostitution and American wives? That prostitutes are very thankful for the attitude of the American wife because she increases her business because of it?*

SANDY: I don't know what to think about American wives. They're gettin' weird lately. I have had women approach me and say, "I don't want my husband going out on me. He wants to screw you, he has told me so. Could we all three go to bed together?" and all this bullshit. And for free! That just really did freak me out. I can imagine. Somebody touch my man in front of me? No way! I couldn't do it. They just act like it's no big thing nowadays. They're really weird. Hell, I know a guy who hasn't been home in four months and his wife is still there, patiently waiting. And he calls her every couple of weeks. It's like the wife, once she got him hooked or has the security of his wealth or maybe it's just his name, I don't know.

QUESTION: *How much do you usually know about the men you sleep with?*

SANDY: Nothing.

QUESTION: *How about a first name?*

SANDY: They tell you a name. You don't know if it's theirs or not. I took time ordinarily, unless I was just stone flat backin' it at a fast pace, just ch, ch, ch, ch, where half the time you don't even undress. If they act like they're not even going to play with you, you just throw your skirt up. When I was in a more relaxed position, and if I had the time, I would always take the time to sit and have a drink or cigarette with them, or lay in the bed with them. That's a trippy time. You've just finished doing it and they're satisfied and you're satisfied, you've taken care of the man. You've got a pocket full of money and you can take time for a cigarette. You don't have to treat him like a dirty dog. I really get down on some of them about their shit. They just talk to their men so bad. Course, some men dig that too.

QUESTION: *Do you have any idea what percentage of the men you slept with were husbands?*

SANDY: Seventy percent, I guess, offhand.

QUESTION: *Before you had the relationship, did you get the money first?*

SANDY: You get that money before you even undress! Well, that too depends, cuz if you're trickin' with a regular, you don't have to worry. But a first or one-night thing, you get the money before you take off a hairpin! You'll not get it back any other way, because he doesn't want to spend it, but he wants you worse than he doesn't want to spend it. Or a piece of ass, not necessarily you.

QUESTION: *What has therapy done for you?*

SANDY: It gave me a big hand. I got into some heavy therapy. I'm very aware of why I do the things I do, what caused me to do the things I did, and all that stuff. But nobody tells me how to, uh, what to do with what I know. In other words, they say, "Well, you're lonely. Don't be lonely." "What the hell you mean, 'Don't be lonely'?" I said, "Where do you go not to be lonely?" And they tell you go to church. If they're

a little bit more realistic they'll tell you, "Well, go out. Meet somebody."
I just can't get dressed up and meet somebody. Number one, if I go to a
night club I've got to be a pickup, just from the getup. So that puts it off.
I don't know. I don't know where to go to meet men that might interest
me. To become unlonely. I don't know what to use instead of dope to
fill whatever it is that needs filled. I see a lot of people in our culture
say, "Well, trip out on the birds and bees and flowers." Well, screw the
birds and bees and flowers! I don't like birds, bees, and flowers. It
doesn't turn me on.

QUESTION: *You say you don't know what to use instead of dope,
and yet you're not willing to date someone who doesn't use it. I'm wondering how much you're willing to take the responsibility for your changing if that's what you want to call it.*

SANDY: I think that I'm probably to the point to where I feel a
little bit old, a little bit used, and I'm a little uptight about that. Twelve
of my years have been given to the state and I'll never see that again.
Twelve years. I've got scars, inside and out. I don't know what I'm waiting for. I really don't. I'm on parole; I'm on probation. I still get therapy
and I sit and help everybody else. I don't get helped. I still get high. I
don't get anything. I don't hear anybody giving me anything to take the
place of dope. So I sneak around, and I keep a full bottle of urine at all
times so that if my parole officer slips up on me, I'll have it. And it's
really a bummer. I don't know where I'm going. I don't even know what
I want.

QUESTION: *Why do you keep the urine on you?*

SANDY: CRC is the center for narcotics addicts, and you have to
be tested once a week, two surprises a month. You urinate in a bottle
and they send it to a lab to see if you've used any kind of drugs. If
you have, then you're violated.

QUESTION: *What kind of drugs do you use?*

SANDY: Uppers and downers, no heroin and no weed. I don't
know why no weed, I just don't use it.

QUESTION: *I've just finished reading the* Elegant Prostitute, *which
I think you might enjoy reading. And there was one girl who said that
quitting was really hard and that psychotherapy was helping her.*

SANDY: I wonder if it really helped. I'm really curious. Even
people that I do communicate with, which is mainly ex-offenders. . . .
They get going; they find their way; they find their fix, so to speak. And
they go right on. And the more successful they get, if you really dig them
and like them, you'll stay away from them cuz you're not successful.
And if you go down, you don't want them to go too. You also don't

want to impose on their lives. They say, "Call me if you need me. Two or three in the morning, that's groovy." I'm not going to call them, one of my friends, at two o'clock in the morning, take him away from his wife and kids after he's worked all day. You're an imposition on your friends when you're like this and they're doing okay. You have to let them go on.

QUESTION: *Going back to your high school days, did you run with a group or were you a loner? Did you date?*

SANDY: I was 5 foot 2 by 5 foot 2 and always a foot taller than everybody else was. Men come taller now or something. In my day I was always taller, like they always came up to my neck. Like I said, I was 5 foot 2 by 5 foot 2 and wore glasses. I just wasn't too lovely. So when the other girls started dating, I started running with the rough group and acting like I didn't care. I guess we attracted each other cuz I was so hostile. I took it out on the teachers or anybody else that was around. I got into the group fairly easily. I had a boyfriend, before I got sent up when I was fourteen, that I had known before. But, heck, we only kissed a couple of times. And then I got sent away and I never saw him again until I was seventeen. And when I got out all my fat had gone away. And I was lovely, like a butterfly, and all the men wanted me and I was in my glory.

QUESTION: *When were you sent to prison?*

SANDY: I got sent up when I was thirteen and I didn't come out until after I was seventeen. To Norwalk and then to Las Willicas, then to Ventura without getting out.

QUESTION: *What was that for originally?*

SANDY: Incorrigible. I just needed twenty-four-hour supervision is what it amounted to. That's what they said, anyway.

QUESTION: *What was it? Did you fight with your mother?*

SANDY: No, I had been sent to juvenile hall twelve times for everything from shoplifting to runaway to, you name it almost.

QUESTION: *After that time then, did you run around with a tough group, hard guys?*

SANDY: Yeah, well, I didn't realize it 'til many years later. You know, I helped someone kick heroin once. He told me that he had the flu and I was seventeen. Two years later I suddenly went WOW! I was really dumb and young. By the time I got out I though I was gay cuz I had never had a man. I was always carrying on with my women. Then I met Dave's father and we started dating. I dated him for about two months. When I met him he was about thirty-two and a three-time loser already and I was sixteen going on seventeen. I guess you'd call him pretty hardcore.

QUESTION: *Have you ever been arrested for prostitution?*

SANDY: No, I never did get arrested on that rap. I don't know why because I tricked with two or three policemen. In fact, that time I was going to turn a trick after being out, when my house got burglarized, that guy was a cop and he said, "Don't bother calling the cops." And I said, "What do you mean, don't bother?" And he said that he was a cop and that it wouldn't do any good. But at that time I was so mad that I was going to blow it anyway. And he had already blown it by agreein' to trick with me. And he just finished smoking a joint of mine.

COMMENTARY

Statements made by our informant seem to support the "pull theory" and also some of those emphasizing background factors.

Sandy came from a broken home, but since she never saw her father, there is really little basis in Sandy's case for the Freudian theory (excessive hatred or love for the father). Sandy never experienced any male contacts in her mother's life. "My mother has not been out with a man since my brother was born that I know of." Thus, there is no basis to believe that her mother's relations with men set the pattern that Sandy later emulated. Her mother (not on tape) is a store clerk, and she has led a fairly pristine life. We see no evidence that her mother's relation with men led to any pattern of "masochism," and Sandy denies any such tendencies on her part:

> I didn't steal from my tricks. Not because I don't steal, but because, well, working the same area daily, they're going to be seeing you again. I don't like to be whipped on. I am not a masochist in any manner. I might be hurting myself in other ways, but I don't like anyone hurting me or making me hurt—not physically.

Nor is there any evidence of "infant mentality," since Sandy has been very much on her own from an early age. She was not seduced at an early age. She kept her virginity until age seventeen.

One aspect of personality theory seems to bear out somewhat in Sandy's case. She might fit the category "emotionally dangerous to men." She has admitted to privately that she finds it hard to keep a man because she "always ends up castrating him." When asked about her romantic relations, she replied:

I'm so aggressive it's going to be my way or no way at all, so that things never lasted very long. I'd either get mad and throw him out or he'd just get to where he couldn't take it anymore. It just gets to a point where it won't work.

Whatever may have been her childhood background, it seems that her "career" as a prostitute has its roots in her early official labeling as a delinquent and subsequent institutional treatment. Sandy, somewhat left alone as a child, was overweight and unattractive as a teen-ager, but she was able to get the attention of some delinquent peers through her aggressive behavior in school. Her associations with this "tough crowd" led at the age of thirteen to institutionalization (charged with incorrigibility). Her experiences in institutional custody may have been quite significant, not only in terms of the stigmatic effects of labeling and the influence of delinquent peers she met, but also because while in institutional care, she engaged in acts of homosexuality. She admitted to us privately that she committed lesbian acts then, and actually thought of herself as a lesbian up to her first heterosexual experience at age seventeen. This lesbianism may have been significant in breaking down normative barriers to sexual deviance, rendering Sandy open to a drift into prostitution.

At seventeen, she experienced her first heterosexual relations, and became pregnant and gave birth to a son. Her husband was sent to prison. This led her to resume her contact with delinquent peers who introduced her to drugs and with whom she was sexually promiscuous. At this point, differential association seemed to explain the transition to prostitution:

My girlfriend and I were talking about that. She was always telling about how she could turn tricks and all the money she was making. . . . And I just listened to her. And then I pulled that first one and we talked about it. And she said, "Well, tomorrow night we'll go out and see how much money we can make." And I just said, "Right on." We got loaded and got dressed up and went out and made some money.

Sandy was attracted to prostitution based upon her economic need to provide for herself and son and also based upon her need for drugs (primarily amphetamines). But we should also comment that Sandy was also "pulled" into prostitution. She actually enjoyed "the life" for some time, and it gratified her strong inclination to "crave attention." She actually enjoyed her contacts with her "tricks" (and in fact at this time is living with a former trick), as revealed by her statement:

With the tricks, I managed to develop some real good relationships. I like those men out there—those poor misled husbands. They're honest and generally very, very nice. Only about 25 percent come on bad.

The "pull" factor is also found in Sandy's comments about the prostitute way of life. She claims she was "not suckered into it." She made favorable comments about the easy money and hours. Most impressive, however, is her belief that many prostitutes engage in prostitution not for the money per se, but because they are "hooked on prostitution."

In many ways, the interactional process whereby Sandy became a prostitute fits the model of typing and labeling described by Nannette Davis. Davis's model is based upon an exploratory study of thirty prostitutes who appeared to drift into prostitution from institutionalization during early adolescence, to increasing promiscuity, to initial prostitute experiences, to final adoption of the deviant identity.[7]

Certainly Sandy's comments indicate some dismal aspects of prostitution—addiction to drugs, the beatings by her pimp, venereal disease. But the overwhelming impression our informant gave us was that prostitution was a way of life worth justifying. Sandy decried her years in prison, but not her former life as a prostitute. Such comments appear to reflect the inadequacies of external control mechanisms in curbing prostitution when internal control factors are absent. The Reckless' model of containment would appear to be thus supported. In addition, Sandy's attitudes of ambivalence may be reflective of a more general attitude of ambivalence toward prostitution in the larger United States society. This ambivalence will be expanded upon later in this chapter.

SHIRLEY: A Masseuse

Bryant and Palmer have proposed a typology of four varieties of massage parlors. They are categorized as: "genuine massage parlors" that provide physical therapy, usually staffed by masseurs; "rip-offs" that promise erotic satisfaction without delivering either a legitimate massage or sexual gratification; "disguised brothels" that provide "a full repertoire of sexual services," and the "massage and masturbation only" parlors.[8] Our next interview is with Shirley, who appears to be employed in a parlor that would fit Bryant and Palmer's third type, a "disguised brothel." Shirley appeared before our class and described her more "modernized" profession.

QUESTION: *Do you consider yourself a prostitute?*

SHIRLEY: Yes, as well as a masseuse, and a healer, and a couple of other things.

QUESTION: *Why do you consider yourself a prostitute if you're simply engaging in an art of massage?*

SHIRLEY: Well, I'm not. I'm also engaging in sexual services for money.

QUESTION: *How is this accomplished? How does this happen without your having been arrested?*

SHIRLEY: I'm smart and I have never been arrested. Hopefully, I never will be.

QUESTION: *Could you explain how you protect yourself from being arrested?*

SHIRLEY: Oh, I should mention, in case anybody in here is a Junior Cop. No, I won't. That's something that we girls keep among ourselves. There are a couple of things we know about people which help us to tell if they're police. Solicitation is breaking the law. You can come in and get a massage and get so turned on you're climbing the walls and unless you solicit me, too bad.

QUESTION: *So a person has to kind of know the ropes, it's not something that just automatically happens.*

SHIRLEY: Right, but that might be in other parlors.

QUESTION: *What is the usual routine at a massage parlor?*

SHIRLEY: I tell him to take his clothes off.

QUESTION: *You do this to him or he takes his own clothes off?*

SHIRLEY: I do it to him. It depends on what kind of massage he buys as to whether I take my clothes off. I'm working in two different places at the moment and one of the places offers a ten-dollar half-hour nude. The guy's a fool if he doesn't buy that. I'm going to take my clothes off for ten dollars, which is what I prefer. I'd rather get my clothes off. I'm a lot more comfortable giving a massage, and who wants to be standing over somebody and he's all stretched out on the table and he doesn't have any clothes on, and there I am fully clothed and I'm supposed to be trying to arouse this man sexually? It's a lot easier if I take it off. And besides, then he can touch me and if he touches me, then a rapport builds up. Now, it depends upon the way he touches me, too. I don't want him grabbing me. So sometimes you have to kinda calm somebody down while you're arousing them in another area. It does get tricky.

QUESTION: *The guy would know the terms, or would he bluntly ask you for sexual intercourse or something?*

SHIRLEY: Most people are pretty suave and debonair. Somebody who comes in and flatly states what he wants is not going to get good service, at least not where I work. He might at some place down the street that has lights around the window and is open twenty-four hours, but I cater to men who come in in suits who have professional jobs. They're doctors, they're lawyers, they're professors. I've got a lot of high school teachers. I don't cater to sailors or the people you see running around downtown. So the men who see me are not going to ask something bluntly. They're going to do it with a little savoir-faire.

QUESTION: *If they're professional people, aren't they kind of concerned about protecting their own identity too?*

SHIRLEY: I haven't run across anybody who has protected his identity to the point that I didn't know exactly who he was. For one thing, all I have to do is go out and read his license plate and I can tell real easy, but I'm not interested in tracking anybody down unless they rip me off, and I've only been ripped off about three times.

QUESTION: *So you have a kind of professional ethics protecting the client's confidentiality?*

SHIRLEY: Oh, right. I wouldn't mention anybody's name and I know that I've done some people whose names you would recognize.

QUESTION: *What percentage of masseuses would you say engage in acts of prostitution?*

SHIRLEY: I don't know them all. Most of my girlfriends are prostitutes, but I would say there are three parlors in town that I know of that are straight, so you can take it from there.

QUESTION: *Do massage parlors have any kind of union?*

SHIRLEY: Right, exactly. It's like Thursday night. One of the girls who used to work where I work got busted, and she heard the "officers" speaking about a raid they were going to do Friday night, this past Friday night, so her ears perked up. When she was released—all they did was hassle her because she hadn't done anything to be busted for—and we put up with a lot of this, and she called up and said: "Hey, I got busted and this is what I heard, and if you know anybody who's working in a parlor, call them up and warn them there is going to be a raid in the city." One of my girlfriends is going with our Fuller Brush man who is a young long-hair and he caters to massage parlors. He knows quite a few girls, obviously. So he went in and told some of the girls, "Hey, there's going to be a raid tonight—watch yourself!" He went into one. I'm sure everybody's seen the Soft Touch. Obviously, I don't work at the Soft Touch. He went into the Soft Touch and he said, "There's going to be a raid tonight!" and they said, "How do you know?" And he said, "My lady's in the same business you are." "Well, how does she know?" "Well, she found out there's going to be a raid—watch yourself!" They got busted. And there is a lot of cooperation going on, if the other girls will let it. But most girls in this business are so jealous—they're so upright—that they won't let anybody else in even if it's in a helpful way. But I would say there are four or five parlors where there is some cooperation. I mean, sure, we're competitive, but there's cooperative competitiveness.

QUESTION: *Is that because there's enough business for everybody?*

SHIRLEY: Sure, I wouldn't be making so much money if there wasn't enough business for everybody. The better you are, the more business you're going to have. We like to think that we're one of the very best in town.

QUESTION: *But there is a certain element of rivalry or competition?*

SHIRLEY: Oh, definitely competition. You look at the ads on Sunday morning and you see all the different ads. I'm always trying to come up with a different ad, because—"Ask for our special, whoop de do"—everybody has a special going.

QUESTION: *You mentioned before class that you were aware of female undercover officers coming in to work as masseuses.*

SHIRLEY: And they're going extras and the whole bit.

QUESTION: *She was actually doing it?*

SHIRLEY: Yeah, yeah, but luckily, for some reason that day everybody was very cool. I think the girl she was working with wasn't feeling well and said, "I'll answer the phone, you take the customers." And this undercover agent did all the people, did all the extras, got all the money. And the lady who owns the place found out about it and said, "Bye bye." Somebody called her up and said, "You have a snitch working for you." She was gone in no time. We were lucky.

QUESTION: *Does it become a matter of policy? Are the girls pressured?*

SHIRLEY: Well, I've never worked for a man and I will never work for a man. Nothing against you guys, now, but you don't know how to run massage parlors. Unless you're in it as a lifetime customer, and that's bad too, you don't know what goes on in the room between the girl and the customer, and only another female can relate to that, and therefore only she can run a business where you're going to be comfortable. And most men who run a business are in it strictly for the money. They don't give a fuck about the girl. As a matter of fact, all they want out of the girl is her money, occasionally her body, and as far as I'm concerned, that's pimping. I won't work for a pimp.

So I only work for ladies, and I'm sure that all the ladies I've worked for know what is going on because they're participating. I work with women who work with me, which makes it a lot more comfortable. I'd rather work with someone who's going to work with me than just sit back and go, "You do this, and you do that." I don't like to feel I'm being bossed. As a matter of fact, I'm managing one of the places I work for now. I've learned a lot over the last two years. If the people you work with don't feel like they have a boss, they're going to work a lot better and be a lot happier and they're going to make you a lot more money. A place doesn't make money unless it gives extras. There is one here in town that is virtually straight and the reason that it makes so much money is that it's situated near downtown and it caters to sailors and a lower element and the come-on is so strong, like "Miss Love." If I was a dude and I bought a massage from "Miss Love," I'd think I was gonna get the works. You don't. You get a good massage. They give excellent massages there, but that's it.

QUESTION: *You mentioned before class that you were married. What are your husband's feelings about your profession?*

SHIRLEY: For seven months we both pretended like he didn't know what I was doing and that I really wasn't doing it. You have to understand I've been married to this man for ten years. He's got long hair and a beard. He's a fox. We were separated for three years and two years ago we got back together. Just as I started this business, like, I'd been working fifteen days and he decided we'd get back together. And I couldn't stop. After fifteen days, I was hooked. I really liked it. So we pretended like nothing was going on, and then one night we were having a fight and he said, "Well, you really don't expect me to believe that you're as straight as you try to palm yourself off as?" And I said, "No." And that was it. Ever since then we've gotten more and more honest with each other. As a matter of fact, a couple of weeks ago somebody asked him, "Well, what does Shirley do?" And he said, "She's a prostitute." He's passed with flying colors. He's doing beautifully. Other than the fact that he's an alcoholic, he's doing great.

QUESTION: *Were you influenced by economic necessity to become a prostitute?*

SHIRLEY: Oh, very definitely. The rent was due. Money was the reason I got into it. I was coming from a place, I don't know if any of you remember the big commune. I lived in this commune with all these hip people, you know, who gave it away every night. You know, the place was filled with men, and there was all this sleeping around going on and the next thing I know I'm out of business and the commune closed down, the shop closed down. I had to live by myself and I'd never lived by myself before. Here I was twenty-eight years old when this happened. I had to figure out some way to make some money. I had been a secretary. I had been a cashier. I had worked for finance companies and construction firms. I was a waitress at a local restaurant. I don't want to do any of that stuff any more. I wanted to do something where I made a lot of money, I was in control, I wasn't working for a man. I turned into a feminist. I just didn't want to work for a man. This was the only way to do it. I have a lovely girlfriend who was going to come here with me today, who started me in the business and I thought, she's beautiful, she's intelligent, she's getting away with it. If she can do it, I can do it.

QUESTION: *So, actually, you didn't have a delinquency background as a teen-ager?*

SHIRLEY: I broke as many laws as anybody else in my day.

QUESTION: *I mean as far as going to juvenile court.*

SHIRLEY: I was never in juvenile court. I was never molested. My mother is a divorced lady who brought my sister and I up. She was a secretary here at State for a number of years. She's a *lady*, you know, and she brought my sister and I up to be ladies, and hopefully I conduct myself as a lady. I was never a bad kid. I threw a wild party once, and the police came and broke it up. I used to get drunk occasionally.

QUESTION: *As a teen-ager, what were your relations with peers? Were you an insider?*

SHIRLEY: I was a grind when I was a teen-ager. I was a bookworm. I got really good grades. I was rather dull. I didn't know anything about makeup. My mother was not very wealthy, obviously, if she was working here. I didn't have nice clothes. I never got anything that was fashionable when it was fashionable. Remember the white sharkskin pleated skirts? The week they went out, I got one. Remember flats, everybody wore flats? My mom made me wear oxfords because they were good for my feet. "There's nothing wrong with my feet, Mother. Let me wear flats." I led a deprived childhood in the manner of clothing. Other than that, plenty of food, everything was great, my mom loved me.

QUESTION: *Did you go to a decent high school?*

SHIRLEY: I went to a middle-class local high school.

QUESTION: *So you weren't in with a rowdy crowd and you were pretty much of a loner?*

SHIRLEY: Yes, like, I was never rushed for a social club. I started here at State in '63, and I think one sorority sent me a notice. They knew. They could tell right away I was not sorority material. At that time I was a virgin. I was a virgin till I was nineteen years old, and this was back in the days when you were supposed to be a virgin when you got married. You saved it for your husband. How dull! If I had it all to do over again, fourteen years old, man. I was full-figured when I was fifteen years old and I saved it for another four years. I don't know why.

QUESTION: *I'm trying to figure out what kind of crowd you hung around with when you were in high school.*

SHIRLEY: Hey, listen. I remember going to a restaurant on New Years Eve in my pajamas with two other girls and this guy came and picked us up. There was a slumber party. Remember slumber parties? In high school, I was at a slumber party. That's how dull I was. So this guy conned us into getting into his car in our pajamas and drive through the restaurant in our pajamas. I remember the days of the guy who urinated as he was driving through a drive-in restaurant on the top of a truck. I'm so glad people have grown up. I haven't heard of anybody doing that in a long time.

QUESTION: *Then you sort of entered the hippie movement?*

SHIRLEY: With a vengeance.

QUESTION: *Was this after you left college or during college?*

SHIRLEY: Yes, I went here, I got spinal meningitis in the beginning of my second year, and on top of that I couldn't handle the phys ed classes. I was still under twenty-two and you had to have phys ed. I couldn't get up early enough in the morning and go out and jog or do calisthenics, or whatever it is. I made it through modern dance and then I keeled over and died. So my second year at college took a nose dive and I ended up getting married.

QUESTION: *To the same guy?*

SHIRLEY: No. I've been married twice. I was nineteen, almost twenty. This was a long time ago. I'm thirty years old. He was in the Army, stationed on the East Coast, and I moved back there. Had a great time. Came back to San Diego, and three months later we were split up, and I was living with my present husband. I had no intentions of ever getting married again. I'm smart, I'm not ever going to get married again. And between him, and a dog bite, and my mother and stepfather, I got conned into getting married New Years Eve, 1967. This dog bit me, and it scared the heck out of everybody, including me. It was a big dog, and I got chewed up. And Bob came rushing into the house, and I knew by the look in his eyes that he really loved me. Oh, what the hell! We'll get married. We got married. We've been together for ten years. We were separated for three, and now we're back together again. What was the original question?

QUESTION: *The original question was your involvement in the hippie movement?*

SHIRLEY: OK, right. Bob and I started smoking grass together in 1966. We toked up for the first time, had some Acapulco Gold, got really loaded. This was right here in San Diego in an apartment on 32nd Street, behind closed doors and pulled blinds. We were so paranoid. We got so stoned. I've never been that stoned. We decided, this is great, we're gonna get stoned, but we're never going to take pills. I think it was seven months later we were dropping acid. For three years we dropped acid. I quit my job and drew unemployment. This really good friend was living with us, and he'd been run over by a train. I've got some weird friends. He was getting disability. So we paid the rent and bought food with his disability check, and we bought the acid and the grass with my unemployment check, and for as long as this lasted, we had a great time. One whole summer was nothing but dropping acid and driving around —we had a Porsche at the time. Don't ask me how we financed a Porsche, but we did. We just dropped acid and drove around Mt. Soledad and Mt. Helix and had a good time, and all of a sudden we came back to earth with a bang. We had to give the car back because we didn't have any more money. Bill moved away, so there went his disability check. My unemployment was about to run out, and Bob and I had to face the fact that we were going to have to get jobs soon, and all of a sudden there we were.

We were working hippies, and we worked for the next four years, I guess. We worked together. We worked separately. We were going to buy a home in Lemon Grove. We were just the model couple, except that we had long hair and we were frequently very red-eyed, and sometimes didn't answer our doorbell, and then something started happening. I started going into a yoga, vegetarian bent and Bob didn't want to do that, and at that time I was so insecure that I didn't want to do it by myself, so we broke up, and he went off and lived with this lovely lady named Marg for a long time, which made me very jealous. I became a groupie. I used to hang out at a local night club and I knew all the big musicians that came in. It's the roadies that are nice. Don't be a groupie for the musicians. Be a groupie for the roadies. And then I got into this commune and I was there for two years. Just had a great time. Met some wonderful people, had some wonderful—I quit dope. When I moved into the commune everybody thought I was a narc because I wouldn't smoke or drink, and one night they held me down and poured a can of Schlitz down me, and then they used to wake me up in the morning and had me a bottle of Schlitz and a joint and that was how I was waking up about four summers ago. It was a nice summer. Anyway, now I'm nice and respectable. I'm so dull and respectable now, other than my job. I stay at home and watch television a lot. I've got a lot of plants. I've got six cats and a dog and my husband and this nice big house, and a nice big yard, and I do a lot of gardening. I'm dull. What can I say?

QUESTION: *Does your husband work currently?*

SHIRLEY: Hopefully, he'll never work again. There are some people who should not work for somebody else. If he could work for himself and make money, that would be fine, but he's not cut out to work for somebody else.

QUESTION: *One thing that is exceptional, compared to other cases, is that you apparently have a stable relationship with your husband, and as you know, the literature characterizes prostitutes as emotionally dangerous to males.*

SHIRLEY: I have no bad feelings toward males unless they do something to me first. I'll take everybody at face value. Sure, there are a lot of men who don't treat me like a human being. I am a seminal sewer, a sex object, fluff brain, whatever, but there are a lot of women who treat me like that too. I spoke in a women's studies class out here, and I have never been so horrified in my life. I don't think that solving the world's problems between men and women is going to be solved by castrating men. There's no way you can convince me that that's going to make anything better. I think that the way to work things out is to show men that we are intelligent, thinking, human beings and that we can fend for ourselves. I piss more men off because I *am* making good money and I *am* independent. There's nobody who's telling me what to do.

Some guy came into one of the shops where I work—big, real big —and he says, "For twenty dollars a month you can have my protection, and I'd do this, and I'd do this, and I'd do this, and the next time I come in I don't want to see you wearing pants." "Why?" He says, "Well, are you gay?" "I'm bi, what difference does that make?" He says, "Well, I just wondered." But listen, if you're wearing pants, and some guy wants to rip you off, while you're putting your pants back on, he's going to grab the money and run. And I'm thinking, what, I've been doing this for two years, and that never even crossed my mind. What difference does it make? If a guy grabs my money and runs out the door, I guess he needs it. He needs it worse than I do. And besides that, I have no compunction about running outside without my clothes on. I would do it. But we got to talking and he wanted to know why I was wearing pants. I'm comfortable in pants. I hardly wear anything else but pants. He naturally assumed I was gay, which I'm not, and then he said something about we still run a check every three or four hours. We come by and make sure that everything's OK. I felt like saying, "Hey, listen, buddy, ten minutes after you leave, somebody could come in and beat the shit out of me." As far as that goes, I just don't believe that I need a body guard. If there isn't something that I can take care of myself, then I'll call the police who will be there shortly. It's on University Avenue in a well policed area. I'm not worried. So then he says something about, "Every woman needs a man's protection," I said, "Listen, nobody takes care of me but me, myself, and I. I support myself. I take care of myself." He goes, "Well, where do you live? I'm going to come over and uh, uh, uh..." Ahh..., now that's a male chauvinist pig. You know, he thinks he can take care of me, until I tell him that I can take care of myself and him too, and then all of a sudden he wants to move in. Those are male chauvinist pigs. Those are the ones whose minds I either have to change or ignore.

Now, if I can't get to them, then I don't want anything to do with them, because I'm not going to waste my energy. But there are a lot of men who don't realize that we have validity. We are human beings first, all of us, then we break down to male and female, black and white, young and old, or whatever it is you get labelled, but we all have this common denominator called human being. You just can't get away from that. Let's relate to each other as human beings, and then we'll get down to taking our clothes off, and you know, you show me yours and I'll show you mine.

QUESTION: *You mentioned before class that you had taken heroin. Is this a factor in your prostitution? Are you feeding a habit?*

SHIRLEY: No. I took heroin three years ago. I was doing everything I could to get my husband back. I really loved the guy and I was making an ass of myself every time I turned around. So I thought, I'll become a junkie, he'll feel sorry for me, move back into my life and take care of me. It didn't impress him in the least. "Shirley, get out of here." Anyway, yes, for three months I was a junkie. I'm glad I did it. I have a lot more sympathy now for people who need crutches. That's what it was. It becomes a crutch. I don't know if anybody else in here has ever done heroin. It wasn't that hard to give up, but the big scare about heroin's addicting once you do it. It took me about a week and a half to get over it. I didn't feel that good and I had a runny nose and I wasn't real pleased with myself, but I did it and it's all over with and I'm glad. It was no big deal. It had *nothing* to do with this job, nothing at all. I want to emphasize that me being a prostitute and me taking heroin happened independently and happened two and a half years apart.

QUESTION: *Would you say that your entering prostitution was something you did consciously and for rational economic reasons?*

SHIRLEY: It started out of economic need and now it's become a cause. I'm definitely into changing the image of prostitution. I'd like to see the sexual attitude of America drastically changed. I want to get into educating children. Do you know that last May at a high school my gynecologist went out to give a talk to the graduating class, the seniors, now, seventeen, eighteen years old? And out of these approximately two hundred kids, twenty of them wrote, and I saw the slips of paper that they had written their questions on, twenty of them wanted to know how a man had a baby. Are you ready for that? That's sad. There's something really wrong if somebody still thinks—does anybody in here think that men have babies?

COMMENT: There's a million dollars willed by some eccentric millionaire to the first man who has a baby.

QUESTION: *Since you're making a career out of this . . .*

SHIRLEY: Oh, wait a minute. I'm not making a career out of prostitution. What I want to make a career out of is sex education.

QUESTION: *What I was wondering is, eventually every prostitute gets to a point and age where they lose their sex appeal.*

SHIRLEY: I figure I've got ten years left, baby. If I take good care of myself, I can make it till I'm forty.

QUESTION: *A lot of women in ancient Greece had the same attitude that you're telling us, then, of course, Greece fell shortly after that.*

SHIRLEY: Listen, I hope there's no correlation there, but if there is, I'm doing my best to keep things going, folks. One of the problems there was that the prostitutes were religiously involved, and I'm an agnostic so I'm sure I'm clear of that. The thing is that if a girl is a good hooker, she's gonna care about her customer, and if she cares about her customer, she's going to release him of his frustrations, and unfortunately, men are still running things around here. The more men's frustrations I relieve, the better off all of us are, cause the more good vibes you put out, the more creative . . . I look at this job as a way to heal people. I'm versed in healing massage, and if somebody comes in and they're in pain, I really can alleviate their pain plus their frustrations. I do a lot of therapy work—people who have premature ejaculation or the inability to get a hard on. Some men just don't like women. They're latent homosexuals and they should be seeing men, but they can't because of their backgrounds. I've helped a couple of them. You know, I don't care about anybody's sexual preferences as long as he doesn't hurt me. That's cool. But there are not enough girls who care about what they're doing. Most girls go in and do it for the money and then scram. They'll work for a month or two. They'll make a large amount of money, and then you don't see them for a month or two until their money's run out and then they're back in it. Well, I've been doing this steady for two years now. I care.

QUESTION: *I don't go to prostitutes because it would only give me short-term satisfaction.*

SHIRLEY: Don't knock it till you've tried it! This is for women only. If your man is going to a prostitute, or a masseuse, or whatever he or she wants to call themselves, you are so much better off. There is no emotional involvement. A man comes to see me. He spends a half an hour to an hour with me. There is an exchange of money. Therefore, nobody feels like anybody's owed anything after he walks out the door. He's gone, and he's relieved, and he can go do whatever. Most men go home to their wives directly after they see me. I have them come back a week later and say, "I was so horney," even though they got off with me, it's like the more you get, the hornier you get. They'd go home and have a great time with their wives and come back and tell me about it the next week. That's great! I hope he gets his wife off. I'd relate to men in a positive way and show them how they can help their wives. Most men don't know how to get their wives off. Most men are really inept sexually. The majority of men I've come across have no idea what gets ladies off, and it ain't fuckin', unless you're very rare.

QUESTION: *What do you find is the most widely requested sex act?*

SHIRLEY: Blow jobs.

COMMENT: Yeah, I heard that.

QUESTION: *Why do you think that is?*

SHIRLEY: Because most women in the forty- to sixty-year-old bracket wouldn't go down on their old man for any amount of money.

QUESTION: *How did you learn this? Were you influenced by your relative who was also a prostitute?*

SHIRLEY: No, I didn't know it at the time. I found out because a lot of my customers go see her. They say she gives the best head in town.

QUESTION: *The best* what?

SHIRLEY: The best head in town. That's another term you can use. OK, you can say blow-job, B.J., French, oral technique, head. Some young guy came in and he said, "How much for a header?" And I didn't know what he was talking about. The only headers I knew about were on cars. Every day I learn something new.

QUESTION: *Did you pretty much come in cold turkey, or did you know someone who worked in a massage parlor?*

SHIRLEY: I knew someone who worked, a very lovely lady who I am very proud to know, who, well, she's just beautiful. She's beautiful to look at and she's got a very beautiful heart. What more can I say?

QUESTION: *Did she teach you anything? Is there much to learn?*

SHIRLEY: You either got it or you don't, and I'd been told the whole time I was in the commune that I had it. So I figured, well, everybody else was pleased, might as well make some money with it. I had a friend named Jim who, unfortunately, is now dead, but Jim for years tried to get me to go to Las Vegas. He wanted to . . . he had some friends and he had had some girls. He used to be a pimp, and he wanted me to be a clothes horse up in Las Vegas. I'm going—Oh, no. I don't know what that leads to. Not me. Not me. I guess it was, maybe the idea would have been attractive to me if he hadn't been involved. I just wouldn't work for a man. There's no way, even Jim, who was someone that I knew, a friend. I wouldn't give him any money off of my body. Nobody's going to get any money off of my body but me.

QUESTION: *What about your sexual relations with your husband?*

SHIRLEY: Bob and I have talked about that. I'm glad you brought that up. Bob and I have talked about that about a month ago. We both stayed up all night and we were going to get it on. I mean, it was one of those, ohhhh, let's get in bed, and as soon as we got in bed and cuddled up we just started talking. And we talked, and we talked and it got to be five o'clock in the morning and nothing had been done with all this talking, and we came to the conclusion that, after ten years, we're going through a brother-and-sister phase. We don't really feel like getting it on with each other. I know he's got a couple of lady friends who are my lady friends too, and if he wants to be with them, that's fine, because I'm for sure being with a lot of different people. It's like, I get off at work sometimes. Not a lot, but occasionally I get off at work, and I'm O.D'd on sex sometimes, so when I come home I don't want anything from Bob because it would overamp me. I'd probably blow it, because when I'm with Bob, whatever I do with him gotta be special, that's gotta be different, like, you know, the tops, and if I don't feel up to it, then I don't want to give him anything less than the best. So, at that moment, our sexual relationship is in a slump. We're taking a two-month vacation from each other. We're going up to Hearst Castle this week, and I'm sure that staying in a motel will, rrrrrrrraaaa.

QUESTION: *When you said you get off at work, that implies that you are not always emotionally indifferent.*

SHIRLEY: I am never emotionally indifferent, unless—I am never indifferent. Let me say that. Somebody can come in and I can despise them, you know, I never want to touch this man again, but I feel obligated to finish the massage and excuse myself gracefully, and remember never to do him again. If he wants to come in and see one of the other girls, that's fine, but it's my prerogative not to have to touch somebody I don't want to, and I don't, because I'm not going to be fair to them. But, no, I am never emotionally indifferent, because everybody comes in, even if they're kind of creepy. The biggest problem I had when I first got into this was, Oh, my God, what if somebody ugly comes in? What if an old man comes in? What if somebody fat comes in? Well, I got all of those wrapped up into one, my second night of work. What can I say? I'm still in the business. As a matter of fact, last night I did a guy who weighs 342 pounds and he's not much taller than I am, and the only thing that I could do was be up front with him. There are some problems that people have that I just ignore. Like, there's a friend who comes in, he has became a friend, but he had polio when he was little, and his right side is kind of withered. I've never said a word. I've known him for a year and I've never said a word about it, but when this guy came in last night, I just kept going, "My goodness, we can't get too close to each other, can we?" and I kept patting him. I went, "God, how much do you weigh? It's all compact, right in the middle." Hopefully, he'll go home and do something about it because it's unhealthy. No, I'm never emotionally indifferent. I get involved with everybody.

QUESTION: *The other thing I picked up on was you never worked for a man. Is this because you've had trouble in the past?*

SHIRLEY: No, but why should a man make money off of my body?

QUESTION: *Critics will probably say that this shows a hatred of men or something.*

SHIRLEY: There's no hatred of men. It's just that most men don't run a female oriented business as well as a woman does, and the place I'm working now is more of a cooperative kind of thing, and the woman I work for is not even in town. She quit the business and she's somewhere else, and we girls are running the shop and it's running along beautifully.

QUESTION: *Aren't most of them male-run?*

SHIRLEY: Yep, most of them are. Most of them have timers. Listen to this. They set it up. You can get a half-hour massage. After the half hour's up, you hear this *ding*. What if the guy hasn't got off yet? You're supposed to rush out, or else you have to pay the extra money, or get him to pay the extra money. So he stays five or ten minutes extra.

So what? It's inconceivable to me that I would work for someone who would set a timer on me and then bang on the door if I didn't come out immediately. I'd be nasty.

QUESTION: *Have you ever had any gays come in?*

SHIRLEY: What? Gay women?

ANSWER: Yeah. How did you react to that?

SHIRLEY: I'm bi. There are a lot of men who call up and want to know if we do couples, they want to bring their girlfriend in or whatever.

QUESTION: *Would you be in favor of decriminalization or legalization of prostitution?*

SHIRLEY: I am in favor of everything being legal, if it's a victimless crime. The only thing that I would be afraid of is the I.R.S. getting in and getting complete control of how much I make. I make a lot of money. I don't want them to take my money and kill people with it. I'm sure that everybody in here feels the same way. I knew several big dope dealers, and I know that the man is never going to get ahold of their money. So, until the I.R.S. can tap their money, I don't want them tapping mine.

QUESTION: *What do you consider prostitution to be?*

SHIRLEY: Selling one's sexual services.

QUESTION: *It is illegal, but do you feel it's immoral?*

SHIRLEY: I can't say that I feel it's immoral. I'm sure that it's immoral when some people do it, because they're not doing it right. To me, immorality is when you're not doing it properly. In other words, when you're not making your client feel good about what he is doing, then you're being immoral.

QUESTION: *What about adultery? Most of your clients are probably committing adultery.*

SHIRLEY: Oh, I guess for about a half an hour, but it's a lot better than their going out and getting a six-month affair that upsets everybody including the wife. The wife never knows about me, and I'm never going to encroach on her territory. Her man goes home to her, and takes good care of the kids and probably takes excellent care of her. I've got a couple of customers who came in and saw me and complained that the reason they were seeing me was that their wives didn't enjoy sex and I asked them why and they said that they didn't know what a clitoris was, so I showed them. Haven't seen them since.

QUESTION: *Do any of your friends in your profession feel the same way you do?*

SHIRLEY: Most of the women I work with. I work with a lot of really fine ladies who are not as willing as I am to become a scapegoat. I think, because of my position, my mother knows what I am doing. My husband knows what I am doing, and I am not afraid to set myself up as an example. This is what I'm doing. Now, me, I am a prostitute. Do I look like the proverbial whore? Let's change the image, I'm very much into this. If I got busted, I haven't, but if I did, I would stand out on the streets and wave placards, and I'd do everything I could do to get the public aware of what the "law" is trying to do to me and girls like me, because if there wasn't a necessity for my position, I wouldn't be making as much money as I am.

QUESTION: *Could you describe step-by-step what happens when a customer comes to the door? Can he be a stranger?*

SHIRLEY: Oh, for sure. Eighty percent of our business is return, but the other twenty percent come in cold and hopefully they're greeted normally if they haven't been before, and especially if it's the first time they've been in. There was a young man who came in last night, and it was his very first time in a massage parlor, but he handled himself very well. Usually, shaky hands, flushed face, jittery movement. This guy was very calm, apparently, until he got to the back room, and the other girl did him, and he kind of fell apart. But most of the people, when they come in, ask what our prices are. We don't have a sign. It's all in our heads, and so we say we have a ten-dollar half-hour nude, a fifteen-dollar half-hour topless switch, and a twenty-five–dollar half-hour nude switch. And they always like the ten-dollar, because that way everybody gets their clothes off, and the girl feels a lot more comfortable if she is without her clothing. He pays for the massage out in the lobby, the front desk area, and when he gets into the back and lays down on the table, the girl asks him whether he would like a powder or an oil massage. You can find out a lot just by what kind of a massage they want. If a guy sincerely wants a massage, he'll ask for an oil massage, because you get a really deep, heavy massage that way. If he wants the powder massage, he usually wants the sensuous, fingertip kind of thing. So, ah ha, right away this guy wants to get turned on. The law is that when you turn them over (they're on their tummies, you're massaging their back and their buttocks and their legs), you're supposed to take a small towel and drape it over them like a diaper. I guess we're not supposed to look at what they got . . . You see one, you seen them all. I've heard that term applied to women so much that I'm using it in reverse now. If the customer doesn't like the towel over him, he usually flings it away. "What's this?" and you know right away that he's going to want an extra, and as you massage the front of him, he will usually ask you several leading questions like (*whispers*), "How much are your B.J.'s?" Or, "How much to get it on?" Or, "Do you give extras here?" A new customer will, if he's got any class, and hopefully most of our customers have class, will kind of pull you down and whisper in your ear, "Do you do anything besides a massage?" And then I go, "What do you mean?" Anyway, there is this exchange where we establish that he is soliciting me, and as soon as that comes down, we get down to the nitty-gritty, and then we figure out whether he wants what is called a local or a hand finish, as I've heard it referred to lately, which is the least expensive service you can get—fifteen dollars, or header, French, blow job, B.J., oral technique.

QUESTION: *Do you enjoy sex or is it a job?*

SHIRLEY: Depends on who I'm doing it with. If it's someone who knows how to touch a woman, and most men, unfortunately, don't know how to touch women. Most men can't get it through their thick skulls that I'm softer than they are. Every woman in here, although she has a higher threshold of pain than you do, has softer skin. The mucous membrane area in her vagina is very, very tender . . . You should never put fingers in vaginas. Fingers carry germs. My gynecologist says, the only things that go in there are tongues and penises. That's a rule. No fingers.

QUESTION: *In other words, you worked other jobs in business, you have a college background, and yet you went on to prostitution. Why? What's a nice girl like you doing in a job like this?*

SHIRLEY: All those other jobs are boring. What's a nice girl like me doing in a place like this? For one thing, I'm not that nice. I have people all the time telling me, "Oh, you're so sweet, you're so nice!" I hate that. I want to be something sultry and sexy. I was to be a Sophia Loren. Nobody takes me seriously. I'll be a comedy hooker, I guess. This job is so much more fulfilling than any other job I've had, and all the other jobs I've had I've had to work for a man or at least under a man, and nothing against you guys, but you're horrible bosses, and I would never, never work for a man in this job. There are several women in town who are running massage parlors. Those are the ladies that I work for.

QUESTION: *Did you have any apprehensions?*

SHIRLEY: I was scared to death. I had never touched anybody that I hadn't wanted to touch. I never went on a date with somebody that I didn't feel was attractive.

QUESTION: *You stated that men can be physically abusive. How does that make you feel toward men? Do you think that this form of prostitution encourages lesbianism?*

SHIRLEY: The way I feel about that is almost all of us are bi. I don't know anybody who hasn't had a dream or some kind of fantasy about making it with a member of their own sex. I took a long time to come out of the closet, but when I finally made love to a woman, I went, that wasn't as bad as I expected. I'm not afraid of it any more. It's not something I pursue but it's something that is available if I should want it. I don't think that prostitution encourages lesbianism, but I think that because you're working very closely with girls, and when there aren't any customers around, you sit and you talk, and because of the intimate nature of our business, we talk about very intimate things, and the more you get to know somebody, and the warmer and closer your relationship is, sometimes it develops into something else. In the place that I'm working in right now, we've kind of made it an unspoken rule that we don't get it on with each other because that could be bad for business. I know that there are a lot of homosexual relationships where the jealousy is paramount, you know, more prevalent than in any heterorelationship. What was the first part of your question?

QUESTION: *How do you and your friends feel about men?*

SHIRLEY: I really like men. I like people. I'd really like to see people being nice to people. For the most part, I think, I like men. There are a few men I don't like, but there are a few women I can't stand either, but I don't think that my job is hurting my attitude toward men, and if a man is rough with me and he won't straighten up his act, then I won't give him a massage anymore, but most men don't realize that they're being rough. It's up to us to train them. Men need training when it comes to sex. It's not something that comes naturally. Most men think that because they've got a dick and they can (*clap hands*) do this trip with it, it's all over. Bullshit!

COMMENT: But most women are the same way. It doesn't come naturally to most women who haven't had the training that you've had.

SHIRLEY: I don't think that I've developed any more skills than any woman in this room. All I'm doing is being up front about where I am. Most people don't talk about sex. Most women won't tell you whether they've gotten off or not, and most men don't care enough to find out, and this business about, "Did you come?" afterward. If you've got to ask, there's something wrong with your sexual prowess, but most men, I'm including you or any one here, most men think that because they've got a dick, they're gifted with something that women don't have. Most women don't get off, getting it on. There are other things that you have got to do to women. If you read *The Descent of Women*, you'll find out that women are not biologically set up to get off because we've uprighted our bodies. When we were on all fours, before we became homo sapiens, we got off every time we got on. We don't any more. We've rearranged our genital area, and the clitoris is set up so that it's not touched by the penis.

QUESTION: *Is your parlor part of a chain?*

SHIRLEY: Uh, uh.

QUESTION: *So it's not controlled by organized crime?*

SHIRLEY: I don't know how organized we are, or how criminal we are. No, we're definitely not part of organized crime. Somebody asked me once if we were paying off the cops, because we never have any trouble, and I answered them, "No, every time they come in we offer them a massage and they run out saying, 'No, we can't. Not while we're on duty.'"

COMMENT: In a course I had last semester we had a lawyer in and he said the cops aren't after all massage parlors, but just the ones that roll the sailors or whatever.

SHIRLEY: Right, and those places are giving my place a bad name, and I'd like to see them closed down too.

QUESTION: *When is it considered soliciting?*

SHIRLEY: When I say, "Would you like to have an extra?" and I quote him a price.

QUESTION: *What if he asked you?*

SHIRLEY: Then he's soliciting me.

COMMENT: That's entrapment.

COMMENT: Then in court it would be thrown out?

SHIRLEY: If I had a good enough lawyer.

COMMENT: So that guy who solicited you in the lobby, you couldn't get busted because he solicited you.

SHIRLEY: But there, again, I'm a prostitute, I'm a criminal. Are you going to take my word against this police officer? Did anybody hear of the gal who a couple of years ago was arrested for knocking the officer off of his tricycle? She is a friend of mine. I know this lady very well. We were roommates, and she has forty percent use of her arm because somebody shot her by mistake. She was judged by twelve of her peers against this officer. This officer was thrown off the force for statutory rape of a fourteen-year-old girl.

QUESTION: *Do you find any deviant sexual styles, say, bondage?*

SHIRLEY: I had one bondage customer, and I'll never do him again. I didn't think I would mind being bound or doing a bondage customer, but it was different. It's kinky. I wanted a little more money for it, and especially since he hurt me. He used his belt. Now, if he used a scarf or something, I might have been more into it. I'm not into belts, and buckles and black leather and all that stuff. He tied me up with his belt and I had to take it off. I had this beautiful turquoise bracelet. It cost me a lot of money, and I took it off so he could wrap his belt around me, and I stuck it under the pillow, and I forgot to get it and I guess it went to the laundry. So somebody has a nice turquoise bracelet at the laundry. Then he wouldn't pay me what I asked. Like, I spent extra time with him, and . . . anyway, that whole episode didn't please me. We do have a customer, this guy had an operation on his spine about ten years ago. He has no feeling in his genitals at all. The only thing that arouses him, does him any good at all, is spanking, hard spanking. And he comes in and you spank him for a half-hour, really hard spanking. I worked up a sweat. I don't consider that deviant behavior, and yet my grandmother would probably think that that was horrible.

QUESTION: *What's your relationship with your parents like?*

SHIRLEY: Really nice. My mom and I had a nice long talk not too long ago. She's got a new boyfriend. My mom's divorced. She's fifty-five years old, she's got a forty-four-year-old boyfriend, and I think she's getting off for the first time in her life.

QUESTION: *When was your mother divorced?*

SHIRLEY: When I was five years old.

QUESTION: *Do you have any memories of your real father?*

SHIRLEY: Yes. He's not real nice.

QUESTION: *Alcoholic or something?*

SHIRLEY: I don't know about that. All I know is that his second wife shot herself in the head, and my stepsisters came home from school and found her, so I don't feel real good about my real father. He used to beat my mother in front of me, so my feelings about my real father are not very good. My stepfather, though, I am very fond of, and I'm really sorry that he and my mother have split up, but I'm glad that she's got this boyfriend. Like, I asked her when we finally had an honest talk if dad had ever gotten her off, and she said, "No." I'm really happy that she's happy.

QUESTION: *What do you think of the concept of the happy hooker?*

SHIRLEY: I am not the happy hooker. I am happy, yes, and I am hooking when I'm working, but I am not the happy hooker. I don't live it. I live it as far as I enjoy coming and speaking and getting things out in the open. I would like to get some things changed. But I don't walk down the street and people can go, "Look at her. She's a prostitute!" You couldn't tell me from the girl next door.

QUESTION: *I spoke to a street prostitute who looked down her nose at call girls because they engaged in "perversions."*

SHIRLEY: Did she define perversions?

ANSWER: Oral sex.

SHIRLEY: Oh, my God! Sounds like my mother!

COMMENT: She was opposed to group sex as well.

SHIRLEY: I'm not opposed to anything as long as everybody involved is having a good time. I don't understand how anybody can be opposed to something that somebody else is doing if they're not being hurt by it.

QUESTION: *What do you think about women's liberation?*

SHIRLEY: I spoke to a women's studies class here and they didn't approve of me at all because my job furthers men's egos, or whatever, and I kept trying to explain to them, "Listen, I can do more good for women in my job if I can show just one man how to get his old lady off and relieve her sexual frustration, don't you think that that's a valid position?" They didn't want to hear that. They're speaking from a political standpoint and not an emotional standpoint. They would really like to castrate men, and I can't believe that that's the answer. I don't really think we're going to change things by alienating men. Let's use our femininity. I'd rather con a man into agreeing with me, before he even realizes that he was ever against me. All of a sudden he's on my side, because I've been nice to him. I've cajoled him. I've swayed him to my way of thinking by using my intelligence, and before you know it he's going to think, yeh, I guess she does have something to say, or something to think, or whatever.

QUESTION: *Do you find that most of your clients come to you because they're having problems finding sex outside?*

SHIRLEY: A lot of them, but a lot of them just come and see me because they need more sex than what is usually available. Most women are stuck at home with three to five kids, nothing interesting going on in their lives, and their husbands are away a lot. They're working. They're involved in their jobs. The wives are bored, and they portray that boredom in bed. So when the men want something exciting, they have to go see somebody who's being paid to be exciting.

QUESTION: *Do you feel that you support monogamous marriage?*

SHIRLEY: Let me say that I support relationships. I don't necessarily support marriage, because I've never found a marriage to ensure a relationship. No, man is not monogamous. I know very, very few people who are monogamous throughout their lifetimes. What happens is that you get bored with yourself, when you're only relating to one other person and that person is a mere image of you. If you're lucky enough to find a soul mate, then you've got it made. I think I've found mine. After ten years, I'd better believe that! I've got a nice relationship and I think it's a soul mate relationship, but I don't know too many people who've been lucky enough to do that, and I don't think that you need to get married to ensure that it stays that way. After two marriages, I'm kind of jaded about marriage. But I'm not jaded about relationships. I think relationships are the greatest thing in the world. I think my mother has finally come to that conclusion. She's fifty-five years old, and she's discovered that she can have a relationship with a man, and she doesn't need to get married, and that he's not going to marry her even if she needed him to marry her. He's been married too, and he doesn't want to get hurt any more. Why do people think that if you get married, you're going to be hurt, whereas if you just have a relationship, you're not going to be hurt?

COMMENTARY

Shirley, like Sandy, is the product of a broken home but there is a lack of information in her interview to indicate that any relationships (or lack of them) with her father influenced her later career. She denies any hatred of men that would support Freudian theory, but in some of her remarks one detects an ambivalence regarding her relationships with men.

> I have no bad feelings toward men unless they do something to me first ... Sure, there are a lot of men who don't treat me like a human being ... I piss more men off because I am making good money and I am independent.
> Well, I've never worked for a man and I will never work for a man.

In some ways, Shirley's remarks may reflect an influence by the women's movement rather than supporting a psychoanalytic model.

Unlike Sandy, Shirley does not fit Davis's process model. She did not experience early institutionalization, promiscuity, or labeling. She claims to have been a virgin during her teen-age years and a "bookworm" rather than a "bad" girl. Like Sandy, she has experienced lesbian relationships and states that she is bisexual.

The greatest similarities between the two prostitutes appear to be in the existence of "pull" factors that led them into the life-style for economic reasons. Although Shirley used drugs to some extent, she does not see her entrance as influenced by drugs. She did, however, seek out another individual in the subculture to teach her the profession. Thus, the learning processes and economic incentives were similar for both women, and Shirley, like Sandy, became "hooked" on prostitution at an early stage.

Shirley, again like Sandy, eventually adopted the deviant identity as "prostitute." However, perhaps due to her "higher status" both in earlier life and within her career, Shirley claims to be more than just a prostitute. She states that she is not the "proverbial whore," and although she is a prostitute she is also a "masseuse, and a healer, and a couple of other things." She views herself as an educator and one who helps marriages rather than harming them. Indeed, these attitudes match closely what James Bryan has termed the "occupational ideologies of call girls." Bryan termed such attitudes as functional for the prostitute in managing public stigma.[9] So they appear to be for Shirley.

Any role of organized crime in the "Mafia" sense (as will be described in Chapter 8) is denied by Shirley. On the other hand, there is a strong indication of cooperation in the subculture of massage parlor prostitutes to avoid control by legal authorities. This exists in spite of indications of strong competition within the "business" generally. This cooperation and other means of avoiding legal entanglements, combined with Shirley's relative lack of fear regarding criminal sanctions, indicate the ineffectiveness, once again, of external controls. Since Shirley manages her own self-concept, overcoming whatever internal control mechanisms might have existed, support is indicated for Reckless' containment model. Further indication of society's ambivalence and, to quote Shirley, "hypocrisy" toward prostitution, are contained in the interview.

THEORETICAL IMPLICATIONS

If we analyze both interviewees within our broader theoretical frameworks, we find no indication of physiological or genetic explanations for their behavior. Indeed, our prostitutes appeared to represent two extremes of physical "beauty" in their earlier years. Sandy described herself in rather unflattering terms. Shirley seemed to be attractive long before her first experience as a prostitute or even before any degree of promiscuity. The most that might be said for physical features is that they could only play a minor role by interacting with psychological and sociological factors within any explanatory framework. With this behind us, let us now examine the implications of our insights toward the psychological and sociological explanations that have been advanced.

Psychological and Psychiatric Theories

There seems to be little support for the Freudian model in analyzing these interviews. There is a conspicuous lack of information regarding if a person were to conclude that the subjects had personality defects. Only a few hints of ambivalent feelings toward men are given in the interviews. These would seem to be explained at least equally as well by effects of a prostitute career rather than the "causes" of such a career. Whatever psychological factors appear to be present seem to better fit the labeling model that resulted in a deviant self-image and the internal control concept of social control theory. Thus, we see again the possibility of interaction of psychological and sociological factors within a process model of explanation, although not completely fitting the sequence of factors within the Davis model.

Sociological Theories

Several sociological explanations of prostitution seem to have logical conceptual connection with various aspects of our subjects' histories. Let us view each of them specifically as we have in previous chapters.

ALIENATION   There has been some attention given in the literature to the manner in which capitalism and the resulting pursuit of monetary gain have served to alienate and exploit females who pursue such gain through prostitution. In addition, several authorities have commented upon the exploitation of females through treating them as sex objects. They claim this is found in its extreme in prostitution. Certainly, there exists a certain "alienation" of Sandy and Shirley from society and from men in particular. However, to place this factor within a Marxist perspective would appear to depend on one's overall acceptance of such a framework in explaining the state of society in general. It should be said, however, that conflict theorists might find some basis in the interviews to support this perspective.

ANOMIE OR OPPORTUNITY THEORIES   Considerable support seems to exist for an anomie framework and a corresponding "pull" concept according to the Lemert opportunity application. Both Sandy and Shirley used illegitimate means or opportunity to obtain the culturally defined goal of economic reward. It is still important to point out that this "pull" was from middle class backgrounds rather than a "push" from lower socioeconomic status groups as is often envisioned by interpretations of Merton's model.

DIFFERENTIAL ASSOCIATION AND SUBCULTURAL LEARNING   It would seem that a combination of differential association theory and subcultural explanations of prostitution serves as a most satisfactory framework to explain the initial entrance of our subjects into prostitution. Both Sandy and Shirley, while attracted to the financial rewards of prostitution, were initiated into it as a source of income and instructed in techniques involved by members of the existing subculture. Their experiences fit the descriptions of an "apprenticeship" model detailed by Bryan[10] and the "teaching" of new prostitutes by madames as outlined by Heyl.[11] It must be again emphasized that no evidence is provided that the subculture exists due to any lower class value system or extreme economic deprivation.

SOCIAL CONTROL THEORY AND LABELING   A similar case of combination might be made by employing both the labeling perspective and Reckless' containment model to further elaborate upon the *process* of becoming a prostitute. Sandy's case history demonstrates the labeling process whereby she developed a self-concept or lack of internal control mechanisms prohibiting prostitution. Shirley appears to modify the deviant aspects of such a negative self-concept by incorporating positive aspects (such as "healer") within her identity.

The lack of effectiveness of external mechanisms of control stands out. Kingsley Davis has described these as "supply" and "demand" factors existing in our society and encouraging prostitution.[12] Other authors have called for legalization of prostitution throughout our society in order to avoid hypocrisy, citing also the influence of organized crime, an increase in the tax base, the control of venereal disease, a decrease in police corruption, and a better utilization of law enforcement through concentration on crimes with victims.[13]

There has been a great deal of comment regarding the legalization issue as it relates to the ambivalence shown in our society toward prostitution.[14] It is pointed out that prostitution is illegal in all states except Nevada, which permits it on a "local option" basis. Nevertheless, it is relatively undisputed that prostitution exists and has existed in every state as it has in almost every culture. Thus, it is frequently termed "the oldest profession" in the world. Laws exist, it is often argued, largely for their symbolic effect in upholding the institutions of marriage and family. At the same time, it seems that many of the individuals who support such laws claim that the existence of prostitution as an outlet for sexual release and sexual initiation is beneficial.

Perhaps this ambivalence is indicative of an even greater equivocation regarding sex in general within our society. This should be borne in mind in the following chapters dealing with homosexuality and transsexualism.

QUESTIONS FOR DISCUSSION

1. Do you agree or disagree that the definition of prostitution should be limited to "sexual bartering"? If not, how would you define prostitution?
2. Do Sandy and Shirley seem to be neurotic, psychotic, or in any way "emotionally unstable"? If you think so, what do you think is the basis of their personal disorganization? If not, how do you think they have been able to escape personality disorganization in the light of their backgrounds?
3. Do you think Sandy really "likes men"? Does Shirley?
4. What relationship do you think being labeled a delinquent had to Sandy's becoming a prostitute? What other aspects of juvenile incarceration might have contributed to her prostitution?
5. In ten years' time, what do you think Sandy will be doing? What do you think Shirley will be doing?
6. What trends in our society do you believe have contributed to the proliferation of massage parlors? Do you believe prostitution is increasing as indicated by this proliferation, or is it merely taking on new forms? Do you believe there are social class differences in the patrons of the various types of massage parlors and of prostitutes generally?
7. Do you attribute any of the attitudes of Shirley as indicative of "the new feminism"? What, in your estimation, might be the effect of the women's movement on prostitution?
8. Give arguments for and against the legalization and control of prostitution.

RELATED READINGS

Bode, Ken, "New Life for the Oldest Profession," *The New Republic* (July 8 and 15, 1978), pp. 21–25.

Bryan, James, "Apprenticeships in Prostitution," *Social Problems*, 12 (Winter, 1965), pp. 287–297.

———, "Occupational Ideologies and Individual Attitudes of Call Girls," *Social Problems*, 13 (Spring, 1966), pp. 441–450.

Bryant, Clifton D., and Palmer, Eddie C., "Tense Muscles and the Tender Touch: Massage Parlors, 'Hand Whores,' and the Subversion of Service," in Clifton D. Bryant, ed., *Sexual Deviancy in Social Context* (New York: New Viewpoints, 1977), pp. 131–145.

Committee on Homosexual Offenses and Prostitution, *The Wolfendon Report* (New York: Lancer Books, 1964).

Davis, Kingsley, "Sexual Behavior," in Robert Merton and Robert Nisbet, eds., *Contemporary Social Problems*, 4th ed. (New York: Harcourt, Brace & Jovanovich, 1976), pp. 221–261.

Davis, Nannette J., "The Prostitute: Developing a Deviant Identity," in James M. Henslin, ed., *Studies in the Sociology of Sex* (New York: Appleton-Century-Crofts, 1971).

Goode, Erich, *Deviant Behavior: An Interactionist Approach* (Englewood Cliffs, N.J.: Prentice-Hall, Inc., 1978).

Greenwald, Harold, *The Call Girl* (New York: Ballantine, 1958).

Heyl, Barbara Sherman, "The Madam as Teacher: The Training of House Prostitutes," *Social Problems*, 24 (June, 1977), pp. 545–555.

Hollander, Xaviera, *The Happy Hooker* (New York: Dell, 1972).

Jackman, Norman, et al., "The Self Image of the Prostitute," *The Sociological Quarterly*, 4 (Spring, 1963), pp. 150–160.

Kinsey, Alfred, et al., *Sexual Behavior in the Human Female* (Philadelphia: Saunders, 1953).

McManus, Virginia, *Not for Love* (New York: Dell, 1960).

Maurer, David, "Prostitutes and Criminal Argots," *American Journal of Sociology*, 44 (1939), pp. 546–550.

Millett, Kate, ed., *The Prostitution Papers* (New York: Avon Books, 1973).

Rosenblum, Karen E., "Female Deviance and the Female Sex Role: A Preliminary Investigation," *British Journal of Sociology*, 26 (June, 1975), pp. 169–185.

Shoemaker, Donald J., "The Teeniest Trollops: 'Baby Pros,' 'Chickens,' and Child Prostitutes," in Clifton D. Bryant, ed., *Sexual Deviancy in Social Context* (New York: New Viewpoints, 1977), pp. 241–253.

Szasz, Thomas, *The Second Sin* (Garden City, N.Y.: Doubleday, 1973).

———, *Heresies* (Garden City, N.Y.: Doubleday, 1976).

Thomas, W. I., *The Unadjusted Girl* (Boston: Little, Brown, 1924).

Winick, Charles, and Kinsie, Paul M., *The Lively Commerce: Prostitution in the United States* (Chicago: Quadrangle, 1971).

═══════════ NOTES

1. Norval Morris and Gordon Hawkins, *The Honest Politician's Guide to Crime Control* (Chicago: University of Chicago Press, 1969), p. 21.

2. Edwin Lemert, *Social Pathology* (New York: McGraw-Hill, 1951), pp. 246–247.

3. Ibid., p. 247.

4. Robert W. Winslow, *Society in Transition: A Social Approach to Deviancy* (New York: The Free Press, 1970), pp. 275–276.

5. Morris and Hawkins, *Honest Politician's Guide*, p. 21.

6. James Bryan, "Apprenticeships in Prostitution," *Social Problems*, 12 (Winter, 1965), p. 287.

7. Nannette J. Davis, "The Prostitute: Developing a Deviant Identity," in James M. Henslin, ed., *Studies in the Sociology of Sex* (New York: Appleton-Century-Crofts, 1971).

8. Clifton D. Bryant and Eddie C. Palmer, "Tense Muscles and the Tender Touch: Massage Parlors, 'Hand Whores,' and the Subversion of Service," in Clifton D. Bryant, ed., *Sexual Deviancy in Social Context* (New York: New Viewpoints, 1977), pp. 134–135.

9. James H. Bryan, "Occupational Ideologies and Individual Attitudes of Call Girls," *Social Problems*, 13 (Spring, 1966), pp. 441–450.

10. Bryan, "Apprenticeships in Prostitution," pp. 287–297.

11. Barbara Sherman Heyl, "The Madam as Teacher: The Training of House Prostitutes," *Social Problems*, 24 (June, 1977), pp. 545–555.

12. Kingsley Davis, "Sexual Behavior," in Robert Merton and Robert Nisbet, eds., *Contemporary Social Problems*, 4th ed. (New York: Harcourt, Brace & Jovanovich, 1976), pp. 248–250.

13. Ken Bode, "New Life for the Oldest Profession," *The New Republic* (July 8 and 15, 1978), pp. 21–25; Gilbert Geis, *Not the Law's Business? An Examination of Homosexuality, Abortion, Prostitution, Narcotics and Gambling in the United States* (Rockeville, Md.: National Institute of Mental Health, Center for Studies of Crime and Delinquency, 1972); Norval Morris and Gordon Hawkins, *The Honest Politician's Guide to Crime Control* (Chicago: University of Chicago Press, 1970), pp. 1–28; Alexander B. Smith and Harriet Pollack, *Some Sins Are Not Crimes: A Plea for Reform of the Criminal Law* (New York: New Viewpoints, 1975).

14. Erich Goode, *Deviant Behavior: An Interactionist Approach* (Englewood Cliffs, N.J.: Prentice-Hall, Inc., 1978), pp. 328–330.

The "Gay' Life: Male Homosexuality and Lesbianism

6

Perhaps no area of human conduct today is, on the one hand, more widely regarded as deviant, and, on the other, defended as a matter of preference that should be tolerated, than is homosexuality. Recently the issue has been given strong emphasis both inside and outside of sociology. This is in sharp contrast to the hushed nature with which the subject has been traditionally approached. The new interest has not entirely removed the extreme difficulties in researching the phenomenon, nor has it removed the public ambiguities surrounding homosexuality. There remain also conflicting definitions of homosexuality and numerous and conflicting theories of its "causes." Indicative of changing views regarding sexuality and sex roles, the term "homosexuality" is increasingly used, as it is here, to include both male and female homosexuality, or lesbianism. However, we find that not only is the phenomenon usually thought of as a male "problem" by the public, but there has been far less attention paid to lesbianism among scientists than has been given to male homosexuality. We will investigate each of these issues in this chapter.

THE NATURE OF HOMOSEXUALITY

Depending upon how homosexuality is defined, estimates of the total number of homosexuals in society vary from around 4 percent to 100 percent of the male population and from 2 percent to 100 percent of the female population. Broadly speaking, we may define homosexuality as "a sexual propensity for persons of one's own sex." [1]

According to the psychoanalytic school, following Freud's concept of infantile sexuality as "polymorphously perverse," a homosexual propensity (whether conscious or not) exists in everybody, and thus homosexuality may be universal (among males and females). Although this way of viewing homosexuality is thought-provoking, it is quite far from what is generally termed homosexual, either publicly or by academicians. Generally speaking, there must be some past or current sexual behavior in relation to one's own sex before we can apply the homosexual label.

We may also consider the quantitative dimension of how much behavior as exceedingly important in the definition of homosexuality. Kinsey found among the white population of the United States that 37 percent of the males and 13 percent of the females have had at least one overt homosexual experience to the point of orgasm between adolescence and old age; 25 percent of the males and 10 percent of the females have greater than incidental homosexual experience for at least three years between the ages of sixteen and fifty-five; 10 percent of the males and 4 percent of the females are almost exclusively homosexual for at least three years after puberty; and 4 percent of the males and between 2 and 3 percent of the females are exclusively or nearly exclusively homosexual throughout their entire lives. [2]

The amount of sexual contact is so variable in American males that Kinsey considered sexuality not as dichotomous (homosexual versus heterosexual) but in terms of a homosexual-heterosexual continuum on a 7-point scale, with a rating of 6 for sexual arousal and activity with other males only, 3 for arousal and acts equally with either sex, and 0 for exclusive heterosexuality. Perhaps because the term *homosexual* seems to convey the misleading impression that all such people are exclusively homosexual and never engage in heterosexual contact, the term *gay* seems to be preferred in the homosexual community. There is probably no definition of gay or homosexual that can be agreed upon by scientists, but one that gets close to the common meaning of the term is proposed by Hoffman (if modified to include females):

> I am going to use the term "homosexual" in this book to refer to those individuals who have a sexual attraction toward partners of the same sex, over at least a few years of their lives.... When I use the term "homosexual" to describe a man (person), by this I do not mean that he (or she) may not also be heterosexual, for there are a significant number of people ... who are sexually attracted to and seek out sexual partners of both sexes. [3]

This definition is probably a bit broad because it may include persons who are placed in special circumstances that prohibit contact with the opposite sex (e.g., in prisoner-of-war camps, on ships, in prisons) and who engage in homosexual acts, although they revert to heterosexual behavior when the opportunity affords.

Another definition of homosexuality, from the perspective of the labeling approach, is proposed by Kitsuse:

> I shall proceed on the principle that it is only when individuals are defined and identified by others as homosexuals and accorded the treatment considered "appropriate" for individuals so defined that a homosexual "population" is produced for sociological investigation.[4]

This definition, by contrast with Hoffman's, is probably too narrow because it excludes those who perform acts of homosexuality in anonymous circumstances (as in a homosexual "bathhouse" or public lavatory) but are never caught and whose identity is never known, even to those with whom they have sexual relations. Kitsuse, however, makes a valid distinction in his exclusion of the "latent homosexual" or "closet queen," as it is termed in the argot of homosexuals.

Despite the appeal to homosexuals who may wish to proselytize others to their own behavior, when we include people with "homosexual tendencies," we are going too far afield from the common conception of homosexuality. We thus must reject the Freudian definition of homosexuality. We might, however, employ Hoffman's definition as a general definition of homosexuality with the proviso that the individual is "free to choose" males or females as sex objects (i.e., one is not institutionalized in a single-sex institution). We might adopt Kitsuse's definition as a fair definition of overt homosexuality.

METHODOLOGICAL CONSIDERATIONS

The nature of homosexuality and the stigma attached to it amplify the problems that we have discussed in regards to other forms of deviance. We have, perhaps, more questions regarding representativeness of samples of homosexuals than with any other form of deviance. The problem of the individual who is not known as a homosexual or to have engaged in any homosexual acts lies at the heart of the difficulty. Lowney, for instance, describes the case of "Jim," who, in spite of a high degree of rapport and honesty regarding drug use and other deviant activity during observations and interviews, denied any form of homosexual activities or concerns. However, when a final interview had been completed, the subject asked Lowney to help him with a "problem." Jim realized that if he told the problem to another person, it would be solved. Jim finally disclosed that he had engaged in minor homosexual activity during puberty. He experienced severe psychosomatic symptoms for over six years as a result. Lowney had another subject who denied any type of homosexual incident or involvement. However, other members of the subject's family reported that he had been seduced unwillingly by an older male several years earlier.[5] We have had several students admit privately that they had not checked an item regarding homosexual activity within a "self-report" of crime and delinquency administered earlier, even with full assurances of anonymity and confidentiality.

Survey researchers report less cooperation and frankness from lesbians than from their male homosexual counterparts.[6] In short, we see that both "subjective" and "objective" methodologies display hazards that may call into question findings concerning homosexuality.

These difficulties of repression and/or denial leave the researcher who would rely on a questionnaire technique with serious doubts as to whether or not those admitting homosexual acts within a survey are representative of all such persons. It would appear that those whose activities were known through other sources would be most likely to admit the behavior within such a format. Thus, we are left with those who have been discovered, most likely by police or through mental health treatment, and those who have admitted publicly that they are homosexuals. The nature of most homosexual (and heterosexual) acts lends itself to privacy and secrecy. It might be questioned as to whether those persons who engage in these activities in a manner in which they might be discovered by police (even through undercover "entrapment") are truly representative of homosexuals any more than voyeurs are representative of heterosexuals.

For many years, explanations regarding homosexuality revolved around reports obtained through psychiatrists and other professionals. Thus, the data were dependent upon individuals who felt they were in need of mental health treatment or "sick." Little wonder, then, that earlier theories centered strictly around such a psychoanalytic "disease" concept of homosexuality. In recent years, the American Psychiatric Association has declared that they no longer consider homosexual preference, *per se*, as an illness. Finally, we must question the representativeness of those who have, in gay subculture terms, "come out of the closet." Such individuals have received a great deal of attention in recent years in the news media in relation to the "Gay Liberation" movement.

The gay subculture has also been the focus of several recent sociological studies. Hoffman, Warren, and Weinberg and Williams have noted the selectivity of this subculture and the manner in which its members resent others who due to fears of being discovered (their marriage, profession, job, position, and so on) refuse to reveal themselves.[7] Thus, the subcultural studies may have a bent toward the unmarried, uprooted, and those holding less prestigious or less vulnerable social and economic positions. Such a bias appears to have been discovered by Laud Humphreys (whose own sample may be questioned). Humphreys did a participant observation study of homosexual encounters in public lavatories or tearooms from April 1966 to April 1967 in New York, Chicago, St. Louis, and other cities.[8] Posing as a "watchqueen"—another homosexual who serves as lookout—Humphreys observed hundreds of homosexual acts. He followed his observations with interviews and, some time later, with a household survey questionnaire of respondents he had identified by the license numbers of their automobiles. Based upon observation of over 100 men, and follow-up interviews and questionnaire study of fifty tearoom participants, he was able to develop a classification of types based upon their sexual preferences, occupational characteristics, marital status, and other related information. Humphreys found restrooms second only in popularity to private bedrooms for homosexual encounters. He found they tended to attract a large number of covert homosexuals, the majority of whom were married (54 percent) and living with their wives in a stable union, and who did not conceive of themselves as homosexuals. A large number of Humphreys' subjects had incomes exceeding the national median and were of relatively high social status.

The Humphreys study has been criticized on grounds of ethics and confidentiality more than its misrepresentativeness. While Humphreys has answered these critics,[9] such a study would now be prohibited by Health, Education and Welfare Department regulations regarding the protection of human subjects as well as by the codes of ethics of various sociological and psychological associations. The matter of ethics and the consequences for the human subjects presents even more obstacles in the research of homosexuality.

With these limitations in mind, let us now view the differences in male and female sexuality that should be considered before examining the homosexual subculture and explanations of homosexuality.

SEXUAL IDENTITY: Male and Female Sexuality

Sexual differences begin with the biological distinctions. (In the following chapter we shall address the issue of hormonal and other differences that may account for transsexualism but which are shown to have few conclusive implications for homosexuality.) While these physical differences distinguish the sexes, acquiring one's gender-identity is the result of a process of interacting psychological, social-psychological, and cultural factors. The end product is a degree of masculinity or femininity. There have been two major schools of emphasis regarding this process. One school of thought has developed within Freudian theory. The other takes a broader view and considers, to a greater extent, the learning process involving familial and societal influences. Before we present summaries of each, let us point out that each notes a difference in the process that involves males as opposed to females. At the same time, it should also be pointed out that the role of the father is the more important in sex-typing involving his interactions with both his sons and his daughters.[10]

Green synthesizes Freudian models as follows:

> By the end of the third year significant differences in male-female development were considered to be unfolding. Crucial to this phase was the child's awareness of anatomic genital differences between males and females. For the male child, awareness of the existence of persons without a penis evoked "castration fear," fear that something destructive could happen to a part of his body from which he was deriving considerable pleasure. For the female, awareness that males have something where she apparently has nothing aroused "penis envy."
>
> Children of both sexes were believed to enter into a love and jealousy relationship with their parents. For the boy, love for his mother is accompanied by the wish to replace his father. Fear that his *father*, who is also admired, would retaliate against this wish was seen as arousing anxiety that the punishment would be loss of the boy's penis. During this phase . . . , the boy ultimately reaches a compromise. He will *behave as a male* (like father) and will later seek out another female (perhaps like mother). On the other hand, the girl, blaming her mother for her lack of a penis, *turns to her father* as an object of love. Realizing the impossibility of her aspiration to replace her mother, she then *identifies with her* and will later seek out another more suitable male.[11]

According to Freud, without the above process of development males and females could revert to their primordial psychic bisexuality.

Social-learning theories propose that a child learns to be a male or a female by the manner in which it is treated by its parents. The parental expectations and parent-child relationships are influenced by what the larger culture defines as masculine or feminine:

> When a boy behaves like a "little man," say, by not crying when hurt, this "brave" behavior is reinforced. If, on the other hand, he does not behave in a masculine-stereotyped fashion, perhaps crying when hurt, this behavior may be negatively reinforced, that is, by his being called a "sissy." The development of the appropriate sex-role identification for the girl is, in many ways, the converse of that for the boy. However, the girl does not receive comparable reinforcement for adopting the feminine role, or comparable punishment for adopting the masculine one, since our culture is masculine-centered and masculine-oriented.[12]

Two points are crucial and appear to be the focus in most theoretical explanations. First, is the role of the father in gender-identification. Next, is the greater emphasis upon masculinity as opposed to femininity. Thus, we might expect father-absence or lack of an adequate father role model to produce greater degrees of homosexuality. Next, we might expect that the masculine identification, as idealized, would be more difficult to attain and, if not manifested, to be sanctioned more severely. Indeed, this appears to be the case. Male homosexuality seems to be more prevalent than lesbianism. Likewise, male homosexuality is more severely sanctioned, even within state laws, than is lesbianism. The process begins quite early—"tomboy" does not have the negative connotation implied within "sissy" (let alone "faggot" or "queer"). Let us now examine specific theories as to the manner in which homosexuality develops; that is, in spite of anatomical characteristics one's gender-identification is such that the individual prefers sexual activity with a person of the same sex.

EXPLANATIONS OF HOMOSEXUALITY

To some degree or another, most explanations of homosexuality are rooted in one of the above two schools of thought regarding sexuality.

Psychoanalytic Explanations of Male Homosexuality

Psychoanalytic theories generally view homosexuality as a form of mental illness or abnormal behavior resulting in some way from defective socialization of the individual. It is this "sickness" perspective, as we will see, that has been hotly contested by advocates of gay liberation.

CASTRATION ANXIETY THEORY   This theory states that homosexual behavior represents castration anxiety, or the fear by the male homosexual of the female genitals. Homosexual men are said to be terrified at the sight of a partner without a penis because of their own unconscious fear that they themselves might be subject to castration. Or, to put it another way, what the homosexual really wants is a girl with a penis and, although he is naturally attracted to women, he is afraid of penisless sex objects. Since it is impossible to find women with a penis, homosexuals choose boys or prefer boys because boys have a maximum of girlish and feminine traits.[13]

MATERNAL IDENTIFICATION THEORY   According to one variant of maternal identification theory, homosexuality is due to the boy's identification with his mother. If his mother becomes a role model, he comes to desire to perform sexual intercourse in the way he imagines his mother does. This may lead to a desire to take the receptor role in anal intercourse, and it may also lead the boy to take on effeminate traits. The homosexual male may, on the other hand, take younger partners as his sexual objects and behave toward them as he would have liked his mother to behave toward him.[14]

In another variant of this approach proposed by Irving Bieber,[15] the homosexual has a mother who is overly close and overly intimate and because she is afraid of losing her son, she is possessive to the point that she demasculinizes him. She favors the prehomosexual son over her other children and even over her husband, and encourages alliances with him against the father, so that the son is alienated from masculine identification. She is herself sexually frigid, but sexually stimulates the son so that he is aroused and simultaneously inhibited in the presence of a woman. The result is a severe inhibition of masculinity and assertiveness on the part of the son. The mother desires and often succeeds in keeping the boy away from other women and retains him as an unconscious incestuous object.

SACRAMENT THEORY   This theory is an attempt to explain the compulsive behavior of some homosexuals who frequently pick up rough-looking young hitchhikers and try to persuade them to submit to fellatio. These homosexuals are typical clients of hustlers, and are frequently assaulted and occasionally found murdered. According to this theory, there is a diminished vitality or self-esteem that the homosexual is seeking to restore through incorporating some of the masculinity of the person he fellates.[16] The homosexual act often occurs after there has been a blow to the individual's self-esteem, resulting in a feeling of acute restlessness that he tries to resolve by going out cruising in his car, looking for hitchhikers, sailors, or hustlers. This explanation is said to fit the well-known emphasis on penis size among male homosexuals.

Psychoanalytic Explanations of Female Homosexuality

Psychoanalytic theories of lesbianism derive from the Freudian idea of infantile sexuality and polymorphous perversity. The psychodynamics are somewhat different in females from those in males. The castration complex figures also in female homosexuality, but in a different way. The female child who sees a male penis at approximately age three experiences the trauma of thinking that she has already been castrated or has not been provided with equal sex apparatus, thus causing her to feel inferior to the male. Several psychoanalytic theories derive from this Freudian assumption. One explanation has it that the girl develops an Oedipal feeling toward her father (Electra complex) and comes to think of each eligible man as a father figure, creating in her an unresolvable incest taboo in regard to all men. Another explanation is that the girl has been rejected by the father, and this rejection causes the girl to identify with the father (identification with aggressor) and to seek

a love object representing her mother. A third explanation is that lesbianism results from regression to the infant stage. Normal sexual development depends upon separation of feelings of sexual love for the
mother and identification with her as a role model. If the girl becomes
ultimately incapable of identifying with the mother as a role model,
either because the mother is seen as too domineering over a loving father
or, on the other hand, masochistically compliant, a girl may either maintain her infantile sexual relationship with her mother in respect to other
girls who serve as mother surrogate or take the role of father in respect
to other girls.

Sociological Theories of Male Homosexuality

Sociological approaches to homosexuality commonly show how homosexuality can derive from forces in society exterior to the family. These
factors, however, are not mutually exclusive with explanations that focus
upon the family.

ANOMIE   One theory, compatible with Merton's theory of anomie,
views homosexuality as a result of economic factors. The homosexual
way of life starts with male prostitution not necessarily based upon any
sexual desire for other men. This "career" in prostitution culminates in
homosexual relations pursued for their own sake and not for the money.
According to this theory, it could be that some homosexual behavior
never has more than a utilitarian, profit-seeking purpose behind it.

MASS SOCIETY   According to this view, homosexuality arises in mass
society from the need on the part of many men for some basis of identity. Being a homosexual gives the person an identity around which to
center his self-concept and behavior. It also makes him a member of a
deviant community, and wherever he goes he can find a group of his
comrades with whom to associate.[17]

A Sociological Approach to Female Homosexuality

There is not as much disparity between sociological thinking on lesbianism and psychoanalytic thinking as there is in other areas of deviance.
Preliminary work in this area has been done by Gagnon and Simon.[18]
They base their analysis upon interviews with a small number (unspeci-
fied) of lesbians. Their quarrel is primarily with popular conceptions of
lesbians, rather than with the psychoanalytic ones discussed above. They
argue against a common conception of homosexuality which makes that
behavior into a master status for the individual. In lesbianism, the homosexual behavior is a very small portion of life organization and identity,

so that in lesbianism the term refers even more to a "way of life" rather than a choice of partners in the sex act. This consideration is helpful, they say, in understanding lesbianism as compared with male homosexuality. In male homosexuality, erotic involvements with other males generally occur earlier in adolescence and prior to any romantic emotional relations. For lesbians, erotic involvements usually take place late in adolescence or in early adult years and only after extensive and intense emotional involvement with a person of the same sex. Thus, in the sense of the "romantic complex" (though not in the sense of sex object), lesbians conform to the norm regulating females in our society. Contrary to popular explanation, lesbian careers do not generally begin with a seduction by an older woman. This is very largely a rationalization sometimes used by lesbians.

Attempting to explain the development of lesbianism, Gagnon and Simon located two factors common to those they interviewed: a preponderance of broken parental homes and of expressed preference toward one of the parents. Such preferences were found almost equally divided between male and female parent. This finding is consistent with the psychoanalytic explanations of lesbianism as either an Oedipal love for father (identification with aggressor) or a regression to infantile sexual dependence upon the mother. However, there is by no means proof of the psychoanalytic explanations in these findings. In fact, Gagnon and Simon observe that such factors are evident in many women who do not become lesbians and state that the additional factors leading to lesbian commitments are not yet known and probably will not be known in the near future. They reject the explanation that excessive masculinity is the factor or one of the factors, since they found no such consistent appearance in their sample. Evidence of a common factor of social rejection based upon social ineptitude was found, particularly in handling relationships with the opposite sex. Another possible factor may be entrance into the "gay community" through going to lesbian hangouts such as a bar known for lesbian patronage. However, Gagnon and Simon maintain that such gay world activities are less frequent for lesbians than for male homosexuals, possibly because of the acquired "techniques of repression" that lesbians share with other females in our society, so that their sexual energies do not as often lead to open expression and are kept in abeyance.

The roles of "butch" and "fem" that characterize homosexuals of both sexes are an interesting and uncritical distinction made in the lesbian community. However, the "butch" role, Gagnon and Simon found, was not traced to masculinity, since almost all of the women interviewed saw themselves as women relating to other women. The "butch" role, instead, was probably a way of reducing dissonance with conventional ideas of male-female relationships, an explanation of why a female has been chosen as a sex partner. This overreaction takes place primarily early in the lesbian career. It may also result from having to meet the demands of life without men and assume culturally male functions of work and responsibility.

Gagnon and Simon's analysis gives us a preliminary sociological framework within which to view lesbianism. In contrast to homosexuality, early childhood factors of overidentification with one or the other parent seem to be primary in lesbianism.

A Symbolic Interactionist or Labeling Approach to Homosexuality

This view holds that homosexuality arises either from failure to learn heterosexual modes of behavior or from a sequence of experiences of being labeled a homosexual and coming to accept the label that has been publicly applied to oneself. The first view is that homosexuality is behavior learned in the same way as heterosexual behavior. Heterosexual behavior is more often the sexual pattern learned because of the greater amount of stimulus for heterosexuality from peer group, parents, and media. Most persons take heterosexual behavior as given or "natural" and do not even conceive of alternative homosexual forms of behavior. In some families, however, heterosexual feelings are discouraged as being wicked, and the child may get the message that homosexual behavior is less undesirable than heterosexual behavior.[19]

The second possibility, according to this approach, is that through social interaction with peers a person may come to suspect himself to be a homosexual, or be driven to alternative homosexual relations due to inability to make heterosexual contacts. After being labeled homosexual by peers, the person may come to adopt the label of homosexual and act in accordance with that label. Alternatively, the individual may engage in homosexual behavior, not really defining it as such, but later develop a homosexual self-image.[20]

Peer group labeling in terms comparable to those of male homosexuality ("sissy," "fag," "queer") does not appear to be as strong a factor in lesbianism. In fact, if anything, a self-labeling process may result from experiences of social ineptness in dealing with males in dating and other situations. We have no knowledge of what kinds of relationships might lead to this self-labeling.

The Overt and Covert Homosexuality Subcultures

A great deal of the more recent sociological research has been devoted to the homosexual subculture or the "gay community." We divide these studies into two groupings. The first are those that deal with what we term the "overt" homosexual subculture. While this subculture provides its members with a degree of secrecy from outsiders, it consists of those who frequent the more public homosexual places and gatherings. Its members, in gay terminology, have "come out of the closets." The "covert" homosexual subculture overlaps with the overt but a majority of its members do not wish to acknowledge their homosexuality to nonmembers or their identities to other homosexuals. The vast majority of these studies have concentrated upon the male homosexual subculture rather than a lesbian subculture. Here, too, there is overlap in bars and so on, but the emphasis has been toward males and it appears there is much less developed female homosexual subculture. This may reflect a lesser number or the lower degree of stigma attached to lesbianism. It may also reflect a tendency for female homosexuals to form more stable relationships, thus eliminating the need for social networks in which to meet others.

The overt homosexual community has been described by several authors as serving as a means for identity and community for homosexuals.[21] Weinberg and Williams, in an extensive cross-cultural study of homosexuals, report that homosexuals who "come out" and take part in the overt subculture are more psychologically healthy and socially well-adjusted than other portions of the male population.[22] Serving as an adaptation to the stigmatization of society, the homosexual subculture provides the individual with a means of social contact and involvement and strong sense of community. The cohesion of the group is strengthened through its own language and information system. The members of this community are involved within certain locations within many large cities. Bars, baths, movies, and other entertainment facilities that service the gay community are located within these areas. A large portion of the members of the subculture frequently live in or near these areas. Their social network provides information regarding parties, gay rights and liberation, and police activities against homosexuals, as well as contact with each other. This subculture is frequently noted for "camping" or stereotyped homosexual behavior (limp wrists and falsetto voices, for instance). Recently, however, there has been a trend within this group toward more manly gestures and dress.[23] While this subculture is somewhat overt, it probably represents only a small portion of homosexuals.

There are a variety of other homosexuals who take part in what we term a "covert" subculture. While a small percent of these take part in the overt subculture as well, the majority are persons who have a very limited contact with other homosexuals primarily for sexual activity only and who keep such activities as secret as possible. Humphreys pierced this subculture to a large degree in his study of public lavatories mentioned earlier. He lists six types of homosexuals who frequent these "tearooms."

Trade homosexuals The first type included 38 percent of Humphreys' subjects and were called "trade" in the argot of the homosexual subculture. He found all were either married or formerly married, and most were working as truck drivers, machine operators, or clerical workers. Humphreys termed these "married men with dependent occupations." In 63 percent of the cases, either husband or wife or both were Roman Catholic, and generally conjugal relations were very rare among those interviewed. Humphreys suggested that diminished intercourse plus religious teachings may have in some way combined to cause the husband to search for sex in the tearooms. Trade do not think of themselves as homosexuals, but are only seeking a form of orgasm other than masturbation. These men are marginal to both the heterosexual and the homosexual worlds and shun involvements in the gay subculture.

Ambisexuals Ambisexuals are "married men with independent occupations." They think of themselves as bisexual or "AC/DC," and have rationalized their deviant tendencies as like those of the great men of history and certain movie stars. Ambisexuals do not hide their deviant tendencies from their friends but in fact discuss them openly and may as employers hire people who share their tendencies. While trade prefer the role of "inserter" in fellation, ambisexuals may serve either as inserter or insertee, the latter being the one who performs fellation. Ambisexuals may engage in anal intercourse, again either as inserter or insertee. Ambisexuals constituted 24 percent of Humphreys' sample.

Gay guys Gay guys are "unmarried respondents with independent occupations." Since they participate in a strong subculture that utilizes bars, bathhouses, and other marketplaces for overt meetings of homosexuals, they are rare visitors to tearooms and constituted only 14 percent of Humphreys' sample. These are admitted homosexuals with definite tendencies for the same sex, and they have little preference in sexual roles ("depends on the other guy"). They seek personal sex on a more permanent basis than the public tearoom offers. Their appearance at a tearoom may be coincidental to waiting for a friend who uses the tearoom as a "watering place." [24]

Closet queens Closet queens are "unmarried men with dependent occupations." They, like the "trade," prefer the role of inserter but must yield to insertee role when they confront the crisis of aging. Closet queens comprised about 24 percent of Humphreys' respondents.

Male hustlers Humphreys distinguishes still another type, the homosexual prostitute, operating from the streets, theaters, and certain bars in urban centers. These "midnight cowboys" share a heterosexual self-image, though Humphreys feels the exchange of money serves more to justify and neutralize a deviant sex image than to meet economic needs. An earlier study revealed the existence of "adolescent male hustlers" or "punks," who demand money in exchange for sex relations.[25] These are delinquent boy prostitutes who permit a homosexual to fellate them in exchange for money. The boys follow a strict code that the relationship must serve strictly as a way of making money and not as a means of sexual gratification, the relationship must be limited to oral genital fellation, and it must be affectively neutral.

Call boys Humphreys notes the late arrival of "call boys," who advertise in underground newspapers as "models" and charge an average of $100 for a night and $25 for an hour. Pittman[26] has noted the existence of male houses of prostitution, run by a "madam" who recruits and screens the new boy prostitutes, and trains them in their duties. These call boys are generally versatile in their sexual preferences (either anal or oral intercourse, inserter or insertee), either homosexual or bisexual in sexual identification, and may progress in a fairly lucrative though somewhat short career as a "model." Call boys cater primarily to affluent white professionals or businessmen in their forties or early fifties who, because of age, have been unable to compete for youth in the homosexual subculture. Call boys and hustlers are stigmatized in the homosexual subculture, primarily on the grounds that, although homosexual behavior is often promiscuous "one-night-stand" activity, there is no exchange of money in ordinary homosexual relations. Partly because of this stigmatization (but also because of advancing age), a call boy's career usually ends in his late twenties.

Two recent works have provided additional insights into the subculture surrounding boy prostitution and pederasty. Lloyd found that many of the boys who fall into prostitution are the products of unstable homes, are frequently runaways, and are lured into prostitution and/or pornographic posing out of a need for money as well as attention.[27] Rossman did a wider study of sexual experiences between men and boys and found that the youths frequently were seeking adventure as well as money and affection. The older males frequently were married and represented a cross section of social and economic backgrounds.[28]

Unfortunately, there is a vacuum within the literature regarding lesbian covert subcultures.

ART AND TOM:
Male Homosexuals

How do these various concepts, types, and theories relate to individual cases of homosexuality to which we might address ourselves? The following two transcripts provide us with firsthand testimony of two overt male homosexuals, both of whom would now be classified as "gay guys." The first transcript was taken from a tape prepared by GLF, a San Diego homophile organization.* The person talking, Art, is a 21-year-old college student, and his analysis of himself, plus his mother's analysis (also on the transcript), is very much

---

* This transcript was taken from a radio program entitled "Self-Portrait of a Homosexual," produced by Paul Marshall, David Craven, Kriss Beveridge, and Carole Marshall. The Executive Producer was Jay McMullen and the program was broadcast over KPBS–FM, California State University, San Diego, on June 20, 1971.

directed to the question of what homosexuality is and what causes it.

Our second transcript was taken from a talk given by another member of GLF, at the time the director of the Gay Information Center of San Diego. Tom, our speaker, shows a self-awareness and knowledge of the homosexual community that provides insights transcending what we could derive from reading technical and scientific literature on homosexuality.

Art

MOTHER: Our son, Art, is an average American boy. He's twenty-one now and has gone through all the schools and colleges. He's a pleasant personality, I would say; if you saw him on the street you would think of him as a fine American. Although one day he came to us, his parents, and said, "Dad and Mom, I think I'm a homosexual."

ART: I was at the dinner table one evening carrying on a very casual conversation. I said to my folks: "There's something you guys ought to know; I like guys better than I like girls. I know that's not the way it's supposed to be but that's the way I feel and I just wanted you guys to know about it."

. . .

ART: I like to go to friends' houses and sit around and listen to records and play piano. I love to play piano. Got a piano in my room as well as a guitar. That's one of my major hobbies, I guess—music. I don't think about girls that much. I think most homosexuals stop and think to themselves quite often during the course of a day about males. I was an only child, born in Indonesia, and lived there for eight years. When Sukarno kicked all the people out, my parents and I decided to move back to Holland. My father loved it but we only lived there for two years because the climate was just too cold for my mother. Consequently, my mother got the bright idea to come to America. I came here not knowing English. By the time I was in sixth grade I was keeping up with everybody else as far as the math and language was concerned.

MOTHER: He was bored, of course, because compared to European schools the schools in America offered too much freedom. He didn't know what to do with his free time, especially the first eighteen months.

ART: Everybody was really interested in me; this new fellow that can't even speak English. That whole trip. But I got one really close friend that lasted all the way through high school. That was Dennis. Dennis was the first one that I ever had a sexual experience with. I used to go to Dennis's house on Fridays when I knew his parents wouldn't be there and we'd do things together, watch television and stuff. We got into intricate sexual interests later but at the time I thought of it as a completely normal thing. Our sex acts weren't really that extensive considering we were just naive thirteen- and fourteen-year-olds. But I enjoyed being indoors with him naked and fondling him and having him fondle me. And I didn't think anything of it. I figured everybody does it at this age and I'll grow out of it eventually. I remember dressing in front of a mirror and he turned to me and said, "You know what you are, you're a homo." And I said, "What?" I didn't know what that meant. It had no impression on me at all, although I found out later that there was such a thing as a homosexual.

It started somewhere in junior high school. Dennis and a couple of friends that I'd been going to bed with, well, they finked on me. They just spread my reputation all over the school. It led to a point where I was being persecuted by various people. I was called names, and I was getting scared. I knew what I liked and I was scared because what I liked was what I wasn't supposed to like.

MOTHER: He would come to us and confide and say there is something that I can't cope with. He was very honest and open with us.

ART: I told my parents when I was sixteen that there was something wrong; that I didn't know what was wrong. I told them I liked looking at guys and that they seemed a lot more attractive than girls. They in turn told me that it was because of my growing-up experiences. Three different culture adjustments, etc. They threw the Freud theory at me and basically told me that I would outgrow this stage.

MOTHER: People in early life have homosexual tendencies and I believed that was the stage Art was going through.

ART: High school really suppressed me. You had to dress, look, and talk a certain way. You had to associate with certain people. And since I had this urge to be part of the in-crowd, I followed these trends of conformity. I dated girls but at the same time was still cruising guys.

MOTHER: My husband and I got a note from the high school principal asking if we could come to his office, that he had to talk to us. I didn't know what he wanted but when we got there he told us that we had a homosexual on our hands. I asked him how he arrived at such a conclusion. What has happened? He said nothing had happened but that they felt he was because he had asked for psychiatric help.

ART: Realizing that the society doesn't want you around is a pretty big jolt to accept as far as your self-concept is concerned. This is really mentally a hard thing to go through. I went through two nervous breakdowns. Sitting home all weekend crying your eyes out, not knowing why you're crying. Can't sleep, can't eat, can't do nothing except cry all the time. Three weeks before I graduated I ran away from home; I didn't want to face my friends. Instead, I took off for San Francisco. I spent a month up there in the Haight-Ashbury district when it was really flowering. I had some really good experiences up there living as a "hippie."

MOTHER: He's very impulsive and if somebody plants an idea in his mind he'll do it.

ART: When I got into college I was still suppressing my needs. I knew what I was, yet I still wouldn't allow myself to come out in the open with it. I did date girls during this period and the brothers did look upon me to fulfill my duties in that aspect. It wasn't until later in the fraternity that I became involved with this girl that I felt was falling in love with me. I knew that I didn't want to hurt her. I just let her have it with, "I like boys better. I like to go out and have a good time with you but as far as marriage and the rest, that's out." She was shocked and dumbfounded. We walked around the block. She just broke down and started sobbing. I felt bad; I really felt bad. But I thought I better tell her now before it really gets heavy.

MOTHER: My husband believes this (homosexuality) is a fear to express yourself toward the other sex. He can't believe that it's something permanent.

ART: I'm not repulsed about being with girls, I always seem to communicate with them very well; but as far as an actual sex act with a girl, it doesn't appeal to me at all. I remember one time I was at a fraternity party with a girl and all of a sudden she was gone. I went out looking for her and then went out to my room. It was pitch black as I went to my bed. I felt somebody grab my leg and there was this girl nude in my bed smiling the most seductive smile I've ever seen in my life. I just thought, "Oh God, I can't have this!" So I turned around and walked out as fast as I could. I told one of the guys that I wanted her out of my bed and they asked me why. I just made up some excuse like I was too tired or too drunk.

I got to be good friends with this guy Steve. We moved in together but he was completely straight; he had no idea what was going on. But he had a beautiful body. Broad shoulders, great muscles, and thin waist. Black hair and beautiful blue eyes. He had the most childlike smile; God, he was beautiful! I was in love with him for six months and finally couldn't contain it any longer. I told him I was in love with him, that I was a homosexual. He didn't even know what the word meant. I told him and he moved out the next day.

From then on I figured, the hell with it. I'm not gonna have any more nervous breakdowns and I'm gonna accept myself for what I am. No more straight life for me. Alfred was this guy I was introduced to by a friend of mine at school who was supposedly straight.

ALFRED (ANOTHER MEMBER OF G.L.F.): When I first met Art he was literally in a closet, and he came over to my house one week-

and when we had a gay party going—you know, listening to records. Anyway, when Art found that he could identify with the people there and that they were friendly he literally came flying out of his closet.

ART: I had been going to Alfred's house, like, every weekend. There would be parties there and I met quite a few people. I was confused but still I was satisfied because, sure enough, these people were homosexuals but still I was having a good time. All these Queens screwin' around having a good time. I felt comfortable but, like I said, I was still rather confused.

ALFRED: To suddenly come upon this is like discovering a new world; it is, in fact, like another world, a subculture. To bounce into this is kind of a groovy experience for a kid "coming out." I think Art found it so fascinating that he went right into it.

ART: I've always been an extrovert as far as my personality goes. When I "came out" I did it with the proverbial "Bang!" Sometimes it takes people about a year or two to come out as far as I did, but it took me less than two and one-half months. The main thing I thought about was to try everything I could, so I tried everything to see how things worked. Alfred's place, his friends, etc., was the path and point of reference from which I learned the ropes of the homosexual world. Every time the guys left the house they made sure to leave me with a young "chicken"—an underaged homosexual. Everybody would tell me about the bars and I was really looking forward to being twenty-one.

The first time I went to a homosexual bar was about last year at this time. Bill and Bob and Fred and I went to a pretty popular gay bar in L.A. I walked straight in, the doorkeeper didn't even catch my I.D., and ordered a beer; here was this place packed and wow, not one girl in sight! We just split up. All guys, a few of them really good looking. By this time I was somewhat educated as to the different types of people that composed our subculture such as the different types of Queens, motorcycle types that would stand up against the bar throwing out their chests looking very brutal, as well as a couple of "Fems," just running around screaming with their hair all done up—you know, bleached-blonde Clairol jobs; screaming at each other about their last trick. It was a pretty general type crowd, businessmen types as well. Everybody was dancing, but, as I said, there were no girls. The place was just packed. I really kind of enjoyed myself, you know, it was kind of nice.

ALFRED: Art was very popular and very active in what he did. Actually, he even went to the extent of forming the Gay Liberation Front in San Diego. He was the first president and actually guiding hand of the organization. And then all of a sudden he stopped his activities; you know, going to bars, and being part of social life. He kind of turned inward to himself and almost dropped out completely.

ART: It became a passion with me, it became an obsession to go to the club and dance. After a while it became rather boring. Seeing the same people and faces every Friday and Saturday night. Most of the people there seemed to be very hung up, very lonely people who could easily be spotted by the look in their eyes. It's a weird loneliness they have; they're looking for something. The extreme and only interest seemed to be, "Who am I gonna trick with tonight?" It seemed to me to be a very desperate type of situation. It all seemed very sad.

I'm really down on hustling. Because it's a bad thing, because I almost did it, man. In fact, I did do it once; I once sold my body for a hundred bucks. He was a dirty, ugly, filthy leech of a man. It was the worst experience I've ever had in my life. I found him in some ad in one of the underground papers, you know, "Swinging businessman wants young boys from San Diego to swing with"—that type of thing. I was selling something that I was trying to think very highly of. That's the only way any of those old men can get sex: pay for it. I don't know of any young, good-looking men who would pay for it. It's really the younger looking men that turn out to be hustlers while the old, decrepit ones turn out to be customers. I don't know if that's the reason I'm really down on it, but I personally would rather have a close personal relationship with somebody.

ALFRED: Yeah, Art had some disappointments. One thing is he was looking for security. Loneliness is the worst thing that can happen to someone and in the gay world it's even more profound. Art found one fella where things started off beautifully and then it suddenly ended.

ART: Specifically, what I was looking for was a husband, at the time. That's about the only way I can say it. I was looking for someone I could settle down with, someone to take care of me and make decisions for me. Consequently, I picked the first one that came along that looked halfway decent to me and managed to get hung up on him. This kid fell head over heels over me and I threw myself into him as far as my emotions were concerned. We moved in together about a week after that, a completely abrupt type of situation. I decided this is it. I withdrew all my money from the bank and paid for everything. He was a husband in the family. He went out and worked and I did the cooking and kept the house clean. I was the hostess when people would come over but three weeks after we moved in together he shafted me and it psychologically tore me up. I just couldn't take it.

ALFRED: To be lonely, to be singularly by yourself is a very frightening factor, and it happens quite a bit in a gay situation. This can lead to several things, like, for instance, suicide.

ART: I have never seriously considered suicide. Even during this time when I was going through this loneliness and depression. My mind just isn't stretched that way; I just can't really think about suicide. I mean, every time I stop and think about something like that, man, good things come into my head and pretty soon my depression is over, if only temporarily. Quite recently I almost did kill myself. I was somewhat drunk, and it wasn't because I lost a lover or anything like that. I really thought of myself and my life ahead of me and it was quite a shock. It seemed to me at the time that I just wasn't achieving anything and I had no future. I was living at home at the time. I just stormed out, said to hell with my Mom, Dad, and the house and just hopped on my motor-cycle and took off. I just wanted to live my own life, or die if I want to. Right after I said that, I decided to kill myself; like I said, I was rather polluted. I was riding down the freeway and figured, okay, this is the best way to do it, so I hit about 90 mph, let go of the steering wheel and just leaned back. If anything would have happened, that would've been it for me, no doubt about it. I was really thinking at those moments, there's really nothing to live for anymore, I've done everything I've wanted to do and I've discovered everything that's going on and I felt there was just nothing going on anymore worth living for. Then all of a sudden I sat up, man—it was really far out. It was really a coincidence because I was sitting there thinking of all the things people had done for me throughout my life, how nice they'd been to me; all these memories were going through my head as I sat parked on the side of the road. I just sat there and thought. About ten minutes after I stopped there, these two guys came by on these beautiful Harleys and they stopped. One of the guys sat and looked at me for about a minute and I looked at him, and he looked at me and said, "Anything wrong, man?" Those were his exact words, I'll never forget them. I looked at him and said, "No, I'm all right." And he looked at me again and kind of smiled and said, "All right, man," and just took off. Man, right there my tears just started falling, I just started crying like a sonofabitch. And I thought to myself, "Wow, I'm glad I didn't kill myself." I cried for about fifteen minutes 'cause I was so happy. I just turned around, took off on my bike, went back home, and went to sleep. I don't know, I guess that may have been a turning point in my life. It really kind of forced me into a very deep reflective attitude in which I decided to take some months off and do some super-serious thinking. I'll just go back into the straight life because it's one of the easiest ways to live; it's very hard to live as a homosexual; I just have to do the kind of serious thinking I've been doing lately.

ALFRED: Art has gone just about the full cycle now. He came crashing out of his closet, and because of doubts, doubts like we've all had, he's gone back into his closet. But Art's got to find something very soon; otherwise, he's going to be quite out on a limb, I think.

ART: Where do I stand right now? I really don't know. I'm kind of in limbo, compromising between the gay and straight life. What can you do? I'd like to find a lover and settle down, take it easy, but right now the chances look very slim; I don't think it'll happen. I guess as I grow I'll have to accept the fact that I'm going to spend the rest of my existence all by myself. There must be other guys that are in the same position that I am right now; that are looking for something and that just don't feel comfortable with either the gay or the straight worlds. I hope someday I'll run into one of these people.

Tom

TOM: I want to first talk about the "gay minority." You are all very, very aware of the black minority, the brown minority, and certain other minorities, but you are not really aware of the gay minority—and yet, we are as large, if not larger in number, than any minority at all. At least 10 percent of you out there belong up here with me, and it is a good possibility that if it wasn't for the social structure and the poor socialization process, the prejudice thing, a good 20 percent of you might be up here with me. An additional 20 percent might occasionally come up here with me. What I mean to say is that homosexuality is natural. It is not particularly universal, and everyone is not going to indulge in it, but if you consider human sexual response from a nonsocial context, from not just our cultures, but from all cultures of the world, then you'll see that homosexuality has been with us since the dawn of man. In certain cultures, notably the Greek and the Roman, it has been socially acceptable. If not sometimes more desirable. For instance, in ancient Greece, particularly Sparta, you were laughed at if you didn't go with a woman and have children; however, love for another male was considered to be pure and noble—it was true love. So the problem with the homosexual today is not a psychological problem, but it is a sociological problem—the problem of what this culture and this society does to its people. Homosexuals are raised in this antihomosexual climate. I can remember being warned about homosexuals at a time when I was practicing homosexuality on my own—I mean, I wanted to. I wasn't exactly laughing when my mother warned me about the people that I was chasing. It was really difficult not to be aware. I am twenty-two now and have been indulging in some form of homosexuality since I was about four. I am not exclusively homosexual. I have a girlfriend and I live with girls occasionally, but I identify with homosexuality; it is a thing I really prefer.

There are three subcultures with the homosexual subculture. If you will pardon the expression, these are three mating patterns. This hierarchy tends to be aristocratic in nature. For instance, there is the "tearoom queen," the one who cruises the bathrooms, the people you might see at the Plaza or walking up and down Broadway, and the people who walk around the park a lot. This is the lowest level on the status scale. The second group is the one which you might say I personally prefer, and this is the gay bar scene. This includes the bars and the baths that are gay meeting places. They are places where we go that you would never dream of—they could be right next door, in fact, and you would never know. And then there is the very aristocratic group, which is comprised of the people who are afraid to be identified as gay. They have these little circles of places where they could not be publicly identified. There are a lot of doctors and lawyers who cannot afford to get a reputation. Now, from the standpoint as a member of the Gay Liberation Front, I consider both the other two groups "cop-outs." The tearoom queen is copping out because he is living the trip that the heterosexual culture puts on him. He can do his own thing as long as he does it in guilt and shame, and cruises bathrooms and sneaks around in the dark. The other extreme, the aristocratic circle, can do their thing in comfort and ease, as long as they don't let their clients know about them, again letting the heterosexual trip fall on their heads. Most of the people who go to Gay Liberation Front are from the bar-type scene. These are the ones who are particularly afraid of having some possibility of running into their employers, or their brother-in-law. GLF is an attempt to take homosexuality out of the dark. It doesn't belong there because it is a groovy thing and homosexuals are groovy people and most of what people know about them is a result of prejudice, fear, and many other uncool trips.

GLF was born in a riot, the Christopher Street Riots of 1969, sometime in the summer. I don't know how many of you will be shocked at my statement, but occasionally the Police Department has been known to take graft, particularly from the gay people. On Christopher Street there was a bar, I cannot remember the name of it, but the bar was not paying enough to the police and they decided it was about time that they crapped out on these evil, degenerate people. So they emptied the bar and had all the gay people out on the street, and they were going to take them down to headquarters and harass them a little bit—they weren't going to do anything terrible to them, but just harass them. Along with the birth of liberation movement, you might say that the parent of Gay Liberation is the Black Liberation, or Black Power Movement. We are following their example. And so this do-your-own-thing movement and this feeling of no guilt and no shame that is coming upon the people is all part of the spirit of the people who went to this particular bar. The gay people proved to the police that there is no flaw and they went down the street throwing rocks and wiping out a lot of the establishment's things. We have a bar here in town and I have a feeling that if the police tried to empty it and were a little too heavy at the wrong time, there would be a riot here. GLF is basically composed of younger people who are not going to take it any more. Gay Liberation is going to be more and more in the front lines of liberation movements.

One of the things we did recently was at a psychology convention at a hotel here. Panel speakers from L.A.'s GLF came down and we were there to discuss homosexuality with psychologists. We are anti-psychology, you might say, in a lot of ways. Psychologists have had the attitude that we are to be converted for a long time. This is the thing we were attempting to point out to them—that we don't want to be converted. We dig what we're doing and all we want is to be left alone. We had a very good experience with these people talking to them. I think we have helped a lot of psychologists. We also had this city's first Gay-In, which was very peaceful, and in which I am very pleased to say that the police department was fantastic. They patrolled the area around the place to protect us, and there were some detectives who were actually, as a matter of fact, out looking through the bushes to see what was happening. They were making sure that people didn't get too violent. We have had all kinds of great things and great things are being planned, so look for more activities of GLF.

I want to talk a little about Alpine County. The major purpose of Alpine County hasn't been accomplished, even though the Alpine County affair result is not going to be taken over. The whole purpose of the Alpine County thing is to focus the world's attention on Gay Liberation Front. It is the kind of subject that most people want to shun, it doesn't exist, these people are not really asking for their rights, they just think they are. But we got the attention and that is the important thing. However, I have something to lay on you that you might like or you might not like, you might get uptight or you might not, I don't know. I hope it doesn't make you uptight. If it does, I don't care. The first successful total gay community is probably going to be in this county. Our county is going to be the first to be blessed by this happy event. There was a little town about sixty-five miles east of here. It's in the county and it's owned by one little old lady who wants to sell it and she wants two hundred and thirty thousand dollars for it. It is almost paid for by now, by gay people. It is called Mount Love Corporation and it is going to be called Mount Love. It is a beautiful location right out Interstate 8 and it can grow and grow and grow—like a flower or cancer, depending on your point of view. I just thought you might be intrigued by this. This city's GLF owns property there and we are going to, in all probability, build a convention center, or small headquarters for Gay Liberation Front, which means that this city may host Gay Liberation Front International. This means basically that this city may be the Hollywood Boulevard of Southern California. Gay Liberation's attempt is not to make gay Americans; its attempt is not to bribe the straight people out; its attempt is not to induce the straight people to become gay. Gay Liberation Front's main purpose is to induce the straight world just to leave us alone. We don't want to be treated like people or anything else, but just to be left alone. Your culture is rabidly anti-homosexual and it destroys people. I had a friend, for instance, who was working for the government for about seventeen years. He had an excellent record, but they found out he was gay and he lost his job, which brings us to an interesting paradox within the government. If you want a government security job and you are gay, you cannot have it. Therefore, if you want that job, you cannot tell them that you are gay, and therefore you are a security risk because you can be blackmailed. However, if you tell them that you are gay, you are not a security risk because you cannot be blackmailed, but you cannot have the job because you are a security risk. This is the logic of our government, that is, some of the members of our government. I might go on to mention that many members of our government are members of our brotherhood. The Gay Minority has an exceptionally good grapevine, an exceptionally accurate grapevine because it is centered in so many pin-pointed areas—the bars, for instance. There is a great deal of evidence that your most respected men, not only the artists like Tchaikovsky and DaVinci and Michelangelo and others are gay, but the political leaders, the members of armed forces are also gay. Let me say that there are two basic roles in the gay society—there is the "butch" and there is the "fem." The "butch" would roughly correspond to the male role and the "fem" to the female role. A "fem" spends most of his time on his stomach, if you get what I mean.

QUESTION: *What about homosexuality in prison? Are those people really homosexuals?*

TOM: Now we have to come to sort of a definition of homosexuality. My personal definition of homosexuality is anyone who has homosexual experiences and enjoys it can be classified as homosexual. If you consider what this means, homosexuality is not so opposed to heterosexuality, as one on one hand and one on the other, but there is heterosexuality and then deep variations of sexuality on that same theme. A lot of people, when confined, and away from females, do practice and enjoy homosexual relationships. There is not a male or female in this room who, under the right circumstances, could not have a homosexual relationship and enjoy it. You can enjoy it physically, but if your head isn't really into it you will not psychologically get satisfaction from it, and that is the important aspect. But there isn't one person who cannot have a homosexual experience and enjoy it, physically, and in certain situations, mounting pressures push you into relieving them. Prisons are an example of this, also boys' and girls' schools, and the military. This is the type of homosexuality that is really the concern because these people tend to want to go back to heterosexual affairs. I get more satisfaction out of sleeping with guys and I much prefer it, and I am not going to change. I could be put into a girls' school, for instance, and I would sleep with girls, yet when I got out, I would go back to sleeping with guys. That is my interest and that is what Gay Liberation is attempting to do, and so, prisons and such are not really properly our concern. My opinion is that if a person psychologically wants a woman, he should have a woman and he shouldn't be forced to go and sleep with guys if he doesn't enjoy it that much—this is where the wives and girlfriends come in.

Let me talk to you about the major problems in the homosexual way of life. It is a rough way of life; it is not easy. It is a lonely way of life. But really, the problems are not any worse than what heterosexuals experience. The only real problem is society's attitude toward it. I am speaking of male homosexuality because I am not an authority on female homosexuality. A boy goes through a series of traumas. By the time he is about fourteen, fifteen, or sixteen, he becomes aware of the little games he played as a child he still likes, but most of his friends aren't interested in that anymore, so he begins to feel different, and he doesn't understand it yet. Along the time he is about seventeen or eighteen, sometimes not until he is twenty or twenty-five, or even thirty, he begins to identify his behavior as what they call homosexual, and that is the first trauma for him. If you consider his feeling, there are negative slang terms in every group. For instance, you find the term "nigger." There are all kinds of names for particular groups. But most groups just have one or two names. The gay people have more negative names than any other group—"pansies," "fairies," "queers"—there are dozens of them. So he has all these negative names that he can choose from and it becomes very very rough. And then he goes through a period in which he is very alone. He may meet a few friends and get interested in the gay life. After awhile, in the gay life, he goes through a series of traumas of bad affairs and experiences, and the rather unusual subculture of the bars and things like that. And then, in my opinion, probably the worst trauma he goes through, I am going through mine right now, is when you reach your early twenties and all of your childhood friends are getting married and having children and you really feel out of it, you really feel like a spare tire. In fact, when I was a child, the boy with whom I used to indulge most of my homosexual play with, well, he now has a daughter. I am sitting here thinking that I can remember when we were children talking about getting married and having a family, and I sit back and realize that things just didn't work out the way I wanted them to, and you really feel strange, and then you go to the bar and have a drink to pick up what is called a trick, a person for the night. So you see, the homosexual is born with the same attitudes of what is right and normal, but he doesn't fit into them. He has these periods of adjustment to go through in order to wipe out his past and impose a new socialization on himself, a new way of living. And then you see, in a mature group of gay people, much more excitement. I can walk into a straight bar and the people are not exciting at all, and I do not necessarily mean the possibility of the chase, or finding someone to take home or whatever. There is just no social interaction, or it is very stilted and very dull. In a gay bar, the emotional level is higher, everyone is either more excited or more depressed. Gay people tend to be more extreme about everything, and it is much more exciting. But it is a rougher life. For instance, I never came home last summer before two or three in the morning—every single night, and I would often come straggling into my apartment at eleven or twelve in the afternoon the next day. I'm sure you've all seen how terrible someone who has been out all night looks. At that time, my neighbors did not know about my activity and they would see me come straggling in. It is the kind of life that a lot of gay people lead. It is a swinging life, a lot of parties, activities, and events, and it is very exciting, but it is not that Anglo-Saxon sort of Protestant life that everyone talks about and it is rough to be a person. He attempts to make himself fit, he tries to lay the heterosexual trip on himself and that means that a guy wants a lover, sometimes they use the terms husband and wife, but it is basically a companion for sex and other purposes—to live together, to buy furniture together, that sort of thing, and it doesn't always work out. This results in a lot of unhappiness when this heterosexual trip doesn't work.

Let me tell you a little bit about the movement—some of the activities and things—here in town. We have several organizations. There is Gay Liberation Front, which I pointed out to you and unfortunately it meets tonight at this time for those of you who come to this class and cannot make it to the meetings. Next semester, or next summer or whenever, I would like to welcome you to the meetings because they are not for homosexuals only. Gay Liberation Front is open to anyone, male or female. If you are a guy and you are afraid to go because you think you will get seduced, let me tell you it is really hard to get a trick if you are not out to get one—no one is going to put the make on you. We have some really good meetings. Actually gay people aren't really that much different than you. The second group is Gay Information Center. Undoubtedly some of you know homosexuals—one out of every ten of your friends is probably gay—remember that the next time you tell a gay joke at a party. You never can tell when a problem with homosexual people might come up. You might even find out that your father's gay. Gay Information Center is a referral information and counseling service for gay people—even for old people who just want information on what homosexuality is or what is happening with the gay movement. And then there is a group called the Metropolitan Community Church. I might also touch the religious aspects of this activity, too. This is a gay church. Again, if you want to go you are welcome because it is not exclusively gay. It is the most liberal church you will go to, and the people there will not be down on you for anything. Everyone is entitled to their hang-ups, even Christians. The other major group is Tre Fem and this is an exclusive girls' group, particularly lesbian girls; however, straight girls are welcome. Tre is French, meaning very, and fem is for feminine—very feminine, although they're not, but they are delightful women—almost got beat up by one the other night. Transsexuality is not homosexuality. It is the actual feeling that you are in the wrong body. If I were transsexual, I would be aware of my male body, thinking

I was female. There are some girls who make very attractive males and no one would ever know she was female. I asked one a very sensitive question and said, "What would happen if for some reason you became pregnant and it became very apparent that you were not male?" She got up with her fists clenched and said, "How would you feel if you got pregnant?" She was really terrified at the idea. Let me get to the religious thing for a second. How many of you are Presbyterian, Methodist, or Lutheran? Your churches do not officially condemn homosexuality as that terrible thing it was always thought to be. Those three churches have changed. In fact, the Methodist Church has opened up its facilities to Gay Church. It is changing and reinterpreting the Bible. The Bible is perhaps the one book in the world that will facilitate interpretation more than any other book and even though many of the churches are now reinterpreting it, I somehow resent that for the past two thousand years somebody's wrong interpretation has sent many gay people to their doom. For instance, the same passage in the Bible that condemns homosexuality condemns women for wearing red dresses. A woman who wears red dresses is equally as sinful as a man who sleeps with a man. A lot of the people who were burned in the middle ages who were thought to be witches were really homosexuals. Charlemagne had men in his harem as well as women.

QUESTION: *If I have friends who I believe are homosexuals, but it has never been brought out in the open, how should I approach the subject? Are people born homosexual?*

TOM: This is a funny predicament and I think that the best thing you might do in this situation is to somehow, sometime, drop a line letting them know that you are not prejudiced toward homosexuality. Let them know that if you do find out, they can trust you. Or avoid the subject completely, depending on your own feelings.

There is some indication in what you might call birth defect, that people are born homosexual, but this is very rare—one out of every thousand homosexuals, maybe. There is nothing to do with the hormone balance. This has been proven. I have had my hormones tested myself and I have very normal hormones. I believe it is conditioning—a psychological thing. The theory is that when you are born you have sexuality but not sexual direction. You are not a heterosexual or a homosexual to begin with, but it is what happens to you when you grow up is what gives you this determination. As for the people who might still insist that it is a genetic thing, that it is born, I would answer it this way: homosexuals tend not to procreate, and as they do not procreate, they would have a tendency not to procreate these genes that create homosexuality, so over centuries, homosexuality is evolutionary and would disappear because they are not being procreated. So this proves that it cannot be born.

QUESTION: *Is it true that the Metropolitan Community Church performs homosexual marriages?*

TOM: This is part of that uncool trip again, and I do not approve of marriages. I am not personally in favor of heterosexual marriages. I think marriage in many ways is an outdated institution. So I hate to see this outdated institution of yours come into our group. However, some people, even if they are gay, feel this social pressure and want to get married. It is not against the law to take a marriage license if you are both the same sex and the Metropolitan Community Church has had maybe three or four marriages of this type. Two women friends of mine are married and two of my male friends are planning on getting married, so it is an increasing thing and it does happen.

QUESTION: *Do you adopt a certain role when you are homosexual?*

TOM: My own feeling is that you do get pushed into a role when you hang around gay circles. I have been pushed into the queen, sort of a "fem" role. I dress like a queen when I go out to the bar. I like to do unto rather than have it done to me.

Let me talk about what is called camping first. Camping is something which needs explanation. GLF once had an executive board meeting when sixteen of us went into a restaurant with our GLF arm badges on and we were doing what is called camping. Camping is a form of getting humor. A lot of groups, such as black people, have their own form of humor. That of gay people is the twisting of the roles of he and she. If you were gay and in my circle, you could call me she instead of he, and if a gay person were sitting next to me I could say, "Hey, girl. . . ." It is a form of laughing at the he or she role of homosexuals because they do not mean that much to us, and most of the raging femininity you see within us is a form of camping—everyone does it some time or another. Though it seems quite sadistic on my part, we enjoy the reactions of the straight people around us and we laugh at them because they do not understand the reasons we are doing it. As for my own femininity thing, right now I am camping.

QUESTION: *Why do homosexuals tend to exaggerate in camping?*

ANSWER: It all has to do with the way you speak, move, and carry yourself. When we exaggerate, we are satirizing the feminine role, and the more we do it, the funnier it is. Though some may think this would tend to single us out more and create more prejudice, we are really a very invisible minority for being so large. Most of the camping is done in bars or within gay groups. To be very honest, when I camp where there are straight people, I do it for revenge. I enjoy tormenting people in this way because I have been pushed around so much, particularly in our high school, because I was gay. We are laughing at ourselves just as much as anyone else. I believe the ability to go camping in public shows a very unhung-up attitude toward homosexuality.

QUESTION: *I get the impression that from what you have said so far, a homosexual's life consists of a lot of different affairs, and if people assume the role of heterosexuality in homosexual relationships, they are copping out. Is this what you mean?*

TOM: No, this is not what I mean. The copping out is when they attempt the man-wife thing and it becomes very monotonous. This would be the heterosexual. I have never seen a monotonous homosexual affair. The best relationships are those where the two partners agree they can both go "tricking out" with other gay people. Love is very easy. The homosexual affair is basically unstable because of jealousy. Affairs cannot last this way. Jealousy is perhaps the most destroying emotion. When gay people try to devote themselves to just one other person, it almost invariably fails. Therefore most homosexuals are quite promiscuous and I think that is one of the problems. Homosexuals run from affair to affair, attempting to find something, and the reason they cannot find it is because society will not leave them alone. If society would leave them alone, I believe homosexuality would become more stable. I myself am not promiscuous and most of the people at GLF are not.

QUESTION: *Why are you homosexual?*

TOM: I have my own theories about me. I had a very difficult childhood. At seven, I came down with a fatal heart disease and was supposed to die. I was in the hospital for a very long time and when I got out of the hospital, I was under the total authority of my grandmother. After that, I was forced to lead a very passive life without much stress or activity. I couldn't play sports. I learned to embroidery—it was something to do with my nervous energy. I read a lot and did many indoor things, and most of the indoor things were girlish things. This could have led me to identification with a passive type role, and therefore made me homosexual. I really don't know.

QUESTION: *When you speak of your friends that are getting married and having children, do you wish you were not the way you are?*

TOM: No, I am very happy being gay, but I love children and would like to have some of my own. However, with society the way it is now, I do not place children in my life because I would have to raise them to do exactly what they want. However, I have been able to do a lot with children. I worked with Head Start for a summer and Red Cross, so I have had a lot of contact with children. I think that my desire to have children can be satisfied in some other way. I would really like to adopt children, but again, because of the way society is, I just can't.

QUESTION: *Is your girlfriend more or less something for your own protection?*

TOM: No, she is a fantastic and groovy person. However, she's married and I cannot propose. We carry on quite heavily actually, but her husband is not afraid because he thinks I am exclusively gay. If she wasn't married, I would marry her but I wouldn't have children because I could not raise them the way I would want to, again because of society.

QUESTION: *Do you ever approach straight people and if you do, how do you go about it?*

TOM: I sleep with guys I know and I turn on to people I care about and if they turn on to me frequently a sexual relationship will result, but they prefer their sexual life and I prefer mine. In fact, the best sex I ever had was with a straight guy—the most responsive person I have ever had. But I am not shallow with sex. I like sex with people not bodies, and I am not that horny, you might say. There was a physically attractive straight guy at my apartment last night and he spent the night. I am sure I could have had him if I had decided to take him, but I didn't because I didn't think it was good for him.

QUESTION: *Are you in favor of Women's Liberation?*

TOM: Yes, and the reason I am is because I can understand Women's Liberation in a way none of you can, because they are talking about this fanatic male sexism. The gay people have the same problem —the male ego thing. This is what Gay Liberation and Women's Liberation are all about. There is a joke that strikes me as funny because those who tell it do not realize that what they are saying is not a joke, but the truth: Delegates from Gay Liberation got together with delegates from Women's Liberation to discuss their differences, only to find that there were none. This is true. Our object is the same thing: Freedom.

QUESTION: *Are your parents aware of your situation?*

TOM: No, my parents are not aware. My parents are extremely unstable. They are going through some family problems with my brother related to drugs right now. I am a very successful person with a lot of ability and I have managed to make use of my ability. I have always gotten good grades in school and have built up a good reputation. My brother grew up in my shadow and he feels inferior to me. They are having problems with him and I don't want them to have to face problems with me. I am very adjusted to being gay, but I remember once my mother told me on the telephone that she thought homosexuality was the worst thing that could ever happen to anyone. I think my mother would rather see me dead, and so I am going to wait until she is strong enough to accept it. I will tell her eventually.

QUESTION: *Are you aware that transvestites inject hormones to change their body?*

TOM: These are transsexuals and I am not a transsexual. Massive doses are used for special reasons. There are two major hormones; they are testosterone and estrogen. Testosterone, when injected into the male or the female, will do nothing more than increase sexual drive. Estrogen injected into either female or male will decrease the sexual drive and enlarge the breasts—period—that is all it will do. Again, this cannot be genetic because we would have evolutionarily disappeared because our genes were not being procreated. I cannot see any malfunction physically in me but I do see a lot of things in my childhood that happened which I feel relate.

QUESTION: *Are you really happy now?*

TOM: Yes, I am really quite happy. The only thing that makes me unhappy is that I have a fear of your prejudice and your opinion of me. I am really as normal and human as you and I can suffer just as much as you, and if any one of you were put down constantly by large numbers of people you would be uptight too. I mean, it is really a wonder I am not psychotic with the problems gay people have to face today—just because I am a simple, everyday neurotic links me closer with you.

QUESTION: *I have misunderstood a few things you said. First, you say that homosexuals do not procreate, but some of them lead perfectly normal lives. Second, you do not believe in marriage, but you said you would marry your girlfriend if she were not already married. Why bother if you prefer men?*

TOM: It is very possible for homosexuals to be leading normal family lives with children involved. All right, what I am saying is that I wouldn't want to marry her but I would like to live with her because I am very fond of her and because she is a very groovy person. I would bother because I simply like her as a person. My whole life is not oriented around sex.

QUESTION: *Don't you think you are just as prejudiced toward my way of thinking, if not more so, than I am of yours?*

TOM: I am overreacting in this case. What I am simply saying is that your life is not that much better than mine, and from my point of view, it definitely has its drawbacks.

QUESTION: *I get the impression that the homosexual is very wrapped up in sex and that this is his primary goal. Is this true?*

TOM: That one summer I told you about, my only interests were drinking and sex. I am only twenty-two and I think most men my age are interested in pleasures. I didn't have to work at the time because I had plenty of money. My father was able to support me through school, so I spent this time mostly getting my head together. My own interests involve political involvement with Gay Liberation Front, socially involved with Gay Liberation Center, and these are not sexually oriented. I am what you might call an intellectual leader in the area in the field of witchcraft; I have worked with Head Start and Red Cross, and I am taking twelve units at State College. I have many hobbies and many interests and most other gay people do too. Of course, some of us are totally wrapped up in sex, but then some heterosexuals are totally wrapped up in sex. I have been talking mostly about sex tonight because that is the topic of discussion.

QUESTION: *Have you been hassled a lot by the police or is this decreasing?*

TOM: Yes, they do hassle us. In fact, right before election time there was vast harassment. They are very uptight.

COMMENTARY

Both of these transcripts give us insights about homosexuality that may help clarify some of the points made in the literature. What is homosexuality to a male homosexual? Quite clearly to these two homosexuals, Art and Tom, homosexuality is not an abnormal phenomenon, but is instead something that is quite "natural" under given circumstances. Tom seems to think that almost everybody would be "homosexual" if he or she overcame societal repression. A homosexual is:

> ... anyone who has homosexual experiences and enjoys it. ... There is not a male or female in this room who, under the right circumstances, could not have a homosexual relationship and enjoy it.

This assumption may be a major one in the formation of the Gay Liberation Movement of which Art and Tom are both a part. That is, the movement contains the assumption that there is nothing wrong with homosexuality, nothing unnatural, and homosexuals should unite to assert their right to be homosexual. This assumption is quite antithetical to the psychoanalytic theories of homosexuality reviewed earlier in this chapter and in the introductory chapter to this text. Psychoanalytic theories assert that homosexuality arises from a defect of socialization (despite the fact that Freud asserted the "naturalness" of polymorphous infantile sexuality). Some psychoanalysts view homosexuality as sickness (however widespread it may be), which can or should be cured through therapy. By contrast, the two homosexuals in our transcripts unite in their opposition to the psychoanalytic approaches, and their testimonies seem to underline the relevance of sociological theories, especially labeling theory. Both Art and Tom seem to have gone through a common development involving three stages: 1) a stage of early homosexual behavior without it really being defined as such by the participants; 2) a stage of passage in which the label *homosexual* is applied, and 3) a stage of social ostracism in school as an outsider, a "sissy," a "queer," or a "fag." In Art's case, he appeared to be an outsider in junior high school perhaps because of his foreignness, and this led to his close relationship with Dennis and early homosexual behavior. Dennis's application of the homosexual label appears to be significant ("You know what you are, you're a homo"). And when Dennis later "finked," Art's homosexual identity became public, thus further solidifying his homosexual self-concept. This may have proved to be a self-fulfilling prophecy. In high school and in his later experience in his college fraternity, he could not sexually relate to females (although he did date) perhaps because he was already convinced that he was a homosexual.

Tom reveals a slightly different order of events. His early illness and domination by his mother and grandmother led to a totally indoor ("feminine") mode of existence. He, too, engaged in childhood and early adolescent homosexual behavior without defining it as such. Like Art, Tom was labeled "homosexual" in high school, "tormented in high school because I was gay." This treatment may have served to lock in homosexual self-identity.

While in these two cases there is little or no evidence that "hustling" was a factor in the early development of the deviant career, there is some evidence in both transcripts of the "search for identity" as a factor in the later "coming out of the closet." Art was enthralled by the gay scene parties at Alfred's house, and these gave him a sense of identity for the first time since adolescence. Tom reflects his partiality to the gay scene in his statement that gay bars are more exciting and more lifelike than straight bars.

There is some minor commentary on two of the psychoanalytic theories: castration anxiety and maternal identification. Art reveals in the fraternity incident that he had an aversion to the nude girl in his bed. However, from his statement, his aversion seemed to be less a morbid fear and more an avoidance reaction based on his belief that this wasn't "for him."

Maternal identification is partly indicated in Art's case by his mother's involvement in the transcript, and from her comments indicating her apparent reverence for Art. However, contrary to the maternal identification role model idea, Art in his sexual preferences seeks the company of especially masculine males (though not compulsively). Tom, however, seems to contradict somewhat the maternal identification theory in respect to his own mother (though not his grandmother), since his own mother seems to be harshly condemning of homosexuality to the point that Tom has not even confronted his parents with his own homosexuality (despite the fact he is active in GLF). Thus, as an overall assessment, the psychoanalytic theories seem to be inconsistently applicable to these cases of homosexuality, while the sociological theories of labeling and possibly mass society seem to apply to both. While we have intended these case studies as only illustrative rather than as empirical proof, there may be some indication that the psychoanalytic theories have arisen out of particular casework patient samples and do not come to grips with actual cases of homosexuality outside of the patient population.

PENNY AND CLAUDIA: Lesbians

The following is a transcript of a classroom talk and interview with two lesbians, Penny and Claudia. Penny and Claudia are both middle-aged women, and although their appearance was somewhat masculine, they brought with them other younger lesbians who were quite feminine in appearance. The speakers made a concerted effort to provide a self-analysis that, considering the paucity of literature available on lesbianism, may be quite helpful.

QUESTION: *Could you define what you mean by lesbian; some of the possibilities would be covert, overt, and certain vulgar terms they use like closet and drag and so forth.*

PENNY: A lot of these terms are slang terms. I would define a lesbian as a woman who partakes in sexual acts with another woman.

QUESTION: *Frequently, regularly—can it be just a one-time thing or more often?*

PENNY: No, always. One who just wants a woman, always a woman. No one who wants a woman today and tomorrow a man; that is bisexual. One who partakes in the sexual act with another woman and wants it that way.

QUESTION: *Thus lesbians are women who would like to have sex with other women only, and reject men as the source of sexual gratification.*

PENNY: Not necessarily rejecting men; this is where everybody gets the whole idea confused. They think just because you are a lesbian that you hate men, and if you mention the word M A N, it's a repulsive word. But this gets the whole thing so confused it makes me kind of ill. I have nothing against men whatsoever. As far as when I talk to a man, I feel like I'm on the buddy-buddy system. I mean, I wouldn't want to be a lover to a man, but I would want these other things.

CLAUDIA: We do have quite a few friends in an organization called Sir. Quite a few of these men come down and we have social activities with them. No man is allowed to come to any of our meetings, but as far as social organizations, we all feel the same. Like, we had a discussion with some of the men, and the only difference between a boy and a girl dating and us going out is we just have no sexual contact with them. We are friends with them. I have quite a few male friends at the house. And this is the only difference; they enjoy my company and I enjoy theirs, but this is about as far as it goes. At the present we have a social worker, a minister, we have a priest, in case people have problems and you have to go talk to someone. And you say to yourself, if I go to my next-door neighbor and say, "Hey, I'm a lesbian," and they say, "Oh yeah, it was nice knowing you." Now the thing is, if you knew a person as an individual, now maybe the girl next to you could be, you know her as a woman, you know her as a friend, you've known her maybe many years, but if she turned around to you and said, "I'm gay; I'm a lesbian," the first thing you think of is goodbye. Think of the person as an individual, not as a name. I've known many many people in my life and after a while when they became friends to me they told me things, but I look at them as individuals, not as a name. And you know that over in Ireland, you're Catholic? Well, forget it. You're Protestant? Well, I don't want to know you, either. And this is the same difference, and this is what people don't understand. It's a name, a word, and people fear what they do not know, they fear what they do not understand. What the public does is hide their head in the sand and we don't see you so you are not recognized, but we are here and we are willing to try to educate people, to try to make them understand. But how can we do it unless you let us? A lot of men would say, "Well, you're hurting my ego because you go with a woman. Why doesn't she go for me?" If he understands, maybe he can help somebody.

PENNY: I'm not much of a speaker. Let's put it this way: are there any questions I can answer?

QUESTION: *When did you first realize you were a lesbian?*

CLAUDIA: If I remember way back, I remember I had a newspaper route, and this pretty little girl lived in the town with me and I was spending all my money on her, but I really didn't realize I was a lesbian, but I was spending all my money on her. We went to school together, and when she graduated and got married it hurt me. I didn't really understand until I was about nineteen years old.

QUESTION: *Do you seek out girls to be love partners?*

CLAUDIA: Let me answer that one. No, absolutely not; in fact, I'd rather not seek out another lesbian, but that is my own personal thing. If it happens, it happens. But I'm not bragging or anything 'cause I have a very good relationship with the girl that I'm with and she was not a lesbian when I met her, and we've been together now for almost six years. In fact, all the girls I've ever gone with have never been lesbians to start with. It's just something that happens. Maybe they look at me in a different aspect. Physically I'm a woman; mentally I'm not. Then you could classify me under the subtitle of being a transsexual, which comes under the title of a homosexual. So many people don't understand there are so many titles under the title of homosexual that you can't just say every person who participates in a love affair with a person of the same sex is a homosexual, because she could be a transsexual, and that is probably the reason why a girl who is straight and falls in love with another girl, she doesn't fall in love with that girl because she's a girl, she falls in love because she's a person first.

QUESTION: *I have heard most homosexual relationships are very short-term; are there many who have lasted as long as yours?*

CLAUDIA: I can tell you about some personal friends I know. I know two women who live in Long Beach and have been together for twenty-seven years, I've got some friends in Boston who have been together for forty years, I know two men in San Francisco who have been together for seventeen or eighteen years. Now, there are short relationships, too, just like in straight marriages. You go and marry someone and what happens? After about six months or a year you find out you're not compatible, so the best thing to do is not keep living with one another. It's the same as it is in straight life, in gay life.

QUESTION: *What happens to your relationship with your family and close friends?*

CLAUDIA: Well, let's put it this way. My family loves me, I know they do. I come from a large family—a broken family, but a large family, and I've gotten all the love in the world I wanted from them. They know about me; they've always known about me, I think, I'm pretty sure. They've never done anything about it until it was too late. They wanted to then, but they knew that my mind had already been set in this way and it was. If people could accept us as well as my family has accepted me, this is what we are trying to do. We're trying to make society accept us. Our parents understand us, they know the kind of relationship we have, they know it's not a fly-by-night thing. They're right, it's true, it's a real love, we're happy, we do things together, and they can see it's something warm. And my family, sure, it hurt them first of all, but you've got to get them to understand you, not us to understand them; they got to understand us first. We have to educate them in the way we are. If they can understand us everything's just great, beautiful. It's a great thing between parents and yourselves.

QUESTION: *How do lesbians in general feel about male transsexuals and those males who want to be like females?*

PENNY: Why not? His mind is the mind of a woman, his body is the body of a man; it's just where his processes are. If he's got the mind of a woman and he's walking around with the body of a man, I mean, it's all right, it's ok except you're in the wrong body, I mean, you function as a woman, but you still have the physical characteristics of a man. It's the same thing with a woman. I mean, your mind overcomes your physical being. I say, go ahead and get it done.

QUESTION: *Do you feel homosexuals need professional help?*

PENNY: If they want it. I mean, you take a person who has been happy all his life the way he is or the way she is, and you say I'm going to give you some help, go see this doctor. If this person doesn't want help, if this person is so happy and really fulfilled, you're just going to mess him up that much more. No, if a person wants help he'll go after it.

QUESTION: *Do you think there is a better argument for being a female homosexual than a male?*

CLAUDIA: Well, a lot is known about the male, but very little is known about the female.

QUESTION: *I believe from what I've read, male homosexuality is condemned more than female. Do you agree with that?*

PENNY: Yes, because theirs is made too public. With men, they more or less cruise in public places and it's more or less a night thing. They just want someone for tonight and someone else tomorrow. They don't even go by or could care less what your name is—most of them. It's just one of those things, variety or I don't know what.

CLAUDIA: But naturally, as we are females and women, we don't jump into things like the men do.

QUESTION: *Is it pretty much the opposite of the male situations? Different people play different roles; one person plays the female role and one plays the male?*

CLAUDIA: Let me answer that one. I can point out two women who are extremely feminine. There is such a thing as a role being played when you're a single. There are what they call "butch" and "fems," but a lot of times when there are two women living together they are two women. I mean, there is no way to cut it.

QUESTION: *So you think of yourselves as women and . . .*

CLAUDIA: See, each one thinks different.

QUESTION: *What I'm trying to get at is, in male homosexuals, you often have an overreaction to the role and you have men acting very feminine.*

PENNY: You have the same thing with lesbians. I mean, if you're one way and you think one way, how can you all of a sudden say that, . . . well, a true homosexual is one girl who wants another girl. She could care less if she's a fem as long as she has the physical appearance of a woman. Now, they don't want a butch, or a woman who acts like a man; they just want all girl. But that sort of thing usually won't last because you've got to have one more dominant than the other.

QUESTION: *Are there physical characteristics about a woman you may see just passing by that can attract you to her physically?*

PENNY: To me it would have to be more personality.

CLAUDIA: Well, now you are talking personally. If I see a pretty girl walking down the street I'll take a look. And I'll think she looks nice and I'd like to get to know her. But I agree, personality has everything to do with it in the first place. The physical attraction is there.

QUESTION: *Would a butch, more than a fem, be more likely to have had prior heterosexual activity?*

PENNY: Not all your butches or even fems have ever had heterosexual relationships.

CLAUDIA: I can tell you from experiences I've had, quite a few women, both butch and fem, have been married to men before. But you can't blame the man for the girl becoming a homosexual. It's something that just . . .

QUESTION: *Do lesbians generally develop the same division of labor as husband and wife in heterosexual marriages?*

PENNY: It depends on the way you want the relationship. We both work and we both share not as individuals but as one. We take care of more or less each other. It's the kind of relationship I would say my mother and father had, actually. I mean, if something happened to her I would assume all responsibility and I know she would do the same for me.

QUESTION: *Would lesbian couples like to adopt children if possible?*

PENNY: Definitely.

QUESTION: *But there is probably no way for you to get a child.*

PENNY: Yes, there is. California has already said that single people can adopt children, if you are financially prepared for this. I wouldn't want a child right now because I don't think I'm financially prepared for this. I want to bring up a child and give him things and not to have him scrounging out in the street. Yes, I would want a child in my household, very definitely.

QUESTION: *Would you consider using artificial insemination to have your children, rather than adopting them?*

PENNY: That is something else. You've got to have a pretty close relationship with your partner, if you want to call it that, and this is something you've really got to discuss thoroughly and something that you've both got to want, and again, I can only take my own views as an example, I would want my partner, if she wanted her own baby, and we had the money, she would definitely have artificial insemination.

QUESTION: *Have you ever had any trouble with the law?*

PENNY: No. If you are doing things that aren't harming anybody else, I mean, if you're on a street corner doing some sort of sex thing, anybody, whether they're a heterosexual or a homosexual, you're going to be picked up. But if you are in your own home and you're doing everything within the law as far as you're concerned, and you're not harming anyone outside, why should the law bother us?

QUESTION: *One of the speakers we had lately was picked up on a complaint lodged by a neighbor. Have you ever had this kind of trouble? Do your neighbors give you static or bad looks?*

PENNY: No. I've had experiences as some of my neighbors found out I am a homosexual and I asked them, what do you think, do you want me to move? They said, "No, now that we know you, we recognize you as an individual, we know you, you've done us no harm, we've gone over to your house for supper." I've had many friends who are heterosexual, and both know about me.

CLAUDIA: The same thing with me. I have a lot of heterosexual friends and after a period of time I decide that I know them well enough to want to share this with them, and their acceptance of me makes a closer friendship between us. After I told them, all they had to say was, "So what? We like you as you, yourself, Claudia."

QUESTION: *I think people are much more condemning of male homosexuals, because people are really uptight about Liz and Jackie [male transsexuals]. In fact, two out of four of them have been arrested recently, one for going out to pick up the paper in her negligee.*

CLAUDIA: Gee whiz. I mean, for me it would be the same way, if I came walking up to a woman and said, "Hi ya, kid. Let's go." I mean, that's something else. And there are children around; you can't expose yourself, like a man walking out in a negligee to pick up the paper. Children around can run home, "Mommy! Daddy! There's a funny looking thing dressed in what mommy wears!" All they have to do is use a little common sense, Good Lord!

QUESTION: *You have talked of having children. Have you thought of the problems you might encounter, not inside the house but eventually the child does have to go out.*

CLAUDIA: I know, I have discussed this with my girl. We discussed the whole thing, and if we had a child, we want one from infancy. If we were to adopt we would adopt an infant, not a child four, five, or six years old, because we would show them our love for the child first of all. I think love conquers all, I really do. Even in an affair such as ours, if we could show the child how much love we had for the child and bring him up in that way so when he gets older and he's going to school, there are going to be kids that are going to say, "How come you got two mommys?" or something like that, like, "Is that your mommy or is that your daddy?" or something like that. I think that the child's mind and his feelings will be so secure with us as far as being fully loved by more or less his parents, I think love will conquer all, I really do. I think after a while the sarcasm from other children, which can be very mean at times, I think it would just bypass. I think if we could get the child to understand how much we do love him and how much we are trying to do everything for him, like I said, I think it has to start from infancy.

PENNY: I'd like to say one thing that happened to me. My sister got divorced and I had her five children, which I took care of for about two or three years and the oldest one was seven at the time. And I was a little leery of taking care of the children at the time because I didn't know what would happen. So after two years, my sister came back with her second husband. I got a letter about a year ago and it was the most beautiful letter that anybody could ever receive, I wish I had it right here to read to you. That letter said, the boy is in college—he is studying electronics and I taught him to, and he said to me, "Aunt Penny, I know, I've known all about you for many years, yet you have given us the love, the understanding, the security when mother was not home. And as far as we are concerned we will always love you, no matter what anybody says." I wish I had the letter. Actually, when I read the letter I almost cried. Because normally when people find out, they just don't want to know you. But I got this letter from a boy. I read it to his mother and his mother had tears in her eyes. For a college boy, to write a letter to me like that, I cried. And he even brought some of his college buddies out to my house, and I said, "Are you sure? I mean, what are these guys going to think, you know?" And he said, "Well, Penny, I told them about you, I told them how you raised us for a while and I told them about all the years I've known you, and they said they all wanted to come out and be friends, and I said so be it." But I wish I had that letter with me. I've got it in a little frame.

QUESTION: *Do you think of yourselves as women or men?*

PENNY: I think of myself as a woman. I am a woman.

CLAUDIA: I think it depends on the individual. My girl looks at me as a man, rather than a woman, because she's always been straight, and that is why she fell in love with me, because she got to know me as an individual, the way I think, the way I . . . everything else. I can't say this to the public, I mean, I work with the public and, well, gratefully my job is working strictly with men all the time. I have a man's job more or less, although more women are getting involved in being a barber. And I have some of the greatest men who come in and sometimes I've gotten to know them well enough where I can more or less stop living a double life and I can more or less start expressing my own ideas to a man and get to know them and they get to know me, and they are really terrific, they really are. They start understanding me as an individual as I really am, not just Claudia here, and Claudia here. These people are really fantastic when you get to know them, but when you don't know them . . . they scare me, actually.

QUESTION: *Would you raise your child to be a heterosexual or a homosexual?*

PENNY: I would let him choose his own way. If I had a little boy I would teach him to be all boy, I would play baseball and football and everything. And as far as sex is concerned, he's still a boy, a normal boy, and he's going to have an attraction for girls and he's going to ask questions that little boys want to ask when they are growing up, and together we would try to answer them as best as we could. If I couldn't I would find a man who I respected as a man to help me out as far as giving him good advice. But if he chose a homosexual life, I would talk to him and make sure he knows what he is doing. He's going to make mistakes. I've made a million. He's allowed a few too.

QUESTION: *Claudia, I'd like to ask you the same question that was asked of Penny. At what time in your life did you realize that you were a lesbian?*

CLAUDIA: Seems like it always was. I've been trying to pinpoint it for a long time. And, like I said, I came from a very large family with six children. My oldest sister died at birth and the next to the oldest was another girl and my father had always wanted a boy ever since the first one, so when I came along, and he really wanted a boy badly, when I came along he more or less started raising me as his only son. Then I came along and again there were three girls in a row, and he wanted a boy real bad to go fishing with, play baseball, and I was being brought up as a little tomboy. It was cute at first; everybody thought I was really terrific. But my ideas started forming then of how I wanted to be like my father. He was a terrific guy, and I wanted to think like him, I wanted to do everything he did, take the car apart, jack it up, anything I could do that he did I wanted to do. Like I said, at first it was cute but as I got older it wasn't so cute. But, anyway, my Dad always had the philosophy, like the first time I had my hair cut real short was in the fifth grade. I had long hair and he decided that one summer he was going to cut it off, which he did and my mother had a fit. Anyway, he said to me. "Claudia, never mind what other people say; you have to live with yourself. If you are satisfied with yourself that is all that matters, and if you are not, then change." And I've remembered that ever since the fifth grade, and for me that has been a fantastic philosophy to follow, and I am happy with myself.

QUESTION: *If you were to have children what would they call you?*

PENNY: I have known other people and a lot of the children call one an aunt, associate her as the aunt. A lot of women get together and simply say this is my cousin, my sister-in-law, or something like that.

CLAUDIA: One would be known as his mother, and I guess I would be known as his aunt.

QUESTION: *You've always talked about having a little boy. What about a girl? How do you feel?*

PENNY: The same way. If we adopted we would have a choice, but if we used artificial insemination, then if it were a little girl then I, or she would have her own ideas and I wouldn't be teaching her how to play baseball. She would be raised like a little girl.

QUESTION: *Do you feel you have an ideal way of life?*

CLAUDIA: It all depends on your point of view. . . .

PENNY: We know so many lesbians, and men too, who have been kicked out of their own homes by their parents for admitting to their parents that they are this way.

CLAUDIA: Penny and I are both from the East, and everybody there is pretty old-fashioned, and they only know what they think, or what they've heard. They have done absolutely no research and they have done absolutely no listening as far as somebody who is that way. They don't want to. They think it's like a contagious disease. This is what we are trying to eliminate, to make people understand, that's all. We don't ask for too much.

QUESTION: *Are there lesbians who force themselves on other women?*

CLAUDIA: Do I know anybody? No, but I'm not saying there aren't lesbians who force themselves upon other women. Like I said, we have our sick people too, and those people do need help, and those are the kind of people to talk to, to try to get them to get help; if you can't get it from another person, get it from a professional.

QUESTION: *Do you think if a child begins exhibiting symptoms of this behavior at an early age, do you think they should have psychiatric help?*

CLAUDIA: Yes. As I said, we do have a minister, and priest. I have had people come to me and say, I don't understand my little boy or my little girl, he is acting such and such and such, what do I do? If I cannot find an answer for you, I will refer you to someone who can help, and who will help. Not psychiatric care, but understanding care is more like it.

QUESTION: *Do you feel if you hadn't been raised by a father who wanted a son you would still be this way? Do you believe it is an inborn characteristic?*

CLAUDIA: Yes, I do. I don't think I could have been raised in a better environment. I come from the best family, I don't come from a "good" family or anything like that, but my home was filled with all the love that a child needs. If my father hadn't raised me as a son, you mean? Well, after me, I did have two brothers and I had a brother born after myself. But my father still felt, well, he thought he had an athletic daughter, is what he thought. And he didn't know that my mind was thinking about, well, I just worshiped my father. Like, I know a lot of straight girls whose fathers are the same way. I mean, they had a fantastic relationship with their father as far as being brought up as a tomboy, but they outgrew it. I didn't outgrow it.

QUESTION: *A lot of little girls go through a tomboy stage. Why is it some don't grow out of it?*

PENNY: Because I think the girls who do go through the tomboy stage are daddy's girl. The girl who doesn't go through the tomboy stage is a mommy's girl. Some like daddy and they'll do everything daddy does, but others would rather be in the kitchen making cookies in a little apron and a little dress.

QUESTION: *But many girls go on and become feminine. What is the difference?*

PENNY: There is no difference. Like myself, I feel it was just meant to be, I mean, I'm not saying it was fate or anything, it's just the way I want to be. I didn't think I was even doing anything wrong when I started having attraction toward the first girl I ever had an attraction to. It just seemed like it was, it came to me normally, I didn't consider anything wrong.

QUESTION: *When girls get into junior high they want to go to dances and proms and . . .*

CLAUDIA: Sure, I did all that stuff too. I even started dating and everything else, but it seemed more wrong than right. Every time, I didn't feel repulsive; in fact, I even gave it the old college try to really become straight. I didn't know what the word straight or homosexual was, but I dated a few boys, and stopped every time, you know, they'd try to kiss me or put their arm around me; I thought this is really queer, you know. I felt it wasn't a natural thing for me, I felt more embarrassed about it, it just wasn't natural. And I'm not all that sick of it either, it just wasn't natural. I am happy the way I am, so . . .

QUESTION: *There have been a lot of movies lately about lesbian love. Do you think these movies are pure fiction?*

CLAUDIA: I haven't seen one yet that is true to life.

QUESTION: *One of the themes that usually comes across is that men are insensitive lovers. Do you think this is fact or fiction?*

CLAUDIA: That depends on the person. I can't answer that for everybody because I had a different feeling. Like I said, I think one way and everybody else may think another way. And everybody may have a different feeling on everything we've discussed today.

PENNY: You see, we are trying to find out what heterosexuals think about us; we're trying to have you understand about us and we're trying to understand you.

QUESTION: *There have recently been articles about homosexuals in various magazines. Do you think this harms you?*

CLAUDIA: No, I think it helps. Was this the one mostly about men?

QUESTION: *Yes, in* Time *magazine.*

CLAUDIA: See, it's just like the one they had in *Look* magazine about transsexuals, that was mostly about men. I wish they'd do more about women. I read the letters that were written in after the article appeared, and they were written in by professional people, doctors, lawyers, nurses—people who have an education and who understand, and they were all excellent letters written in, except one letter by one woman who really wrote a pretty nasty note and she was just a plain old housewife. I mean, she had no education about the subject itself except what she has heard through the grapevine or talking over coffee, and so she wrote a pretty nasty note in there. But every one of them, the other letters were really outstanding. They said that it was helping the public to understand them and that we are not all sick people, but we are people. Because you know there are so many people sitting here that don't realize that their doctor or their nurse or their dentist or even their next-door neighbor who takes care of your children may be a homosexual. I mean, they say that 90 percent of your professional people are. I'm not saying that your doctor or your nurse or your dentist is; I don't want you to look at them weird when you go in, but I am saying this is the statistic on it.

QUESTION: *Don't you think a lot of the problem with people understanding is that we have been brainwashed into believing that there are certain masculine traits that men have and feminine traits that women have and anytime you have an individual straying from the norm you have the problem of people understanding, because then people don't look at them as an individual but as a title?*

CLAUDIA: That is quite true.

===== COMMENTARY

A lesbian, according to our informants, is a woman who partakes exclusively in sexual acts with other women and wants it that way. In their self-analysis, our respondents make a number of statements that seem to corroborate Simon and Gagnon's analysis, although no evidence is presented in their statements for or against the castration anxiety theory. Our respondents agree with Gagnon and Simon that female homosexuality is more tolerated publicly. They seem to believe this is because females are more discreet, but they also cite instances of acceptance by friends, siblings, and parental family that we did not find in the case of male homosexuals.

Our speakers give evidence for the Gagnon and Simon view that femininity is pervasive among lesbians: first, in the covertness of their activities; second, in their adherence to the romantic complex ("We are women who want to have the understanding and companionship. We don't jump into things the way men do."), and third, in the sense that after a relationship is formed, the participants think of each other as two women living together rather than "butch" and "fem" ("There is such a thing as a role being played when you are single . . . but a lot of times when there are two women living together they are two women. I mean, there is no way to cut it.").

There is one departure from Gagnon and Simon's "femininity complex" idea. One of our respondents, Claudia, actually thinks of herself as a man in a woman's body, and in her relationship with the girl she lives with, she plays the masculine role. Her girlfriend is "straight" or heterosexual, and thinks of Claudia as a kind of husband rather than as another woman. Claudia's father, in fact, raised her to be a boy. She was a tomboy, and she idolized her father—a "terrific guy" who taught her boys' activities like fixing cars, playing baseball, and going fishing. He also cut her hair short. He later taught her what seems like a role-maintaining philosophy of "You've got to learn to live with yourself." Perhaps as a result of this teaching, she came to feel that erotic relationships with boys in a dating situation just didn't seem natural, although she notes she is very able to relate with boys and men in a buddy or work relationship. That is, Claudia seems to think of herself as a transsexual, and she is currently involved in a "man's job" of being a barber.

One point may somewhat extend Gagnon and Simon's analysis. Penny seems to model her relationship with other girls after her parents' role relationship. "We both work and we both share, not as individuals but as one. . . . It's the kind of relationship I would say my mother and father had, actually."

It is noteworthy that despite our probing, our respondents gave no definitive answer about what factors support a continued "tomboy"-labeled role and what factors lead a girl to "grow out" of this role. The question was asked, "But many girls go on and become feminine. What is the difference?" Penny replied:

There is no difference. Like myself, I feel it was just meant to be. I mean, I'm not saying it was fate or anything. It's just the way I want to be. I didn't think I was even doing anything wrong when I started having attraction toward the first girl I ever had an attraction to. It just seemed like it was, it came to me normally.

This hardly seems an answer to the question of what factors are the differentiating ones. But maybe this is indicative that there are earlier psychological attitudes that are determinant. The attitude that homosexual erotic relationships are "natural" seems to be a nontypical one. Perhaps if this attitude is somehow taught by the parents along with tomboy socialization, the pattern of lesbianism becomes fixed. Obviously, we are only speculating, and more cases will need to be studied to see how the "tomboy" role is fixed, and to ascertain if there are other social or psychological routes to lesbianism. This would also provide us answers to the manner in which a label is adopted as a self-concept or identity under labeling theory.

THEORETICAL IMPLICATIONS

Let us now examine the theoretical implications of both our male homosexual and our lesbian informants. They provide us with some interesting applications of these major frameworks and point to the need for further research as well.

Biological Theories

We have no data from our informants regarding any biological or hormonal differences. The manner in which biological sex differences interact with other factors is important in the area of sexuality. Thus, it appears there should be continued research as to the manner in which hormonal or other differences may affect or predispose an individual toward homosexuality.

Psychoanalytic Theories

We have found that psychoanalytic explanations may have been exaggerated in past samples. If we view our informants within these theories, we find them only partially applicable. We do find that the father-figure is important in sexual identification. This is so in the case of Penny, who speaks of "Daddy's girl," as well as with Tom, who apparently lacked a proper father-figure when under the domination of his grandmother. Nevertheless, the dynamics of the process as well as its universal application are left somewhat obscure. It is possible that other social and cultural variables must be considered along with the psychological factors to complete the picture. Another question that might be raised is why such explanations lead to alcoholism or drug addiction in some instances and to homosexuality in others. Is it that the alcoholic or drug addict resolves struggles with sexuality by succumbing to the use of substances to reduce the tension while the homosexual gives in? If so, how do we explain the homosexual-addict or the homosexual-alcoholic?

Sociological Theories

DIFFERENTIAL ASSOCIATION   We find the application of learning theories are most valid when our informants were introduced to the homosexual subculture and sexual activities rather than explaining the initial sexual preference itself.

ANOMIE   Merton's anomie is of little value in examining the issue of homosexuality herein. In neither our male or our female homosexual interviews do we find a struggle toward culturally approved goals resolved through the means of homosexuality or homosexual identification. Some may still infer this particularly as regards male homosexuals, but it is not apparent from our informants.

SUBCULTURAL THEORIES   Again, we find that those subculture theories that center upon lower class status are of little benefit in explaining the phenomenon of homosexuality as has been the case in earlier chapters. However, we do see that homosexual subcultures exist and the overt subcultures provide an identity and sense of community for their members. Our informants are necessarily members of these subcultures, but we are left with little explanation regarding those homosexuals who do not take part in overt activities. Such individuals might provide further clues as to the nature of homosexuality in all its aspects.

LABELING   Perhaps the theoretical framework that has the strongest potential for explanatory power is labeling theory. We find that it is more evident in our male informants than in our lesbians. However, we have found that the order and process involved in adopting the label vary. Thus, additional research in this area might be of substantial consequence in revising labeling theory and specifying variations in the labeling process. Perhaps an examination of labeling processes along with psychological propensity or predisposition to adopt such a role or self-concept would be of the greatest significance.

SOCIAL CONTROL   The social control models take on a new dimension within this chapter. Not only do we find the external control mechanisms, both formal and informal, ineffective when internal control mechanisms (homosexual identity, and so on) are lacking, but we find the overemphasis of such mechanisms may contribute, particularly among males, to the adoption of a homosexual identity. If one envisions the legal control of homosexuality as leading to imprisonment, the problems are multiplied within such single-sex institutions. On the other hand, the use of the "medical model" of external control (that of psychiatry) has proven to be ineffective, and rejected by our informants. Informal mechanisms of control, such as the overemphasis upon masculinity, or negative sanctioning through terms such as "queer" or "tomboy," also appear to be counterproductive. Perhaps a normal sexual development is dependent on informal control mechanism but with a less negative tone and within a proper balance.

In the next chapter, we will examine what some believe is a more advanced or progressed form of homosexuality, that of transsexualism.

═══════════ QUESTIONS FOR DISCUSSION

1. Discuss the "sickness" view of homosexuality. Why do you suppose this approach is so vehemently opposed by Gay Liberationists?
2. Do you agree with Claudia's statement that people are much more condemning of male homosexuals than they are of lesbians? Why or why not?
3. How can the recent radicalization and politicalization of homosexuals be explained?
4. What factors might account for the almost complete lack of sociological research into the subject of lesbianism?
5. Which of the theories on the origin of homosexuality seems most plausible to you? Which seems least valid?
6. Do you think lesbian couples should be allowed to adopt children? Why or why not?

═══════════ RELATED READINGS

Achilles, Nancy, "The Development of the Homosexual Bar as an Institution," in John Gagnon and William Simon, *Sexual Deviance* (New York: Harper & Row, 1967), pp. 228–244.

Benson, R. O. D., *In Defense of Homosexuality: Male and Female* (New York: Julian Press, 1965).

Bieber, Irving, et al., *Homosexuality* (New York: Basic Books, 1962).

Caprio, Frank, *Female Homosexuality* (New York: The Citadel Press, 1954).

Committee on Homosexual Offenses and Prostitution, *The Wolfenden Report* (London: Her Majesty's Printing Office, 1957).

Cory, Donald W., and LeRoy, John P., *The Homosexual and His Society: A View from Within* (New York: The Citadel Press, 1963).

Gagnon, John, and Simon, William, "Femininity in the Lesbian Community," *Social Problems*, 15 (Fall, 1967), pp. 212–221.

———, *Sexual Deviance* (New York: Harper & Row, 1967).

———, *The Sexual Scene* (New Brunswick, N.J.: Transaction Books, 1973).

Grier, Barbara, and Reid, Coletta, eds., *Lesbian Lives* (Oakland: Diana Press, 1976).

Hite, Shere, *The Hite Report: A Nationwide Study on Female Sexuality* (New York: Macmillan, 1976).

Hoffman, Martin, *The Gay World* (New York: Basic Books, 1968).

Humphreys, Laud, *Tearoom Trade: Impersonal Sex in Public Places* (Chicago: Aldine Publishing Co., 1970).

Kinsey, Alfred, et al., *Sexual Behavior in the Human Male* (Philadelphia: W. B. Saunders, 1948).

———, *Sexual Behavior in the Human Female* (Philadelphia: Saunders, 1953).

Kitsuse, John I., "Societal Reaction to Deviant Behavior," in Earl Rubington and Martin Weinberg, *Deviance: The Interactionist Perspective* (New York: Macmillan, 1968).

Krich, A. M., *The Homosexuals* (New York: The Citadel Press, 1954).

Leznoff, Maurice, and Westley, William, "The Homosexual Community," *Social Problems*, 3 (1956), pp. 257–263.

Lloyd, Robin, *For Money or Love: Boy Prostitution in America* (New York: Vanguard Press, 1976).

Magee, Bryan, *One in Twenty: A Study of Homosexuality in Men and Women* (New York: Stein and Day, 1966).

Pittman, David, "The Male House of Prostitution," *Transaction*, 8 (March–April, 1971), pp. 21–27.

Reiss, Albert J., Jr., "The Social Integration of Queers and Peers," *Social Problems*, 2 (Fall, 1961), pp. 102–120.

Rossman, Parker, *Sexual Experience Between Men and Boys* (New York: Association Press, 1976).

Schofield, Michael, *Sociological Aspects of Homosexuality* (London: Longmans, Green & Co., Ltd., 1965).

Ward, David, and Kassenbaum, Gene, "Homosexuality: A Mode of Adaptation in a Prison for Women," *Social Problems*, 12 (1964), pp. 159–177.

Warren, Carol A. B., *Identity and Community in the Gay World* (New York: John Wiley and Sons, 1974).

Weinberg, Martin S., *Society and the Healthy Homosexual* (New York: St. Martin's Press, 1973).

Weinberg, Martin S., and Williams, Colin J., *Male Homosexuals: Their Problems and Adaptations* (New York: Oxford University Press, 1975).

Weltge, Ralph W., ed., *The Same Sex* (Philadelphia: Pilgrim Press, 1969).

West, D. J., *Homosexuality Re-Examined* (Minneapolis: The University of Minnesota Press, 1977).

Westwood, Gordon, *A Minority: A Report on the Life of the Male Homosexual in Great Britain* (London: Longmans, Green, & Co., Ltd., 1960).

NOTES

1. Committee on Homosexual Offenses and Prostitution, *The Wolfenden Report* (London: Her Majesty's Printing Office, 1957), p. 11.

2. Alfred Kinsey, Wardell Pomeroy, and Clyde Martin, *Sexual Behavior in the Human Male* (Philadelphia: W. B. Saunders, 1948).

3. Martin Hoffman, *The Gay World* (New York: Basic Books, 1968), pp. 30–31.

4. John I. Kitsuse, "Societal Reaction to Deviant Behavior," in Earl Rubington and Martin Weinberg, *Deviance: The Interactionist Perspective* (New York: Macmillan, 1968), p. 21.

5. Jeremiah Lowney, "Drug Use Among Young Males," unpublished dissertation (Lexington, Ky.: University of Kentucky, 1976), pp. 377–384.

6. D. J. West, *Homosexuality Re-Examined* (Minneapolis: The University of Minnesota Press, 1977), p. 18.

7. Hoffman, *The Gay World*; Carol A. B. Warren, *Identity and Community in the Gay World* (New York: John Wiley and Sons, 1974); Martin S. Weinberg

and Colin J. Williams, *Male Homosexuals: Their Problems and Adaptations* (New York: Oxford University Press, 1975).

8. Laud Humphreys, *Tearoom Trade: Impersonal Sex in Public Places* (Chicago: Aldine Publishing Co., 1970).

9. Ibid., pp. 167–173.

10. David B. Lynn, *The Father: His Role in Child Development* (Monterey, Cailf.: Brooks/Cole Publishing Co., 1974), pp. 140–166.

11. Richard Green, *Sexual Identity Conflict* (Baltimore: Penguin, 1975), pp. 18–19.

12. Ibid., p. 23.

13. Otto Fenichel, *The Psychoanalytic Theory of Neurosis* (New York: Norton, 1945).

14. Hoffman, *The Gay World*, p. 146.

15. Irving Bieber et al., *Homosexuality* (New York: Basic Books, 1962).

16. Hoffman, *The Gay World*, p. 142.

17. Kitsuse, "Societal Reaction to Deviant Behavior."

18. John Gagnon and William Simon, "The Lesbians: A Preliminary Overview," in *Sexual Deviance* (New York: Harper & Row, 1967), pp. 247–282; and "Femininity in the Lesbian Community," *Social Problems*, 15 (Fall, 1967), pp. 212–221.

19. Hoffman, *The Gay World*, pp. 152–153.

20. Alfred Lindesmith and Anselm Strauss, *Social Psychology* (New York: Holt-Dryden, 1956), pp. 315–321.

21. Hoffman, *The Gay World*; Evelyn Hooker, "The Homosexual Community," in James O. Palmer and Michael J. Goldstein, eds., *Perspectives in Psychopathology: Readings in Abnormal Psychology* (New York: Oxford University Press, 1966); Warren, *Identity and Community in the Gay World*; Weinberg and Williams, *Male Homosexuals: Their Problems and Adaptations*.

22. Weinberg and Williams, *Male Homosexuals: Their Problems and Adaptations*.

23. Humphreys, *Tearoom Trade: Impersonal Sex in Public Places*.

24. Laud Humphreys, "New Styles in Homosexual Manliness," *Transaction*, 8 (March–April, 1971), pp. 38–46.

25. Albert J. Reiss, Jr., "The Social Integration of Queers and Peers," *Social Problems*, 2 (Fall, 1961), pp. 102–120.

26. David Pittman, "The Male House of Prostitution," *Transaction*, 8 (March–April, 1971), pp. 21–27.

27. Robin Lloyd, *For Money or Love: Boy Prostitution in America* (New York: Vanguard Press, 1976).

28. Parker Rossman, *Sexual Experience Between Men and Boys* (New York: Association Press, 1976).

Transsexualism

7

Perhaps due to the recent publicity surrounding the sex change operation of Dr. Renée Richards and the controversy over whether such an individual should be permitted to participate in sports as a female, there have been heightened awareness of and interest in transsexualism. One of the interesting aspects of transsexualism is the terminological difficulties this subject invites. We must, first of all, distinguish between sexual inversion and homosexuality.

> Inversion refers to the assumption of a female role by a male and conversely of a male role by a female. Inversion is a term descriptive of people and not of the sex act. ... Homosexuality, on the other hand, means sexual or love relationships between members of the same sex. Since male and female counterroles are usually involved in the sex act, even homosexual partners often play opposite-sex roles.[1]

Transsexualism is a form of sexual inversion, and it is distinguished from homosexuality (even though transsexuals may perform "homosexual" acts). Armstrong makes a distinction between homosexuality and *eonism*, or the desire to take on feminine mannerisms and wear women's clothes:

> 1) The crucial characteristic of the homosexual is the desire for a physical sex relation with a person of his own sex. The eonist is repelled by the physical aspect of a homosexual relationship. 2) Homosexuals do not want to change their sex and identity. This is the fundamental anomaly in eonism. 3) A conspicuously feminine appearance and a lifelong preference for feminine games and activities are far more common in eonism than in homosexuality. 4) . . . preference for the feminine role in eonism is evident from early childhood. 5) The fantasies of pregnancy and the passionate longing for a maternal role together with the desire for castration in an attempt to achieve anatomical resemblance to a woman are characteristic of eonism.[2]

A further distinction is made between transvestites and transsexuals. A *transvestite* is a person who feels the desire and need to dress in the clothing of the opposite sex. *Transsexuals*, on the other hand, not only want to dress like the opposite sex but also wish to have their bodies medically altered. The male transsexual feels he is in reality a female, imprisoned in a male torso. Since transsexuals identify with the opposite sex, they consider relations with members of their own sex to be heterosexual rather than homosexual.

These terminological distinctions are not usually made by the lay public, and, in fact, there is no total consensus in the scientific community over the use of these terms. This may be because, as will be shown by the findings of one important recent sociological study, these various forms of sexual deviancy are not entirely separate, but, in fact, the same person may pass from one form to another in an ordered progression of stages.

METHODOLOGICAL CONSIDERATIONS

While many difficulties inherent in the study of other forms of deviance are overcome in analyzing those who are no longer "hidden" as deviants following medical alteration, other problems arise. First, is the lack of adequate numbers of transsexuals from whom to draw samples. More important is the difficulty in studying initiating and predisposing factors *ex post facto* either a sex change operation or the decision or desire to undergo one. Thus, most studies of transsexualism rely, as does ours, upon depth and processes as recalled rather than breadth or statistical generalizations.

EXPLANATIONS OF TRANSSEXUALISM

There are numerous explanations of transsexualism, most of them psychoanalytic or psychological. Biological approaches are less than satisfactory explanations. A recent sociological approach to transsexualism has been developed; however, because the problem has been of direct concern to psychologists and psychiatrists, who have treated transsexuals clinically, the bulk of the theories are in those two fields.

Biological Explanations

Various biological explanations of transsexualism have been disappointingly unsuccessful when compared with their initial allurements. Through the years, such approaches have attempted to explain the phenomenon by anatomical deficiencies in the brain, chromosome abnormalities, and hormonal imbalances. Studies of prenatal infants, identical twins, and nonhuman primates appear to reveal, at best, interaction of physiological changes (such as testosterone levels) with psychological state (such as stress) within social situations (such as military combat).[3] The manner in which any "predisposing" biological trait may interact remains an area for continued research.

Psychological Explanations

PSYCHOANALYTIC THEORY   Most psychoanalytic writings on transsexualism are based upon the teachings of Freud and trace it mainly to efforts to counteract castration anxiety. However, contrary to the idea of castration anxiety, transsexuals do not overtly fear castration but instead actually seek it.

Another more promising psychoanalytic approach focuses upon separation anxiety and a separation complex, especially in regard to the mother of the transsexual. This theory has been developed extensively in an important study by Stoller,[4] and because it is the most plausible of the psychoanalytic approaches, we shall review this theory in detail.

The primary focus of Stoller's theory seems to be upon the development of the mother as a role model for her son. If the primary role model for a male child is his mother, he may play the female role. This is probably somewhat true for all boys, but boys who will become transsexuals have special infant and childhood circumstances. Their mothers are generally bisexual and "boyishly" feminine. They wear their hair short, wear very little makeup, and prefer mannish clothes. The mother might be termed neuter as opposed to masculine or feminine. The father is generally characterized by his physical absence from the family and introverted silence or preoccupation when home. All of this leads to an early and excessive identification with the mother. It has been observed that the mother of a male transsexual often has an abnormally close physical relationship with her son, holding him close for many hours of the day, sleeping in the same bed, seemingly unable to permit the separation of the child from her body. This ego absorption continues on into childhood until age four or five. Thus, the male child comes to play the female role, having completely identified with a female role model, and this is the role he will continue to play through life.

Other psychological theories of transsexualism have been proposed based upon common stress on the importance of unhappy childhood and conditioning to the female role.[5]

PARENTAL REJECTION   A boy's parents have wanted a child of female sex and, rejected by his parents, the boy becomes dissatisfied with himself and regards his genitals as the reason for his failure.

NUDITY IN THE FAMILY   Children who view their parents nude may come to have faulty sex identification, such that a child's transsexualism may be traced to a parent's exhibitionism.

IMPRINTING   The establishment of gender role is *imprinting behavior*, or learning that takes place early in life and is incapable of extinction. Thus, if a child is assigned a gender contrary to his chromosomal, gonadal, or hormonal sex before the age of eighteen months, reversal of that gender assignment leads to severe mental conflicts after that time. This theory applies, it should be noted, mainly to hermaphroditic children, those having both external and internal male and female sex organs (while this is the exception rather than the rule in most cases of transsexualism we are considering).

Sociological Theory

SOCIAL-SEXUAL APPROACH   A recent study done in San Francisco helps to unravel some of the anomalies in the above literature.[6] James Driscoll lived with transsexuals for one year in a hotel whose chief occupants were transsexuals or their "husbands." Through participant observation and depth interviews he acquired detailed life history data on seventeen transsexual prostitutes. Driscoll developed through his study a list of "universal generalizations" about all cases (such that his analysis qualifies as "analytic induction" in Cressey's sense of the term).

He found that all had gone through (or would probably follow) a series of stages. These are stages of changing sexual identity, each with its own underlying set of explanatory factors. Driscoll shows in these stages how public and self-labeling and differential association interplay to produce a deviant career in what Becker has called a "sequential role model." [7]

1. Effeminate Childhood As in much of the psychoanalytic literature, from infancy to puberty the gender of the "girls" * was treated inappropriately or ambiguously by their parents (or parent). Every one of the subjects came from a broken home. In almost all of the cases, the mother was the dominant figure, and the father did not provide a good masculine image. Feminine behavior was rewarded by gifts of girls' toys and playthings, the use of female dress, and by encouragement to have hair grown long. The subjects were taught at this stage to avoid the rough activities of boys, and all feminine behavior was reinforced positively. Thus, these children were taught to be girls and the female role was prescribed for them.

2. Labeling of Female Behavior What was seen as normal between parent and child was considered deviant by age mates once the girl reached school age. They were alienated from boys, and disliked undressing in front of boys and playing boys' games. Their behavior led to ridicule and rough treatment, and at this stage they were lonely, being able to associate with neither boys nor girls. They were often punished for trying to urinate in the girls' rest room.

3. Homosexual Stage In their late teens, they performed homosexual acts, eventually coming to conceive of themselves as homosexuals, entering the gay world. In the gay world, they thought of themselves as "hair fairies" or "drag queens." They learned much about dressing as a female from other such homosexuals. However, they experienced little or no curiosity about how "real" girls dressed. Such participation gave them a sense of identity and self-certainty. At this stage, the girls left home. In some cases this was due to police rousting, while in others, parents ostracized them, expecting them to act masculine. This treatment made them contemptuous of society's rules, and after that they began other illegal activities such as petty theft and male prostitution.

4. Transvestite Stage At this stage, female attire was worn day in and day out, and the girls tried to attain a feminine way of life. They met other transvestites and tried to learn from them. By being transvestite, it was impossible to hide a "homosexual identity," so the

---

* Driscoll prefers to call his subject girls, based upon his experience of coming to think of them as girls, and based upon the fact that they think of themselves as girls and call each other "girl" and refer to other transsexuals as "she" and "her." We shall use the same appellation based upon similar experiences with the transsexuals in our transcript.

girls lost their jobs or simply quit, and became involved in male prostitution as a livelihood. They learned about dress (pads and gaffs) from other transvestites. They learned how to avoid arrest, and about police informal policy. They then regarded the "hair fairy" with disdain. They experienced relative happiness at this stage; however, this stage lasted only a short time, from three to eight months.

5. *Transsexual Stage* When the girl learns about the conversion operation and that it is possible for her to be a woman physically, she may pass into the next stage, transsexualism. At this stage, the girls regard themselves as women in every sense except their possession of male sex apparatus. Now they deny they are homosexuals. They take estrogen and seek the change of sex operation, an operation involving excision of the penis and creation of an artificial vagina. They will embark upon full-time prostitution and think of themselves as a woman during the sex act, and often try to pass as a woman by fooling their "tricks." They wear pads and a "gaff," a cradle made of canvas or denim pulled up tight at the crotch, flattening the genitalia. The drag queen is now regarded by them as a sort of freak. At this stage, there is no discontinuity between what they were taught to be as a child and what they are in fact. However, they find hustling to be a highly disagreeable aspect of their lives, view their customers with disdain, and get little pleasure out of their acts. They would like to get married and adopt children.

6. *Feminine Stage* At this stage, the girls want to live the lives of normal women, so they give up prostitution and find a job (twelve of the sample of seventeen had done this at the end of Driscoll's year of observation). Hormonal changes have occurred, making the transsexuals softer in manner and action. At this stage they "come out as women." They want to live a normal middle class life. At this last stage, they take an active interest in the way women act and are especially attentive to transsexuals who have made the successful transition to the ordinary world. They seek out the company of women and try to find out how a normal girl lives. Though they have not necessarily obtained the change of sex operation, they now have great hope of doing so and they band together with other transsexuals in hopes of overcoming their minority status in society. Driscoll notes the creation of a transsexual organization in San Francisco called COG (Correction of Gender), which was successful in getting the police to drop their use of the charge of "impersonation" and to allow the girls to use public ladies' restrooms. At this stage the girls have matured, have gained self-respect, and now see themselves as law-abiding citizens, entitled to their rights.

Other authors have commented that this final stage is a continuous "ongoing" process of gender identity. According to this interactionist approach, the final stage is the process wherein the deviant discredits the former stigma and adopts a new, acceptable self-concept.[8]

JACKIE AND LIZ:
Transsexuals

The two participants in the following transcript, Jackie and Liz, have spoken on several occasions to classes at various local colleges. They have been picked up by the police frequently on charges of prostitution and impersonation, and thus have become known to local law enforcement officers. The talk we taped was given before a large classroom audience, and lasted two and one-half hours. The questions asked of the girls were varied, and some were extremely personal. The girls, nevertheless, seemed to hold up quite well during the evening and related not only academic knowledge and personal detail, but quite a bit of wit, evoking hilarious laughter at various points. Much of the laughter was a response to sexual innuendo, but also to the quickness and sharpness of the speakers' retorts to many questions. The use of wit is perhaps indicative of a fair amount of adjustment to a marginal minority status of being a transsexual.

LIZ: Let me start out by saying that we're all men. Umm, we're male prostitutes, I guess you could call us. We're known as transsexual transvestites. Jackie and I started out about two and one-half years ago and we dress like this twenty-four hours a day. We couldn't seem to work dressed as women so we resorted to prostitution. And it was kind of hard at first but we got used to it. And we work more or less downtown and sometimes down on hotel circle—we do on occasions, and we charge $20 minimum and it goes up to $30—that's for a half hour, sometimes longer.

JACKIE: You'll have to excuse me. I'm kind of nervous. Recently, about two months ago, we got two new partners, we are breaking them in. They have the same problem about work. Most of our clients are heterosexually oriented men who have families and kids. And because of the heavy patrolling downtown, the prostitution is not rampant at all; it's very restricted. As a matter of fact, according to vice officers we're the only prostitutes who are allowed to walk the downtown area as long as we abide by three principles: that there is no soliciting to minors, uniformed military personnel, and no jackrolling. As long as we abide by those three principles we have no friction from the police officers. We haven't been out in the county areas as yet but we imagine that there would be just as little problem. And because of our—how should I say it?—virtues—what we have and are soliciting from clients, police have grown used to us and our service is not really that detrimental to the community. And because of this, men are less apt to rape people, they're less apt to contract venereal disease because we have daily checkups. We each have a private physician who takes care of us. Each one of us here has gone to the UCLA Identity Clinic, which deals with the transsexual, and we are both; Liz and I are both registered candidates for sex reversals and we are all under estrogen treatment to physically alter our bodies to that of a female. It will take about two years of intensive psychiatric study to really validate our intentions and make sure we have real, sane desires to change our sex. And that's where the conflict arises, that's why we're misfits, because society refuses to accept the transvestite. And in the economic field we are more or less condemned to enter theatrical occupations. And when you don't have any theatrical talent you have to go on welfare or resort to prostitution. And we picked the latter because, well, really, it's easy money. We don't really hurt our clients because, as I said, the city is really well patrolled and prostitution is very limited. And strangely enough, our clients are not restricted to sailors and the military services exclusively. A lot of executive people, a lot of conventions open up new frontiers for us in clientele. We all do our own makeup and our own hairdos and we don't have one stitch of men's clothing in our house and, as Liz says, we live like this twenty-four hours a day. I myself was a student at this college for two years—'66 and '67; then I embarked on my proclivity of dressing as a woman. It was incongruous with being a student; the administration wasn't exactly happy with it. Since then I've sent some feelers through and [names another college] is going to accept me on this basis.

QUESTION: *How much money do you make an evening?*

LIZ: On the average, about, between four of us, $225 a night. But we don't work every night, only about two nights a week.

QUESTION: *How old are you? Do you feel like women?*

LIZ: I'm twenty, and Jackie's twenty-one. I myself feel completely as a woman. I don't have any male thoughts, really. The only thing is my body structure and, other than that, I consider myself a female.

QUESTION: *How long have you been doing this, and what are your reasons for wanting to convert?*

LIZ: I cannot live as a man, no way. As a man I was spotted, people would harass me about it.

QUESTION: *Do your clients know . . .*

LIZ: They know immediately we are men, we tell them. Therefore we can never get stuck with a prostitution rap, because we tell them we are men.

QUESTION: *Could you describe an average evening?*

LIZ: We start out getting ready about 4:00 and get out about 10:00. We go downtown, we always go around the Plaza once to let everybody know we're in town. Word travels fast around the Plaza. We break into teams. Jackie takes one of the new ones and I take the other one, and our favorite place is the place we call "the mirrors." We stand there and when traffic goes by you can see about eight of us at once, and it's a dead traffic stop. They go around the block again and again and again. It's a good place to get clients. A lot of people will come by and stare at us, because we hold a pose and they think we are mannikins and they come to touch us and we move and they about die. There is a lot of harassment, young girls come up and call us names and I give them an ugly look and they run away, and get their boyfriend who is going to come and beat me up, and I take care of him and it's all over.

QUESTION: *Where do you go to the bathroom?*

LIZ: Using the bathroom, okay, we have to use the community bathroom. There's places in town where they share the bathroom and it's no problem.

QUESTION: *When did you decide that you wanted to be a woman instead of a man?*

LIZ: My father passed away when I was very young and I was brought up by my mother. I idolized her. I wanted to be her . . .

QUESTION: *Didn't she try to discourage you?*

LIZ: She tried. She tried.

QUESTION: *How long does it take to find a man?*

LIZ: It doesn't take long, it doesn't take long at all. Well, that depends. A lot of people know us, a lot of people don't believe that we're men. We tell them and they're curious, so they'll pay to find out. And when they do they just stay anyhow. But it's no problem to find clients.

QUESTION: *Would you describe their reaction when you tell them that you're men?*

LIZ: Well, a lot of them think, okay, you're giving us the brush-off and we'll leave—and they do. And then they'll find out that we are men from sailors or someone down the street and they'll come back and then they'll start the name-calling. And then we just say, "Well, you asked for us, we didn't ask for you," and it shuts them up and they go away.

QUESTION: *How did you feel with your families? Emotionally, I mean.*

JACKIE: Well, I never felt adequate as a male. I never even really got warmed up to what constitutes standard measures of masculinity in heterosexual society. I more or less picked up the feminine role in life and it just developed into an overt transvestite.... And that later developed into transsexualism with the desire to alter one's body physically to that of the other sex. And all of us here are taking what they call maneuvers to change our sex.

QUESTION: *What is the difference between masculinity and femininity?*

JACKIE: Basically it's a matter of aggression and passivity, which we have a lot of the latter and little of the former.

QUESTION: *The centers of your style of life are San Francisco, Los Angeles, New Orleans. Have you ever been there?*

LIZ: No, not really. I've lived in L. A. for a while.

QUESTION: *Well, did you live in a type of environment where there were other people of your particular life style?*

LIZ: There are some up there but L.A. is as far as I've gone. Up there they're a bunch of dopers. They cannot go out or talk with anybody unless they're completely wasted on something. We do not deal with them whatsoever.

QUESTION: *Do you feel the need to surround yourself with the environment where there is a male playing the female role?*

LIZ: No, we'd rather not.

QUESTION: *Do you feel uneasy in a city where there is no particular place where an individual like you would feel at home?*

LIZ: No.

QUESTION: *Are you afraid of women?*

LIZ: No, not at all. I've had sex with women and I was almost married once. Now I just couldn't do it....

QUESTION: *Are there any similarities between your clients and the general public? I can't understand the person who would want a person who appeared to be a woman and was actually a man.*

LIZ: They're just like you.

QUESTION: *Do you ever see yourself as attractive? Do you ever notice attractive women?*

LIZ: Oh yeah, I always feel attractive.... I notice attractive women, but all I feel toward them is envy.

QUESTION: *When you go shopping for dresses, how do you handle that? Have you been arrested?*

LIZ: Jackie has been arrested for that one time. She went out to a shop and she told the lady that she was a man and asked for a private dressing room, which she was given. And a couple of minutes later this woman came in and interrupted her when she was undressed. So she proceeded to give her back the dress and when she came out she was arrested by the security guard there, for disturbing the peace. And she was given permission. Now, when we go in, we tell them or else we just buy things we know that are going to fit.

QUESTION: *After your operations do you consider getting married?*

LIZ: Definitely.

QUESTION: *What kind of training program are you giving the new girls?*

LIZ: It's private; top secret.

QUESTION: *Do you notice any types in terms of your clients? Age group, etc.?*

LIZ: Naturally, your younger ones you don't see as much because a young man will not pay for sex. A lot of them won't. More or less you see the age group between, let's say, the late twenties and on. That can still cut the mustard. Definitely not sailors, executive types and such.

QUESTION: *Have you ever been hassled by the draft?*

LIZ: The draft? Well, I tell you, I would like to get drafted but they refuse.

QUESTION: *Do you have any problem with the female prostitutes?*

LIZ: They won't even talk to us. The female prostitutes downtown come out looking like they've been through a ringer. Bleached hair, roots out about eight inches, chopped off, never curling it. They look very rough. They have on men's clothes more or less. They have on old sloppy shirts and a pair of slacks—men's Levis, just sloppy.

QUESTION: *Do you ever go into bars?*

LIZ: No.

QUESTION: *How many people are there in town that you know are in your situation?*

LIZ: In my situation? Well, there's some colored but they stay down more or less south of Broadway and we never see them except when we go to jail. We're the only four uptown.

QUESTION: *Which section of the jail do they put you in?*

LIZ: Queenstown.

QUESTION: *What are your long-range goals in life?*

LIZ: To become a woman and to be married.

QUESTION: *Is the desire to become a woman linked to a genetic malfunction?*

LIZ: No, it isn't. It hasn't been determined as of yet.

QUESTION: *Will the transformation be complete after your operations?*

JACKIE: Yes. Legally our birth certificates will be altered to say that we are female.

QUESTION: *How long will the operation take?*

JACKIE: Well, there's various ways of doing it. You can have the breasts done and the vagina or one at a time. Usually they do it one at a time and they can extend it over two years. Usually they would rather start them out on hormones and have breast development before an irrevocable operation—a penisectomy.

QUESTION: *In injecting estrogen, is there any problem with cancer?*

JACKIE: No, Not that I know of. No correlation between estrogen and cancer.

QUESTION: *Don't you ever feel hesitant about going through with it?*

LIZ: No.

QUESTION: *Is sex kinda rough while you're still a man?*

LIZ: Not at all.

QUESTION: *Doesn't the constant legal harassment discourge you?*

LIZ: No, not anything we can't handle. Like, Jackie's been arrested eighteen times and there were no convictions.

QUESTION: *When you are arrested are you put in the women's ward?*

LIZ: Oh, no, in the men's ward.

QUESTION: *Explain your relationship with your father.*

LIZ: The way I look at it, my father favored my brother more. My mother didn't, more or less. There were four of us—two sisters and two boys and we paired off. My little sister and I were my mother's, and my older sister and brother were my father's.

QUESTION: *How do your brothers and sisters feel about this?*

LIZ: My older sister detests it completely. My brother is very free-minded about it. And my little sister thinks it's great. She likes to go shopping with me and she says I'm her mother when we're out shopping. And nobody knows the difference. It's really great, no problem.

QUESTION: *How do you have sex now before the transformation takes place?*

LIZ: It'll cost you twenty to find out. There's no thing like the real thing.

JACKIE: But you aren't the real thing.

QUESTION: *Will you ever be able to have a child?*

LIZ: At this time I don't know.

QUESTION: *Would you like to?*

LIZ: Very much.

QUESTION: *What do the doctors say about the possibility of .. a uterine transplant?*

JACKIE: It's feasible at this time but there just hasn't been any experimentation along this line.

QUESTION: *Haven't you ever come across someone you found so attractive that you'd be willing to give him a free ride?*

JACKIE: You mean, do it for nothing? Yes, this has happened.

QUESTION: *Would you ever consider adopting a child? Would you be allowed to?*

JACKIE: Yes, definitely.

QUESTION: *Do you associate with women who want to be males?*

LIZ: Oh yes, lesbians they're called.

QUESTION: *If you were to get married would you want to marry a female or a male?*

LIZ: A regular man.

QUESTION: *It seems that you can be more feminine than a female; have you considered the designing business, or cosmetology?*

LIZ: I'm an interior decorator and a beautician, cosmetologist.

QUESTION: *Will you continue in prostitution until you marry?*

LIZ: Yes, or until society lets us dress like this and work, we'll continue in prostitution.

QUESTION: *You're all dressed sharp. How much do you spend on clothes?*

LIZ: About $200 a month.

QUESTION: *Are there any males that you'd like to go out with?*

LIZ: Oh yes, I have a husband at the moment.

QUESTION: *Do you pay income tax?*

LIZ: No. I have savings but that's mine and nobody touches that.

QUESTION: *Is your voice always that high?*

LIZ: It can be changed. Yes, when I have to go out as a boy I have to change my voice to a man's voice.

QUESTION: *When do you have to go out as a boy?*

LIZ: Well, say, I wake up and I have an appointment at the doctor's or something and I don't have time to put on all the crap—ah, makeup. I have to go out as a boy.

QUESTION: *Do you wear a wig?*

LIZ: Ah yes, this is a wig. Jackie has all her own hair. My own hair is long. I wear my hair sometimes when . . . when I have to go out as a man I lower my voice like that.

QUESTION: *Would you lower your voice?*

LIZ: Do I have to? Well, when I go out as a man I talk like this. [Lowers voice.]

QUESTION: *How do you make contact with your prospective clients when working as a team?*

LIZ: Well, Jackie and I just started out as a team and we've known Kelley and Joni for about a year and a half, two years, about a half a year after we started going together. They wanted to come along with us but at the time we just didn't think it was right. And so we started territories. And things just sort of went together.

QUESTION: *Do you think you will bring more of you people together?*

LIZ: No, it will never get any bigger than this.

QUESTION: *When was the transsexual first recognized in medical science?*

JACKIE: With the phenomenon of Christine Jorgensen.

QUESTION: *Where do you live?*

LIZ: We have our own home in town. The neighbors are, well, we get odd looks once in a while because she'll come running outside with no shirt on, just a pair of old levis and all this and all that hair. And the nextdoor neighbor boy, well, when we first moved in he started flirting with her and then one day she ran out of the house like that and jumped into the car to go to the store. Well, he hasn't flirted with her since. And the lady next to us is too old to worry about it now. She has one leg in the grave and the other one going quickly. I mean, she can't really tell.

QUESTION: *If you're wearing your hair, how do they know?*

LIZ: Well, honey, you try being a boy on estrogen and running outside with no shirt on. I mean, they work but they're just not that fast.

QUESTION: *Isn't it a traumatic experience to go out downtown a male dressed as a female and prostitute?*

LIZ: Well, I'll tell you. When you're walking down the street for a while and you run into a partner, you might say, and you try it and you make this mad money and it comes easy, it doesn't really bother you at all. I like money. I like nice things. It's no problem.

QUESTION: *Do you ever think about getting old?*

LIZ: Yes, very much. I think, what if I don't get the operation, I'm going to be an old, old transsexual. But, I mean, things are . . . society is changing.

QUESTION: *So you think that by the time you're old things will have changed and you'll be married?*

LIZ: Oh, yes.

QUESTION: *What do you do on the five nights you're not working? Does it take you from 5 until 11:00 to get ready for work?*

LIZ: On our nights off we stay at home. I guess it takes us about five hours. More or less. The way we work it. There's one bathroom in the house and we try to get four girls in the bathroom and there's one big mass of makeup and everybody's grabbing for everything at once. It's too much, so we just take turns.

QUESTION: *How many people in the United States have had the sex change operation?*

LIZ: I don't know. Jackie, do you know anything about that?

JACKIE: There's been estimates at about 10,000. County Hospital here has done its first sex reversal, but authority for that filtered down through the university. Johns Hopkins University has a clinic for it and various other universities have opened clinics to just deal with the problem by itself.

QUESTION: *Is your boyfriend feminine or an honest-to-god man or what?*

LIZ: He's completely heterosexual.

QUESTION: *Does your femininity bother him?*

LIZ: Not at all.

QUESTION: *You said that you hope to have children someday. Will you ever tell your children?*

LIZ: I don't feel any need for it. Possibly it could be detrimental to them. It could be and if I was to be changed, I would not live anywhere around this area; I'd probably move completely out of California.

QUESTION: *Do you plan to go to a hospital for this operation?*

LIZ: We plan on going to the university hospital for the operation if possible. We're on a candidates' list right now for it but we cannot have an appointment with the doctor until January.

QUESTION: *What will be the diagnosis on your chart when you are admitted?*

JACKIE: Transsexual.

QUESTION: *How would you feel if you had a son and you found out he was like you?*

LIZ: I would understand him. If those were his true feelings I could accept him.

QUESTION: *You said before you would not tell your children about yourself, but how would you explain comments other people would make?*

LIZ: Well, like I said, I'd move completely out of the state. If someone confronted me I'd deny it.

QUESTION: *How do you protect yourself?*

LIZ: Self-defense? I can handle myself great, honey. I've thrown little old sailors across that plaza many a time. Even the officers know how mean I can get.

QUESTION: *In having your body changed do they help your mental change?*

LIZ: No, it's just a bodily change.

QUESTION: *Do you have a satisfactory way of life that is worth passing on to others?*

LIZ: I don't recommend it unless they are very strong-minded and ready to pull a hard load, a hard and heavy load.

QUESTION: *Do you have any part-time pimps?*

LIZ: I don't need one.

QUESTION: *Have there been any attempts to put through legislation that could make your situation easier?*

JACKIE: They just changed a law and made male prostitution legal, I don't know the section number. Illinois is the only state I know that has homosexual behavior legalized.

QUESTION: *What about the sodomy laws?*

JACKIE: I don't perform sodomy; my services are strictly oral.

QUESTION: *Do you feel you have a mission to enlighten the public?*

LIZ: We'd all like to see the laws changed.

QUESTION: *Do you enjoy being a prostitute?*

LIZ: It has its ups and downs.

QUESTION: *Jackie, doesn't this lower your self-respect?*

JACKIE: No. When I engage in my business I do it on a very impersonal level. I do it like I do the dishes. There is no emotional contact with the person. It is purely a physical service I perform and that is all.

QUESTION: *Well, Jackie, when do you become emotionally involved?*

JACKIE: Well, I have a lover, if that is what you wish to call him. I give him certain physical outlets I wouldn't give clients, which, besides the emotional attachment, is the only way you can differentiate between him and my clients.

QUESTION: *Liz can make her voice higher. Can you do that, Jackie?*

JACKIE: Yes, on occasion, but with me it is an unconscious thing while Liz has trained herself. There has to be a stimuli which I'm not aware of myself, because Liz has noticed I do speak like that myself under certain circumstances that I can't control.

QUESTION: *Will the estrogen level raise the timbre of your voice?*

JACKIE: Over about five years it will. It also nourishes the hair, makes the skin softer, prolongs your life too. Sex reversal rejuvenates your life five years.

QUESTION: *Do you ever have sex among yourselves?*

LIZ: NO! I'm sorry for being so blunt about that but I'm so sick of that question. It would be queer, like going to bed with a woman.

QUESTION: *What do you think of the new feminist movement? Do you think women are ridiculous to be throwing away their bras and not wearing makeup?*

LIZ: I don't know. If I had a set of them, good sized, I'd throw it away too. But women can get very lewd in their dress. You can wear a see-through blouse in good taste. But women who are about ninety years old and are sagging down to their waists and are wearing a see-through blouse, uh huh. No way, it just doesn't look right.

QUESTION: *What is jackrolling?*

LIZ: Rolling your trick, taking them out and stealing their money.

QUESTION: *Do you discriminate against race, creed, or color?*

LIZ: I do stick to my own color.

QUESTION: *What do you think of women's liberation? Do you think it is silly?*

LIZ: Not at all.

QUESTION: *How much is the operation going to cost, and how long will it be before you can call yourself a woman?*

LIZ: It will set us back quite a bit, thousands. And it will be years.

QUESTION: *You say you only work two nights a week. . . .*

LIZ: Let me clarify that: we push two nights a week; the other nights during the week, if opportunity strikes we're not going to look down on it.

QUESTION: *Well, both you and Jackie say that you have men that you enjoy emotionally. Do you have, like, parties that you go to where there are women who are physically women, and do you get along with these women?*

LIZ: Oh, yes! Definitely.

QUESTION: *What is the operation like? Is it a vagina transplant or what?*

JACKIE: It is artificial, but it has been done so well that it has fooled gynecologists upon examination. And it can be made custom made to the dimensions of the husband too. Well, they don't exactly castrate the person. They insert the penis inside out and retain certain nerve endings so there is sexual excitement and climax too. And they can either remove the testes or insert them in the thigh region where they would not be seen or felt. Then the plastic surgeon comes in and does the external part.

QUESTION: *How do your lovers feel about you being prostitutes?*

LIZ: It's our business, our work. They have to accept it.

QUESTION: *What kind of men do you appreciate?*

LIZ: Horny types.

QUESTION: *After the operation you will be able to feel stimulation?*

JACKIE: Yes, the surgeon retains certain nerve endings and places them, at his discretion, along the tract of the vagina.

QUESTION: *Aside from being a prostitute, do you have a social life? I mean, do you have a group of friends with which you associate, do you attend concerts and other social functions?*

LIZ: Oh, yes. Jackie and I go to concerts quite a lot.

QUESTION: *Do you prefer a homosexual to a heterosexual?*

LIZ: Definitely not. I don't go to bed with homosexuals. I am like this because I want to be a woman, I want to go to bed with straight men, and straight men want a woman, not a man. And I just don't feel comfortable with a homosexual.

QUESTION: *You mentioned a percentage of your clientele were curiosity seekers. Do these people become repeaters or are they a one-time phenomenon?*

LIZ: They often become clients, yes.

QUESTION: *Have you ever been under a psychiatrist's care? Or did you ever notice yourself going through a transference at one time and seek help because you didn't want this to happen?*

JACKIE: No, I'm not amenable to psychotherapeutic efforts. Most transsexuals aren't. It's a very fixed psychosexual phenomenon that is predetermined very early in life. Most transsexuals do start off as prostitutes and even after the operation continue as prostitutes.

QUESTION: *Will you get married also, Jackie?*

JACKIE: My intentions are to do so.

QUESTION: *Have any of you taken part in any athletic events?*

LIZ: I was on the football team.

QUESTION: *Do you get any physical pleasure out of your relationships with your clients, or with your boyfriends?*

LIZ: When I am with a client I dismiss all thoughts of everything. When I'm with my boyfriend that is different. I do not experience an orgasm. The pills I am taking, the estronals, they . . Jackie, would you explain that for me?

JACKIE: They cut the libido off.

QUESTION: *Doesn't this make sex kind of a waste?*

LIZ: Not at all.

JACKIE: No, if I was to become sexually stimulated it would be a conflict with my identity. This is a biological denial, what I am doing right now. I never feel I need a release.

QUESTION: *Why do you take the clients back to your own house rather than renting a motel room? It seems like a lot of traveling.*

LIZ: No, this way it is in the privacy of our own home.

QUESTION: *You no longer practice cosmetology?*

LIZ: I do style hair, but more or less I do it for people I like.

QUESTION: *When you are at home, how do you delegate the household tasks, do you hire a gardener?*

LIZ: Joni [another transsexual] does the gardening; she likes to do outside work; right now we are remodeling the house and Jackie and I are doing most of that. And Kelley more or less does all the household chores, vacuums and such.

QUESTION: *How do you protect yourself from venereal diseases?*

JACKIE: Well, it all depends on the mode of intercourse. As long as you restrict yourself to oral, and unless there are open sores in your mouth, it is very difficult to contract the disease because the body heat immediately kills the germ. And we have regular checkups.

QUESTION: *Are any of you religious, or are your parents religious?*

LIZ: I believe in God, I'll leave it at that.

QUESTION: *Do you have a church you attend? How are you treated by the minister?*

LIZ: Yes, I attend church. I'm not worried about the minister. That's his problem.

QUESTION: *What are your feelings on marijuana?*

JACKIE: I have nothing against marijuana or the use of different stimuli or depressants if they are used with a certain amount of discretion.

QUESTION: *How much education have you had?*

LIZ: I have been through high school; Jackie had two years of psychology.

QUESTION: *Didn't you want to finish, Jackie?*

JACKIE: I'm coming back as soon as I have my reversal. I'll change my major to literature, as I could never get licensed as a practicing psychiatrist with my criminal record.

QUESTON: *Do you have any career plans?*

JACKIE: Yes, I want to go through college, finish my education. I'd like to be a teacher or do some research work.

QUESTION: *Can you attend a college dressed as you are?*

JACKIE: No, I can't. It's not illegal, but the code they have is very broad and it comes under the heading of disturbing the peace, and it does. It would be hard for a classroom . . . perhaps after the first few weeks it could function, but the administration just frowns on it.

QUESTION: *Can you recall any puppy love affairs you had when you were in school?*

LIZ: No. In my youth I was attracted to two females quite strongly but they were both relatives, cousins. We were more or less the same way and when our families got together we were paired off this way. One of them got married and the other one and I hung around together for a while; then she got married.

QUESTION: *When you were young did you find girls attractive at all?*

LIZ: No.

QUESTION: *Have you ever been convicted for anything other than traffic violations?*

LIZ: Never been convicted, no.

QUESTION: *While you are in jail do you get the same treatment as the others?*

LIZ: No, the queens are always given the best treatment. We get our own cells, we are never put with anyone. But we can always get out.

QUESTION: *Jackie, could you tell us something about your family?*

JACKIE: Yes. My father is a senior assistant design engineer, and we've lived here for ten years. In my childhood he was remotely distant to me, there was never any father-son relationship, and I was overly dependent on my mother. My identity more or less became fixed on my mother.

QUESTION: *How do your parents feel about your transsexual activities?*

JACKIE: Well, my parents have been in Europe for the past few years. They just got back and I haven't really seen them, so I haven't discussed it with them. I believe they are here but I haven't had physical contact with them.

QUESTION: *What do you think your parents' reaction will be?*

JACKIE: I couldn't care, really. It's not going to deter my ambitions. They will probably have ambivalent feelings toward it.

QUESTION: *If society would accept you as you are, what jobs would you take up?*

LIZ: I'd take up cosmetology, work in a beauty shop.

JACKIE: I'd continue in school.

QUESTION: *Could you tell us what your favorite hobbies are?*

LIZ: I like football, tennis, swimming, water skiing. Just a lot of sports.

JACKIE: I like to work on my car, and I have a large collection of pornography.

QUESTION: *How did you meet each other?*

LIZ: I went over to a friend's house, and the first time I walked in Jackie was running out with her hair in curlers, on her way to the laundromat. And I saw more of her and more of her, and then we decided to tell the guys where to get off and get our own house.

QUESTION: *Why does it help to work as a team?*

LIZ: Well, we more or less always travel in pairs for self-protection. There are people who will get mad sometimes and we smack them down a few times and they are all right.

QUESTION: *How did you get your names?*

LIZ: Well, Jackie got hers from the jail. And I just adopted mine; it was given to me.

QUESTION: *Did you ever have a movie star that really appealed to you?*

LIZ: Marilyn Monroe, Jayne Mansfield.

JACKIE: Irma La Douce.

QUESTION: *Have you ever been physically assaulted by any of your clients?*

JACKIE: No.

▬▬▬▬▬ COMMENTARY

As to the truth of these statements, there are two kinds of verification that can be offered. First, all four transsexuals referred to in the transcript have been observed by us and by students in their transsexual female attire in the vicinity of the downtown area known as the Plaza. The four are known to local police, according to reliable informants, as homosexual prostitutes. Other details are open to the reader's own verification.

Our informants bear out the descriptions and explanations of transsexuals in the literature. We find several factors: 1) complete and early feminine sex identification, 2) complete identification with mother and estrangement from father (or father's death), 3) development gradually from transvestite to transsexual, 4) preference for heterosexual men in sex relations and avoidance of homosexuals and other transvestites as sex objects, and 5) a background of harassment by peers and reluctant attitude of physicians to help. The existence of these expected factors is our second form of verification that the statements made are indeed truthful.

We may find in the transsexuals' statement various data relevant to the theories we have examined. Maternal identification seems to characterize both Liz, who was raised by her mother after the death of her father, and Jackie, whose father was remote from her and whose "identity became fixed on her mother."

There is no evidence that as children our respondents were rejected by their parents, and in Liz's case, there were several siblings who were raised in their biological sex.

It is difficult to tell what relevance body image plays in etiology in these cases. We do know, however, that before the use of estrogen, our respondents were average in weight for their heights. The use of estrogen was accompanied by a rapid weight loss, and now, of course, our respondents are quite feminine in appearance.

There seems to be in these respondents much corroboration for Driscoll's excellent sociological analysis. There is evidence of: 1) early femininity and maternal identification, 2) a period of hazing by peers in school, 3) a homosexual period during adolescence (this was not discussed in the transcript but came out in subsequent untaped conversation during which the respondents said they performed homosexual acts with "football players" and others), 4) a period of development to transvestism and dressing in women's clothes twenty-four hours a day, leading to the perceived necessity of prostitution due to loss of job and expulsion from school, and 5) a transsexual stage in which the subject thinks of self as a woman, refers to others as "she," and seeks the change of sex operation and marriage. There is evidence of passage to step (6) in Jackie's reduced sex drive (due to estrogen), and maintenance of residence in a middle class neighborhood (we are familiar with the area in which they live) living as a "family" obeying a kind of incest taboo.

THEORETICAL IMPLICATIONS

The above comments leads us to some conclusions regarding transsexualism that are similar to the theoretical implications regarding homosexuality.

Biological Theories

We have no basis on which to accept or reject biological factors from our informants. As is the case with homosexuality and as stated earlier in this chapter, the manner in which such factors may interplay with others appears to be an area ripe for further research.

Psychological Theories

We see with both Jackie and Liz either the absence or the emotional distance of the father-figure. There are indications of early maternal identification. As with our homosexual subjects, these early factors are related to other social factors in a developmental process. It is, perhaps, the larger sociological process that distinguishes our transsexual informants from our homosexual informants.

Sociological Theories

There appears little need to comment upon the models of *differential association, anomie,* or *subcultural theories* beyond what has been noted in the previous chapter. They appear to be of only limited value in explaining transsexualism other than a degree of learning involved from other transsexuals within an existing subculture.

LABELING AND SOCIAL CONTROL THEORIES   The convergence of *labeling* and *social control* seems to provide the best explanatory framework following the initial psychological factor of early feminine identification. While external mechanisms of control again prove ineffective, the latent effect of peer hazing and societal rejection tend to reinforce the deviant self-concept and hasten new gender identification. This labeling process appears to culminate in discrediting the stigma associated with the negative label as a new identity (female) emerges.

Recently, within United States society, there has been a trend for sex roles and symbols of gender to be less rigidly defined. Perhaps to a lesser degree, formal and informal sanctions have decreased for those deviating from sexual norms (particularly an increased acceptance of homosexual acts). If these changes continue and become more widespread, one should consider the long-range implications within social control and labeling frameworks. It is possible that early rejection of individuals who do not "measure up" to a rigid sex stereotype will be less severe. Consequently, there may be less likelihood that the process will continue and that such individuals will adopt the stigmatized label (a new sex identity). On the other hand, some would argue that if sex roles are not clearly defined and individuals do not have definitive symbols with which they may identify their own masculinity or feminity, then increased homosexuality, transvestism, and transsexualism will result. These questions point to the complexity of human behavior and the need for continuing research.

QUESTIONS FOR DISCUSSION

1. What are the main differences between transsexualism and homosexuality? Compare transvestites and transsexuals.
2. Discuss some of the special infant and childhood circumstances that may be correlated with transsexualism. Do you think the existence of such circumstances nullifies the possibility of sociological explanations of transsexualism?
3. Give a brief summary of Driscoll's six stages of changing sexual identity. At which stage is Jackie? Liz?
4. Neither Liz nor Jackie expresses any interest in joining together with other transsexuals (organizing). Can you think of any reasons for this?
5. In what ways are Jackie's and Liz's childhoods similar? In what ways do they seem to have been different?
6. According to Jackie, what is the basic difference between masculinity and femininity? Do you agree with her definition? Why or why not?

RELATED READINGS

Bryant, Clifton D., ed., *Sexual Deviancy in Social Context* (New York: New Viewpoints, 1977).

Driscoll, James, "Transsexuals," *Transaction*, 8 (March–April, 1971).

Green, Richard, M. D., *Sexual Identity Conflict in Children and Adults* (Baltimore: Penguin Books, Inc., 1975).

Green, Richard, and Money, John, *Transsexualism and Sex Reassignment* (Baltimore: The Johns Hopkins Press, 1969).

Kay, Barry, *As a Woman* (New York: St. Martin's Press, 1977).

Sagarin, Edward, *Odd Man In* (Chicago: Quadrangle Books, 1972).

Stoller, Robert, *Sex and Gender* (New York: Science House, 1968).

Walinder, Jan, *Transsexualism* (Goteborg, Sweden: Akademiforlaget, 1967).

NOTES

1. Alfred Lindesmith and Anselm Strauss, *Social Psychology* (New York: Holt-Dryden, 1956), p. 318.

2. C. N. Armstrong, "Transvestitism," in D. R. Smith and W. M. Davidson, eds., *Symposium on Nuclear Sex* (New York: Interscience, 1957), p. 84, as cited in Jan Walinder, *Transsexualism* (Goteborg, Sweden: Akademiforlaget, 1967), p. 3.

3. Richard Green, M. D., *Sexual Identity Conflict in Children and Adults* (Baltimore: Penguin Books, 1975), pp. 29–42, 205–210, 304–305.

4. Robert Stoller, *Sex and Gender* (New York: Science House, 1968).

5. Walinder, *Transsexualism*, pp. 14–15.

6. James Driscoll, "Transsexuals," *Transaction*, 8 (March–April, 1971), pp. 28–37, 66, 68.

7. Howard S. Becker, *Outsiders* (New York: The Free Press, 1963).

8. Thomas Kando, "Passing and Stigma Management: The Case of the Transsexual," in Clifton D. Bryant, ed., *Sexual Deviancy in Social Context* (New York: New Viewpoints, 1977), pp. 149–159; Edward Sagarin, *Odd Man In* (Chicago: Quadrangle Books, Inc., 1972), pp. 122–124.

Organized Crime

8

It usually comes as somewhat of a surprise to the beginning student in criminology and deviant behavior that organized crime has not, until recently, been given any real attention or study by social scientists. The popular interest in the subject has generated a considerable amount of fiction, sensational journalism, and such movies as *The Godfather*. However, there is little work that could be called scientific study. The difficulty in studying a phenomenon that, by its very nature, demands secrecy can be appreciated. During the 1950s and 1960s, a concerted interest in organized crime developed largely as a result of three federal government investigations: the Senate Committee to Investigate Crime in Interstate Commerce (the Kefauver Committee); the Senate Committee on Operations, Permanent Subcommittee (McClellan Committee); and the President's Commission on Law Enforcement and Administration of Justice. The participation of social scientists on the President's Crime Commission, namely, the contributions of Donald R. Cressey to that commission, may even be considered a starting point to the scientific study of organized crime.

Thus, relative to a scientific framework the systematic study of organized crime is still within a beginning stage. Very little is known empirically about the subject and, at this stage of our knowledge, a major controversy has centered around the very concept and nature of organized crime itself. There are several divergent views on the subject. The three major ones have been 1) organized crime as the "Mafia," 2) organized crime as the "Cosa Nostra," and 3) organized crime as "diffuse independent collectivities." We will examine these three views and compare them to those of informants who have spoken on the subject before our classes. We will then examine other recent research regarding organized crime that may allow us to study the phenomenon within our larger theoretical models as presented in Chapter 1.

While the views of our informants are presented as illustrations rather than empirical proof, so much of the "knowledge" or the early study of organized crime has been based upon the testimony of one or a few informants (particularly Joseph Valachi) that our interviews might well qualify as "evidence" rather than mere illustration.

ORGANIZED CRIME AS THE "MAFIA"

The belief that there is a nationwide crime syndicate controlled by Sicilians (with roots in Sicily) that dominates organized crime in this country dates back to the nineteenth century. In 1890, New Orleans Superintendent of Police Peter Hennessey was murdered. Hennessey had been investigating the activities of the Matranga brothers, a gang of Sicilians who allegedly gained complete control of the New Orleans waterfront in 1890. Residents assumed Sicilians to be responsible and nineteen gang members were arrested, then subsequently acquitted. An irate crowd lynched eleven of the nineteen, resulting in an international incident and considerable coverage in the news media blaming the event on the "Mafia" or "Black Hand." This allegation in the news media led to reaction in the Italian community, and many Italian community leaders vehemently denied the existence of the Black Hand. In 1907, however, these leaders organized the White Hand Society, a society whose acknowledged purpose was to combat the Black Hand, and thus themselves confirmed the existence of the Black Hand.[1] It is possible that the Mafia as a large-scale organization did not even exist in this country before all the national publicity. It appeared to flourish in the early 1900s but then became less influential in the 1920s when the Black Handers joined in with the mainstream of American gangsterism.

The term *Mafia* became popular when the Kefauver Crime Committee began to uncover testimony about a national crime syndicate in the United States. The term *Mafia* implies that organized crime in this country is dominated by Sicilian-Americans, that the organization is of nationwide scope, and that it is actually rooted and currently based in Sicily.

> *Behind the local mobs which make up the national crime syndicate is a shadowy, international criminal organization known as the Mafia, so fantastic that most Americans find it hard to believe it really exists. The Mafia, which has its origin and its headquarters in Sicily, is dominant in numerous fields of illegal activity—principally narcotics—and it enforces its code with death to those who resist or betray it.[2]*

The Mafia is believed to have arisen in Sicily during the early part of the nineteenth century. It began as a protective organization of the peasant classes formed to resist oppression by the feudal land barons. The Mafiosi, however, launched a reign of terror—murder, rape, robbery, extortion, and kidnapping. Landowners acquiesced to Mafia demands and made deals with the Mafiosi to protect their estates, and the Mafiosi in turn became crueler tyrants over the peasants than the gentry ever were.

Based largely on testimony by Harry Anslinger, Commissioner of the Narcotics Bureau at that time, the Kefauver Committee uncovered several alleged characteristics of this organization: 1) a secret code called *Omerta*, or "death to informers"; 2) an inner circle of organized crime known as the "family"; and 3) a Mafia grand council that governed local families. The evidence for this view consisted primarily of testimony by Anslinger and other Narcotics Bureau agents (much of which was kept secret); systematic *denials* of the existence of the Mafia by alleged gangsters who testified ("evidence" for the code of Omerta); and reference to various violent crimes that "had all of the earmarks of the Mafia." The international head of the Mafia in Italy was believed to be Charles (Lucky) Luciano, who, after serving ten years in prison, had been deported to Italy by Thomas E. Dewey.

While the "Mafia" concept appears to be that which is most accepted by the public generally, we will shortly examine sociological views that have treated it as a "myth." First, let us examine a modified but competing concept of organized crime, that of the "Cosa Nostra."

ORGANIZED CRIME AS THE "COSA NOSTRA"

While the term *Mafia* implies a national organization rooted in Sicily, the term *Cosa Nostra* represents another perspective, namely, a national organization of Sicilian origin but centralized and controlled in the United States and with a somewhat unique organizational structure. This perspective came to light largely as a result of the testimony of Joseph Valachi before the McClellan Committee in 1963, although the term was known to the FBI and other agencies before Valachi's testimony.[3] Valachi, by his own testimony a *soldati*, or soldier, in the Vito Genovese family, revealed in detail the organizational structure of Cosa Nostra, named the major bosses and numerous subordinates, and told the history of Cosa Nostra and how it became transformed from the Sicilian-based Mafia to Cosa Nostra, its Americanized counterpart.

Based largely on the McClellan Commission findings, Valachi's testimony, and a consultant paper by Donald Cressey, the President's Crime Commission gave a detailed description of Cosa Nostra in an attempt to bring its existence to public attention.[4] The President's Commission pinpointed this structure to twenty-four exclusively Italian groups (5,000 individual members) operating as criminal cartels in large cities throughout the nation. Together they are said to control most of the illicit gambling and loan sharking in the country and are heavily implicated in narcotics trafficking and labor racketeering. The President's Crime Commission estimates of annual intake are from 7 billion to 50 billion dollars from gambling, several billion from loan sharking, and 250 million from heroin trade. In addition, Cosa Nostra is said to exercise a virtual monopoly over many legitimate enterprises such as cigarette vending machines and juke boxes. These twenty-four groups work with and control other racket groups, whose leaders are of various ethnic derivations. In addition, the thousands of employees who perform the street-level functions of organized crime's gambling, usury, and other illegal activities represent a cross section of the nation's population groups.

Each of the twenty-four groups is known as a "family," with membership varying from as few as twenty men to as many as 700. The organization as a whole (previously known as the Mafia) is known as the Cosa Nostra and has a membership of approximately 5,000 people. Each family in the organization is headed by one man, the "boss," whose primary functions are to maintain order and maximize profits. His authority in all matters relating to his family is absolute. Beneath each boss is an "underboss," the vice-president or deputy director of the family. He collects information for the boss, relays messages to him, and passes his instructions down to his own underlings. On the same level as the underboss, but operating in a staff capacity, is the *consigliere*, who is a counselor or adviser. He gives advice to family members, including the boss and underboss. He thereby enjoys considerable influence and power. Below the level of the underboss are the *caporegime*, or lieutenants, some of whom serve as buffers between the top members of the family and the lower-echelon personnel. To maintain their insulation from the police, the leaders of the hierarchy (particularly the bosses) avoid direct communication with the workers. The *caporegime* fulfill the buffer capacity. Other *caporegime* serve as chiefs of operating units. The lowest-level members of a family are the *soldati*, the soldiers or "button" men who report to the *caporegime*. A soldier may operate a particular illicit enterprise—such as a loan-sharking operation, a dice game, a lottery, a bookmaking operation, or a smuggling operation—or he may "own" the enterprise and pay a portion of its profit to the organization, in return for the right to operate and perhaps for being backed by the capital and resources of the organization. Beneath the soldiers in the hierarchy are large numbers of employees and commission agents who are not members of the family and are not necessarily of Italian descent. These are the people who do most of the actual work of various enterprises. They have no buffers or other insulation from law enforcement. They take bets, drive trucks, answer telephones, sell narcotics, tend the stills, and work in the legitimate businesses.

The President's Commission viewed the threat of Cosa Nostra not only in terms of millions of dollars lost to Americans and corruption of public officials, but also in terms of the violence or threat of violence that allegedly accompanies organized criminal activities. At the lowest level within the structure of Cosa Nostra, the previously discussed *soldati*, who do the work of the organization, run their enterprises through use of extortion and bribery. The *soldati* may actually be designated "corrupters," functioning to establish relationships with public officials and other influential persons whose assistance is needed, or they may also specialize as "enforcers," whose function is to maim and kill recalcitrant members.

In terms of control, however, the most threatening aspect of Cosa Nostra, in the view of the President's Commission, was its nationwide centralized control by a ruling body known as the "Commission." This is an oligarchical body serving as a combination legislature, supreme court, board of directors, and arbitration board. Family members look to the Commission as the ultimate authority on organizational and jurisdictional disputes. It is composed of the bosses of the nation's most powerful families and has authority over all twenty-four. The composition of the Commission is said to vary from nine to twelve men.

It is nearly impossible for law enforcement agencies to penetrate top levels of Cosa Nostra because of a "code of conduct" which stipulates that underlings should not interfere with the leader's interests and should not seek protection from the police. They should be "standup guys" who go to prison in order that the bosses may amass fortunes. Loyalty, honor, respect, absolute obedience—these are inculcated in family members through ritualistic initiation and customs within the organization, through material rewards, and through violence. The boss may order the execution of any family member for any reason, and deviance is quickly discovered through an elaborate system of internal informants.

The structure and history of Cosa Nostra were described in even greater detail by Donald Cressey in his book *Theft of the Nation*, a book developed from his consultant paper to the President's Crime Commission.[5] Cressey's information came from "police reports, informants, wire taps, and electronic bugs." Cosa Nostra, Cressey holds, differs from the Sicilian Mafia in several respects. The term *Cosa Nostra* came into use when a group of "young Turks" headed by Lucky Luciano emerged triumphant from a struggle with more traditional Sicilian "mustache Pete" leaders, including Salvatore Maranzano and Giuseppe Masseria. The term *Cosa Nostra* might have come into use to rid the organization of the Sicilian image created by the term *Mafia*. The current "Commission" is an American innovation to Cosa Nostra and not just a transplant from Sicily. It differs from Italy's counterpart in its more diffuse division of power resembling a *cosca*, or stable union of families within a given district rather than a *consorteria*, or society-wide Mafia. Thus, in the United States, based largely upon a breakdown in ties resulting from immigration, migration, and urbanization, there is a less cohesive relationship between families than in Italy (and also less cohesion within families as evidenced by the creation of fictive families as compared with the often real family ties of Italian "families"). Despite a lessening of family alliance relationships, in this country Cosa Nostra today is said to maintain an important element of nationwide direction by way of the Commission. Family alliance is based upon exclusive Sicilian or Italian descent. In addition, families are linked to each other, and to non-Cosa Nostra syndicates, by understandings, agreements, and treaties, and by mutual deference to the Commission. In addition to their conspiracy to commit crimes, the members of Cosa Nostra, Cressey maintains, threaten a behind-the-scenes takeover of the government of this country on the local, state, and federal levels in that some government officials and judges are considered, and consider themselves, members.

INDEPENDENT COLLECTIVITIES

Although the existence of a nationwide syndicate (Mafia or Cosa Nostra) has been affirmed by a national commission and two Senate investigating committees, the idea is not without opposition among academicians, and in fact the opposition runs parallel to the major government investigations. The idea of the Mafia in this country was sharply contested by Daniel Bell and he termed this view "The Myth of the Mafia."[6] The Crime Commission's portrayal of Cosa Nostra was held to question by Ramsey Clark in his book *Crime in America*,[7] and the Commission's view plus those of Donald Cressey were given careful scrutiny by Hawkins and Morris in *The Honest Politician's Guide to Crime Control*.[8] There is more recent evidence, cited by Francis A. J. Ianni,[9] that there is a "new" form of organized crime controlled by black and Hispanic groups in a "process of ethnic succession" of immigrants and migrants. The main theme of these analyses is that although organized crime does exist, it is not centralized on a national basis. Rather, it consists of independent collectivities organized mainly in the major metropolitan areas. Thus, "local" syndicates without any real national or even regional ties to one another pursue "business" within their localities.

These perspectives indicate that organized crime is not dominated by any one particular ethnic group (such as Sicilian-Americans or Italian-Americans), but cuts across ethnic ties, among both lower-ranking participants and top leaders. These various analyses are important and have separate emphases, so we shall take them up in turn.

The Myth of the Mafia

Bell, focusing exclusively upon the Mafia concept of the Kefauver Committee, examines first the evidence adduced by the Kefauver Committee and then the sociological assumptions made when we speak of the Mafia.

The Kefauver Committee, Bell says, failed to produce any tangible evidence of the existence of the Mafia in the United States.

> Neither the Senate Crime Committee in its testimony, nor Kefauver in his book, presented any real evidence that the Mafia exists as a functioning organization. One finds police officials asserting before the Kefauver Committee their *belief* in the Mafia; the Narcotics Bureau *thinks* that a world-wide dope ring allegedly run by Luciano is part of the Mafia; but the only other "evidence" presented—aside from the incredulous responses both of Senator Kefauver and Rudolph Halley when nearly all of the Italian gangsters asserted that they didn't know about the Mafia —is that certain crimes bear "the earmarks of the Mafia." [10]

Bell believes that organized crime is not a Sicilian-American invention nor do they monopolize it, but it is instead part of the American way of life and a "queer ladder of social mobility" used by all newly arriving immigrant groups in this country.

> The salient reason, perhaps, why the Kefauver Committee was taken in by its own myth of an omnipotent Mafia and a despotic Costello was its failure to assimilate and understand three of the more relevant sociological facts about institutionalized crime in its relation to the political life of large urban communities in Amerca, namely: 1) the rise of the American-Italian community, as part of the inevitable process of ethnic succession to positions of importance in politics, a process that has been occurring independently but also simultaneously in most cities with large Italian constituencies . . . ; 2) the fact that there are individual Italians who play prominent, often leading roles today in gambling and in the mobs; and 3) the fact that Italian gamblers and mobsters often possessed "status" within the Italian community itself and a "pull" in city politics. These three items are indeed related—but not so as to form a "plot." [11]

Bell states that gambling was overrelated to gangsterism in the Kefauver report, there being only a minority of gamblers who are also gangsters. It is, moreover, a less violent route to fortune than that used by many of today's wealthy families, and certainly less violent as compared with the means used by the "captains of industry" and "robber barons" of the nineteenth century in this country. In fact, because of the requirements of running large-scale business enterprises, many of the top "crime" figures have long ago forsworn violence and their incomes are in large part derived from legitimate or quasi-legitimate but socially respectable sources, such as gambling casinos.

What, then, is the source of the concept of the Mafia? It derives from the American tendency to find a scapegoat as a means of dealing with problems of life:

> There is, . . . in the American temper, a feeling that "somewhere, somebody is pulling all the complicated strings to which this jumbled world dances." In politics the labor image is "Wall Street" or "Big Business"; while the business stereotype was the "New Dealers." In the field of crime, the side-of-the-mouth low-down was "Costello." [12]

Limits of Organized Crime

The President's Commission on Law Enforcement and Administration of Justice was appointed by Lyndon B. Johnson. Ironically, Ramsey Clark, who was the Attorney General under Johnson at the time the Commission published its results, had views on organized crime diametrically opposed to those published by the Commission. His published views stand, in fact, as a penetrating critique of the Commission report on organized crime.

The President's Commission stated that organized crime was influential in every part of the country. Clark, in turn, stated:

> Whole nations today are free of it as are entire states and regions in this country. Nowhere is it the principal part of crime, but in some of our major cities its tentacles wield power over many people and reach into high places.[13]
>
> President Johnson's Crime Commission surveyed seventy-one cities and found evidence of organized crime in only twenty-five.[14]

Clark even intimates that organized crime for the most part involves crimes of a minor nature:

> Organized crime supplies goods or services wanted by a large number of people—desperately needed cash, narcotics, prostitutes, the chance to gamble. These are its principal sources of income. They are consensual crimes for the most part, desired by the consuming public. This fact distinguishes the main activities of organized crime from most other crime. Few want to be mugged, have their assets embezzled or their cars stolen, but it is public demand that creates the basis for the activities of organized crime.[15]

Clark corroborates Bell's earlier statement about the trend away from violence among crime bosses:

> Legal activities tend to make organized crime conservative. The bosses no longer need to run the high risks of constant criminal activity. They have vested interests and a stake in the status quo. The occasions on which violence or other unlawful activity is a sound risk diminish. The strict discipline essential to daily criminal conduct is not necessary. They go soft in comparison to their earlier days.[16]

Clark even doubts the estimates of earnings of the syndicate made by the Crime Commission:

> The high estimates of syndicate income would average $1 million a year for 26,000 individuals and the low a million each for 6– to 7,000 persons. Even the lower estimate of the Crime Commission is wildly improbable.

Directing his attention to the Crime Commission's view of Cosa Nostra, Clark admits the organization exists but reduces its importance in the overall picture of organized crime in America.

> As with all crime, we oversimplify our definition of organized crime. There is far more to it than La Cosa Nostra. Our society is much too complex to expect only a single syndicate or type of illegal activity. There is no one massive organization that manages all or even most planned and continuous criminal conduct throughout the country. There are hundreds of small operations that engage in organized criminal activity—car theft rings, groups of burglars, safecrackers working together, gangs of armed robbers, combinations that occasionally smuggle and distribute marijuana and dangerous drugs—scattered throughout the nation.[17]

Like Bell, Clark suggests that the whole emphasis upon Cosa Nostra and organized crime smacks of scapegoating:

> Organized crime is something everyone can hate. . . . It is cheap to handle, too. Arrest a bunch of Sicilians and the latest "crime wave" is over—and America lives happily ever after. For many, organized crime is the alien conspiracy that absolves us of responsibility for crime in America. This self-deception only causes a serious diversion from the real problems and urgent needs of crime prevention.[18]

ORGANIZED CRIME AND GOD

Morris and Hawkins have satirically drawn a comparison between "the demonology of organized crime," that "there exists a single, mysterious, omnipotent organization that is responsible for much of it," and the belief in God as a matter of faith. While God is said to be, in theology, invisible, immaterial, eternal, and omnipotent, organized crime is indirectly attributed with the same characteristics since there is little empirical "evidence" as to definitive existence beyond the persistence of the belief in it and scanty, secondary "patterns" of data. Morris and Hawkins critically examine the major sources of data, stating: 1) the Valachi testimony is analogous to "the knowledge of Standard Oil which could be gleaned from interviews with gasoline station attendants"; 2) Cressey's argument that by outlining the detailed structural skeleton of Cosa Nostra demonstrates the existence of such is a *nonsequitur*; 3) the Valachi testimony, though it comprised the prime source of the knowledge of the skeletal structure, is uncorroborated by any other testimony; 4) the Valachi testimony contained internal inconsistency—for example, despite a code such as "one for all, all for one," Valachi testified the organization offered him no immunity from prosecution; 5) the Valachi testimony was contradicted by others; 6) with regard to the alleged "meeting at Appalachin" on November 17, 1967, which has been used as "proof of conspiracy," there was a) conflicting testimony as to how many top leaders were there, and b) the conviction of twenty arrested there was reversed on appeal and conspiracy was not proven legally; and 7) there are members even in the Crime Commission Report who are of non-Sicilian ancestry.

Morris and Hawkins concur with Bell and Clark that the crime conspiracy idea involved in Cosa Nostra is probably traced to scapegoating tendencies in this country and "The Paranoid Style in American Politics."

THE NEW MAFIA: Black and Hispanic?

Francis A. J. Ianni, in recent articles, treats organized crime as "an American way of life." [19] He views the economic system of the United States as a continuum with "legitimate business . . . at one end and what we call organized crime at the other." [20] Thus, "organized crime" provides "successive waves of immigrants and migrants" as a means of economic and social mobility. Hence, according to Ianni, organized crime is not limited to any one ethnic group, such as Sicilian-Americans or Italian-Americans. Ianni views organized crime as in a state of transition wherein Italian domination is giving way to domination by blacks and Hispanics.

Employing field methods of research including interviews and field observations, Ianni portrays a model of organized crime whose membership is recruited from legitimate social and business relationships as well as from prison acquaintances. Its "criminal links" are rather loose and similar to those of legitimate enterprise, including employer-employee relationships, joint ventures, buyers and sellers, and leaders and followers. The "code," according to Ianni, is merely an extension of prison and youthful gang relationship rules, including such norms as "Don't tell the police," "Don't be disloyal," and "Don't be incompetent in your job." [21]

Ianni maintains that whatever former hierarchies have existed within organized crime were based upon Italian ethnic and family relationships, but these are now disappearing as that wave of immigrants have moved within legitimate businesses. The hierarchy that is replacing Italian-Americans is composed of blacks and Hispanics, mainly Puerto Ricans, as legitimate means are unavailable to these groups within the economic structure. In addition, the current activities of organized crime, numbers-racketeering, prostitution, and drugs, better suit the "needs" of these groups as "customers" than those within Italian neighborhoods or communities. Ianni maintains that the organizations are rather loose and neither regional nor national in scope, but that greater police enforcement could bring about the destruction of the weaker members and, thus, a stronger hierarchy as well as a coalescence of black and Puerto Rican leadership.

Thus, while Ianni would appear to agree with many of the points made by Bell, Clark, and Morris and Hawkins, he would combine their assessments and take them one step further in explaining why organized crime exists:

> ... blacks and Hispanics must continue to face the same basic dilemma which confounded earlier generations of Irish, Jews and Italians: How do you escape poverty through socially approved routes when such routes are closed off from the ghetto? Organized crime resolves the dilemma because it provides a quick if perilous route out.[22]

RALPH, TONY, AND PEDRO:
Participants in Organized Crime

With all the mystique of secrecy and alleged code of "death to informers," we anticipated we would never find anybody who had participated in organized crime who would be willing to be interviewed. To our surprise, however, we came across three opportunities to hear from people who could serve as informants. Our first informant was a person of obscure background who spoke to the class as a self-proclaimed participant in organized crime. He was brought to class by a student of Italian-American origin, and he identified himself only by a first name—Ralph (fictitious). Ralph owned and operated an auto repair shop in New York. During the course of his business he repaired police cars, and through his association was able to "fix tickets." He also repaired cars owned by gangsters. Ralph is related by marriage to a man who owned a bakery in whose ovens the mob disposed of its bodies. Ralph claims he witnessed an assassination of a gangster and was told to keep his mouth shut about it. He did so and, in his words, was "rewarded by the syndicate for doing so." We make no claim as to the verity of his statements, but his interview is nevertheless included here because of numerous thought-provoking statements about organized crime in relation to the American social structure along lines quite similar to those of Daniel Bell.

Our second tract, perhaps more significant, was taped in the office with an ex-convict who had spoken to the class on another subject. We can make no further identification of him. However, as it turned out, his class lecture did not prove to be of such value to be included as a chapter, so this informant does not appear anywhere else in the book. Our respondent, whom we shall identify as Tony (fictitious, but he is a person of Italian-American background), presents a picture of organized crime very similar to that presented by Ramsey Clark.

Our third informant, Pedro, spoke to the class regarding his youth as a Puerto Rican growing up within the city of Milwaukee. His class lecture was for purposes other than those in keeping with the context of this work. However, we have known Pedro, recently ordained as a Roman Catholic priest, under other circumstances and have recorded those portions of his life story that shed light upon the study of organized crime. Pedro's comments are very much in line with the description of organized crime and the place of Hispanics as presented by Ianni.

Ralph

QUESTION: *Many magazines and news articles put forth the idea that organized crime is dominated by Italians.*

RALPH: Not necessarily so. The main syndicate, the Mafia, which people say have changed their name and is now La Cosa Nostra, but it is still the Mafia. It's only moved into a different racket. And the Cosa Nostra, so to speak, is now just the plain hoodlums. They are now not allowed to associate with the Mafia because Mafia is now big business and they can't afford to associate with hoodlums because they are now part of the society.

QUESTION: *You mean the Establishment?*

RALPH: Yes, [names well-known bank] is part of the syndicate; so are your biggest bankers. If you want to get rid of organized crime in the United States today, you must get rid of the United States because that is who controls the government, controls everything that exists in this country today, is crime. Politics are part of your crime syndicate. I dare say there is anybody here who doesn't know it. If you don't you're living in a dream world because crime is so prevalent among politicians because they are the ones who are allowing it to go on. The only way you're going to get rid of the crime structure is to get rid of your whole present-day structure and this is something that is not bound to happen because money loves money and people are always going to go where the money is and nobody is going to go the other way to fight crime, and if he does he's just finished.

QUESTION: *You mentioned something about the bakery business, lead shoes, and some lake in New York before you began speaking. Could you elaborate?*

RALPH: There are lakes in upstate New York called Louise and Marie and during the time that Murder Incorporated operated out of Brookline [sic], they would take those who got in the way and make cement shoes for them and drive them up to this place that is about 100 miles north of New York City and drop them in. And there was others who disappeared into concrete pavings and also in the ovens. There was bakers who would take these bodies and put them in the oven and no one would ever see them again. I mean they could make people disappear, and other people who say these things happen had to keep their mouth shut or you'll be in the oven with them.

QUESTION: *[Names reputed gangster] was named as a Lieutenant in La Cosa Nostra. What do you know of him?*

RALPH: He's a mere cog in the wheel. He's nothing. There is something with organized crime. They always have the fall guy and their main purpose is to distract. It is like the old game. They put somebody up in the forefront to take the brunt of the blame for whatever goes on, and meanwhile they're operating someplace else, wide open and reaping everything in.

QUESTION: *What about all these well-known people, from Lucky Luciano to Vito Genovese and Frank Costello?*

RALPH: They are all hoods. They are not even considered the upper bracket in the society of the Mafia. They are expendable, like, most of those people die from heart attacks, brought-on heart attacks. Look at the crime record. Al Capone died of a heart attack and so did Lucky Luciano. These people all died of heart attacks and they all had good hearts. They even have doctors in the organization. It's a hard thing to beat them.

QUESTION: *Don't they have to answer to somebody?*

RALPH: They work together. It's a close-knit organization. In fact, they have teletype and all the modern conveniences to contact one another and they do it in code. They don't have to operate in the open like they did in the old days. All they use these gangsters for these days is their dirty work, but they don't even need them. The Cosa Nostra is nothing.

QUESTION: *Is there one big boss?*

RALPH: No, it's a group of men, a whole group. They are not only here in this country. They are in every country in the world. They are in Taiwan, in Japan, they are all over. Matter of fact, they've got a big business going in Japan. The Mafia is in Japan and Taiwan and Hong Kong. You can imagine, it's not a local organization. It's a worldwide organization. Each man answers to himself in that it is not done collectively. They come with teletype machines and they do it through the teletype when they operate.

QUESTION: *Do they have much to do with world conditions?*

RALPH: You can trace this to them also, because they control the money. They can stir up money in any part of the world if they want, and make you believe you are fighting a war for some reason or other.

QUESTION: *Can you give us an idea of how you came by your information?*

RALPH: Like I said, associations in New York, childhood all the way up. Matter of fact, I left New York in 1960. I been here now ten years. But I go back, every couple of years I go back. It's the same situation. It still exists, and those areas where they were remain the same. They don't change. The main operators are out in the suburbs, the bigger wheels. They are in politics. The main organization, the Mafia itself, originates in Palermo, and that organization is still alive. They are not the controlling interests of the world because every country now has its own which is linked with the international Mafia. Now you have Interpol, which is the international police, to cope with them, but they are bought and sold also, so they can't do anything either. You cannot fight organized crime. It has gotten too far out of hand. This is my contention, and the only way you are going to stop them, you'll have to go for broke.

===== COMMENTARY

Ralph's story seems fantastic, incredible. Some might even write it off as nothing more than the ramblings of a paranoid. However, a number of statements he made have a ring of truth. It seems to follow that if the term Mafia was used in the twenties, and that if members of that organization rose, as Daniel Bell suggests, to become wealthy "legitimate businessmen," then the old Mafia could in fact operate now in the sphere of legitimate business, as the organization would have moved up along with its members. It should, however, be equally possible that other ethnic groups could have moved up in the same way such that Mafia members would be only a faction within the larger power elite in this country.

It is also true, perhaps, that, as Sutherland stressed in the 1940s and 1950s, big business is rife with "white collar crime," and in many of its activities actually more criminalistic than some organized crime activity. In our ranking, gambling is ranked as less serious than embezzlement. The President's Crime Commission has stated that when organized crime takes over legitimate business, it ceases to be legitimate business. Is, then, the evidence on white collar crime adduced by Sutherland, and more recently by Ralph Nader, not at the same time evidence of the movement of organized crime into legitimate business? Thus, our informant introduced an interesting hypothesis, one apparently not entertained before, that white collar crime and organized crime are really the same problem.

Ralph also suggests that Cosa Nostra as an allegedly Sicilian-American organization is merely a scapegoat for organized crime. This idea is, as we have seen, held by Bell, Clark, Morris and Hawkins, and Ianni. Ralph's emphasis is different, however. He suggests that the conspiracy goes beyond Cosa Nostra and is in back of the American social structure. Thus, his analysis is really closer to the Kefauver view, but also incorporates Cressey's Cosa Nostra idea. It does seem tenable, however, that if the Mafia controlled the United States government, it would be useful in deflecting public attention away from its influence to point an accusing finger at a group of mobsters calling themselves Cosa Nostra. However, what doesn't fit is that public inquiry into Cosa Nostra might lead to inquiry into the larger historical infiltration of legitimate business. At any rate, it seems at least consistent with the idea that Kefauver was getting close and it was necessary to put forth the notion of Costra Nostra and have certain persons named as "fall guys."

Tony

While Ralph's views on organized crime are interesting and certainly thought-provoking, we feel a much more realistic "insider's account" is given in Tony's testimony. Also, we know something about Tony's background. He is of Italian-American descent. He is an ex-convict born and raised in New Orleans. We know he spent time in prison for robbery. We know he at one time owned a bar and was associated with a "syndicate in New Orleans." In his own words: "I worked with a wire service that was associated with an organization, like most bookie joints are. It was my job to keep those bookies who weren't associated with them out of business. They were very generous. They gave me a salary and I could also keep their bankroll when I closed them down." We be-live Tony was an "enforcer" in the New Orleans syndicate. It seems, at any rate, more likely that he would have gained some firsthand knowledge of organized crime, in or outside of prison, than in the case of our first informant.

QUESTION: *Speaking of the public view of organized crime, have you read* The Godfather?

TONY: Yes, but Puzo dwells more on the individual relationships of the people and the stereotype they represent. I find that even with all the elaborate investigating equipment of the FBI, they find it hard, if not impossible, to get a clear picture of what constitutes organized crime, how it comes about, and what its purposes are.

QUESTION: *We've talked about this nationwide conspiracy, about the "Commission" or the "Boss of Bosses." Right now they're talking about Joseph Columbo and Carlo Gambino in New York.*

TONY: I find this hard to believe. I know a number of people who are involved at that level, and I find it hard to believe that Gambino is really a "boss." If there is or ever was a boss of bosses and all that it entails, it would have been Vito Genovese. I don't believe in the theory of a national conspiracy, that it is a complex organization with tentacles stretching out into every city. It's developed on a local level and always on a local level there is someone who controls, someone with the most influence and who loosely bosses the criminal endeavor such as prostitution, drugs, stolen goods, this type of thing.

QUESTION: *In contrast to that, I know there was the meeting in Appalachin of some eighty-five . . .*

TONY: There were sixty-seven, and I know two of the men who were there. I think that what was actually happening was an attempt to organize on a national scale, and it was broken up. Nothing was ever accomplished and there were no more attempts.

QUESTION: *What about the Valachi testimony?*

TONY: Oh, Valachi was an old line, minor criminal. I'm not sure why Vito Genovese swore him dead. I am sure that he did swear him dead, but Valachi was looking for some reason to keep alive and he tried to get this by giving Bobby Kennedy and others some reason. I think that he had a great imagination and there was probably some truth in everything that he said, but I think that he exaggerated them. I don't doubt that he was a gunman. I don't doubt that he executed the people that he said that he did in the time that he said that he did. He hadn't done anything recently, if you remember. The information was fifteen years old.

QUESTION: *What was his rank in the organization?*

TONY: I don't think he was much more than I was when I was involved, just a gunman, a muscle man.

QUESTION: *Then he wouldn't really have known all that much.*

TONY: No. I didn't really know that much. I knew something about the inside, about the formations of it, how it comes about, and some about how the criminal employees exercise their power on local, state, and even national government. I don't know what their plans are— I'm glad I don't—I don't want to know. What's happened today is that the Al Capone era is over and done with. You now have highly educated men in high places and they make far more money legitimately than they do illegitimately, I think. It might be questionable how they gained control of this company or that company, but what they do is offer legitimate organizations through which illegitimate acts can be carried out. For instance, I know of an old bank that used to be on my criminal route. This bank will exchange money for securities, bonds, monies that you shouldn't legally have—for a percentage. There's millions of dollars every year just in percentages. But it always develops on a local level and local crime leaders get hold of something, then viciously give up their money to have certain officials elected and thereby get control of legitimate companies and control of the government until it pyramids and he finds he has a tremendous influence and power. He has his hands in electing officials for mayor, state governor, and even Congress. He becomes the boss locally and, in that sense, there is organized crime. Now, when you talk about the Mafioso or La Cosa Nostra, which I personally think was invented by Valachi, but these people who control at a local level have knowledge of each other. Sometimes they're even related by blood or marriage. The thing, though, that prevents this so-called national conspiracy is the great amount of suspicion that these men have for one another, their distrust, and the jealousy that they have in regard to their own ability and power. It's inconceivable to me that the people that I know could ever get together and appoint an absolute boss over them. It's contrary to their personality. It's contrary to the Italian personality since we're probably talking more about Italians.

QUESTION: *Do you agree with that? What the President's Commission says, that it is primarily Italians?*

TONY: Oh, I agree with it, but, of course, I'm talking about only my experience with it and it's in the Southern states, with the exception of Miami.

QUESTION: *Is the organization pretty much New York-based?*

TONY: No, Detroit. The first persons to start anything in Miami were the remnants of what used to be called the Purple Gang out of

Detroit. They were the first ones to recognize the potential of South Florida. There is a family succession thing. If a guy has six brothers, they're all involved to a greater or lesser degree, and their children are all in college or graduated and practicing in law or medicine and they're aware, of course, but they don't feel badly about it because they've grown up with it.

QUESTION: *What about the organization itself? Is it a pretty coercive thing? Is there a lot of violence?*

TONY: Not a whole lot any more. Of course, there is a forced secrecy, and it does date back to the Mafia, which comes from Sicily, which was something entirely different than what it is today here and in Sicily. It was at one time almost like vigilantes. They came to this country and some wise guy twisted it to his own purposes. Originally in New Orleans they preyed only on Italian immigrants for protection. "We'll get you jobs, we'll do this for you, if you pay us." Then they say, "Well, we've done this so successfully with our own, let's expand and take over the whole city or state." And they did. And they killed a few police and the D.A. of New Orleans.

QUESTION: *They were acquitted of it, weren't they?*

TONY: Sorta, some were killed by uprisings and other methods.

QUESTION: *But wasn't it still a small-scale operation then?*

TONY: Yes, in the sense that it only encompassed the city of New Orleans.

QUESTION: *It started in New Orleans?*

TONY: It started in this country in New Orleans, brought from Sicily by the dockmen. Then it spread because this guy would leave and then another and so on. But they didn't leave like a conspiracy. They just went. They developed a personal thing. It wasn't "our thing." It was *my* thing. They were able, of course, to call on each other for assistance in influencing different things, but that's as far as the alliance goes. They exercise an enforcement, but now it's done like a businessman. If he wants to cooperate, he will cooperate or he will lose his business. They can cause him hassles with licenses or other things, like political influence.

QUESTION: *They don't have to use strong arm anymore?*

TONY: No, because they can will the law. They have control of the people who write, interpret, and enforce the laws. And they do this. I'd say some 60 percent of the Congress has obligation to some particular crime boss, and it's the same in the Senate, whether people want to believe it. I mentioned Cuba because I worked an area that was predominantly a gambling outfit with bookies and gambling houses in New Orleans. It's against the law, but any cab driver will take you to a house and they've got everything that they got in Vegas except the floor show. They had complete control of Havana. They paid Batista millions. How do you think Batista amassed all those millions that he has? And what they had was complete freedom with him, and this young idealist Castro wasn't going to go for that. People ask why did we back a dictator, when Batista was talking all the ideals of freedom much like the early days of this country. But it was the gambling influences on the Congress in the United States. It's just that simple, but people won't believe that. But I believe that and I have reason to believe that. I've seen what gambling can do and the kind of people who control the money and what purposes they can use it for. They've just arrested our rackets-fighting district attorney, and you know whose payroll he's on? The man I'm telling you about now, the boss of New Orleans gambling.

QUESTION: *One of the primary interests seems to be gambling. Is that true?*

TONY: Yes. There's a movement now completely away from narcotics. Prostitution has been left to the freelancers for quite some time now, ever since Luciano was racked up so badly for it years back.

QUESTION: *Wasn't he deported to Italy?*

TONY: No, to Sicily. He was pardoned from all his time and released to assist in organizing the Sicilian invasion and to relay messages to the allies. He was killed some time back.

QUESTION: *Do you think that a lot of the top businessmen are running and perpetuating the syndicate or Mafia?*

TONY: I think that a lot of them are involved. There are several top businessmen in several large cities that I know of that, although they aren't prime leaders, they are associated with the syndicated activities in their area. They do favors and provide fronts. This includes bankers and corporation heads.

QUESTION: *Do you believe, in most cases, the syndicate is really breaking laws that shouldn't have been laws in the first place? Except for heroin, gambling and prostitution are services that should probably be provided rather than labeled as crimes.*

TONY: That's basically true. They have always appealed to human weaknesses. Gambling has provided the largest amount of funds for any organization. The public helps make a young man ambitious, like the kid telling me that he'd rather be a Mafia Don than the President because then he could tell the President what to do. Being successful at crime doesn't discount you anything. You get all the respect, prestige, and material goods anyway. The key is being successful. You'd be surprised at how much this influences the guys that I worked with. What a lot of these burglars and gunmen want is to be noticed by some Don who'll say, "Hey, man, you're just what I need." The public adds to that; the movies add to that; yellow newspapers add to that. Then, after you condone this big man up here, and you punish this little man down here, and then, when you let him out you treat him like some kind of alien being. Society doesn't want to take any responsibility for creating this little man. They want to believe that he just happened out of some unexplainable spontaneous environmental phenomenon. What I'm talking about is hypocrisy, I guess, because they are providing the fertile ground for crime at any level—organized or freelanced. The people who are involved in big crimes, such as narcotics, can't say, "Hey, you can't traffic this area anymore." What they are saying is that if you jeopardized any of us because you're handling it, that we will fight for survival. Narcotics are just too hot to handle. An agreement is made as a majority thing or boss of bosses. They can get together enough for their own protection, but the minute you mention a boss of bosses, every one of them thinks of himself as the one qualified.

QUESTION: *I think that one of the reasons that we call this organized crime is that it is very difficult to deal with organized crime at the national level.*

TONY: You can't fight it. All they can do is uncover something here, indict someone there, prosecute someone here, and send them to jail for a while. The law enforcement agencies aren't going to make it happen. I don't know how to bring it about. The only people who can effectively end organized crime are those people of the community where organized crime exists. I'm talking about elected officials who must be able to say, "I don't care if you can make me a cinch for this election; I would rather not win than be indebted to you." And then expose them. Or even use them to get into office and then expose them. We're talking about honesty, courage, awareness, and involvement as opposed to ignorance, apathy, and self-seeking rather than for the good of the whole. And how do you go about changing that? You just work at it. I mentioned revamping corrections and the justice system. Planting the seed and hoping that it will flourish and that someday we can successfully accomplish this change.

COMMENTARY

Tony makes a number of points that seem to corroborate the third view, "independent collectivities," discussed above.

1. Nationwide conspiracy is very difficult to achieve.
2. There are local organizations, but there is so much rivalry among leaders that they could not agree upon a national boss or even a central council, and the Appalachin meeting, rather than proof of a prior organization, was in fact a first attempt or recent attempt at centralized coordination.
3. Valachi may have exaggerated the scope of organized crime so that the government would give him protection, and much of his testimony may have been fabrication, since he was a very low echelon member of the organization—a soldier.
4. The organization is getting away from the violence of the Al Capone era and today is heavily infiltrated into legitimate business (in agreement with Ralph's statement above).

The picture of organized crime that Tony gives seems to make sense of the various views discussed above. As stated by Daniel Bell and our informant, Ralph, organized criminals or their collaborators are often involved in legitimate business. There is also, as stated by Clark and Bell, a rudimentary criminal organization, although primarily at the local level. However, Italian-Americans share an American trait of "individualism," so the idea of a national or international conspiracy embodied in the findings of the Kefauver Committee, the McClellan Committee, and the Crime Commission is perhaps an overstatement or exaggeration today.

Pedro

QUESTION: *Tell us something about yourself and your background.*

PEDRO: I was born in Puerto Rico, but my family moved to Milwaukee when I was about a year old. First of all, we lived in a, you know, kind of middle class neighborhood. You know, it was mainly white, Anglo, and so on. Then, when I was junior high age, we moved to the other side of town. My Dad bought these apartments and he wanted us to live in one of them so he could keep his eye on them, because that was a different kind of area altogether. People there didn't have as much and there was a lot of vandalism and that kind of thing.

QUESTION: *Was this mainly a Puerto Rican neighborhood?*

PEDRO: Well, it depends on what you want to call "neighborhood." It was mainly Puerto Ricans right there, but the whole area was mixed. There were Cubans, Mexicans or Chicanos, other Spanish-speaking people, and then nearby there was most everything, blacks and other groups. But, yes, it was mainly Puerto Rican where I lived. That was the funny thing. When I went to the new school in that area, we hung around with our different groups. The teachers, especially your newer, younger ones, didn't know the difference between Mexicans and Puerto Ricans and Cubans, and so on. And if we hung around in groups, they thought you were a "gang." You know, just if people looked alike or dressed alike, then they thought you were a gang. It was kind of funny, but, then, the police were the same way. Like, guys would fight over girls. You know, you just don't whistle or make wolf calls at a girl that is a member of another group. And if this would happen, well, it was necessary to defend the reputation of the girls. Because, if you didn't, that was like saying she was "easy." So, anyway, these were no big deal, but the newspapers would have a big headline, "Puerto Rican Gangs Fight" because we were the biggest group, there were more of us. But they really didn't know the difference because, to them, all people who are Spanish-speaking look alike, so they call them all Puerto Ricans. We really didn't have any gangs, but they thought we did.

QUESTION: *Was there any form of organized crime in that area?*

PEDRO: What do you mean? Like the Mafia?

QUESTION: *Yes.*

PEDRO: Hah! That's a laugh, you know! Maybe they have that in Chicago or New York, with Mafia and Italians and all, but that wasn't the way it was in Milwaukee. It is kind of funny, because we had organized crime, if that is what you want to call it. But do you know who was the head of it? The Chinese! That is, at least, as far as the numbers racket, and everyone played that. I mean, everyone. You see, it is just a little bit to play. You can play a quarter a day or whatever, and, sure, your chances of winning aren't too good, but if you do, it is quite a bit. So, these people didn't have much money, you see, but they could afford to play a quarter or so and, if they won, well, it was pretty good for them. But all that wasn't the Mafia. That was primarily played by people in the neighborhood, Puerto Ricans and others. But the big people, the people who ran it all, were Chinese. They were the ones who made all the money.

QUESTION: *How do you know this?*

PEDRO: [*Laughs*] Well, you see, my uncle, he had this store and he got caught, was busted. He was pretty heavily into it, and he went to prison, did time.

QUESTION: *How high up was your uncle? Could you explain more about this and how he had ties with the Chinese?*

PEDRO: Well, you see, you have to know how it operates. You see, if you have a store, particularly if it is a laundry or a small store where you have charge accounts or numbers you work with, then there is no way they can catch you. You see, you pay your quarter and you pick your number. Well, a storekeeper, he keeps a list of the numbers and amounts and, if he gets caught, he just says these are the account numbers and the amounts people owe him, or their laundry numbers, and there is no way they can prove him wrong. Then, you see, he just turns the lists and the money over to the pick-up man and keeps a copy. If he has a winner on his list, it is given to him and he pays off his customer. Again, he can keep a list of winning numbers and just say it is a part of his accounts. My uncle got in deeper because he was a pick-up man. He would, you know, take the lists from the different stores. He got caught that way. He had too much, and so on, on him. Some undercover agent caught him. But he wasn't going to tell who he knew was his contact person. He didn't do very long because they really didn't have that much on him. They threatened him, but he wouldn't tell. Anyway, you see, he knew it was the Chinese who were the head of it all. But everyone knew that. I mean, everyone but the police or whoever if you believe all these stories, you know, about the Mafia and Italians and all. It is a joke!

QUESTION: *Were there any other forms of crime in this area, like prostitution or drugs? Were these run by the same organization?*

PEDRO: Hah! Of course! There is always prostitution. That goes on everywhere. Oh, yeah, we had a lot of streetwalkers on some streets and all, but you know who picked them up? It was the nice people from other parts of town, a lot of them. But they didn't have anything to do with organized crime or the numbers. That stuff goes on all over. It is the same way with drugs. Oh, yeah, when I was growing up you had your glue-sniffers, and pot, and all that. Later, some of those guys went on to use other things, some of them, but a lot of them became alcoholics, I think. I really didn't get into a lot of that because, I guess, about that time was when I started to hang around the church and at the rectory a lot. But, anyway, I don't think there was any connection between any of those things and the numbers. You always have your pimps and your drug dealers, but they were all different people. I don't know. I guess, maybe the Mafia, or whatever you want to call it, does control heroin and that stuff, you know, at the top, but I don't know. I guess somebody has to. But I'm not sure it is like in the movies and on television.

COMMENTARY

Pedro's perspective is at a different level than that of either Ralph or Tony. Pedro was not really a "member" of organized crime but was close to its everyday workings within his neighborhood. Thus, while his level of knowledge would not allow one to confirm or deny the existence of a large nationally organized "Mafia" or "Cosa Nostra," his view from a Puerto Rican enclave would appear to support the "independent collectivities" view of organized crime. Pedro's story would appear to particularly uphold the contentions of Ianni that a new succession of immigrants and migrants, mainly blacks and Hispanics, has replaced the earlier Italian and Sicilian members. What is curious in Pedro's story is that the "big people . . . who ran it all were Chinese." This, too, may fit Ianni's view even though he did not mention the Chinese specifically. The Chinese to whom Pedro is referring may not have been fully integrated into the "legitimate business" and of the spectrum of American life. All three groups may, thus, be utilizing this means of working their way out of poverty with socially approved ways being presently closed to them.

Pedro's comments regarding the views of "outsiders" to the neighborhood, as opposed to those who lived there, deserve particular comment. One may regard some of his comments as, in part, upholding a labeling theory perspective. The outsiders labeled the Mexicans, Cubans, and Puerto Ricans all as Puerto Ricans, but, even further, as Puerto Rican "gangs." The fact that the perspective of the "insiders" was quite different is reminiscent of the findings of William F. Whyte in *Street Corner Society.*[23] Whyte, as a participant-observer, found that an Italian-American neighborhood that was viewed as a "disorganized" slum area by outsiders was actually quite highly organized within its own value system. Such an "outsider" perspective, on a larger scale, could lead to the creation of a "myth" of a Mafia by a similar process of labeling without concrete evidence in support of such a "reality." Whyte, in the 1930s in the Italian neighborhood of Cornerville, found similar patterns of residential playing of the "numbers rackets" as Pedro described among the Puerto Ricans more recently.[24]

The picture of organized crime that comes from the three accounts —Ralph's, Tony's and Pedro's—is that there is a diffuse influence of varied ethnic groups (heavily influenced by Sicilian immigrants in the first two accounts but influenced by Chinese and Puerto Ricans in the third account) and that organized crime exercises a strong influence in the American business community and has many collaborators there.

Let us now examine organized crime within our larger theoretical network.

THEORETICAL IMPLICATIONS

Several theoretical links may be drawn from the three accounts. We have mentioned that organized crime, or, at least, the "Mafia" and "Cosa Nostra" views, may be the creation of a "labeling" process. We may also see the following theoretical explanations:

SUBCULTURAL THEORIES An "organized network" would, in itself, be considered a "subculture." However, the persistence of such an organization within certain areas and among certain ethnic groups could be explained through various subcultural theories. Most likely to come immediately to mind are those subcultural theories which imply a "lower class" link to deviancy through lack of legitimate opportunities or through innate features of lower class life itself. These would include the "Drift" theory of Sykes and Matza, Cloward and Ohlin's "Differential Opportunity Theory," and Miller's theory of lower class subcultural as a "generating milieu" for delinquency. Ralph and Pedro both allude to the subcultures of their neighborhoods and differing value systems as "petty gang thievery" and "numbers" as compared to the larger society. Such subcultural links would also appear to fit the Ianni perspective of organized crime.

DIFFERENTIAL ASSOCIATION Sutherland's theory of Differential Association would also appear to fit the accounts of our three informants. The acceptance of "definitions" of numbers-playing, prostitution, and petty thievery as "a way of life" would appear to constitute acceptance of such rationalizations. Indeed, Ralph's reference to "associations" in New York and Tony's description of the acceptance of the authority of the leaders could be interpreted within a framework that allows a set of definitions in favor of crime to prevail over those definitions opposed to crime.

ANOMIE The implications of Pedro's interview and the following comments of Tony would tend to indicate that Merton's theory of anomie has special relevance in explaining organized crime:

> Being successful at crime doesn't discount you anything. You get all the respect, prestige, and material goods anyway. The key is being successful. You'd be surprised at how much this influences the guys that I worked with.

It could be this was Merton's prime referent when he developed the theory of anomie, particularly in his discussion of innovation, and it may be indeed that this is where it has its true relevance.

SOCIAL CONTROL THEORY Perhaps the Reckless' containment model of social control could serve both as an explanation for the existence of organized crime and as a link between the forms of deviance discussed in Chapters 2 through 7 of this text and those that will follow. It could be said, in other words, that organized crime exists because "external" control mechanisms (if conceptualized at a national level) are ineffective (these would include the inability to arrest "big national crime bosses," if any exist; the bribery of policemen and other officials inherent in organized crime; and the inability of officials to halt the everyday practice of numbers-playing, prostitution, and drug use in certain neighborhoods) and because "internal" control mechanisms are inoperative among those whom organized crime serves (the "buyers" of such services would include those who either through compulsion or pleasure seek gambling, sexual activities, drugs, and so on). Indeed, rather than attempting to control organized crime through external means, a more effective control might be to legalize or decriminalize "victimless" crimes, as has been advocated by Morris and Hawkins, Geis, Schur, and others.[25]

In earlier chapters we examined some forms of "victimless" deviance. Although there has not been a great deal of evidence that organized crime has engaged in the "marketing" of all of these activities (social nudism, homosexuality, and transsexualism, for instance), it can be seen that organized crime does engage in providing services, such as drugs, prostitution, and gambling, that would otherwise be unavailable on the legal market. In the following chapters, we will examine, in part, "career crimes" or "professional criminals." Cressey has described the "professional" as one who pursues crime "as a regular day-by-day occupation; the development of skilled techniques and careful planning in that occupation; and status among criminals." [26] This description would imply some degree of "organization" and "hierarchy" that characterize most views of organized crime. Regardless of which of the three major perspectives one might accept, we may merely be discussing the degree of professionalization, organization, and hierarchy that may or may not be present among embezzlers, robbers, or even murderers. We would exempt the rapist and the victim from this analysis, although they too will be examined in later chapters.

QUESTIONS FOR DISCUSSION

1. Ralph maintains, "If you want to get rid of organized crime in the United States today, you must get rid of the United States because that is who controls the government." What truth, if any, lies behind this rather extreme statement? What kind of society would it be if indeed organized crime did control this country? Is it that way indeed?

2. From what you may know of the nature of formal organization, what factors endemic to formal or complex organizations (as suggested by Tony) would limit the power and control of syndicated crime in this country?

3. Do you think that the apparent growth in ownership of "legitimate" businesses by organized crime indicates, as Bell maintained, that people who were once gangsters are "going legit"?

4. What hope is there, if any, of combatting organized crime in this country? Is it desirable to do so?

5. It is often said the United States is a "materialistic" society. How might a de-emphasis on material values provide a setting less conducive for organized crime to flourish? Discuss this from the perspectives of: a youth growing up in a ghetto, a policeman, a politician, and a "legitimate" businessman.

RELATED READINGS

Bell, Daniel, *The End of Ideology* (New York: The Free Press, 1965), pp. 138–148.

Clark, Ramsey, *Crime in America* (New York: Pocket Books, 1970).

Clinard, Marshall B., and Quinney, Richard, *Criminal Behavior Systems: A Typology*, 2nd ed. (New York: Holt, Rinehart and Winston, 1973).

Cressey, Donald, *Theft of the Nation: The Structure and Operations of Organized Crime in America* (New York: Harper & Row, 1969).

Einstadter, Werner J., "The Social Organization of Armed Robbery," *Social Problems*, 17 (1969), pp. 64–82.

Geis, Gilbert, *Not the Law's Business? An Examination of Homosexuality, Abortion, Prostitution, Narcotics and Gambling in the United States* (Rockville, Md.: National Institute of Mental Health, Center for the Study of Crime and Delinquency, 1972).

Hills, Stuart L., *Crime, Power and Morality: The Criminal-Law Process in the United States* (New York: Chandler Publishing Co., 1971).

Ianni, Francis A. J., *Black Mafia: Ethnic Succession in Organized Crime* (New York: Simon and Schuster, 1974).

Kefauver, Estes, *Crime in America* (Garden City, N.Y.: Doubleday, 1951).

Kennedy, Robert F., *The Enemy Within* (New York: Harper & Row, 1960).

Maas, Peter, *The Valachi Papers* (New York: Putnam, 1968).

McIntosh, Mary, *The Organization of Crime* (London: Macmillan, 1975).

Morris, Norval, and Hawkins, Gordon, *The Honest Politician's Guide to Crime Control* (Chicago: University of Chicago Press, 1969), chap. 8.

President's Commission on Law Enforcement and Administration of Justice, *Task Force Report: Organized Crime* (Washington, D.C.: U.S. Government Printing Office, 1967).

Savitz, Leonard D., and Johnston, Norman, *Crime in Society* (New York: John Wiley and Sons, 1978), pp. 573–690.

Sutherland, Edwin H., and Cressey, Donald R., *Criminology*, 10th ed. (Philadelphia: J. B. Lippincott, 1978), pp. 265–297.

Tyler, Gus, *Organized Crime in America* (Ann Arbor: University of Michigan Press, 1962).

Whyte, William F., *Street Corner Society* (Chicago: University of Chicago Press, 1943).

NOTES

1. Humbert Nelli, "Italians and Crime in Chicago: The Formative Years, 1890–1920," *American Journal of Sociology*, 75 (1969), pp. 373–391.

2. Estes Kefauver, *Crime in America* (Garden City, N.Y.: Doubleday, 1951), p. 14.

3. Donald R. Cressey, *Theft of the Nation* (New York: Harper & Row, 1969).

4. President's Commission on Law Enforcement and Administration of Justice, *Task Force Report: Organized Crime* (Washington, D.C.: U.S. Government Printing Office, 1967).

5. Cressey, *Theft of the Nation.*

6. Daniel Bell, *The End of Ideology* (New York: The Free Press, 1965), pp. 138–148.

7. Ramsey Clark, *Crime in America* (New York: Pocket Books, 1970), pp. 51–67.

8. Norval Morris and Gordon Hawkins, *The Honest Politician's Guide to Crime Control* (Chicago: University of Chicago Press, 1969).

9. Francis A. J. Ianni, "New Mafia: Black Hispanic and Italian Styles," *Society,* 11(3) (March/April, 1974), p. 26.

10. Bell, *The End of Ideology,* p. 139.

11. Ibid., p. 141.

12. Ibid., pp. 140–141.

13. Clark, *Crime In America,* p. 52.

14. Ibid., p. 54.

15. Ibid., p. 52.

16. Ibid., p. 56.

17. Ibid., pp. 57–58.

18. Ibid., p. 66.

19. Ianni, "New Mafia," p. 26.

20. Ibid.

21. Ibid., pp. 34–37.

22. Ibid., p. 39.

23. William F. Whyte, *Street Corner Society* (Chicago: University of Chicago Press, 1943).

24. Ibid., pp. 111–146.

25. See Morris and Hawkins, *The Honest Politician's Guide to Crime Control;* Gilbert Geis, *Not the Law's Business? An Examination of Homosexuality, Abortion, Prostitution, Narcotics and Gambling in the United States* (Rockville, Md.: National Institute of Mental Health, Center for Study of Crime and Delinquency, 1972); and Edwin M. Schur, *Crimes Without Victims: Deviant Behavior and Public Policy, Abortion, Homosexuality, Drug Addiction* (Englewood Cliffs, N.J.: Prentice-Hall, 1965).

26. Donald R. Cressey and Edwin H. Sutherland, *Criminology,* 10th ed. (Philadelphia: J. B. Lippincott, 1978), pp. 277–282.

White Collar Crime: Embezzlement; "Street" Crime: Robbery

9

Thus far, we have examined a variety of deviant acts, often termed "victimless" crimes, and organized crime, which may link some deviant activities without victims to some of those with victims. We now begin our study of acts which, by their nature, involve victims. This chapter deals with a comparison of white collar crime and street crime—specifically, embezzlement and robbery. We consider white collar crime and street crime together in order to examine what many sociologists and others regard as discrepancies in the manner they are viewed by society. These discrepancies seem to exist in spite of the relative threat each type of crime poses to life and property. The discrepancies exist within public perceptions as well as the legal system. We treat both crimes as having victims even though the nature of the victimization may differ. White collar crime may involve a single victim, many victims, or an entire population, but the relationship between the criminal and the victim is indirect and nonspecific. Some white collar crimes involve loss of life, limb, or health by the victim. Others, including embezzlement, involve loss of property. The relationship between the street criminal and the victim is usually more direct and specific. Street crimes, including some types of robbery, also can result in loss of life, limb, or health as well as property. The main purpose of robbery, like embezzlement and most white collar crimes, is usually financial gain.

White collar crime tends to be regarded as less serious than street crime. We shall examine some of the reasons for the public perceptions of the two types, discuss some general theories that may apply to either type, and then present some specific theories that deal separately with embezzlement and robbery. After presenting the interview, we will make some comments and place the two types of crime within broader theoretical frameworks for comparison.

ACCEPTANCE OF WHITE COLLAR CRIME AND FEAR OF STREET CRIME

Among those deviant acts which have a victim, the public tends to rank white collar crime as relatively less deviant or severe than other crimes such as burglary, robbery, rape, and murder. However, such ranking does not appear to reflect the relative fear of the public regarding specific crimes. The public tends not to fear white collar crime even though they are much more likely to be its victim. This may be due to several reasons, the most important of which may lie within the nature of white collar crime itself. Edwin Sutherland, in his classic study of white collar crime, defined it as a crime committed by a person of respectability and high social status in the course of his or her occupation.[1] Thus, the very "respectability" and status of the individuals involved may account for many of the misperceptions. Indeed, many acts that involve large amounts of financial gain for individuals or corporations and result in serious loss to others, whether the loss be of property, health, or life itself, are not defined in law as "crimes." Rather, many illegal acts, particularly those involving corporations, are dealt with administratively by state and federal agencies such as the Food and Drug Administration, the Securities and Exchange Commission, the Occupational Safety and Health Administration, the Federal Trade Commission, and so on. Such acts, although termed "illegal," are not considered "criminal." Thus, the corporations involved are usually fined and the executives responsible for the decisions may even be promoted.

Stuart Hills describes some of these "white collar criminals":

The white-collar offender is the contractor who intentionally uses defective building materials; the vice president of a pharmaceutical firm who knowingly refuses to report dangerous drug effects to the Food and Drug

Administration or to physicians; the corporate executive who conspires to rig prices, robbing the public of millions of dollars; the industrialist who criminally pollutes streams and recreational areas, endangering health and despoiling the countryside. The white-collar lawbreaker is also the stockbroker who peddles fraudulent securities; the entrepreneur whose home-improvement frauds drive the poor and unsuspecting to despair; the surgeon who splits his fees; the government official who barters his political influence for private profit; and the banker who juggles the books to conceal his embezzlement. Only rarely, however, do these and other kinds of white-collar occupational offenders come to occupy the status of "criminal" and experience its stigmatizing and harsh punitive sanctions.[2]

Given the status of white collar offenders, along with the frequent lack of criminal definition and sanctions in law, it is not astonishing that the public does not perceive white collar crime as something to be feared. This distortion is probably exacerbated by the treatment of various crimes in the media and by differing treatment of those individuals who commit acts defined as criminal in the legal system. In a recent work, Jeffrey Reiman traces this discrimination.[3] In spite of the fact that, according to 1974 Chamber of Commerce statistics, the cost of white collar crime was almost $42 billion, or more than all of the FBI Index crimes combined, and considerably more lives were lost than in "street" murders or other violent acts, Reiman notes the manner in which we perceive crime:

> Think of a crime, any crime. Picture the first "crime" that comes into your mind. What do you see? The odds are you are not imagining a mining company executive sitting at his desk, calculating the costs of proper safety precautions and deciding not to invest in them. The odds are that what you do see with your mind's eye is one person physically attacking another or robbing something from another on the threat of physical attack.[4]

Reiman points to what may be the critical element of effecting public perception, "specificity of intent to do harm." He maintains that the public has accepted a model of crime as one person specifically harming another "one-on-one" as opposed to "indirect harm" (such as the loss of *many* lives in a mining accident due to the lack of adequate safety equipment). The model, in turn, is incorporated within our legal system, which reinforces the public perception even further.[5]

If we look at the specific crime of embezzlement and compare it with other property crimes, we find that the estimated annual cost of embezzlement is $3 billion, or about that of all FBI Index property crimes.[6] At the same time, the chance of arrest for burglary, larceny, and motor vehicle theft is *133 times greater* than for embezzlement.[7] In 1973, the average sentence for robbery was 133.3 months, while the average sentence for embezzlement was 21.1 months. The average time for parole for those sentenced for robbery was 51.2 months, while the average time for those sentenced for embezzlement was only 13.2 months.[8]

THE NATURE OF EMBEZZLEMENT

Embezzlement commonly implies indulgence in "bookies, babes, and booze."[9] The term derives from the French *bezzle*, which means "drink to excess, gluttonage, revel, waste in riot, and plunder."[10] Because embezzlement is considered in criminal law a serious offense, a felony, the definition of embezzlement is fairly clear in criminal statutes. A standard legal definition is cited by Cressey:[11]

> The fraudulent appropriation to his own use or benefit of property or money entrusted to him by another on the part of a clerk, agent, trustee, public officer, or other person acting in a fiduciary capacity.[12]

A shorter version of this definition is given in the F.B.I. Uniform Crime Reports:

> Misappropriation or misapplication of money or property entrusted to one's care, custody, or control.[13]

Cressey found that when he tried to apply these legal definitions of embezzlement to actual cases, he ran into problems. The legal definition excludes some acts that he felt should be included (e.g., larceny by bailee, confidence game, forgery, issuing fictitious checks, conspiracy, grand theft, theft of government property, falsification of a bill of lading used in interstate shipment, and theft of goods in interstate shipment). It also includes some acts that should not be included (e.g., some cases of forgery). Cressey sharpened and shortened the definition of embezzlement to refer to "criminal violation of financial trust" whereby: "First, the person must have accepted a position of trust in good faith. Second, the person must have violated that trust by committing a crime."[14]

THE NATURE AND TYPES OF ROBBERY

A clear definition of robbery is given in the F.B.I. *Uniform Crime Report:*

> ...stealing or taking anything of value from a person by force or violence or by instilling fear, such as strong-arm robbery, stickups, robbery, armed. Includes assault to rob and attempts to rob.[16]

Robbery is a crime of violence against the person. Robbery differs from other crimes of violence (notably, criminal homicide, aggravated assault, and forcible rape) in several major respects. It is the only crime of violence in which whites are victimized more often than blacks, and also the only one that is predominantly interracial.[16] While other crimes of violence are likely to be committed by family members, friends, or other persons previously known to their victims, robbery usually is committed by a stranger to the victim.[17] Thus, robbery may be an offense that the public may justifiably fear as one committed by a "marauding stranger" and constitutes "true crime" in this respect. Unlike the victimless offenses previously discussed, robbery involves a definite personal victim, and, unlike other violent offenses discussed below, the offender is likely to be a criminal rather than a personal friend, acquaintance, or member of one's family whom one has somehow provoked.

There are many ways in which a person can be robbed, different situations of robbery, and varied types of robbers. A British study yielded five kinds of robberies based on data compiled in 1957:[18]

1. Robbery of persons in charge of money or goods in their course of employment (174 cases)
2. Robbery by attack in the open (162 cases)
3. Robbery on private premises (42 cases)
4. Robbery after previous association between victim and offender—mainly for sexual purposes (71 cases)
5. Robbery in cases of previous association of some duration between victim and offender (13 cases)

While types of offender or offender motivation cannot easily be discerned from the above classification of types of offenses, we can derive a classification of offenders from the study of characteristics of offenders and of modi operandi of the crime(s) they commit. Before discussing these data, we may say there are basically three types of robbers, quite like those types discussed in John Irwin's book *The Felon*:[19] 1) habitual thieves with relatively long criminal records, which Irwin calls "state-raised youth," 2) amateur thieves, termed "disorganized criminals" by Irwin, and 3) professional thieves, with considerable skill and specialization. These are listed in decreasing order of their actual prevalence, with professional thieves least prevalent. Robbery is not a crime generally favored by professional thieves since they prefer to avoid violence in their crimes.

The first category, state-raised youth, probably describes the largest group of robbers. Into this same category falls a classic case study, the "own story" of a jackroller, edited by Clifford Shaw.[20] Shaw's jackroller—a person who rolls or steals from drunks—was a person who had been in and out of reform schools until his later incarceration in adult prison. The perspective of the world developed in state schools, with their characteristic brutality and exploitation of inmate by inmate and strict regime of discipline and punishment by the staff, was that of a dog-eat-dog world into which one is thrown. The jackroller saw his world as a world of powerful and powerless people. He became locked into this perception of the world based upon his previous experience in the microworld of institutional confinement. He perceived life on the outside as a place where you temporarily sojourn and engage in wild, abandoned pleasures. The jackroller's "own story" is amazingly similar in these respects to Irwin's description of state-raised youth. The link between this alienated perspective of life on the outside and the actual offense of robbery is quite plain to see. Robbery is a wanton means of getting even with powerful people, of using brute force to achieve one's needs, and a direct route to hedonistic gratification. F.B.I. statistics indicate that the state-raised youth category is the largest category of robbers, the average criminal history of previous offenses for robbers being about ten years, with 91.4 percent having previous offenses.[21]

Irwin's second category, "disorganized criminals," a category that seems to overlap somewhat with state-raised youth, captures another aspect of the kind of person who commits robbery. Disorganized criminals "pursue a chaotic, purposeless life, filled with unskilled, careless, and variegated criminal activity."[22] They are highly available for criminal pursuits and are easily moved by their own impulse or others' encouragement to commit law infractions.[23] In world view, they, like the state-raised youth, see the world as dog-eat-dog and corrupt. Evidence of the prevalence of this type among bank robbers in particular is the high frequency of arrest rates for this offense. F.B.I. statistics for the three summer months of 1964 indicate that within a year of 238 cases of bank robbery, 210 of the 332 robbers involved had been apprehended.[24]

Professional thieves are highly skilled, specialized criminals for whom crime is a means of livelihood and a way of life. Professional thieves have occupied a diminishing representation among robbers. Even so, the major theory of robbery is based upon an "own story" account of a professional thief, and, in fact, this one account presaged much of the textbook view of professional crime utilized in current criminology texts.[25] Quite conceivably, this decline of the professional criminal in robbery is traced to changing technology and police effectiveness, making the "big score," the major preoccupation of professional thieves, more and more difficult to achieve through robbery.[26] Though professional thieves are losing interest in robbery, we should still include them in our discussion because they probably are responsible for big jobs involving large amounts of money and because this type may be a logical outcome of the other forms (state-raised youth or disorganized criminals). Irwin characterizes professional thieves by their good character, rightness, coolness in the face of difficulties, unobtrusiveness, and skill. Characteristically, their world view is that society is corrupt, but they, the thieves, are honest and trustworthy.

THEORETICAL EXPLANATIONS OF EMBEZZLEMENT AND ROBBERY

It is obvious from the above discussion that the nature of and differences between robbers have been far more refined by sociologists than is the case with embezzlers. This is probably reflective of the availability of official data and the differing methods by which the two groups are treated within the criminal justice system. In turn, some theories have developed that are general to property crimes, others are specific to embezzlement, but more appear to have been formulated to explain the specific property crime of robbery.

THEORIES DEALING WITH PROPERTY CRIMES IN GENERAL

Many explanations of criminal behavior are geared toward property crimes. These range from the individual, psychological level to the sociological or cultural level. Because so many of the theories detailed in Chapter 1 have property crime as their focus, directly or indirectly, we will not repeat them in their entirety herein. Rather, we will now focus our attention briefly on the most obvious applications toward the general area of property crimes before examining concepts, elaborations, and combinations of theories that apply specifically to embezzlement and robbery.

Psychological or Psychiatric Theories

Freudian explanations for theft of any sort involve regression to oral or anal stages of development. As mentioned in Chapter 1, embezzlement is due to regression to the late oral stage while armed robbery is due to regression to the late anal stage. Few other psychological explanations have attempted to focus specifically upon property crimes. Most "personality" theories have focused mainly upon sexual behavior, dependency behavior, or more violent offenses. A specific explanation of psychology of embezzlement has been offered by Lottier and will be described shortly. Cressey combined both psychological and social factors in his explanation of embezzlement, which will also be detailed.

Sociological Explanations

ALIENATION THEORIES Alienation theories, particularly those with strong Marxian influence, appear to have their greatest explanatory power in dealing with property crimes, as well as in explaining the differential treatment of white collar criminals as opposed to street criminals. Conflict sociologists have offered several propositions that stem from a critical philosophy that views private property as contrary to the nature of man and the basis of a class conflict between the ruling capitalists and the workers:

1. Crime is defined by the dominant class according to behaviors that conflict with their class interests.[27]
2. The enforcement of criminal laws and treatment of criminals are based upon the threat to the class interests of the dominant class and the social class of the offender.[28]
3. Poverty and economic oppression are "sources" or "causes" of crime.[29]
4. Failure to truly reduce crime oppresses the poor who are its victims.[30]

DIFFERENTIAL ASSOCIATION/ANOMIE-OPPORTUNITY THEORIES Differential association and anomie-opportunity theories utilized in conjunction with one another offer separate explanations that vary slightly for embezzlement and robbery. *Subcultural* explanations and the *labeling* perspective appear to have greater explanatory power when dealing with robbery than with embezzlement. The embezzlers' subcultural ties are typically with other businessmen who may reinforce certain rationalizations. However, the act of embezzlement itself is usually performed in isolation. On the other hand, robbers frequently have an entire network of contacts, which has already been described. Labeling might be best utilized in understanding the differing recidivism rates of robbers as opposed to embezzlers. Thus, it has its most direct application in explaining the "career" nature of the robber as opposed to the embezzler, once apprehended. Roberts asknowledges the rationalized self-concept of the professional thief but contrasts it with the self-concept of the white collar criminal:

> He believes he is only following sharp business practices or doing his job. Most of his work is legal, and he takes the attitude that the American way has always been *caveat emptor* (let the buyer beware).[31]

Thus, the white collar criminal does not see oneself as a criminal, while the professional thief acknowledges deviance even though justifying it through a cynical world view.

SOCIAL CONTROL THEORIES Social control theories offer little specific application to property crimes, although they would explain such acts as a form of deviance. Perhaps what has been said above regarding differing self-concepts would affect internal control mechanisms contributing to a higher rate of white collar crimes, since what one was doing would not be seen as "bad." Likewise, the relative lack of effectiveness of external, legal containment may be a contributing factor in the greater amounts of property and lives involved.

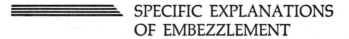 SPECIFIC EXPLANATIONS
OF EMBEZZLEMENT

A Psychological Explanation

Lottier studied a group of fifty embezzlers convicted by a Detroit court and who had undergone psychiatric examination. From this, he developed a model of embezzlement relying on the act as a means of "tension-reduction." The embezzler, according to Lottier, is an individual who has not found other ways to reduce or internalize tension. In addition to the normal biological drives, businesspersons have heightened anxiety and tension due to their competitive, aggressive behavior and position of trust. When this tension is increased in a particular situation (perhaps the threat of personal economic disaster or a domestic problem) and the individual does not have other means with which to discharge this tension, he or she seeks relief through embezzlement. The embezzlement is not merely a relief from financial burdens, but a reduction of other psychic and sexual tensions as well.[32]

Sociological Explanations

Before Cressey's classic work, *Other People's Money*,[33] two major sociological theories were advanced to explain embezzlement. Sutherland, in his book *White Collar Crime*,[34] explained embezzlement and other forms of white collar crime as due to differential association. Sutherland viewed participation in embezzlement as one of the illegal practices learned as one becomes indoctrinated into the subcultural ways of businessmen:

> As part of the process of learning practical business, a young man with idealism and thoughtfulness for others is inducted into white collar crime. In many cases he is ordered by the manager to do things which he regards as unethical or illegal, while in other cases he learns from those who have the same rank as his own how they make a success. He learns specific techniques of violating the law, together with definitions of situations in which those techniques may be used. Also, he develops a general ideology.[35]

The second major approach to embezzlement is a variation of *opportunity theory*, which states that there are opportunities inherent in trust positions that form temptations if incumbents develop antisocial attitudes that make normative violation possible and if the incumbents define a need for extra funds or extended use of property as an "emergency" that cannot be met by legal means.[36] It should be noted that this variation of opportunity departs from that theory's assumption that deviancy is induced by low status position or low income but substitutes "sudden reversal" in place of these variables.

CRESSEY'S METHODOLOGY AND EXPLANATION OF EMBEZZLEMENT Cressey's work, *Other People's Money*, stands as the major contribution in the study of embezzlement. It also, we may add, epitomizes the approach to deviancy that we propose and are using for other areas of deviancy. Cressey's study of embezzlement advances the study of that area of crime to a higher level in terms of understanding the point of view of the deviant actor and in terms of theory development.

Cressey's methodology has received criticism primarily on the grounds that it fails to enhance our abilities to make predictions about the phenomenon at hand (embezzlement); that is, it ignores genetic aspects of causation in favor of systematic ones. In systematic causation we locate a definable conjuncture of events operating at the time of an offense, while in genetic causation we refer to the prior life experiences that have propelled the individual into present circumstances. Although critics assert that through analytic induction we fail to get at prediction, they agree that the method enhances intuitive understanding.[37]

This methodological critique seems to rest upon the ex post facto nature of analytic induction. That is, Cressey examined an accidental sample (i.e., cases at hand) of some 133 embezzlers imprisoned at Joliet, Illinois; Chino, California; and Terre Haute, Indiana. Critics assert that we cannot generalize from this sample to all embezzlers. From our point of view, however, this criticism misses the point of Cressey's research. In questing for universals, Cressey was not trying to formulate scientific laws about a certain behavior, but was merely trying to examine prevailing theories in the light of existing known cases of the phenomenon at hand. If we can find cases of the phenomenon that do not jibe with one or another theory, then the theory is found to be invalid and must be rejected as applied to the phenomenon. This, too, is the whole point of our analysis in this text. So often we find that when we examine an individual case, we can reject a theory or group of theories about that phenomenon. We can then either reshape the theory or reject it altogether. In the final analysis, we are closer to reality regarding that phenomenon, have an intuitive feel for it, and in fact are in a better position to make meaningful predictions about it. It has been argued in reply to critics of analytic induction that perhaps situational factors or "systemic" one are in fact the major ones of concern to the phenomenon of embezzlement, and perhaps to other phenomena.[38] That is, there are no clear-cut personality dynamics or motivational syndromes involved in the phenomenon, and precipitating situational factors are in fact primary. The point has been made more salient in recent years by adherents of the labeling school of deviancy, and of phenomenology and ethnomethodology as has been discussed earlier in this book. Both stress the changing situational nature of "causes" or "exigencies."

Unlike most other forms of deviancy discussed in this text, with embezzlement we have a theory—Cressey's—that seems to fit perfectly the case we have at hand. Cressey has already done the groundwork. First, he rejected the differential association approach to embezzlement, because he found cases in which violators interviewed said they knew the behavior to be illegal and wrong and other cases in which the violators said they knew of no one in their business or profession who was carrying on practices similar to theirs.

"Opportunity theory," the second hypothesis, was rejected because individuals were encountered who had experienced grave financial difficulties earlier in their occupational careers, but had not taken to theft as a solution. Cressey's final generalization (which from our point of view still remains a theory until verified by examination of all cases of the phenomenon) emphasizes the situational factor of *psychological isolation* and posits three conditions considered essential in leading a person to violate a financial trust:

> 1) *When the person conceives of himself as having a financial problem that is nonshareable.... 2) When the person becomes aware that his nonshareable problem can be secretly resolved by violation of his financial trust.... 3) When the person is able to apply to his own conduct rationalizations that enable him to adjust his conception of himself as a trusted person to his conception of himself as a user of the entrusted funds or property.*[39]

This formulation, combining both the social situation and the psychological factor of isolation, fits the case of embezzlement that is presented in this chapter. Even in this case, though, other psychological and sociological factors may be apparent that merit further consideration.

SPECIFIC EXPLANATIONS OF ROBBERY

If a combination of psychological and sociological factors have been utilized by Cressey to explain embezzlement, it should not be surprising that a combination of sociological theories have been used to explain robbery. For a single framework, given the types of robbery stated, it is necessary to employ differential association, labeling, and anomie-opportunity approaches.

The main theory that has been used to explain robbery is differential association. In Sutherland's discussion of the professional thief, robbery is marginally discussed as "mob" activity.[40] Mobs operated under several binding rules including a "no rat rule," expenses shared in common (including court costs), honesty among members, and membership support including "putting in the fix" in case of the arrest of one member. Recent study, however, has revealed that armed robbers do not develop such well-organized mobs, but in fact their organization is more like a temporary partnership of people joined together for a specific purpose. Members are more or less expected to "rat" if they are caught, and partly for that reason, other members will not support the arrested party with either court costs or a "fix." Career armed robbers are "nonprofessional" also in their modus operandi. They do not always, or even usually, make extensive plans for their robberies, but more often resort to "selective raids" on small objectives such as liquor stores and occasionally engage in ambushes or guerrilla-like operations with utterly no prior planning. Also, unlike more organized criminals, they are found to invariably "blow their money" in the event that they pull off a "big job." [41]

Thus, differential association is not a complete theoretical framework. The category of state-raised youth seems to be suggestive of a labeling theory approach. Youthful delinquents who are (in their own perceptions or actually) unjustly stigmatized for minor acts of delinquency and subjected to degradation, stigmatization, and delinquent socialization within institutions progress to serious offenses. Through prison contacts, differential association with criminals takes place, but such contacts serve more as connections and less as apprenticeships for later crime. Perhaps men who become robbers had few work skills prior to imprisonment and gain relatively little by way of crime skills in prison.

Curiously, then, the anomie-opportunity approach also seems to hold in the case of robbery. An unusually large number of robbers, statistics show, are unemployed, unskilled men who quite possibly feel they have nothing to lose from robbery. Bank robbers calculatively "view the consequences of arrest and punishment to be no worse than the consequences of present conditions." [42] Also, we might add, they have accrued few "safer" skills in professional crime that could serve as an alternative to robbery. This "nothing to lose" philosophy might be a result of ex-con stigma were it not for the fact that about one in four bank robbers has no prior prison record for any offense whatsoever.[43] Thus, it may be that robbery is an outcome of oppressive life circumstances, either in or outside of prison, and it can take the form of utilitarian act that Merton describes as "innovation."

With explanations both of the differing and similar aspects of embezzlement and robbery in mind, as well as the broader explanations of property crime in general, the case histories of an embezzler and a robber are presented for analysis.

ALBERT:
An Embezzler

The following transcript was taken in class from a talk given by a former embezzler, Albert. At the time of the transcript, Albert was working as an accountant for a local firm. He is currently married (to the wife referred to in the transcript), age forty-eight, and earns about $10,000 per year. At the time he committed his crime, Albert was almost prototypical of embezzlers who are described as "usually about thirty-five years old, married, with one or two children, living in his own mortgaged home, and driving a medium-priced automobile." [44]

ALBERT: Both my parents are devout, fine, generous people. I attended the public schools in New York. I don't recall any traumatic experiences in my early childhood outside of the various neighborhood fights. The discipline in my family, which was rare, involved not receiving my weekly five cents allowance. My relationship with my brother (three years my senior) was never very close, mainly because of the friction of an older brother not wanting his younger brother to tag along. He was what I looked upon as a symbol of authority—he drove, worked, and overall did things before me. He was a great mixer and social person, whereas I shied away from crowds. I was a good student in junior high and high school. I never smoked, drank, or used drugs— I still don't. I never saw the inside of a police station until I was thirty-eight years old; that was ten years ago. This covers a brief background of my formative years.

I married at the age of thirty-four and at the time of my offense I had two girls, four and five. I should spend some time in talking about my wife. She is nine years my senior, which may have had an effect somewhere along the line. She wasn't a disciplinarian and let the girls turn the house inside-out. During a day's work at the office, I'd get four or five calls from her telling me that Ann did this or Sally did that. This was very embarrassing because I'd constantly be called from a board meeting to the phone. Our sexual life was very poor, so over the course of time I made modifications and when you're involved in this situation you have costly expenditures. (This was at the time I committed this offense and the things leading up to it.) I didn't want to mention this, but I feel this is a part of it.

In our corporation I was the assistant vice-president. The pressures of a corporate executive are very strong. There are many things you must do—it's not a nine-to-five job. As an executive for a multi-million-dollar corporation, I'd arrive at my office at 7 a.m. and stay until 9 or 10 p.m. On Friday when I'd leave for my so-called weekend my briefcase would be bulging. This is the price you pay for a $30,000 yearly salary. This may sound like a large sum of money to you—it is not. When you're making this type of income you must eat, dress, and socialize expensively. I loathed the patronizing of certain people, but the job made it necessary. I might be evaluated by you students of social science as being antisocial. I have very few friends because this is the way I want it. It will be this way until my last day on earth.

The event which caused my condition of crime—I was involved in a financial speculation. You can buy a certain stock on margin; you don't pay for the full price of the stock—you pay a part. As long as that stock retains its financial equilibrium or if it's going up, the stock-broker who you bought from will carry your account. But should that stock decline, you have to make up the margin immediately—if you don't, he will sell you out. Consequently, with my expenses of a mistress and various other things, I reached a point where I didn't give a damn. I suddenly realized one day at lunch, that my home life, which was practically nil, and the answer to my problems might be to appropriate a large sum of money so I could look at the world and say, "Go to hell." My objective was to go to a foreign country with my family. I would not leave them high and dry. It was that afternoon at lunch that I decided to carry out this "fantasy." I did not anticipate that my wife, though her mind was cluttered with problems and ill emotions, would not take part in this type of undertaking. My kids were, of course, too young to understand. It was then that I decided to take as much money as I could. I am not an expert or authority on embezzlement, although in the course of my imprisonment, I did rub shoulders with perhaps half a dozen embezzlers. These other men had spent many months planning. I completed my actions in ninety days—maybe my corporation was more conducive to such a theft.

Let me give you a brief explanation of the mechanics of embezzlement. The structure of a corporation may be condensed into AR and AP. AR stands for accounts receivable; this means the money which is due the company. This does not apply usually in embezzlement. AP, accounts payable, the money which we as a corporation owed, is the area I concentrated on. Basically, the way I completed my theft was that I created pseudo accounts payable. I created fictitious creditors of my company. In the course of seventy-five days I had taken approximately $193,000 out of the company.

QUESTION: *How did it get into your pocket?*

ALBERT: I created these companies out of state in a little town about 300 miles northeast of New York City. I opened up a fictitious bank account in that town using these small company names. My company wrote a check to these fictitious companies and every week I'd go to these banks and extract the money I had defrauded from my employer. Incidentally, don't try this; there are many more controls now. If you asked what circumstances compelled me to commit this crime, I would say a deteriorating home life, financial pressures, as well as the type of person I was at the time.

QUESTION: *You mentioned in the office that there were certain organizational aspects that allowed you to commit this crime.*

ALBERT: Yes, well, the comptroller of a corporation is the chief financial officer. He decides how much money will be spent, paid, invested, etc. Therefore, it wasn't too difficult for a person in this position to get away with embezzlement for a while. Incidentally, there's an interesting point: in this period of time when I had taken $200,000 it could have just as easily have been $2,000,000 if I had wanted it to. It would have been just as simple. Thinking back on another of the reasons I stole from my company was the fact that I was passed over for vice-president of the company in favor of a very incompetent man.

QUESTION: *Was there nepotism or corruption in the people that hired him?*

ALBERT: No, I think it was just a case of his employer being just as incompetent too. I can never tolerate anything less than a man who does his best. Unfortunately, the American business community is loaded with cases of nepotism, of men hiring their son-in-laws when they know nothing about business. The guy they hired was a fast-talking dude who talked his way into a job that paid $50,000 a year. He was basically just a stupid, idiotic actor.

An interesting aspect of my case is the area of my trial, sentencing, and prison. I have had three years of law school and can talk to you from the point of view of being a defendant in a criminal action. Judges and lawyers can talk to you *about* a criminal action but never from the point of view of a defendant. This makes all the difference in the world. The wheels of justice run so quickly at one end and so very slowly at the other end. It doesn't take much to throw sand in the wheels and slow them down. Sometimes they stop and go the other way. I've never been involved with the apparatus of law before. I was shocked at the entire judicial function; the fact that the processes of law which supposedly govern all our actions are so narrow that it's all one can do to get your defense within the narrow confines of the law. I'd like to make one point which I hope you will keep in your minds forever. The whole theory of criminal law is that your defense must be admissible within these very narrow confines. Verdicts in a criminal action must be unanimous—twelve people. The jury system, when you take twelve people who are supposedly your peers and you realize that they're not your peers, you begin to wonder. I recall four of the people who were on my jury and their occupations. One was a taxicab driver, another was a factory worker, a housewife, and the fourth a postoffice clerk. These people were of such mental caliber that you wouldn't let them fill out a tax return let alone let them sit on a jury during a trial which involved very complicated areas of high finance. It's true I stole, but how could these people have possibly given me a fair decision when they could hardly understand what was going on? The cab driver fell asleep twice during the trial. During the course of a criminal trial, the DA and the judge will never tell the jury that they have the right, as the jury, to refuse to apply the law in this case. An attorney in New York tried it and he got five days in contempt of court for abusing the court's patience. In other words, if your defense can fit into this very narrow channel, and is admissible and they can't raise a reasonable doubt, they must acquit. They also should have the right that in the event that a reasonable doubt is not raised, let's say the prosecutor has proven his case, if the jury feels that the applicable law shouldn't be applied, they have the right to withhold the application of the law. They want to keep the jury ignorant and keep the legal channels very narrow. The law exists for people, people don't exist for the law.

My attitude of the judicial process was laughable. I didn't contemplate suicide in my fourteen months at Sing Sing. During that time three people committed suicide. Men who had long periods of imprisonment, twenty, thirty, forty, to life. I looked upon this as an experience which was steeped with misery, humiliation, and all facets of dehumanization. Just the process of booking and arrest is something which strips a man or woman naked. It's an emotional and intellectual stripping which gets down to the very core of your guts. Out of the 3,500 men in there, were about five with which I could carry on a reasonably intelligent conversation.

QUESTION: *I'd like to cover these points. What is embezzlement, what are the different types or subcultures, that is, how do you classify what is serious? Do you consider it to be a serious offense?*

ALBERT: Embezzlement is definitely a very serious offense, a fraction of embezzlement is as minor as misdemeanor or traffic violation— no matter how you rationalize it. A good comment on the subculture is that in 99 percent of these cases the embezzler is a loner. They will do everything possible to remain as anonymous as is humanly plausible.

QUESTION: *Could you have possibly learned to become an embezzler from the people you work with?*

ALBERT: Well, of course indirectly, yes. The business firm per se and its chain of functioning from one process to another is conducive to this kind of thing. To someone who "sits at the top" and ties all the financial strings together. But to answer your question as to someone in the organization who prompted me or similar offenders into embezzlement—the answer is no. The one thing you need to remember is that an organization is a living, breathing—it's an entity. People who occupy substantial positions within an organization will remold and modify it and as an institution it is a shadow of one man. The identity of that one man can reshape an organization for better or worse—depending on personality involved.

QUESTION: *How does someone who sat at the top of a corporation relate with ordinary criminals in prison?*

ALBERT: To converse with murderers, child molesters, bank robbers, sex maniacs is something which you cannot believe. Keep this in mind: I do not look down on these people. I look down on their crimes. I think that basically people who commit these crimes are psychotics. There are psychiatrists that hold that embezzlers are also psychotics. I don't think I am but perhaps from that point of view and that time I was; I don't know.

QUESTION: *How did you get caught? When did you come to California?*

ALBERT: Basically, I think I was caught because I subconsciously wanted to get caught. As far as the laws of extradition, Brazil represents a haven as well as Israel. I had enough funds to leave. I told my wife of the possibility of leaving the country, although I never told her why. She had no knowledge of my crime until the police came around. She, of course, refused. An independent audit came in. This gentleman came in during a period of time in which I had taken off several days; I pleaded personal reasons. It was just a fluke that these auditors came in. So that you'll have an understanding of how a man can come in and put his finger on missing funds, let me explain something about accounting. Accounting is such that each step is based on another. When you find one figure that is wrong, you can be pretty sure that there is something else wrong down the line somewhere. It doesn't take much to find out.

I came to California in 1965 because I felt that it would be a wonderful place to start over. When I first came here I was comptroller of a corporation in Los Angeles paying $20,000 a year. I was there two years and finally became tired of the money game business. Money is just a means of keeping score, really. The L.A. area is filthy; the smog, crowds, and city-jungle bothered me. Consequently, I decided to come to San Diego. The attitudes of my old community were such that during the course of my trial we moved. My wife would go shopping in the market and they would look down their noses at her. They'd point her out. My kids' friends would tell them how they saw their daddy's picture in the paper. Children are very cruel.

I can just see the minds of the jury that decided my case. "There's a guy that makes good money; I'm gonna burn him." You can almost feel the vibrations. You can reach down and put your hands on their puny little minds and feel what they're thinking. Insofar as the problem in finding work, this was a tremendous problem; especially in my position, one in which I am trained to handle funds. My first job I was a clerk in a garage. I quit after three weeks and my parole officer told me I couldn't quit without his consent. I was going crazy doing work that a trained monkey could've done. I wanted something that was more intellectually challenging, so I took a second job as a credit manager. I had this job for a year and then became a bookkeeper. In finishing my parole I had reached the staggering amount of $175 a week. The problems of a parolee are tremendous. I had a few real friends, however. But most men out of prison really suffer. I think that you young men and women are the social scientists of the future; perhaps district attorneys, judges, sociologists, and other overseers of the future. If my appearance here can enhance your understanding and your degree of compassion and love one bit, it's been worth the effort to come and speak here today.

QUESTION: *How many years were you on parole?*

ALBERT: The maximum in New York for first offenders like me is two and one-half to five years. I served fourteen months in Sing Sing and three and a half years on parole. I paid back $50,000 of the money I stole—25 percent. The best way to get out of paying if you've been caught is to file bankruptcy, a debt that can never be paid.

QUESTION: *How much did they recover of what you stole?*

ALBERT: $50,000. The corporation was paid back by the bonding company. If they have evidence that a man has stolen $100,000 and they get back half, most bonding companies will pay for the rest. The reason I was sentenced to state prison was because I would not give them back one dime. The bonding and insurance companies notified the judge that I wouldn't cooperate, so he gave me the maximum allowed by law. During the course of my prison term my lawyer returned to them $50,000. The rest of the money has been spent. If I had given the money back there might have been no prosecution, but the DA was pushing this case so it's not likely that I would have been let off even if I had given back the money. The prosecutor doesn't care if the man returns the money; to him, a crime has been committed and a man must pay.

QUESTION: *Did you at any time feel that your conviction was unjustified?*

ALBERT: I think the defense attorneys had created a reasonable doubt in the minds of the jury. I'm not saying that I wasn't guilty of the offense. I was as guilty as hell. However, I'm talking now from a point of law. The laws say that if a reasonable doubt is raised in the minds of the jury, they *must* give a verdict of not guilty. In our opinion, we had created more than a reasonable doubt, because in the course of the investigation they found that the billing was correct, that these companies had in fact charged my corporation with these bills. You have twelve people on a jury who bring in their individual prejudices and stupidities and all kinds of temperament. There is many a man who has been sent to prison because they didn't like his hair color, nationality, etc. You cannot divorce these factors from the decisions a jury makes. I say this: if your case is strong on law, have it in front of the judge. Simply because the people on the jury don't have the intellect or expertise to render a fair decision. It's the only system we have, but through my first and last experience with juries I have concluded that they're twelve average, little people who don't have the intelligence to render fair decisions.

QUESTION: *How did they decide you were the culprit?*

ALBERT: See, there are two areas of embezzlement. A man has to have the means of acquiring this money. Authority also. The second factor is that embezzlement by its very nature involves dealing with written matter and writing is as traceable as fingerprints. That's how they got me.

═══════════ COMMENTARY

Cressey's theory of embezzlement seems to be epitomized by this transcript. At the time of his embezzlement, Albert was thirty-eight years old, married, had two children, and lived in his own mortgaged home. He perceived himself to have a financial problem—actually two such problems—the "upkeep" of his mistress and his stock market losses. These problems were nonshareable because of Albert's sense of psychological isolation—he is a self-proclaimed loner—and perhaps because of his "deteriorated home condition." He relates how his thinking developed over time and how he came to believe that his problem could be solved by violation of financial trust. Last, he enumerates (consciously or unconsciously) a variety of rationalizations for his behavior. His wife was a poor disciplinarian and poor sex partner. He felt he was overworked and underpaid at the corporation he worked for. A less qualified person was hired and promoted over him. Thus, in Albert's own view, a highly conscientious, scrupulous, competent person came to be an embezzler. Albert's competitive business nature, his state of anxiety over sexual and financial tensions, and his search for reduction of these tensions through embezzlement also fit Lottier's model.

However, it appears that the Cressey theory has greater explanatory power in its comprehensiveness of the situation.

Although Albert received a somewhat light sentence and probation in comparison to many other sanctions for property crimes, he appears to be alienated by the justice system. He appears to feel a sense of injustice even though he admits he might not have been prosecuted had he provided restitution. He is especially critical of the jury, who he claims were not his "peers," referring to factors that indicate their working class status. He, thus, does not appear to accept society's condemnation yet admits his guilt. Albert, even now, does not think of himself as a criminal. He relates (not on transcript) that he never did and that he is disdainful of the offenders in Sing Sing with whom he was forced to live.

During the course of the interview, Albert denies that anyone prompted him or induced him into embezzlement, and states his embezzlement arises from his own unique special knowledge of the system and position of trust. At the same time he states a "loner theory," that embezzlers must of necessity be "loners," a theory that Cressey did not explicitly state as one tested in his book *Other People's Money*, and a theory that may warrant further test. The traits Albert refers to are personality traits (perfectionism, high personal organization, introversion, alienation, etc.). However, there is no reason to suppose that the method of analytic induction precludes examination of *predisposing factors* as part of a universal generalization. In doing so, this method might yield generalizations more acceptable as genuine explanations as differentiated from mere definitions.

STEVE:
An Armed Robber

Our respondent in the following transcript is an ex-convict "doing good," in Irwin's terminology. He is a rehabilitated criminal who is active in a number of ex-con organizations locally. Even so, his current views reveal a number of aspects of life situation and belief that are quite typical of robbers as we have described them. Steve is somewhat exceptional in being white and from an affluent family background. We will see in his interview the dynamics of the development of a criminal career of a state-raised youth.

STEVE: I've been a career criminal since I was eight years old. I don't know whether I'm like the people that have talked to you already; I just want to tell you what I know about criminal justice. I've experienced the total criminal justice system; been through everything past and present that they have to offer. I started, as I said, at eight years old. My criminal career was, I think, an accident. I came from a good home and went to a Catholic school and had pretty nice experiences as a child. At some point in time, however, things happened. I trace my beginning in this to riding my bicycle on the sidewalk and in so doing this I ran into an elderly old lady and knocked her down. At this point it became hit-and-run bicycle. This got me to the attention of the police. I think at the time I was somewhat scared. It wasn't too bad an experience because they didn't do too much. They told me I couldn't ride my bike for thirty days. I lost the shock of this thing after a few days and soon was back on the street riding with another fellow on a Sunday morning and it was raining, so we went into an old garage and started a small fire, which soon spread and burned the building down. Now I'm an arsonist. This time they sent me to juvenile hall and locked me up. The first thing they do in any jail, and a thing that I can't help but equate with the criminal justice system, is that they take all your clothes off. A great deal of my life I've spent running around naked. The Home wasn't a bad place but it was a scary place for an eight-year-old boy. I met kids there that were much more sophisticated than I. I didn't like it so I ran home. Out of this I learned how to steal cars. We used to steal the night watchman's car at the old brewery. We did it every night and finally got caught. My timing is terrible, because I seem to get arrested at a point in time when the authorities want to try new things. So at ten years old they sent me to reform school.

QUESTION: *After the arson experience did you try to explain to them that it was an accident?*

STEVE: Yeah, in fact, the other fella with me ran and got away. I stayed there and tried to put out the fire. I thought that by staying there and trying to put out the fire I was doing right. For some reason, the authorities let the starting of that fire become the sum total of my life. As a have gone through life, people have attempted to sum me up because I rob banks. But, at the same time I robbed banks, I worked with blind children, see, so I'm not just all one thing or another. But, the way we work things, the authorities' involvement was that I set the fire, not with why or my actions afterwards. This is my main criticism.

QUESTION: *Did your previous record prejudice their decision?*

STEVE: No, I don't think so, just the seriousness of the whole thing—I could have burnt the whole neighborhood down. And our solution to these kinds of things is that we take people who do these things and put them in places where they can't do them. Putting me in juvenile hall at that time meant that I would not start a fire. I guess it was presupposed that I would run out and start another one that afternoon. I call this thing a game. I guess I started it by running the old lady down with the bicycle. They reacted to what I had done, I in turn reacted, and it keeps on going. It starts off unconscious, but ends up conscious and deliberate.

QUESTION: *After you escaped from juvenile hall, what were the mechanics, what caused you to steal cars?*

STEVE: On one occasion, I ran away with a fellow who was older than I, and stealing a car came very natural to him. It didn't really seem like a very big thing. He knew how to start it and drive it and at that age it was exciting to have such a big, powerful object under your control.

QUESTION: *Then it was for a joyride; you didn't steal it for resale or anything?*

STEVE: Right.

QUESTION: *Did you come from a poor family, middle class family, or what?*

STEVE: I come from a wealthy family. My parents were show business people. Looking back, maybe I knew more and experienced more than most kids my age, but I didn't understand it any better.

QUESTION: *Do you think your parents' background as show people affected the authorities' reaction to you?*

STEVE: No. I think that they were simply reacting to the incident itself. I was old enough to know the difference between right and wrong, and lighting that fire was a stupid thing; but kids do stupid things.

QUESTION: *Did you bad-mouth them at all?*

STEVE: As I recall, I didn't. I acted somewhat scared, but that's normal. You know that policemen are overpowering in situations like that, besides, that's a long way to go back to try and remember exactly what you did and why. I could do that for the jobs I pulled as an adult, though. Anyway, after all that, I ended up in state reform school, which is our junior reform school. When I arrived, it was at its low. They beat the kids, locked them in stand-up lockers, literally tortured them to death. They had just finished beating one kid to death when I got there, and were hanging him in his room trying to feign suicide. There was an investigation and all kinds of things happened. Father Flannigan of Boy's Town fame was brought out here to try and bring some semblance of order to the place. His philosophy was that there was no such thing as a bad boy. I ran off from him thirteen times. Each time we would pray together and I would swear to him and God that I would go and not sin again, and then in just a short time I'd run. I think he modified his statement after me. I am the only one in the history of State to ever be taken home in handcuffs. They turned me loose to my parents, saying that I was just too much for the reform school. During my thirteen escapes I'd steal cars, and when I was released, I went on stealing them. I just fell in love with stealing cars; some I would try and take back to where I'd stolen them. At one point in time they told me that I had run some 120 car thefts that they knew about; there were some that they didn't know about.

QUESTION: *It is extremely rare that they would release anyone from reform school. What else did you do besides escape? Beat up other kids?*

STEVE: Yeah, I did some of that. I set up an escape from Lost Privilege Cottage. Lost Privilege Cottage was a huge dormitory in which everyone stayed in bed twenty-four hours a day. We weren't allowed to talk, so we learned the deaf and dumb language and planned out our whole escape talking with our hands. And I was elected to attack the guard. There was a big fan because there was no air-conditioning. If you wanted to go to the bathroom, you had to raise your hand and he might or might not acknowledge you, depending on his mood. If he did okay it, you would go up to the desk and he would issue you so much toilet paper. Some were more generous than the others, so I learned when it was best to go and when not. Anyway, my part in the plan was to jump this big guy from behind and then the other thirty or forty little kids would pile on him. But somehow, at the last minute, I decided to change the plan slightly to be me hitting that redneck and stunning him. So I picked up the fan—you know how fans swivel—and when I went to hit him with it, it spun around and mangled up his hair and scalp. Didn't really hurt him bad, but looked awful. So this was one of my offenses at school and there were numerous other things. The reason they turned me loose was that my age precluded them from sending me on; there was nothing to send me on to, and I was just too disruptive to the reform school's system. I found out in later life that I have an ability to stir up trouble. I've done it all my life and I'm still doing it, except in a more socially acceptable manner. I'm just a troublemaker. And I like it and do it well. They were afraid to try and drive me home without some kind of restraint because they were afraid that I might try and run away on the way home, it had reached this point. But, because of further activity, mostly car theft, I was again apprehended. This was at a time when California was recognizing that they had a juvenile delinquency problem.

QUESTION: *Why did you go back to stealing cars? Did you have any peer group influence?*

STEVE: It was fun! Yeah, I ran with a gang, and we'd steal cars and joyride.

QUESTION: *Were most of these kids from institutions?*

STEVE: Some of them I'd met in; some I'd met out. Some were on their way in; they'd just been a little bit slicker than me and hadn't got caught.

QUESTION: *Were they high school age? Let's see, though, you were what age?*

STEVE: I was ten or eleven.

QUESTION: *So it was grade school!*

STEVE: They still do these things in grade school too. Then, about 1940, there was a movement to do something about the juvenile problem. As I understand it, there were many alternatives, but someone hit on the idea that the best thing to do with kids who exhibited the same kinds of behavior I did, had some sort of genetic failing, and that it would be impossible to cure this, and so, probably the thing to do was to pass a law called 7050 of the Penal Code, in which it would give the state the right to sterilize these kinds of people and thereby breed them out of existence. They went all over the landscape collecting juveniles and shipping them off to insane asylums across the country. I was sent to [names school]. I'm reluctant sometimes to go into detail about the treatment there because of so many girls present, but this place was not to be believed. The things they did to people were crazy. They beat people, they killed people, they performed weird operations on people, they forced people to have abnormal sex, perverted sex, they put liniment in your rectum; and this was just standard treatment. I was terrified, and I managed to escape from there—and this is what you're going to find out, is that I'm probably one of the best escape artists. Everyone thinks I'm so slick and keen, actually I'm just scared to death and find a way out.

QUESTION: *How do you escape?*

STEVE: Well, my attitude is this, that if you watch long and hard enough and that's all you think about, somebody's going to make a mistake. And when it happens, you take advantage of it. One of the control features at the school was that they kept everybody naked. We're back to that again! I think there's some kind of psychological hold on people if they're running around naked and the authorities have clothes on. They seem to mean more to you. So when I ran from there, I had to run naked. I ran three days and three nights through those mountains naked and with a shaved head—that's another thing they do. I must have been a sight to see! During this time in the mountains, I broke into this cabin for food and clothes, and I found a rifle. Until that time, I had never come in contact with a rifle, but I knew by instinct that this was power. Then I got the idea that this gun would make all the difference. And I made a plan, and went back to the school. I went back to the ward that they had had me on; I stuck up the guards; I turned everybody loose—if you can imagine 350 naked bodies running all over the countryside—I did things to those guards that they had done to me and some things that you wouldn't believe; and every time I think about it I feel good. I really did bad things to them and it really caused quite an uproar—I pushed the war news right off the front page. I really created a stink, but it did do one thing; it brought an investigation to the school, one of the superintendents of twenty years was fired, several of the guards were imprisoned. It was just a snake pit and they cleaned it out. Now, many years later, I think back that I did do something good even in my madness. About five years ago, though, I was reading an article by some Danish psychologist who visited the place, and would you believe, the same things are happening again? I've come to the conclusion that the system purifies itself and then goes right back to its corrupted state.

QUESTION: *How old were you when you staged this uprising?*

STEVE: Oh, twelve or thirteen. I'd been at the game a long time. After this thing they took me back and damned-near killed me. My family got a court order finally; they moved me back home by ambulance. They didn't think that I was going to live, that's the condition I was in. They had beat on me for days, in shifts. Why I lived I don't know, but I think one of the things was that I just hated them. I found that hate's a powerful weapon. One thing that I'll tell you about later is that I spent some four years in solitary confinement in Folsom Prison and the name of the game is to drive you insane, and the only reason that I survived it was because I hated them so bad that I wouldn't let them do that to me. It's a powerful weapon if you can control it; my problem was that I couldn't control it very well. So, I was brought back here and spent several months in the hospital under guard while I was recuperating. After a while I got well, in terms of my body. By that time my mind was pretty sick. I appeared in front of the local judges, and they said, "While there certainly are some extenuating circumstances, and I think you were even justified in some of the things you did, we just can't turn you loose on society." So they decided that they were going to do me a favor. They were going to send me to a school of industry. Now, this is the senior reform school. I arrived there and it was definitely different, it was really a clever place. They had developed a system there where the guards didn't beat you, they had other cadet officers who worked their fellow prisoners over. And it worked because there was a quasi-military type of thing where if you wanted to be captain of a company, the way to become captain was to beat the present captain up. And for being captain you got more credits, and if you got more credits that meant you went home quicker. It was that kind of a game. When you arrive there, they take you, the four cadet officer prisoners take you into the shower and strip you naked—you're back to that again—and give you a good thrashing. Sort of an indoctrination to let you know where you're at. The thing that they missed about me was that they were amateurs at this beating game and that they hadn't really even hurt me. So I went through all their Mickey Mouse routine, and finally I got my chance to go out on what they call recreation hour. And one of the games we used to play was one guy took a bat and hit the ball out and you tried to catch it. Well, I worked like hell so that I could catch a ball; so that I would have my turn at bat. And when I got my hands on that bat, I went after those four guys who had done this to me and really hurt them. I never had any more trouble at the school. I got to be captain; I got to do anything I wanted. I found out that if you're a bigger animal in the jungle than the other animals, then you do well. I used this philosophy throughout my criminal career. I went through two sessions there. I got through one and they let me out, but by then I was really committed to this thing. I had learned to burglarize and all sorts of things.

QUESTION: *Did you learn that at this institution?*

STEVE: Oh, sure. That's where I learned it all. It was like going to school.

QUESTION: *Did the other kids teach you techniques?*

STEVE: Well, we'd just sit around and talk about 'em. It's kinda all you talk about. And you lie a lot, because you run out of the truth. Out of most of the twenty-four hours you're talking and these are the things you talk about. Now I am in my teens and it suddenly occurs to me that I've got the label of having been in an insane asylum; they'd performed weird operations on me; I really thought that my manhood was in question, a reform school ex-inmate, I'm a thief, I'm an arsonist. Christ, I'm all sorts of things, and I haven't made a nickel. So I decided that, well if this is what I am and this is what I'm going to be, then I had better try and be a little more professional about it. I hooked up with a guy much older than I and started committing armed robberies. And I was quite successful, and I guess I was a pro cuz I didn't just run into gas stations. I planned them; I executed them with what I like to call professionalism. Fortunately, I had been taught by a much older guy who had been a robber all his life, and his philosophy was that a good robbery was one in which you don't hurt anybody. I had trouble learning this because I had a lot of hate and hostility in me. He pointed out to me that to take it out on some broad that's a teller at a bank is really kinda dumb. You don't even know her. I think in some ways, I learned more about being a human being from a bank robber than I ever did from my parents, the institutions, and a lot of other things.

QUESTION: *How did you come to meet this fellow?*

STEVE: Well, when you travel in this kind of circle, you're bound to run into them. And a lot of the old thieves were really curious to meet me, because it looked like I was going to be one of the up-and-coming thieves. I had a pretty good track record at that point, and that's what you look for. Like, you publish things to get it behind your name, in my profession your credentials count. Even getting caught can help, depending on how you got caught and how you conducted yourself.

QUESTION: *You didn't submit a manuscript for consideration, did you?*

STEVE: No, you submit yourself and your reputation.

QUESTION: *How do you go about submitting yourself?*

STEVE: People hear about you and you circulate among the crowd. And when I decided that this was going to be my life, I had everything that I wanted—lots of money, pretty long-legged girls, fancy cars, the works. I'm one of the few people who can say honestly that I've been able to do anything I wanted. The problem is that the retirement system in this life is terrible. I finally got caught, and the sentence for armed robbery is state prison.

QUESTION: *Did you rob banks?*

STEVE: Yeah, I robbed banks, supermarkets, department stores, [names local department store]—I got $6,000; loved that old man!

QUESTION: *Could you tell us how you go about robbing a bank? What are the techniques?*

STEVE: Banks I robbed twice; the third time I couldn't beat the security. My idea of robbing a bank is not what you read in the paper, where you run up to the teller and give her a note asking for all her money because she'll give you $1,500. Some place in that bank might be $15 million. My attitude was that you rob the whole bank. This doesn't mean the branch downtown, because that's too huge. You find rural banks. The one I said that I didn't rob was in Salinas, and I had taken a job as a women's shoe salesman. The store just happened to be right across the street from the bank, so I could watch it all the time, and the store also did business with that bank. That job was the most horrifying experience I've ever had! I spent months looking at this bank and I couldn't beat their security. I could have robbed the bank probably, but not in the way that I wanted to. I'm greedy and if I can't have it all, I don't want any. It's hard to describe techniques. You look for flaws, for ways to get away, you cover every contingency that one can think about. There's always the X factor that you can't control and that's what usually gets you caught. That's what got me caught. Like, for instance, you get all the money into your car and then the thing won't start. But you try the best you can. I always figured that getting caught was one of the occupational hazards. And I was prepared to pay that price. I finally reached a point where I think I had received more time than anyone in this country has ever been given, except for the gas chamber. They were really sick of me, and they had caught me with my pants down, and they got me. And I wiggled and twisted and turned and spent all kinds of money on attorneys. And when it was all settled and done, they really had a case. I went up with robbery and habitual criminal act—I had more life sentences than this whole room could probably do—and they sent me to Folsom State Prison. I then did what probably all long-term prisoners do, I studied law and started fighting my own case when I ran out of money. When you get busted like this, everything gets expensive. They know that they've got you over a barrel, and they really ripped me off good. I was up there about a year, I had lost my appeal in court, I had no more resources, I wasn't in a position to finance myself, and my only alternative was to do it on my own. So I studied law, I wrote writs, I went that route, and strangely enough, I wound up getting a hearing at the Supreme Court; in which I lost. I lost primarily on mechanics, my argument was more philosophical than it was legal. It dawned on me then that I was either going to have to do all these life sentences, which meant fifteen or twenty years before I even thought about getting out. I could have killed myself—I thought about that, but I'm chicken!—or I could escape. And the more I looked at it, the more the escape route seemed interesting enough to try. Nobody had ever escaped from Folsom as a maximum security prison before, so that made it quite a challenge. And as I looked this thing over, I looked for flaws much the same way that I did when I robbed, I found that there was a river that ran past Folsom. It had six machine guns and all kinds of things, but the legend is that no one has ever successfully swam the American River and they really believed that no one could because no one had. Well, one of the things that I had done during my youth one of those inbetween times—and this is what I mean when I say I'm not a sum total of crime—was become a long-distance swimmer. I almost broke the record from Catalina to the mainland. So I thought that if I could get into that river, if anyone in the world could swim it, I could. I was willing to put my life on it that I could. I plotted and schemed, and I finally found a flaw in their security and one day I got in their river. And I swam away and got away. We had the biggest manhunt in California history; there was some 650 policemen had me surrounded with helicopters, hound dogs, everything. I just couldn't believe that I was that important to anybody. During this time, there was one thing that happened that I like to tell because somebody always asks how and when did I get my thing together to make me all right now, assuming that I am all right now. I think everyone has things happen to them during their life, but I've been lucky and always get mileage out of mine. During this escape, we wound up in these Japanese people's home, we were out in this field, I had been bit by a rattlesnake, we hadn't eaten in days, we were out of water, we were really in bad shape.

QUESTION: *You keep saying "we"?*

STEVE: Oh, yeah. My partner went with me.

QUESTION: *He swam too?*

STEVE: Well, I kinda had to help him a little bit, but we made it. We swam, we went down through this tunnel, and—you couldn't believe this river, it looked like Niagara Falls—over rocks, hundreds of rolls of barbed wire in the bottom, six machine guns. We got through all that, got into some placid, beautiful water, almost dead, and crawled out on the bank, and I crawled right onto a sleeping rattlesnake and he bit me. Really, my timing is terrible! Anyway, we watched these people's farmhouse until they left, and then we went in. We'd waited for them to leave because we didn't want any contact with anyone from the community. It poses too many problems when you're an escaped convict, especially when you had as much heat on you as we did. We went in the house to get food, clothing, and whatever else might help us, and we fell into a situation that is an escaped convict's dream. There were two new cars, the keys were in them, there was a safe with money, there was a whole rack with guns, there was clothes, food, medicine. It was perfect. I took a bath, doctored my snakebit arm, shaved; I did all those things. I even used their toothbrush! We were ready to leave and this man and woman came home.

Now, one of the things I got to tell you is that people create images of themselves just like people create images of convicts and other people. And at this time I had me convinced that I could do whatever I had to do and that was up to and including kill someone if I had to. I was out to get away from something that was really big. So when these people came home, it turned into this kind of situation. It became very obvious that to complete this escape, we were going to have to kill these people, and I was prepared to do it. So the man walked in the house and I let him get in and then I stepped out, put this gun on him—his wife was still outside—and told him, "All right, old man, just shut your mouth and sit down." He was a little, wrinkled-up old man about this big, maybe 5 feet. And he walked up and pushed that shotgun aside and slapped me and asked me don't I have any manners, this is his house. This guy was unbelievable, and his wife was just like him. He was about as impressed with us as . . . I can't really put it into words. I can't tell you what this guy made me feel like, but it became quite clear that I wasn't going to kill him. We tried to find some alternatives. We thought of taking him with us; he wouldn't go. We found a cellar and thought we'd just lock them down there; he wouldn't go in the cellar, he had rheumatism, and it was too cold. We thought maybe the closet was the thing; it was too hot, he had breathing problems. We tied him up and it was too tight. We tied him up and it was too loose. He finally decided that the thing to do was to tie him up in his TV chair. Have you ever tried tying someone up in one of those chairs? It's really kind of a frightening experience. I finally reached a point where this man had beat me at my own game. I told him, "Old man, I've had a lot of bad things happen to me, but you're the worst." And with that, we just left him. And it was his phone call that started the manhunt again and ultimately got us arrested.

One other point of this story that really isn't too significant, but maybe I should tell. We wound up in this pond of water in the middle of a ranch some place, and it was hot, in the middle of July, and we needed water. The authorities, the posse—just like you see on Matt Dillon—of cowboys knew where all the water was in the area and they'd been checking each water hole around. And they came to this one place, and we saw them coming, so we just did like Daniel Boone. We took a deep breath and went under water, and I'll be damned if they didn't walk on by. We weren't breathing through no straws or nothing, we weren't that sophisticated, but it worked pretty well, And we heard them say that this place was clear and they were moving on to some place else. And we thought, WOW, we beat them. And it was getting dark, and we felt pretty good about the whole thing. I don't know if you've ever been in the country at night, I'm a city boy myself, but cows come down to drink. And there's always one cow that's the boss cow, the one with the horns. And this cow wouldn't drink, he'd just stare across the water at us. And one of them old farmers—they even know the cows' names up there, you know, like Old Blue—said, "I think Old Blue's seen something up there." He got his hog leg out and came over, and we took our deep breath and laid down in the water. But you can only hold your breath for so long, and when I stuck my horn up for air, he damned-near shot it off!

I guess the moral of the story is that we'd beat Folsom, airplanes, helicopters, all kinds of tracking equipment, and 650 men, but that cow was just too much! Again, it's timing! Anyway, I was apprehended for this, received four more life sentences, and went back to Folsom. I went into solitary confinement and I spent four years and nine months there. I took an awful lot of verbal abuse from my peers then. They had followed the story on TV, on radio, it was a like a serial and they were rootin' for us. And the verbal abuse mainly was that if I had killed them old folks, I'd have gotten away. What the hell's wrong with you? And I remember trying to explain, because you could talk through the ventilating system if you don't get caught, trying to explain why I didn't kill them and finally it just became a useless conversation. And one of the things that bothered me was that I had subscribed to something that maybe I wasn't equipped to play. I'd always wanted the acceptance of these people, I'd always earned it, and if I had to kill that old man and woman for these guys to like me, I had to question what I was, what I had become, and where I was going. If there's a turning point in somebody's life, I would say that that was the beginning of mine. I decided to try and get my things together. I started reading, going to school, doing many things that I'd neglected.

After ten years, they decided to move me down to medical facilities to see the psychiatrist—see, they keep you in so long that they start worrying that maybe they've driven you crazy! So they wanted to check my sanity before they thought about letting me out. I became a clerk in the social welfare department working with statistical matters, and I worked for a woman. Now, I hadn't seen a woman in a long, long time, especially an attractive woman! She terrified me, she scared me to death. I was always afraid that I was going to say something wrong or look at her wrong. And after some time I began to get the idea that this woman had some feelings about me, and that was crazy because you just don't fall in love with prisoners, and vice versa. There's a madness about prisons that any female that works there is somehow "their" female and if they even catch you looking too long they really get crazy and want to beat your brains out. What was worse, as the months went on, I began to get some feelings about her. I tried to examine them in my mind because she was the first woman, she was beautiful, and she was friendly and nice. And the next thing I know, we both wound up with the idea that we'd fallen in love in this insane asylum. There was no real hope that I was going to get out. She had an abundance of faith like most women in love do, more than I did. The first time I kissed her, we thought we heard someone coming and she jumped back, knocking a calculator off the desk and smashed it to pieces. That first kiss cost the state of California $1,600! We carried this romance on for some two years without getting caught, which has to be some kind of record, and I finagled my way with her help and lots of other people's help to get out. We got married the same day, and we're living happily ever after. Since I've been out I've done all sorts of things. I've been research assistant for the associate dean here at State. I was in charge of the narcotics program for the county honor camps for a year, a consultant for vocational rehabilitation for young offenders. I do a lot of these kinds of things. I'm writing a book. There have been some people trying to get me to make a movie about myself, but on their terms, meaning that they get all the money and maybe I get to go to the premiere or something. So we have to work on this before it's finalized. Lot of crooks out here too! I'm staff associate at a behavioral science institute. Recently I'm involved with a thing called Ex-offenders Resource Inc., in which we are now trying to sell to the public that people with my kinds of experience are a resource and could be a creative resource in the system of criminal justice. And, that we would like to be looked on not as ex-convicts, but that maybe we do have a contribution. We're receiving some warm kind of acceptance with this idea. I also think that we need a social action kind of thing, that we've got to make people aware. I, for one, am not going to be satisfied with second class status any longer. I paid my debt to society already, and I'm not going to ride in the back of the bus any more. One of the things that I decided I would attack was the voting. They tell me that I may never vote. You should see the taxes I pay. I've got three children in school and I think I'm a productive member of the community. I try to be, anyway. And they tell me that I can't vote. Personally, I don't want to vote for any of these bums, anyway, but I don't want them saying that I cannot vote.

QUESTION: *Could you kinda tell us some of the things that you did to the guards at the asylum?*

STEVE: Well, I took all their clothes off first! And I had mine on! That was kind of fun! And one of the things they used to use as punishment was soap towels. You take a couple of the large bath towels and soak them in hot water and put this brown soap on them and put them over your face and make you breathe and that stuff would just burn your lungs out. I just put the gun up to their head and made them make soap towels and put them on each other. I made them urinate on each other. I made them put liniment in places . . . I'm sure you know where I'm talking about. I did all those things. And the biggest thing of all was that this guy who was the biggest beast of all them, I just shot him right in the stomach. He didn't die, damn it. You can't kill them, they're like snakes. You've got to cut 'em up into littler pieces. I beat on them, I made them run through an ice cold shower—they had one shower that was hooked up to the drinking fountain system. Then I ran 'em out in the parking lot naked. Looking back on the whole thing, it was kinda fun! I enjoyed it.

QUESTION: *How did the guards react to it?*

STEVE: Now, these guys were tough guys who had done these things to me and others. They sniveled, crawled, one of them was trying to show me pictures of his children, they licked your feet, they weren't even men. We took our beating and our punishment with a lot more dignity and manliness than they did. I learned that the people who do that kind of thing are really bullies, and I can spot a bully a mile off. I hate bullies. What kinda sickens me in looking back is that these kind of people are really cowards down deep but that they've got a good front, and I became just like them because at the time I really delighted in hurting them. I don't like that part of myself and I have to keep a close check on that part of me.

━━━━━━━━━━ COMMENTARY

We see in Steve's self-analysis definite examples of labeling theory and differential association theory. Anomie-opportunity theory, however, seems to have little or no bearing in the sense that Steve came from a wealthy family background and most of his attitudes and deviant behavior patterns seem to emanate from prison or other institutional experiences. However, in another sense, opportunity theory does have relevance here. Steve was from the age of eight a state-raised youth, and the state, as *parens patriae*, did not provide him with the necessary work or intellectual skills to pursue a legitimate career. The illegitimate means he had learned in prison were therefore the only ones realistically open to him when he left institutional custody.

Steve's criminal career started as a result of an accidental fire that he started and the subsequent labeling of the act as arson. At the age of eight, he was processed as a juvenile delinquent and underwent a "status degradation process" of stripping. Steve underwent beatings, sexual abuse, and other forms of punishment at various institutions he visited. He fought back vigorously and escaped frequently.

At each juncture along the way, Steve met up with a "significant other" who taught him techniques of crime. In juvenile hall he met a boy more sophisticated than he who taught him how to steal automobiles. At the state industrial school he learned his "definition favorable to the violation of law"—"if you're a bigger animal in the jungle than the other animals, then you do well." After this he made another contact: "I hooked up with a guy older than I and started committing armed robberies." By this time, Steve had progressed from Irwin's category "state-raised youth" to "professional thief." Most of his robberies were planned, professional robberies. His accomplice taught him the characteristic attitude of nonviolent coolness: "his philosophy was that a good robbery was one in which you don't hurt anybody.... He pointed out to me that to take it out on some broad that's a teller in a bank is really kinda dumb. You don't even know her."

Steve's current work, though representing a "doing good" orientation of some ex-cons, is not entirely inconsistent with many of his previous attitudes. Even during his earliest act of "arson," he expressed such attitudes as "rightness" and "good character." "I thought by staying there and trying to put out the fire I was doing right.... At the same time that I robbed banks, I worked with blind children." Even Steve's inclination to "make trouble" seems to fit somehow into his current work. "I found out in later life that I have an ability to stir up trouble. I've done it all my life and I'm still doing it, except in a more socially acceptable manner."

THEORETICAL IMPLICATIONS

In analyzing both Albert's and Steve's cases, perhaps the strongest implication for science rests in the need for greater specificity in the types of crime and, hence, greater specificity in theoretical models. In both histories, the combination of either psychological and sociological factors or portions of several sociological perspectives results in an almost complete explanation. A variety of such amalgamations each directed to specific types of deviance might prove of great importance. Such amalgamations might best undergo reconceptualization and be placed within a larger, more abstract theoretical scheme than now exists. This might be kept in mind as the existing broad theories are reviewed in light of the case histories presented.

Psychological and Psychiatric Theories

There is little evidence to support the Freudian interpretation of anal or oral regression in either of the interviews. Nevertheless, the method of analysis is inadequate for a proper test of such concepts. Steve, the armed robber, was specific in his denial of mental illness even though he was once institutionalized in a "school" that apparently was meant to treat antisocial behavior. What family background and early discipline information is given does not suggest a psychiatric approach. The applicability of psychological factors from the Lottier and Cressey frameworks in Albert's case suggests that a refinement of the psychoanalytic approach incorporating sociological factors may prove to be theoretically important.

Sociological Theories

ALIENATION OR CONFLICT THEORY   There is reason to accept some portions of Marxian analysis in studying the cases of property crimes. While both Steve and Albert were pursuing, legally and illegally, the materialistic goals of capitalistic society, they were alienated from the system. Albert states that while he was earning a "$30,000 yearly salary" and living a lifestyle accordingly, he "loathed the patronizing of certain people, but the job made it necessary."

Steve claims that he learned not to hate and be hostile from "being a bank robber" and that he learned personal values from an older bank robber rather than from his family or institutions. In viewing society, he states that there are a "lot of crooks out here too!" and that he does not want to vote "for any of these bums, anyway!" Clearly, alienation is present in both individuals, but caution must be exercised somewhat due to the perspectives that may have been gained as a result of their treatment in the criminal justice system rather than as a cause of the behavior that brought them to that system.

Both offenders are from white and at least middle class backgrounds. As mentioned, Steve is atypical of robbers in these regards. With that in mind, and taking into account the fact that Albert still appears to come from a much higher socioeconomic background than

Steve, other propositions from alienation theory appear to have some validity. For embezzling $193,000, Albert received fourteen months in prison and three and a half years on parole (both lower than the national averages according to the data presented earlier). His crime was such that he might not have been prosecuted had he returned the stolen funds. He regards this sentence as excessive, he does not consider himself a criminal, and he especially resents the jury whose class background is of a lower status than his own.

Steve does not state specific amounts of time served for specific amounts robbed. However, as a career thief he had many life sentences in addition to other time. What must be pointed out is that his career began, as he states, when he was unjustly accused of arson at the age of eight. The ultimate victims of the property losses brought about by both men in our complex economic and insurance-laden society would appear to be a wide range of individuals, including the poor. Steve, in fact, appears to recognize that "to take it out (hostility, alienation) on some broad that's a teller at a bank is really kinda dumb."

LABELING THEORY   No further comment is probably necessary on the acceptance of the criminal label by Steve and the rejection of the same by Albert. The differing manner in which they were treated by the justice system, the differing manner in which they accepted such treatment, and their associations with others in the system, all lend support to a labeling perspective. This is especially true if such an approach is viewed in combination with alienation and differential association approaches.

DIFFERENTIAL ASSOCIATION AND SUBCULTURAL THEORIES   Both the differential association and the subcultural approaches do not, at first, appear to apply to embezzlement, the "loner" crime. They are obvious in the case of Steve's career and learning experiences as robber. On the other hand, if such perspectives were refined to include the indirect learning process that Albert refers to as the "chain of functioning from one process to another ... conducive to this kind of thing," an entirely different conclusion might ensue. We are not ordinarily inclined to view businessmen of high status as members of a "subculture" providing the learning experiences and rationalizations for criminal activity. We are more inclined to view a lower socioeconomic area of a city or a group of ethnic or racial minorities in such light. Taking into account the extent and amount of white collar crime mentioned earlier, a reformulation of our thinking in regard to the differential association and subcultural approaches might be in order.

ANOMIE-OPPORTUNITY THEORIES   An anomie approach to the property crimes presented would fail if we merely viewed the legitimate opportunities available to each of our subjects and their socioeconomic background. On the other hand, if the overemphasis of culturally defined goals is considered, anomie may be highly applicable. This explanation is enhanced by our methodology. In considering the perspective of the deviants, the *illegal* opportunities are the only ones *they* perceive as available to them in spite of other viewpoints. This may be particularly true in the case of Albert and other white collar criminals. Such a reemphasis of these concepts from anomie theory may prove of extreme significance in the light of unofficial data regarding crime. It has been the official data, obtained from arrest and court records, that have been cast into doubt by increasing evidence of crime in all social classes in recent years.

SOCIAL CONTROL THEORIES   The implications for social control theories are not as unique as with other theories but should be pointed out. As in previous cases, we find the crucial factor of the containment model to be the breakdown of internal control mechanisms and the ineffectiveness of external measures of containment. Albert's admission that he may have subconsciously wanted to get caught indicates his sense of the lack of his own control and his desire for external mechanisms to restrain him. In his case, as appears to be the case with most white collar criminals, detection and public sanctioning regardless of the severity of the punishment was sufficient to refrain him from repeat offenses. On the other hand, Steve recognized and weighed his chances of being apprehended—"getting caught was one of the occupational hazards. And I was prepared to pay that price." Repeated sentencing was not a deterrent. Neither was his treatment within a medical model of social control (mental hospital). It appears that with Steve it was only when he came to grips with his own internal mechanisms of control that he was able to end his career as a robber. This seems to have been brought about, in part, by his changed self-concept (aided by his wife) and through his assistance of other ex-offenders. As he states, "I, for one, am not going to be satisfied with second class status any longer." The policy issue resulting from the social control model appears to be the overutilization of incarceration as a means of deterrence. This may be further delineated in noting the lack of utilization of the criminal model in sanctioning white collar crimes as opposed to street crimes. Perhaps a proper balance is in order.

══════ QUESTIONS FOR DISCUSSION

1. What reforms do you believe should be made in the justice system in handling white collar crimes as opposed to street crimes?
2. Currently Albert is working as an accountant for a local firm. Do you think he can be trusted not to repeat his offense? Why or why not?

3. Even though acts of embezzlement may occur in isolation from other such offenses, differential association may have some bearing on them. Explain.

4. What aspects of anomie theory seem relevant to the explanation of white collar crime, and what aspects are not applicable or contrary?

5. Based on Steve's career as a criminal, do you think that many if not most delinquent and criminal careers are started by accident? Discuss the significance of this in terms of deviancy theories we have studied.

6. Do you think Steve is aware of the seriousness of his crimes? Can you explain his attitude?

7. What would you say are the main factors in Steve's "doing good"?

RELATED READINGS

Aubert, Vilhelm, "White-Collar Crime and Social Structure," *American Journal of Sociology,* 58 (1952), pp. 263–271.

Chambliss, William J., "Toward a Political Economy of Crime," *Theory and Society,* 2 (Summer, 1975), pp. 149–170.

Cleaver, Eldridge, *Soul on Ice* (New York: McGraw-Hill, 1968).

Clinard, Marshall, "Review of *Other People's Money,*" *American Sociological Review,* 19 (1954), pp. 362–363.

Conklin, John E., *Illegal But Not Criminal* (Englewood Cliffs, N.J.: Prentice-Hall, Inc., 1977).

Cressey, Donald, *Other People's Money: The Social Psychology of Embezzlement* (New York: The Free Press, 1953).

———, "The Respectable Criminal: Why Some of Our Best Friends Are Crooks," *Transaction,* 2 (March–April, 1965), pp. 12–15.

Geis, Gilbert, "Toward a Delineation of White-Collar Offenses," *Sociological Inquiry,* 32 (Spring, 1962), pp. 160–171.

———, *White Collar Criminal* (New York: Atherton Press, 1968).

Genêt, Jean, *The Thief's Journal* (Paris: Olympia Press, 1954).

Goodman, Walter, *All Honorable Men: Corruption and Compromise in American Life* (Boston: Little, Brown, 1963).

Hamilton, Charles, ed., *Men of the Underworld: The Professional Criminal's Own Story* (New York: Macmillan, 1902).

Hapgood, Hutchins, *The Autobiography of a Thief* (London: G. P. Putnam's Sons, 1904).

Hartung, Frank, "A Vocabulary of Motives for Embezzlers," *Federal Probation,* 25 (1961), pp. 68–69.

———, "The White-Collar Thief," in *Crime, Law, and Society* (Detroit: Wayne State University Press, 1965), pp. 125–136.

Hills, Stuart L., *Crime, Power and Morality: The Criminal-Law Process in the United States* (New York: Chandler, 1971).

Irwin, John, *The Felon* (Englewood Cliffs, N.J.: Prentice-Hall, Inc., 1970).

MacKenzie, Donald, *Occupation: Thief* (Indianapolis: Bobbs-Merrill, 1955).

Martin, John, *My Life in Crime: The Autobiography of a Professional Criminal* (New York: Harper & Row, 1952).

President's Commission on Law Enforcement and Administration of Justice, *The Challenge of Crime in the Free Society* (Washington, D.C.: U.S. Government Printing Office, 1967), pp. 47–49.

———, *Crime and Its Impact—An Assessment* (Washington, D.C.: U.S. Government Printing Office, 1967), pp. 102–115.

Quinney, Richard, *Critique of Legal Order: Crime Control in a Capitalist Society* (Boston: Little, Brown, 1974).

Reiman, Jeffrey H., *The Rich Get Richer and the Poor Get Prison* (New York: John Wiley & Sons, 1979).

Riemer, Svend, "Embezzlement: Pathological Basis," *Journal of Criminal Law and Criminology*, 32 (1941), pp. 411–423.

Roberts, Ron E., "Crime for Fun and Profit," in *Social Problems: Human Possibilities* (St. Louis: C. V. Mosby, 1978).

Robinson, W. S., "The Logical Structure of Analytic Induction," *American Sociological Review*, 16 (1961), pp. 812–818.

Schuessler, Karl, "Review of *Other People's Money*," *American Journal of Sociology,* 49 (1954), p. 604.

Shaw, Clifford, *The Jack-Roller: A Delinquent Boy's Own Story* (Philadelphia: Albert Saifer, 1930).

Sutherland, Edwin, *The Professional Thief: By a Professional Thief* (Chicago: University of Chicago Press, 1937).

———, *White Collar Crime* (New York: Holt, Rinehart and Winston, 1961).

Turner, Ralph, "The Quest for Universals in Sociological Research," *American Sociological Review*, 18 (1953), pp. 604–611.

NOTES

1. Edwin Sutherland, *White Collar Crime* (New York: Holt, Rinehart and Winston, 1961).

2. Stuart L. Hills, *Crime, Power and Morality: The Criminal-Law Process in the United States* (New York: Chandler, 1971), p. 145.

3. Jeffrey H. Reiman, *The Rich Get Richer and the Poor Get Prison* (New York: John Wiley & Sons, 1979).

4. Ibid., p. 57.

5. Ibid., pp. 58–59.

6. Chamber of Commerce of the United States, *A Handbook on White Collar Crime* (Washington, D.C.: U.S. Government Printing Office, 1974), p. 6.

7. Reiman, *The Rich Get Richer and the Poor Get Prison*, p. 109.

8. Ibid., p. 119.

9. Herbert Bloch and Gilbert Geis, *Man, Crime, and Society* (New York: Random House, 1962), p. 291.

10. Ibid.

11. Donald Cressey, *Other People's Money* (Glencoe, Ill.: The Free Press, 1953), p. 19.

12. Black's Law Dictionary (St. Paul: West Publishing Company, 1933), p. 633, as cited in Cressey, *Other People's Money*, p. 19.

13. J. Edgar Hoover, *Crime in the United States: Uniform Crime Reports*, 1964.

14. Cressey, *Other People's Money*, p. 20.

15. Ruth Cavan, *Criminology* (New York: Thomas Y. Crowell, 1962), p. 715.

16. Robert Winslow, *Crime in the Free Society* (Encino, Calif.: Dickenson Publishing Co., 1968), p. 13.

17. Ibid., p. 35.

18. F. H. McClintock and Evelyn Gibson, *Robbery in London* (London: Macmillan, 1961), p. 16.

19. John Irwin, *The Felon* (Englewood Cliffs, N.J.: Prentice-Hall, Inc., 1970).

20. Clifford Shaw, *The Jack-Roller: A Delinquent Boy's Own Story* (Philadelphia: Albert Saifer, 1930).

21. Walter Reckless, *The Crime Problem* (New York: Appleton-Century-Crofts, 1967), pp. 303–305.

22. Irwin, *The Felon*, p. 24.

23. Ibid., p. 25.

24. Herbert Bloch and Gilbert Geis, *Man, Crime, and Society* (New York: Random House, 1970), p. 289.

25. Edwin Sutherland, *The Professional Thief: By a Professional Thief* (Chicago: Phoenix Books, 1956).

26. Bloch and Geis, *Man, Crime, and Society*, p. 290.

27. Richard Quinney, *Critique of Legal Order: Crime Control in a Capitalist Society* (Boston: Little, Brown, 1974).

28. William J. Chambliss, "Toward a Political Economy of Crime," *Theory and Society*, 2 (Summer, 1975), p .153; William Bonger, *Criminality and Economic Conditions* (Bloomington: Indiana University Press, 1969), p. 11.

29. Chambliss, "Toward a Political Economy of Crime," p. 154; Reiman, *The Rich Get Richer and the Poor Get Prison*, p. 7.

30. Reiman, *The Rich Get Richer and the Poor Get Prison*, pp. 6–7.

31. Ron E. Roberts, *Social Problems: Human Possibilities* (St. Louis: C. V. Mosby, 1978), p. 158.

32. Stuart Lottier, "Tension Theory and Criminal Behavior," *American Sociological Review*, 7 (December, 1942), pp. 843–844.

33. Cressey, *Other People's Money*, p. 20.

34. Sutherland, *White Collar Crime*.

35. Ibid., p. 240.

36. Svend Riemer, "Embezzlement: Pathological Basis," *Journal of Criminal Law and Criminology*, 32 (1941), pp. 411–423.

37. Marshall Clinard, "Review of *Other People's Money*," *American Sociological Review*, 19 (1954), pp. 362–363; W. S. Robinson, "The Logical Structure of Analytic Induction," *American Sociological Review*, 16 (1961), pp. 812–818; Karl Schuessler, "Review of *Other People's Money*," *American Journal of Sociology*, 49 (1954), p. 604; and Ralph Turner, "The Quest for Universals in Sociological Research," *American Sociological Review*, 18 (1953), pp. 604–611.

38. Don Gibbons, *Society, Crime and Criminal Careers* (Englewood Cliffs, N.J.: Prentice-Hall, Inc., 1968), p. 336.

39. Cressey, *Other People's Money*, pp. 16–20, as paraphrased in Bloch and Geis, *Man, Crime, and Society*, p. 292.

40. Sutherland, *The Professional Thief*.
41. Werner Einstadter, "The Social Organization of Armed Robbery," *Social Problems*, 17 (Summer, 1969), pp. 64–83.
42. Camp, *Nothing to Lose*, as cited in *Man, Crime, and Society*, p. 290.
43. Ibid.
44. Bloch and Geis, *Man, Crime, and Society*, pp. 291–292.

Forcible Rape

10

We may define forcible rape as sexual intercourse by a male with a female other than his wife without the consent of the woman and effected by force, duress, intimidation, or deception as to the nature of the act. In law, the term "consent" has become a grey area subject to contention in court in such cases as alcoholic intoxication of the woman, insanity, mental incompetency, and the like. Sexual intercourse by a male with a consenting female who is under a specified age is distinguished from forcible rape and is termed "statutory rape."

Until very recently, there had been very few studies of rape and rapists. However, the feminist movement has spawned an increased amount of literature in the area. A considerable amount of the recent literature has dealt with the victim of rape, the topic of Chapter 12. The increased attention to the subject has benefited our knowledge of rape even though the theories still remain somewhat rudimentary. As we shall see, some methodological issues exist and earlier data have been increasingly called into question.

METHODOLOGICAL PROBLEMS

As in other areas of crime, many early theories were based upon official data, particularly the FBI Uniform Crime Reports (UCR). As methods of self-reports, victimization surveys, and other techniques have developed, such data have increasingly been called into question. This is perhaps no more important than in the area of rape. It appears from data gathered by the President's Commission on Law Enforcement and Administration of Justice and the National Opinion Research Center that three to four times as many women are raped as report the crime to the police.[1] In addition, recent attention to the issue by women's groups appears to have increased the incentive to report a rape[2] and for the police to record some reports as rapes that previously might have been ignored or termed "unfounded."[3] Studies also indicate that the closer the relationship between the victim and her attacker the less likelihood of the rape being reported.[4] There is a greater likelihood the woman will report the rape if the rapist is younger than she, if she is highly educated, and if the police department has women on rape squads to deal with her case.[5] These findings call into question the extent of and the recent reported increase in rape. Also questioned is the picture of rape as an act committed in an urban area, by a stranger who is young, black, of lower socioeconomic status, and with a prior criminal record. Rape is a rather common occurrence. It is usually an *intraracial* event, where the victim is of the same race as the offender and, more often than not, both victim and offender reside in the same neighborhood area. Alcohol and alcohol problems are frequently factors in rape.[6]

TYPES OF FORCIBLE RAPISTS

Guttmacher divides rapists into three categories: 1) *explosive*—those in whom the rape is an explosive expression of pent-up sexual impulse or a defense against their own homosexual tendencies; 2) *sadistic*—those who want to injure the victim because of their deep-seated hostility toward women; 3) *aggressive criminal*—those who are out to "pillage and rob" and for whom rape is just another act of plunder.[7]

Gebhard and his associates have provided a fivefold classification: 1) *assaultive*—men whose behavior involves "unnecessary violence" who have a "strong sadistic element" in them; 2) *amoral delinquents*—those who pay little heed to social controls and treat females strictly as sexual objects; 3) *drunken*; 4) *explosive*; and 5) *double standard*—those who divide females into good and worthy of respect versus bad and not entitled to consideration despite resistance.[8] Of these, the first is the most frequent, and all five constitute about two-thirds of the rapists Gebhard studied.

THEORETICAL EXPLANATIONS

A great deal of what is stated theoretically regarding rape relates, directly or indirectly, to many other areas of deviant behavior. It would be appropriate to point out particularly that aspects of homosexuality, alcoholism, prostitution, and violent crime, such as armed robbery and murder, all relate to the issues of aggression, sexuality, and control involved in forcible rape. These conceptual links are not fully elaborated herein but are worthy of consideration by those interested in a more comprehensive framework of deviance.

Biological Theories

As in other aspects of human behavior, genetic or physiological explanations have been advanced to explain the act of rape and other acts of human aggression. These have included theories based upon genes, the size and shape of cranial cavities, body size and shape, and so on.[9] More recently, the XYY chromosome pattern has been advanced. This explanation is based upon the presence of an extra (Y) chromosome among those who are criminally-inclined, particularly among those who are involved in sexual offenses and other acts of aggression.[10] Most recent evidence, however, does not point to a causal link and the relationship, if any, appears to be interrelated with differential rates of arrest and other sociological factors.[11]

Brownmiller relies heavily upon the "structural capacity" of men to rape and women's "corresponding structural vulnerability" to build her thesis of the historical, cultural, psychological, and social factors by which men have used rape as a weapon to dominate women.[12] Other studies have examined the link between physiological sexual arousal and aggression in males.[13] Thus, whatever physiological factors are involved seem to necessitate their interaction with other aspects effecting human behavior.

Psychological Theories

We have seen in Chapter 1 that according to psychoanalytic theory, the rapist is a person who overcompensates for bisexuality through aggressive masculinity in the sex act. Bisexuality, however, is only one possible source of aggressive sex behavior. Yochelson and Samenow view this as only one of several characteristics of "the criminal personality." According to their model, rape and homosexual activity are portions of a general way of life marked by the inability to form relationships, treating persons as objects, lack of acceptance of responsibility, absence of guilt, and general antisocial behavior.[14] The sexuality of such individuals is such that they use sex in order to prove their "manhood" and to "conquer" others. The male criminal tends to begin his sexual activity earlier in life,[15] frequently engages in voyeurism and exhibitionism as well as homosexual and heterosexual activity but has difficulty in maintaining an erection and reaching ejaculation.[16]

Sociological Explanations

Most of the sociological theories regarding rape have emphasized the larger, cultural context. Micro theories appear to have less applicability. *Differential association*, for instance, relates only in developing general attitudes regarding sex and in the learning of sex roles. *Labeling* has limited power except in the general label of "criminal" or in the recidivists who are convicted of one rape or sexual offense and continue in a "career." A non-Marxian concept of *alienation* can be seen in those perspectives which emphasize the "alienating" aspects of sex roles within American culture. Three explanatory frameworks seem particularly relevant, however: *subcultural, social control,* and *anomie-opportunity.*

SUBCULTURAL THEORY Subcultural theorists have emphasized the violence of United States society and/or the rigidity of sex roles within our culture. An earlier work by Menachem Amir described the "subcultural theory of violence" among young, black, urban males as conducive to rape and other violence.[17] Such theories have been called into question by McCaghy and others in view of more recent evidence of rape among a broader spectrum of social classes.[18] McCaghy builds a model based upon the general cultural values supporting violence and "values supporting the male as sexual aggressor" to explain how some men in conducive situations are apt to engage in rape.[19] The McConahays have examined cross-cuturally sexual permissiveness, sex-role rigidity, and violence. They conclude that the rigidity of sex roles learned by males leads them to violent acts and to the association of violence with sexual arousal.[20]

SOCIAL CONTROL THEORY Social control theorists have centered upon the impulsiveness of the rapist. Such theorists point to the lack of "conscience,"[21] the inability to identify with laws and mores of society, and the lack of attachment to family among rapists as indicative of the relative absence of internal control.[22] On the other hand, the rapist (along with other criminals) is concerned about the external means of control, "getting caught."[23]

ANOMIE-OPPORTUNITY THEORY   Anomie-opportunity theorists present another source of the "illicit means" approach in regard to rape. This explanation, developed by Bloch and Geis, is based upon analysis of cross-cultural ethnographic studies of rape and employs four factors:

> 1) severe formal restrictions on nonmarital sexual relations of females, 2) moderately strong sexual inhibitions on the part of the female, 3) economic or other barriers to marriage that prolong the bachelorhood of some males into their late twenties, and 4) the absence of physical segregation of the sexes.[24]

Thus, according to this "opportunity theory," we may expect forcible rape among unmarried men who are in proximate contact with females and who are either formally restricted and/or inhibited from having sexual intercourse. This explanation seems to fit our case study ideally.

FRED:
A Rapist

Fred, the respondent in the following transcript, was first introduced to us at a social gathering that we attended at the home of an ex-convict. He was introduced to us as an alcoholic who attended A.A. meetings and was suggested as a possible class speaker on drunkenness. As it turned out, in Fred's deviant background drunkenness was only part of the picture. The interview actually started in the office before class, and as with other informants, Fred "spilled" much of his story before class. So, with his permission, we had the tape recorder going from the start. Fred seems to be an intelligent and self-aware person, and his own analysis is so well organized that it constitutes almost a textbook study. Fred fits the pattern of forcible rape described above quite well, but in one very important respect he departs. His sexual activity was in fact *progressive,* starting with minor offenses and progressing to more serious ones. Only the serious ones, however, led to official arrest and labeling. It could be that minor sexual offenses do not show up on the offender's "rap sheet" because the victims have been reluctant to report them, rather than because the offenders are first-time sex offenders. This is one point that will bear further research. Fred also departs from the etiological picture in that he is white and apparently comes from a middle income family. Other similarities and differences will be noted in our commentary.

QUESTION: *You say you started out as a classic case of progressive perversion.*

FRED: Well, originally I started out as a peeping Tom at about ten to twelve years old, which is normal in that period. I was active in this with four other brothers, but while they grew out of it, I never did. I never got caught but it was close a lot of times. From there I went to simple assaults of women. I didn't beat them up, just reach out and feel them. Like, we used to hitchhike along the road and women would pick us up. We'd feel them up and they'd say, "No, that's naughty" but we'd still continue. Young kids hitchhiking, you know, older women come along and pick you up. It used to be pretty fun to hitchhike, but now I hardly ever do it anymore. For a long time I thought I was ugly; where did my sexuality go to?

QUESTION: *How many kids in your family?*

FRED: Seven. I was in the middle. At home we were taught nothing about sex. Anything we learned we learned on our own. Most people, for instance, stay as peeping Toms but this lost its appeal with me and I gradually progressed. My parents were of German stock and very reserved. Sex was strictly taboo around the house. It was dirty and filthy and not to be talked about. It was strictly physical attraction with no emotion attached. That's the way I was brought up. We all know the sex act is one of the most beautiful things there is. It took me up to about three years ago to really realize this, what motivated me, etc.

QUESTION: *What came next in your progression?*

FRED: Well, as we hitchhiked and felt women up nobody ever blew the whistle on us. They just thought we were naughty boys. I was pretty young looking when I was younger. I don't look my age now. I'm almost thirty-five now. I seldom drink anymore. Well, anyway, from that I progressed to attempted rapes. I was really afraid to have forcible intercourse with a woman. Sometimes I would beat on the woman, sometimes no. Some women liked to be raped and a few times the women thanked me afterwards, that this was what they were looking for. This really bolstered my ego; I was sixteen. From there I went on to realize that I hated my mother for the way I was treated as a child and that all I wanted was to have control of the situation. My little brother used to beat the shit out of me and my mother used to sit there and laugh at me. When I was in the Army, I joined when I was seventeen, I never stopped these activities. I went to an Army psychiatrist; blah, blah, was all he said and nothing was ever done about my situation. I later realized that I loved my mother, dad, and family, but to this day they still ostracize me and don't want anything to do with me. When I came home from the Army my dad tried to whip me and I beat the shit out of him. He never touched me again. He says the reason he never did was because I was the only one of the boys that ever stood up to him and he respected me for that. Coming from a dad, that's quite a compliment. My dad was very shrewd. I was born and raised on a farm in Iowa.

I was the fastest runner in my family, which many times kept me from getting the shit stomped out of me. My dad was also a black belt in karate and he taught us all he knew when we were kids. He taught us when we were about ten. He'd use the handle from a toilet plunger to hit us quite often. To this day I have scars on my hips and on the back of my legs. He beat us until we bled. Both my parents did this; if one of us did something wrong all of us got beatings. For instance, I had been at Davenport, Iowa, with my dad to pick up some supplies and had been working like a dog all day. Got back and Jack, my brother, was supposed to set the table that evening and my old man just got out the stick and started whaling away at every one of us. It wasn't just the boys, it was the girls too, up to when they were late teenagers.

QUESTION: *One of the things I'd like to have you cover is your relations with your peers in school.*

FRED: Well, I was what you'd call a pretty quiet fellow. I didn't date girls—girls were dirty. Mom always degraded the girl, but Dad gave us the car and money when we'd go out. I double-dated and would pick up girls in the pickup truck, but a girl I really liked and respected —well, I'd never tell my parents about her. There was never any sex play when I dated; I was afraid of intercourse. I was very sensitive and had mixed-up emotions; I thought I couldn't satisfy a woman. I had underdeveloped testicles and penis until the chief medical officer at prison gave me male hormones, which helped me to have a more developed penis, but now it is a bit hyper, which presents problems. The advantages are that I now feel more relaxed with myself and trust myself. This new confidence was the thing that got me over this adverse type of thinking. I progressed to simple assaults on women rather than forcible assaults.

QUESTION: *This was in the Army?*

FRED: Yes, before the Army I would kidnap the woman and pull her out in the sticks.

QUESTION: *Did you have sexual intercourse with her?*

FRED: No, I didn't attain orgasm. This is the thing that really shook me up.

QUESTION: *What did you do, pull their clothes off?*

FRED: Yeah, just pulled off their clothes and touched them and kissed their nipples. There were cases where we'd have oral copulation. At knifepoint she'd copulate me back and I still wouldn't have orgasm. I couldn't do anything and would just let them go.

QUESTION: *Now, was this still in a small town?*

FRED: Yes, this is still in a small town.

QUESTION: *Well, how come you never got caught at it then?*

FRED: In a small town they never said anything.

QUESTION: *But you'd still see these people.*

FRED: Yes, you'd see them every day. They kept their secret and I kept my secret with them. Because the virgin really doesn't want to talk about it—the way it was performed and what I made them do, they don't want to retell it in court. Sometimes there was a sexual overtone, an old girlfriend who jilted me or wives who didn't want to tell their husbands. I committed my first forcible rape when I got out of the service in Tempe, Arizona. I was standing at a bus stop, not hitchhiking, when a young woman about thirty-five picked me up. I pulled a knife on her, drove out in the desert about thirty miles, raped her forcibly, took her car and clothes, and left her out there—120 degrees in the sun. I never felt any guilt about it for three years.

QUESTION: *Did you ever find out what happened to her?*

FRED: Oh, yeah, I've seen her since then. I told her there wasn't any way I could undo what I'd done to her and that the best thing for me to do was never let her see me again. Ever since then I've sent her a Christmas card, she sends me one too, and now we're good friends. That was the first time I had orgasm . . . it felt pretty good.

QUESTION: *I can't understand why you didn't earlier. Was it fear?*

FRED: I had a gross fear of sex—I was afraid to screw the women I was raping. It was many rapes until I got down to the nitty-gritty and did it. I now realize that the sex act itself is one of the most beautiful things in the relationship between a man and a woman. Not just that but the foreplay of the sex act too. At twelve I started peeping on other women, especially exhibitionists.

Anyway, I progressed from that to simple assaults on women, reaching out and feeling their butt, run my hand up their legs. I was about thirteen, fourteen, fifteen at that time.

QUESTION: *How many brothers do you have?*

FRED: Four brothers and two sisters. I don't know why they didn't progress like I did. I stayed home, was a mama's boy. I was small and slender. I feel I can take care of myself. They were dating and I was not. I was very withdrawn and nobody gave a shit about me. I felt very inadequate, not able to associate with other people. My parents were very strict. They didn't seem to care what happened to me. Later on we'd hitchhike and feel up women. I'd take women out in the woods and strip them and just look, I couldn't have an orgasm; this shook me up pretty bad. My mother took me to a family doctor when I was about fifteen and found I had a slight case of large nipples. He poked around and made me feel very embarrassed and I ran out of his office crying. I hated my mother for this and didn't talk to her for a year.

In the Army I went to Ranger school, survival school, and learned how to be very, very sneaky. We specialized in guerrilla warfare and I specialized in hand-to-hand combat. I was a bayonet instructor for four years. Taught judo and now have learned Kung Fu. This training has enabled me to trust and feel in control of myself. This is something I never felt before. I've been out of prison about seven months now and I've had no trouble functioning in all ways. I think and thoroughly feel like a real man. This, to me, is an important part of being a mature human being. The only one I feel has ever been a complete human being is Jesus.

I progressed from forcible assaults to forcible rapes. The first rape I committed was when I was twenty-three years old. It was the first time I attained an erection and experienced orgasm. Before this it always shook me up bad not to attain erection and have orgasm.

I've been in prison twice, four years each. The reason I went the second time was for a simple assault on my sister-in-law. My older brother is a Ph.D. in psychology and the night I assaulted his wife we sat and talked. He was my parole officer, by the way, which made it pretty rough at home. I was living with them and found myself falling in love with my sister-in-law. I felt pretty bad about this. In prison I kept getting in fights and they'd keep shipping me around. I lost this tooth in a fight. I learned to keep my mouth shut, pay attention to the therapy, and talk about myself. Really started to learn about myself. I realized that if I wanted to be treated like a human being I had to start acting like a human being, not like an animal. I had also, before, assaulted my mother. I raped both my sisters and felt very guilty about it. I thought about suicide many times and tried to take my life once; hung myself and my eyes were starting to pop out when my mother found me. She cut me down and saved my life. She asked me why I did it and I told her to go screw herself, so she kicked me out of the house. I've never been back, for fifteen years. No one in my family will even talk to me. My mother pretty well controls the family but I love them all and miss them all. Those rapes on my sisters were the worst things I'd ever done. In 1960 I assaulted two police officers, ambushed them, broke their knees with a two-by-four. I was never convicted of that one. I pulled a few armed robberies and rapes simultaneously. Never was convicted. I went into a bank late in the afternoon when just a man and women were there. I made the man lay down and

I screwed the woman. They chased me all over town for fourteen hours before they caught me. They weren't sure I was the right guy 'cause I rubbed Mercurochrome on my face and the camera film from the bank camera came out blurred. Forcible rape in Arizona calls for the death penalty, which is the gas chamber; I helped build the one in Arizona. Anyway, I was found not guilty for lack of evidence.

When I assaulted my sister-in-law I had intended to rape her but I just couldn't do it. I broke down and cried. She was very susceptible to rape. She was very open-minded, nothing shook her up. I told her the problems I was having with myself. As gross as it may sound, going to the joint was the best thing that ever happened to me. I have an AA degree and a BS in horticulture science. Got 'em in prison. In two weeks I'll begin work at [names firm] as a landscaping maintenance supervisor, paying $6.10 an hour, and that's a hell of a job. I love working with plants and have been able to channel my emotions constructively by growing plants.

I've been able to function as a man. In CMC, California Men's Colony, a doctor started giving me testosterone proof 100—100 milligrams of this hormone every two weeks. This male hormone is made from bulls' testicles. My testicles and penis are fully developed now and I'm able to function successfully and completely; it's a hell of a feeling. I feel like a human being again.

QUESTION: *Did you continue with your sexual activities when you were in the service?*

FRED: Yes, I did. I committed an average of three rapes a week, never attaining orgasm until I got out of the Army, and that was in 1959.

QUESTION: *Do you think that most of the Rangers and Green Berets that you knew were compensating for any sexual inadequacies they might have had?*

FRED: Well, most of my outfit were criminals or ex-cons. They were willing to serve in the Army to keep from going to prison, such as I did. I can't say, really, that there were any questionably masculine men in the Green Berets. I will say that most of the guys were always trying to prove something. We pulled some pretty vicious raids. We spent many a day in the stockade for some of the things we pulled.

QUESTION: *I'd like to know how you can tell if women are susceptible to rape and how they respond.*

FRED: All right, I'd say most of the women that are susceptible to rape are pretty broadminded and pretty sexy. Sometimes a woman who tries to hide sexuality is very susceptible to rape. What she's really saying is, "I'm a woman but I'm not gonna let anybody know about it, but I dare you to find out." So you find that she is a woman and most of the time she's the best lay. A woman who's very broadminded such as you, and a few others in here that are smiling. This type of a woman tries to be nice to everybody and sometimes it comes out the wrong way. You sort of sense this. It's just a feeling you have. With me, it was being familiar with women for so many years.

QUESTION: *If you hadn't been successful in raping a woman do you ever think you would have gone as far as to kill the woman?*

FRED: Yes, the first time I went to prison I went to a mental institution in California. This is a maximum security hospital for sex offenders. I was there four years and eight months. The reason I went there was that I committed a rape in Arizona where I cut her nipple off with a knife. I had the knife under the nipple and she jerked away and cut it off. I thought then about killing her, but I didn't. I was deathly afraid of murder. I asked the court to send me to [the hospital]. I knew that if I killed somebody I would take my own life. I didn't want to do that. [The hospital] is a real hellhole.

QUESTION: *How do you spot a developing sex offender?*

FRED: There's really no clear-cut way. A person who fights constantly for no particular reason, shoplifts, or runs away all the time. Likes to bully people. A person who wants to be noticed but goes about it in an assaulting way. I was in trouble in school all the time. We used to pull all kinds of tricks. I got kicked out of a typing class 'cause I dropped a typewriter on the teacher's toe.

QUESTION: *You mentioned that you were in Alcoholics Anonymous because you were having a drinking problem. Why is this?*

FRED: Well, I was drunk a few times when I pulled my last crimes. I was drunk the night I assaulted my sister-in-law. My granddaddy had a still and I started drinking when I was a kid. It has aggravated my crimes. He was a great bootlegger, drunk all the time. He even used to give it to the babies. If you've ever seen a baby drunk it's as comical as all hell. It's pathetic too. Liquor makes me sicker than a dog.

QUESTION: *Are you married?*

FRED: No. Interested?

QUESTION: *What provoked you to ambush the police officers?*

FRED: Well, they accused me of something I didn't do: going 50 in a 35-mile zone. I was in reality going 25. They were drunk when they gave me the ticket. I defended myself and they were suspended for ninety days. The harassment really started after that. I was living up in Linda Vista at the time. There were sixteen cops living in a five-block area near my house, so relations weren't too friendly. I had a civil bond put on them, which is when the courts say the law or police can't mess with somebody. They kept it up, though. I went to each of their houses one night and told them to quit it, to get screwed. It got worse after that. About two weeks after that I ambushed them on two separate occasions. I spent about four hours apiece on them, really worked them over. One of them I saw about three days later at the police station when I went to reregister my change of address.

During one rape a woman actually thanked me. How about that? But then, there were times when they called me every kind of name. That's okay, I'm a crazy bastard but I'm at least enjoying myself. Average age was about twenty-five. For instance, a woman picked me up at the bus station when I was waiting for a ride to Phoenix; this is the same one that writes me Christmas cards. I pulled a knife on her. She had a low-cut summer dress on, no bra or panties. Her nipples were up at this time so I knew she was sexually excited. She looked like she just came from being seduced. She was still sweating, hair matted down and kind of messed up. Her bra and panties were laying in the back seat so I don't know where she'd been. She was thirty-five years old, married, with a daughter thirteen years old. I pulled a knife on her and she said, "What do you want, the car?" and I said, "Yeah, among other things." "I don't have any money; do you want sex?" she said. I told her I was gonna rip her off. She said she'd let me. I put the knife down on the seat and never took it out again until we got out on the desert. I raped her out on an Indian reservation, which made it a Federal crime: kidnap and rape. When we got out there she told me her husband was an invalid in a wheelchair and I undressed her in the car as we were driving along. She didn't have a stitch on as we went down that freeway; people would drive by and really stare. Even though she was willing, because a knife was involved it makes it forcible. All you have to do is indicate that you have a weapon and it makes it forcible.

QUESTION: *Did she report you?*

FRED: No, I got caught on another attempted rape about two weeks later. That's the one where I beat up the woman and accidentally cut off her nipple. I got shook up and told her I was gonna kill her. Cut her a few more times on the breast and in the pubic area. Then I decided I wasn't gonna kill her. She was down on her hands and knees looking for her nipple, said she was gonna put it back on. She was crying on about it, so I just took her clothes and left her there. Ditched her car later. There was an article in the paper about a car being stolen but nothing about the assault at all. I don't know how she got home, but I saw her about two weeks later and she was still blistered up bad. We later became very good friends. At that time I didn't give a damn whether she lived or died. I would've preferred that she died 'cause it would've left me clear. By the way, I wore disposable gloves every time I pulled a rape. No prints.

QUESTION: *If you had a choice between a passive and aggressive woman, who would you rape?*

FRED: Probably the passive one first. The aggressive one would be second choice. I'd be reluctant to rape the aggressive one because I want control of the situation, unlike the way it was at home. There I was pretty much the scapegoat. The best thing to do if you get raped is to go along with it and let the man rape you. Those that get murdered usually resist. The more violent you resist, the more violent the attacker becomes.

QUESTION: *Have you ever had a girlfriend?*

FRED: Yes, when I was nineteen I was going to get married. I was home on a forty-eight-day leave from the Army to get married and the day before the wedding my fiancée got killed. If she was alive today I'd marry her.

QUESTION: *How does society treat you now?*

FRED: Pretty fair. I don't feel any animosity toward anybody. You have to accept yourself for the way you were, the way you are, and the way you're going to be. Have to trust yourself in order to trust other people. When I was at a medical facility under the Department of Corrections in Sacramento I went through an eighteen-month therapy program called the Category "E" program. I had four psychiatric clearances before I went there, which you have to have before you begin the program. I was diagnosed as a paranoid, which was entirely erroneous. This was the way I was diagnosed by the first psychiatrist I'd ever seen and every psychiatrist after that went along with this. The average time I talked to them was five minutes. How can you diagnose or judge a man in five minutes flat? In fact, the one who made the initial diagnosis talked to me for a minute and a half. It stayed on the record all that time until I got to Vacaville, when it was changed. I had my diagnosis changed here from paranoid to "simple rascality." This is what I was when I came there, a rascal. I was a rascal when I was a peeping Tom. All boys do it. Girls peep on boys too, but they're just more sneaky about it and never get caught. We did a lot of things. I didn't have a driver's license till I was nineteen. After I'd been in the service two years I got my driver's license. I used to steal my Dad's truck to go on secret dates. The girls that I would bring home to meet my mother, well, she'd be real nice to them, but when they'd leave she'd really chop them up. They were never good enough for me. She never did this to my brothers. She was very protective of me, especially after I broke my finger.

I have a twin brother who's a lieutenant colonel in the Army. We used to get into all kinds of trouble together when we were kids. About two blocks down the street there was another pair of identical twins, John and Jake; if we were in trouble they were in trouble right along with us. I used to roll toilet paper down the hallways in school and blame it on my best friend. To this day we're great friends and he still doesn't realize I did that to him, and he used to do ten hours of detention every week for that. That's rascality. We'd take rotten Limburger cheese and put it into the school's cooling system and we'd all be out of school for three days. Sweet odor. We had a neighbor and every time he'd take a crap we'd tip it over onto the door so he couldn't get out. This went on for about six years. Another year we put a cow on top of the schoolhouse and it really shit all over everything. Another year we dissected a pigeon and strung it out all over the third floor. We'd ride motorcycles in the school halls.

I was just trying to draw attention to myself. You had a question over there.

QUESTION: *Did you love your fiancée?*

FRED: I loved her very much. If she was alive today I'd marry her. She was the only girl my mother ever approved of too.

QUESTION: *You said your home life was harsh and your mother was protective. Could you explain that?*

FRED: Yes, she was protective to the point that if I did anything wrong, WHAM! Most of the time my dad beat up the kids but she controlled him. They love each other very much. They're like a couple of kids. They never really told us they loved us, but you know, punishment is an expression of love. If we were good there was no praise. But they were just trying to show us they loved us.

QUESTION: *Do you have any problems about your past?*

FRED: None whatsoever. My past doesn't have to happen again. I channel my energies. In February I'm going to college and taking a three-unit course in landscape technology. Once I graduate I have to work for [names a nursery] for five years, which I don't mind at all.

QUESTION: *What kind of jobs did you have in the past before prison?*

FRED: I was in the Army, and nights I worked at the [names hotel] in San Diego. Bakery work. Right after prison I couldn't get a job so I decorated pastries and sold them around the neighborhood.

Made good money. I baked about 400 loaves of bread a week and sold them for 25 cents apiece around the neighborhood. I have a lifetime Master Baker's license, I also hold a State Nurseryman's License and a State Contractor's License. I also work for JOVE and help ex-cons get jobs. The impulse to rape has left me and I have no desire to do so again.

QUESTION: *When you were going through therapy was there anytime when you started experiencing the reality of what you'd done? How did you get through it?*

FRED: Yes. It was almost unbearable. I was in talk therapy. Talk about anything that bothers you, anything. Talk about it so much that you don't feel guilty. Also had a great deal of psychodrama. Helped me get my aggressions out in the open. I'm hostile but no longer aggressively so. In creating good landscaping I'm channeling my hostilities. I'll be off parole on the 23rd of November, which is unusual; only a year to the day since I got out. In therapy we talk about everything and learn to accept it. If I go back to prison it'll be for life and I'm too damn young to spend my life in prison.

COMMENTARY

It is rather difficult to typecast Fred. He seems to fit the assaultive category on some occasions, the drunken on others, and the amoral delinquent on still others. Thus, we have a commentary on the typologies of rapists mentioned above—they are not much help in understanding this individual case.

Fred is white and comes from a middle class background. His sexual offenses were progressive—from minor "peeping Tom" offenses, to simple assault to aggravated assault, to forcible rape. His offense record apparently involves primarily rape.

Fred is typical of rapists in other respects. He is unmarried. He had an alcohol problem and alcohol was involved in his offenses. Like many cases, his victims were often acquaintances, friends, and relatives. Most interesting is his physical disability, underdeveloped penis and testicles, which might have served at least as a perceived barrier to marriage and sexual intercourse. Fred seems to emphasize the role of women as "victims in search of their criminal," especially certain types of women, such as those who seem to say: "I'm a woman but I'm not gonna let anybody know about it, but I dare you to find out."

Some factors in Fred have changed as a result of his prison experience. First, he is older. He has also overcome his barrier to marriage—his sexual underdevelopment. He also seems to have developed some capacity for empathy, as shown by remorse expressed in group therapy.

But in some respects he has not changed. He still seems to orient himself toward that certain kind of woman who he believes is susceptible to rape—as shown by his statements in class. However, he seems able to relate to them socially, perhaps to engage them in an intimate personal relationship without coercion. He claims he is currently engaged or dating a woman with whom he is intimate. Perhaps in years to come he will maintain such a relationship with his ideal woman and will refrain from seeking women he perceives to be "susceptible to rape."

THEORETICAL IMPLICATIONS

There are several theoretical concepts and perspectives that are applicable to Fred's case. Once again, we find that they interact to some extent.

Biological Theories

Naturally, we have no knowledge of Fred's genetic or chromosome structure. However, there does appear to be an interaction of Fred's physical appearance and underdeveloped sex organs with his psychological makeup and labeling ("I thought I was ugly"). It is possible, also, that his concern regarding his "slight case of large nipples" contributed to additional concerns about his masculinity and a need to "prove" his manhood.

Psychological Theories

It is obvious that Fred had feelings of sexual inferiority and inadequacy as postulated by psychiatric theories. Even though we find no evidence of bisexuality in Fred's life, the fears regarding his nipples could have produced the same type of reactions homosexual fantasies or early experiences may produce in others. Yochelson and Samenow's "criminal personality" appears to apply as well. Fred was unable to form adequate relationships with others, particularly females, whom he initially saw as "dirty." He apparently lacked guilt during his "career" as a rapist and engaged in other antisocial and criminal behavior as well. His sexual activity began "as a peeping Tom at about ten to twelve years old" and progressed to forcible rape. He had difficulty in reaching orgasm, perhaps due more to his physical composition than to psychological characteristics.

What is significant in Fred's case is that we have rather deep insight into the early childhood and family background that may have contributed to this personality. We must be cautious in interpreting such information given the possibility that such reality may have been influenced by the considerable psychiatric therapy Fred had undergone. Nevertheless, we are able to view a home life in which Fred resented his father, who was abusive physically, was attached to his mother ("I was a mama's boy"), saw sex as "strictly taboo around the house," and was taught that "girls were dirty." The physical abuse and parental ambivalence regarding love are frequently associated with a psychopathic personality and violent behavior.[25] This aspect can be further interrelated with the learning process of *differential association* within a "subculture of violence" in addition to an understanding of the lack of internal control mechanisms (conscience and guilt). The rigidity of sex roles also may relate to this process.

Sociological Explanations

The application of *differential association* and *labeling* implications in Fred's history have already been mentioned. *Alienation* concepts may only apply in the manner in which Fred viewed or was alienated from females. Other sociological explanations seem to have considerable power.

CULTURAL THEORY   The "culture of violence" dimension as an influence on earning and socialization is evident. Fred's father used physical punishment extensively. In the Rangers Fred later grew to become physically violent himself. He was taught by his parents, first, that sex was something purely physical (as well as "dirty") but also, as he stated, punishment was "an expression of love." Because of this indoctrination, Fred actually seemed to lack any kind of compassion for his victims and even seemed to feel that despite his physical brutality toward them, they responded to him with love in a kind of sadomasochistic relationship.

SOCIAL CONTROL THEORY   Social control explanations apply in the impulsiveness of Fred's acts and his lack of guilt surrounding them. He did not, at the time of his sexual offenses, feel attached to the general laws of society or to his family members, some of whom he also raped. It is surprising that Fred was able to commit so many acts before receiving external control sanctions. He committed one assault on his brother's wife shortly after a "long talk" with his brother, who was both a psychologist and his parole officer. The external measures, both incarceration and psychological therapy, had mixed results in deterring Fred. He claims that he began to face reality when he was engaged in heavy "talk" therapy and psychodrama. This, of course, followed the remedy of Fred's lack of physical development.

An interesting point in social control arises in Fred's case and in other cases. If we accept the fact that Fred was either physically or mentally "sick" or both, we preclude his criminal responsibility. On the other hand, Fred would not have received the medical assistance he apparently was in need of, had he not first been adjudicated under the criminal or legal model. This question, and many related aspects, is an area of needed attention.

ANOMIE-OPPORTUNITY THEORY   The *anomie-opportunity* explanation as presented above has potential in explaining Fred's development as a forcible rapist. First, Fred came to *perceive* restrictions on nonmarital sexual relations with females. His mother limited his selection of girl friends by ridiculing his female acquaintances—girls he brought home. Also, his parents attached taboos to sex and his mother conveyed the attitude that most girls were "dirty." It could be that, at the same time, his mother came to approve of women for Fred who were sexually inhibited, those Fred describes as "rape susceptible." Fred nevertheless experienced barriers to marriage—the death of his fiancée and his own sexual underdevelopment. At the time, living in a small town, he was in close proximity with a number of women. Some may have "led him on" or teased him, and he responded by sexually assaulting them. He was reinforced in his conviction that sexually inhibited women actually want to be raped when a rape victim actually "thanked" him.

In a succeeding chapter, the role of the rape victim will be examined. The other side of some of Fred's claims, that "some women like to be raped," will be discussed.

═══ QUESTIONS FOR DISCUSSION

1. Discuss each of Gebhard's five classifications of rapists and tell how each applies or does not apply in Fred's case.
2. Do you feel Fred will rape again? Why or why not?
3. According to Menachem Amir, rapists have many of the same characteristics as murderers. Discuss this statement.
4. Give a brief description of Fred's childhood. Do you think that childhood factors are the primary determinants in Fred's adulthood rapes and other crimes? If so, what bearing does sociological theory have on the case?
5. Discuss Fred's statement that "some women are susceptible to rape."
6. In what ways does Fred conform to the description of the "typical" rapist given at the beginning of this chapter? In what ways is he atypical?
7. What factors in American social structure might account for high and ever increasing amounts and rates of forcible rape?

═══ RELATED READINGS

Amir, Menachem, "Forcible Rape," *Federal Probation*, 31 (1967), pp. 51–57.

Brownmiller, Susan, *Against Our Will: Men, Women and Rape* (New York: Simon and Schuster, 1975).

Chase, Naomi Feigelson, *A Child Is Being Beaten: Violence Against Children, An American Tragedy* (New York: McGraw-Hill, 1976).

Doshay, Lewis, *The Boy Sex Offender and His Later Career* (New York: Grune and Stratton, 1943).

Ellis, Albert, and Brancale, Ralph, *The Psychology of Sex Offenders* (Springfield, Ill.: Charles C Thomas, 1956).

Fingarette, Herbert, *The Meaning of Criminal Insanity* (Berkeley: University of California Press, 1972).

Gebhard, Paul, *Sex Offenders: An Analysis of Types* (New York: Harper & Row, 1965).

Gelles, Richard, *The Violent Home: A Study of Physical Aggression Between Husbands and Wives* (Beverly Hills, Calif.: Sage, 1972).

Goode, Erich, "Violent Behavior," in *Deviant Behavior: An Interactionist Approach* (Englewood Cliffs, N.J.: Prentice-Hall, Inc., 1978), pp. 395–433.

Guttmacher, Manfred, *Sex Offenses: The Problems, Causes, and Prevention* (New York: Norton, 1951).

Kanin, Eugene, "Male Aggression in Dating-Courtship Relations," *American Journal of Sociology*, 63 (1957), p. 197.

Karpman, Benjamin, "The Sexual Psychopath," *Journal of Criminal Law, Criminology, and Police Science*, 42 (1951), pp. 185–186.

McCaghy, Charles, "Crime in the Streets—Against Person," in *Deviant Behavior: Crime, Conflict and Interest Groups* (New York: Macmillan, 1976), pp. 109–144.

McConahay, Shirley, and McConahay, John, "Sexual Permissiveness, Sex-Role Rigidity, and Violence Across Cultures," *Journal of Social Issues*, 33 (Spring, 1977), pp. 134–143.

Malamuth, Neil; Feshbach, Seymour; and Jaffe, Yorman, "Sexual Arousal and Aggression: Recent Experiments and Theoretical Issues," *Journal of Social Issues*, 33 (Spring, 1977), pp. 110–133.

Radzinowicz, Leon, ed., *Sexual Offenses: Report of the Cambridge Department of Criminal Science* (London: Macmillan, 1957).

Tappan, Paul, "The Habitual Sex Offender," *State of New Jersey Report and Recommendation of the Commission on the Habitual Sex Offender* (Trenton, N.J.: 1950).

Von Hentig, Hans, *The Criminal and His Victim* (New Haven: Yale University Press, 1948).

Wheeler, Stanton, "Sex Offenses: A Sociological Critique," *Law and Contemporary Problems*, 25 (1960), pp. 258–259.

Yochelson, Samuel, and Samenow, Stanton, *The Criminal Personality, Vol. I: A Profile for Change* (New York: Jason Aronson, 1976).

NOTES

1. Menachem Amir, *Patterns in Forcible Rape* (Chicago: University of Chicago Press, 1971); Erich Goode, *Deviant Behavior: An Interactionist Approach* (Englewood Cliffs, N.J.: Prentice-Hall, Inc., 1978), pp. 425–430; Michael Hindelang and Bruce Davis, "Forcible Rape in the United States: A Statistical Profile," in Duncan Chappel; Robley Geis, and Gilbert Geis, eds., *The Crime, the Victim and the Offender* (New York: Columbia University Press, 1977), pp. 87–114.

2. Goode, *Deviant Behavior*, p. 427.

3. Ibid., pp. 426–428.

4. Ibid., p. 426.

5. Ibid., pp. 426–427.

6. Ibid., p. 427; John Gillin, *The Wisconsin Prisoner* (Madison: University of Wisconsin Press, 1946).

7. Manfred Guttmacher, *Sex Offenses: The Problem, Causes, and Prevention* (New York: Norton, 1951).

8. Paul Gebhard et al., *Sex Offenders* (New York: Harper & Row, 1965).

9. Samuel Yochelson and Stanton Samenow, *The Criminal Personality, Vol. I: A Profile for Change* (New York: Jason Aronson, 1976), pp. 57–58.

10. Ibid., pp. 59–60.

11. American Psychiatric Association, "No Definite Link Found Between XYY and Crime," *APA Monitor*, 1 (December, 1970), p. 5.

12. Susan Brownmiller, *Against Our Will: Men, Women and Rape* (New York: Bantam, 1975), pp. 4–7.

13. Neil Malamuth, Seymour Feshbach, and Yorman Jaffe, "Sexual Arousal and Aggression: Recent Experiments and Theoretical Issues," *Journal of Social Issues*, 33 (Spring, 1977), pp. 110–133.

14. Yochelson and Samenow, *The Criminal Personality*.

15. Ibid., pp. 178–180.

16. Ibid., pp. 333–348.

17. Menachem Amir, "Forcible Rape," *Federal Probation*, 31 (1967), pp. 51–58.

18. Charles McCaghy, *Deviant Behavior: Crime, Conflict and Interest Groups* (New York: Macmillan, 1976), pp. 133–134.

19. Ibid., pp. 133–136.

20. Shirley McConahay and John McConahay, "Sexual Permissiveness," Sex-Role Rigidity, and Violence Across Cultures," *Journal of Social Issues*, 33 (Spring, 1977), pp. 133–143.

21. Yochelson and Samenow, *The Criminal Personality*, p. 412.

22. Ibid., pp. 303–304.

23. Ibid., pp. 411–412.

24. Herbert Bloch and Gilbert Geis, *Man, Crime and Society* (New York: Random House, 1970), p. 253.

25. Naomi Feigelson Chase, *A Child Is Being Beaten: Violence Against Children, An American Tragedy* (New York: McGraw-Hill, 1976); Kenneth Wooden, *Weeping in the Playtime of Others: America's Incarcerated Children* (New York: McGraw-Hill, 1976).

Murder

11

Homicide refers to the killing of one human being by another. There are various forms of homicide, including murder, manslaughter, excusable homicide, and justifiable homicide. Our concern in this chapter is murder. In law, murder refers to the killing of another human being *with malice aforethought*. Malice aforethought is a predetermination to commit an unlawful act without just cause or provocation. In most states in this country, malice aforethought is the delimiting condition of "second degree murder," while "first degree murder" involves *premeditation* as well. Premeditation consists of deliberation before the act and intent to commit the act, although in practice only a moment of such deliberation is sufficient to indicate the presence of premeditation. Manslaughter, as distinguished from murder, is killing without malice aforethought and not as a result of accident or legal duty, while excusable homicide refers to accidental killing, and justifiable homicide refers to killing from legal duty (e.g., a legal execution). Although there may be deaths in which homicide is questionable (e.g., poisoning or overdose of drugs), homicide statistics are considered to be relatively immune from vagaries of police practice, political interference, or other sources of bias.[1] However, certain forms of killing of others are not necessarily legally classified as murder. These would include white collar crimes that result in the death or deaths of persons.

Other instances include acts, such as medical malpractice, wherein the legal remedy is usually reserved to the civil rather than the criminal courts. There is also considerable debate today concerning the legitimacy of killing in war and terrorist action, abortion, and by active or passive euthanasia.[2]

ETIOLOGY

Before we move ahead to various explanations of murder, there are some significant correlates of murder that must be reckoned with in the theories we will examine. Studies of homicide data reveal significantly higher rates among certain groups that others. Homicide is higher among males, nonwhites, the age group twenty to twenty-four, and in the lower socioeconomic class.[3] Homicide is found to be more than twice as prevalent in the South as in other regions in the United States.[4] It seems to increase during times of prosperity and decline during depression.[5] Homicide rates also tend to be higher in metropolitan and rural areas than in intermediate-sized cities.[6] The victim of homicide is very likely to be a male, of the same race as the offender, and a close acquaintance rather than a stranger to the killer.[7] He is likely to be killed by a gun in an interaction in which he has affected the emotions of the other party.[8] Alcohol or other drugs are often likely to have been involved in the situation.[9]

CURRENT DEBATES

Stemming from and crucial to the research and theories regarding murder is the public policy discussion regarding the use of capital punishment and gun controls. These policies are advocated as deterrents to homicide. Due to the highly emotional interaction involved in a homicide situation and the frequency with which the victim may precipitate the killing,[10] it is argued that the death penalty is of little or no consequence as an individual deterrent.[11] Former United States Attorney General Ramsey Clark argues that capital punishment demeans life rather than reverences it.[12] Wilson argues that the death penalty is a symbol for life.[13] The most thorough study of the deterrent effect, individual and general, was conducted by Thorsten Sellin, whose conclusions point to a lack of deterrent effects.[14] Gibbs has questioned the logic of Sellin's and other studies in that they fail to take into account the *certainty* of punishment within our justice system. That is, if each offender knew he or she would be apprehended and receive the death penalty, a general deterrent effect could result within a population. According to Gibbs, such reasoning has never been tested adequately.[15]

The United States Supreme Court ruled in *Furman* v. *Georgia* that the death penalty, as it was being administered in 1972, was "cruel and unusual punishment." [16] The court's ruling was based upon the unconstitutional discrimination that was being exercised in the administration of capital punishment. Discrimination, as had been pointed out earlier by the President's Commission on Law Enforcement and Administration of Justice, was working against the poor, blacks, males, and members of "unpopular groups." [17] States have since revised their legislation and, in recent years, executions have been revived beginning with Gary Gilmore in Utah and John Spenkelink in Florida. The debate continues in public and academic circles.

Kleck, in 1979, conducted an elaborate statistical analysis of deterrence factors. He concluded that the deterrent effect of capital punishment is questionable, although there is stronger evidence that the incapacitative effect of imprisonment, if certain, may serve as a somewhat stronger deterrent. However, Kleck found that gun ownership had a very strong relationship to homicide. This relationship was circulatory in that:

> The aggregate level association found in this research between the homicide rate and the level of gun ownership, combined with individual level survey data on reasons for obtaining the owning firearms, strongly suggests that crime is a cause of gun ownership just as gun ownership is a cause of crime. If people own guns because they fear crime, because they see themselves in serious danger of being assaulted, raped, burglarized, or robbed at gunpoint, then the task of reducing violence through the reduction of gun ownership may be a profoundly difficult one.[18]

Thus, Kleck's conclusions appear to be supportive of the "subculture of violence" theory that will be discussed shortly.

THEORIES

Several basic approaches have been developed to explain murder. A great deal of theory regarding violence in general has been mentioned in Chapter 10 and will not be repeated in detail here. Physiological and genetic explanations, including the XYY approach, are among these. In the area of homicide, there has been relatively little interdisciplinary rivalry between the psychoanalytic approaches and the sociological ones. The sociological theories are generally stated in a context of compatibility with psychoanalytic approaches.

Psychological Explanations

PSYCHOANALYTIC THEORY   We have seen that Freud developed a theory that human beings are born with life instincts and death instincts, which are in constant conflict with each other. These instincts constitute the id, which, through the process of socialization, comes to be regulated by the ego and superego. Failure to develop the superego or ego may mean the person cannot handle hostility. Murder and other forms of aggression may result. The personality possibilities for murderers are variable, depending upon the extent of socialization. On a continuum they range from presocial criminals and psychopaths, who have not developed superego controls, to accidental or situational criminals, or "acting out neurotics," who have developed normal egos and superegos, but have developed an obsessive compulsion to kill because of situational pressures.[19] Generally speaking, homicide is seen as resulting from insufficient ego and superego such that aggression comes to be directed toward other persons, while if the superego is sufficiently strong, the aggression will be directed against the self, resulting sometimes in psychosomatic symptoms (such as migraine headaches, asthma, hives, or ulcers) and in more extreme cases in suicide.

In "normal" individuals, what changes might trigger sudden release of aggressive impulses? We might speculate that alcohol or other depressant drugs can act as an uninhibitor, breaking down superego controls. Indeed, as noted earlier, alcohol appears to be a factor in a majority of homicides. Beyond the uninhibiting effects of alcohol or other drugs, we may posit other factors, such as a crisis in one's role relationships, factors more sociological than psychological. Sociologically, a person enters a situation with plural "selves" or roles. One "self" is normally invoked but others are invoked if the situation changes. This is an assumption of the "subcultural theory," which we will examine shortly.

Other psychological theories, particularly Yochelson and Samenow's "Criminal Personality" explanation,[20] that describe violent criminal activity apply to murder as well as to rape, assault, and other crimes.

Social-psychological Explanations

EXTERNAL RESTRAINT THEORY   Henry and Short have proposed a theory that is rooted in psychoanalytic theory but that also takes into account certain social correlates.[21] By trying to view both homicide and suicide in a unified framework, they provide insights that go beyond the frustration-aggression and subcultural approaches. They state there are three major independent variables to be related in discussing homicide and suicide: 1) amount of frustration, 2) the "strength of a relational system," and 3) the "strength (degree) of external restraint." "Strength of the relational system" is defined as "involvement in social or cathetic relationships with other persons." [22] The relational system of the married is stronger than the relational system of the unmarried and stronger among rural people than among urban. "Strength of external restraint" is defined as the degree to which behavior is required to conform to the demands and expectations of other persons,[23] and varies inversely with position in the status hierarchy, that is, socioeconomic class system. With these definitions in mind, Henry and Short hypothesized:

1. Suicide varies inversely with the strength of the relational system and homicide varies positively with the strength of the relational system.[24]
2. Suicide varies negatively and homicide positively with the strength of external restraint over behavior.[25]

Thus, going back to the correlates of homicide, external restraint explains the greater homicide of males, nonwhites, the young, and the lower socioeconomic class, while strength of relational system explains the higher incidence of homicide in the South and in rural areas. Henry and Short found that the data available on marital status and homicide were too poor to draw any conclusions[26] because available data fail to distinguish between those who were single, widowed, and divorced and those who were married.[27] However, this hypothesis is significant in terms of the case to be discussed in this chapter, and may be valuable in explaining "normals" who commit murder (not explained by psychoanalytic or subcultural theory). That is, Henry and Short are proposing that the greater the degree of intimacy, the greater the potentiality for violent conflict, an assumption noted in the literature on conflict theory.

Sociological Theories

CONTAINMENT THEORY   The *social control* theory of Reckless is proposed as an alternative to the Henry and Short formulation.[28] Reckless proposes external containment or control and internal containment to explain violent behavior. "External containment" refers to the holding power of the group whereby society and particularly nuclear groups contain, steer, shield, divert, support, reinforce, and limit its members. External constraint is related to such factors as meaningfulness of roles, availability of supportive relationships conferring a sense of belonging and identity, and degree of isolation and homogeneity of culture, class, and population. High containment is found in folk societies and religious sects, such as the Jews, Quakers, Mennonites, and Amish. The Hutterites of North America, a communal Christian sect, is a case in point. Despite some evidence of mental disorder among the Hutterites and strong evidence of "themes of violence, murder, and stealing occurring in response to Thematic Apperception Tests for almost every Hutterite respondent who took these and other projective tests," these tendencies are not acted out overtly or directly. Antisocial behavior and violence are rare among Hutterites. Investigations have revealed no instances of murder, assault, or rape, and other types of physical aggressiveness are rare. Reckless attributes this lower level of overt aggression to the high level of external containment as shown in strong taboos against violence and childhood socialization against fighting.[29] Thus, among the Hutterites there is a strong relational system and strong external restraint, conditions Henry and Short link with high rates of homicide, and yet the Hutterites fail to show that form of aggression. Though this evidence calls Henry and Short's formulation into question, it may in fact be supportive of subcultural theory.

> For example, the absence of crime among the Hutterites can readily be redefined as allegiance to a *nonviolent* subculture, and psychological traits which result from subcultural allegiance can enter into the "behavior control system" of the individual.[30]

Reckless's implied rebuttal to subcultural and external restraint theories is found in his concept of "inner containment." Reckless and Dinitz have previously argued, contrary to subcultural and opportunity theories, that lower class boys who have a "good boy" or favorable self-concept will not engage in delinquent behavior (inner containment), despite situational or subcultural pressures. Inner containment represents the ability of the person to follow the expected norms, to direct himself.[31] In contemporary society with its diversity, mobility, impersonality, there is more reliance upon inner containment and less upon external containment. Inner containment is composed of essentially four components: favorable self-concept, orientation toward socially approved goals, tolerance of frustration, and retention of norms. Inner containment, in turn, is a direct corollary of attachment to primary groups such as the family and "effective reference groups." Thus, the explanation of homicide among the young, the poor, males, and residents of the inner-city and extreme rural areas can be found in containment. The young, the poor, males, and inner-city groups all can be found lacking in external containment. They also, due to breakdown in family and reference group ties, may be found weak in inner control. This helps to explain the low rates of homicide among the Japanese, the Chinese, the Scandinavians, the Dutch, and the Germans, whose transplanted members establish a high order of containment in the United States, despite past or present poverty. On the other hand, rural homicide (and high rates of Southern homicide) can be explained by the same dynamics as those of developing countries, in which "large segments of the people are emerging from a tribal or semi-tribal life, and weak outer containment must be added to the paradigm and a weak self must also be added." [32]

LABELING THEORY *Labeling* theory has not been frequently employed as an explanation specific to murder. Other sociological explanations that will be described have had minimal application.

One subcultural explanation has had considerable attention and "fits" with psychoanalytic theory. The key link, as mentioned earlier, is the multiple "selves" a person plays. A certain "self" may be invoked by others in particular situations.

SUBCULTURE OF VIOLENCE THEORY   One such "other self" that might emerge at times arises from what Wolfgang has termed the "subculture of violence." This is a subculture emerging especially among youthful, black, urban males (among whom, we have seen, murder rates are high), and this subculture has its own codes and characteristic set of beliefs and attitudes:

> A male is usually expected to defend the name and honor of his mother, the virtue of womanhood . . . and to accept no derogation about his race (even from a member of his own race), his age, or his masculinity. Quick resort to physical combat as a measure of daring, courage, or defense of status appears to be a cultural expression, especially for lower socio-economic class males of both races.[33]

In this subculture, personal assaults are not seen as wrong or antisocial, but in fact are socially approved and expected under some conditions. Wolfgang describes the subculture in psychoanalytic terms as a "collectivization of the id" whereby basic urges and impulses are less inhibited, needs are satisfied immediately, and social regulation is weak. They are several important hypotheses derived from this theory:

1. The greater the degree of integration of the individual into this subculture, the higher the likelihood that one's behavior will often be violent.[34]
2. There is a direct relationship between rates of homicide and the degree of integration of the subculture of violence.[35]
3. Persons not members of the subculture of violence who nonetheless commit crimes of violence have psychological and social attributes significantly different from violent criminals from the subculture of violence; i.e., violent criminal offenders from a culture of nonviolence have more psychopathological traits, more guilt, and more anxiety about their violent behavior.[36]
4. The development of favorable attitudes toward, and the use of, violence in a subculture usually involves learned behavior and a process of differential learning, association, or identification.[37]

Like psychoanalytic theory, the subcultural approach focuses upon the person whose socialization has freed him from ego or superego controls, although the subcultural theory also includes the possibility that normal superego and ego controls are countermanded by the subculture of violence, resulting in antisocial conduct (as opposed to presocial conduct) in which guilt is neutralized by participation in the subculture.

According to its authors, however, this theory is not formulated to explain the murder committed by a person who has not been exposed to the subculture of violence. However, the next theory, external restraint theory, does purport to explain such murders.

The "subculture of violence" theory could be supplemented by, or possibly substituted by, a more general "culture of violence" approach such as that described in Chapter 10. Thus, the total level of violence. in United States society, the degree of gun ownership, and the manner in which males are socialized as aggressors, within all socioeconomic and racial groups, may explain homicide by degree other than that given in hypothesis number 3 above.

DIFFERENTIAL ASSOCIATION THEORY   Both "subcultural" and "cultural" approaches have been complemented by explanations derived from *differential association theory*. Thus, an individual may "learn" violent behavior within the total culture to which he or she belongs as well as from individual subcultures. The differential association emphasis may explain (as it appeared to in the case of the rapist, Fred) the manner in which youngsters may learn to act violently as a result of childrearing practices.

ALIENATION THEORY   *Alienation* concepts and explanations derived from *anomie* theory have had minor application to homicide. We might theorize, however, that differing rates of homicide among lower socioeconomic groups and minorities can be explained by their degree of alienation caused by the economic system. Certainly, the discriminating use of the death penalty, cited earlier, would appear to favor explanations by conflict or alienation theorists. Anomie theory might explain those homicides that result from armed robberies or deaths resulting from white collar crimes as described in Chapter 9.

RICHARD:
A Murderer

In what respect any of these theories apply to our individual case remains to be seen. The following interview was taken in class from an ex-convict who had been convicted of assaulting his wife and murdering his three children on December 23, 1952. His self-analysis is very extensive and is that of a well-educated man. Our respondent, Richard, differs somewhat from the "typical murderer." He is Caucasian. At the time of his offense, he was middle-aged (thirty-nine), was employed in a middle class capacity as a teacher, and lived in a middle class neighborhood. Being an exception to many of the theories discussed above, this case may provide insights that will help shape or reshape the theories.

RICHARD: On December 23, 1952, after a year of estrangement from my wife—in a moment of madness—I took the lives of my three small children and almost destroyed my wife and myself.

My wife and children were my little world. When my wife withdrew her love and affection, when she rejected me again and again, my mind and energy over the months, night and day, were bent on getting her back. When, after attempting to please her, waiting, arguing with her, when my wife said things to me I could not stand to hear, and struck me—when this happened, I felt cut off with terrible finality, violated, betrayed, almost inundated with terror. I could no longer contain myself. It was as though something burst deep inside me. I felt impelled to destroy and did.

While I was attacking my wife, the children came screaming out of their bedroom and my violence was transferred from her to them. It was all over in a few seconds. The explosion into violence, the manner and means of it, what I did to myself afterwards (cut both wrists to the bone and severed my esophagus with a razor blade)—these were not the actions of a sane man. Emotional upheaval had transported me beyond a focus of awareness that included rational decision.

If the ambulance had arrived a few minutes later, I would not be here. At the county hospital, a team of surgeons worked hours to save my life and repair the damage done.

For five days I was given private nursing care around the clock. I could do nothing for myself. My hands and forearms were bound on boards to protect my wounded wrists. A tracheotomy had been done to permit me to breathe. Only my mother was permitted to visit me. I felt strange and frightened. Every time I opened my eyes, a nurse was there looking at me, waiting to care for me. I began to mend, to want to live.

After five days I was arraigned in municipal court and taken by the sheriff and two of his deputies to prison for safekeeping. The authorities there, I was told, would be able to provide medical care and protection not available in the county jail.

After five months at the prison I went to trial. There, after a month-long trial, the jury found me guilty of three counts of murder in the second degree and one count of assault with intent to commit murder.

The judge sentenced me to prison for the maximum sentence he could hand down: three five-to-life sentences and one one-to-fourteen to run consecutively. This meant sixteen years to life. Later these sentences were aggregated by state law to ten to life, which meant I became eligible for parole in three years and four months.

In my first two years at prison, I just put one foot in front of the other. The betting on the Big Yard was that I would commit suicide in the first years. Nights—after a hard workout in the gym on the top floor of an old building down in the alley—when I came out on the fire escape and looked five floors down to the pavement, it would have been very easy to have stepped off.

It was not until I was transferred to a medical facility that I began to find myself. There I had five years of individual and group therapy. Therapy there was much like that at Synanon—hard-driving, uncovering. For months I had diarrhea and difficulty in sleeping. But I learned some things.

I learned that quite early my mother communicated to me an unstated proposal that had far-reaching effects upon my life: "If you love me, you will do everything I want you to do because everything I want you to do is right and good and perfect; and if you do, I will love you above everyone."

She kept the promise—as long as she lived. Even after my offense, she treated me as though I were a god. In her eyes, I had been perfect: I accommodated to toilet and eating and language training earlier than children usually do. I measured up to her moral and social expectations. I became the all-American boy—a scholar, an athlete, a school and campus leader. I became a naval officer, a teacher and coach, a devoted husband and father. For thirty-nine years I lived entirely within the law. I fulfilled her expectations and she kept the promise.

With no father (my father was beaten to death with a hammer when I was six months old) to rescue me in my most vulnerable years, my obsession (to be loved by everyone as my mother loved me) and my compulsion (to qualify for that love by being perfect) took root.

To feel impelled to measure up to and to please others—to be always "right and good and perfect"—in order to feel right about yourself is a terrifying and precarious existence, and when you fail—catastrophic.

My wife and children were my little world—the principal people between me and the terrifying threat of isolation, failure, and self-doubt. Confronted with his threat, having no real identity, ridden with anxiety, dependent on those close to me for constant assurance of love and affection that would stave off anxiety and give me at least some feeling of self and security, it was imperative that I maintain my little world. I could not let it go, accept an altered version of it, or create another. I had to have it. I wanted, desired it so much that I struggled to obtain it until I drove myself beyond the edge of sanity.

In my fifteen years in prison, I refused to think of myself as a convict, an inmate, a number. I accepted responsibility for what I had done; but I fought tooth and toenail to maintain my identity as a person.

QUESTION: *With regard to the offense, homicide, would you say that the best sentence would be the shortest one, in other words, that jail is really not the answer for the person who has committed homicide?*

RICHARD: First of all, from the standpoint of risk, I believe the person who commits homicide is in about the 99 percentile as far as risks are concerned. This is extraordinarily high. About the length of incarceration after a person has committed an offense—of course, every offense and every murder is something different, it is an individual thing. A situational offense, such as mine was, many times is such that the victim is very close to the person who is doing the killing. I think that the important thing about murder, about any offense, is that we find some way in understanding the motivation of these offenses and that we deal with these motivations in a positive way, in a rehabilitative way. I think that probably, in my case, if I had been sent to a clinic or something like that, I believe that I would have had a lot better opportunity for treatment. I would have to learn about dealing with crime from the standpoint of understanding it and to create experiences which are going to be helpful to people.

QUESTION: *Do you feel there is any way, as you say your case was situational, that your actions could be due to your upbringing or your socialization process? Can this be predicted or expected to a certain degree?*

RICHARD: Yes, I was expected to live up to the image of the all-American boy, and people are very receptive when you act this way. I was really not expected to do this sort of thing. People must be able to project themselves in my situation and be able to identify with the condition I was dealing with at the time and my personality.

QUESTION: *Who would be qualified to make the judgment and make a prediction?*

RICHARD: I think that you people are looking in the direction of considering a situation such as this, perhaps among young friends. You might see somebody who is so compulsive and so obsessive and, who, as in the fashion that I was, needs to be loved by everyone. I think that you yourselves can begin to be aware of this and to recognize the damage of protection and then maybe you can make a diagnosis. This person feels the need to qualify for your love or attention, and you cannot reject this person. The attention should just be there in a relationship and that is how you concern yourself with him. If you spot somebody in such a terrible emotional state that there are irrational signs, then maybe you should consult somebody that knows more about it than you do. The point that I am trying to make here is that we need, in our education, a great deal more experience than we have had along these lines, and we need a great deal more awareness and we need to become involved and concern ourselves with what goes on around us.

QUESTION: *In the case of an assassination, is the theory that you look for a person who is kind of a loner true? It seems that all the descriptions attached to a potential offender seem to fit a lot of people. A lot of people would say that this could be just about anybody. Is there any other kind of trigger-type things that a person could look for—any kind of more particular thing, Another thing that occurred to me was that when you were describing your experiences, it sounded like quite a normal person. Do you consider yourself normal, and if so, is not everyone a potential murderer? And secondly, what do you consider to be the best theory?*

RICHARD: Those who assassinate a president, or some act similar, are usually using motivation with some kind of common denominator structure of motivation as far as they were concerned. I think there are a lot of people who are loners, but the real problem is with those who are paranoid with delusions of their goals of love and marriage and who are seriously disturbed and living in a zone of psychotic love. I think the thing that is abnormal about my own situation is that I became obsessed with everything I did and the purpose and way in which I bribed myself, which was to qualify for the love of other people—their appreciation, acceptance, and attention. I became completly carried away in this. But the thing I want to say is that what really causes crime, in regard to the examples of our assumptions and our conclusions, some people have had the education, training and experience, and perhaps the inclination, energy, or some other unknown factors in their personality that qualify them so that they are better decision-makers than most of us—they are innately endowed with this. We can draw the conclusion that because this assumption seems to be true, we want more of these kind of people making our decisions for us. The truth of the matter is that we grow and develop, by assuming responsibility for our successes and failures as well, and learn from them. If we advocate from this possibility of letting someone else do things here and here and here, we are in fault. We become dependent, and as a result, frustrated—we don't like ourselves or the world. I think we must examine our assumptions and conclusions all the way up and down the line. We have got to come up with assumptions and conclusions which are valid and erect new foundations, sociological, psychological, and etc. There are a thousand ways in which to do this and to build new foundations for criminal justice in relation to crime and delinquency. We have to start someplace, the way you people are trying to find out more about what is going on. You must have some kind of confidence in authority and you also want to arrive at some kind of self-authority.

THEORETICAL IMPLICATIONS AND COMMENTARY

The foregoing case seems to run contrary to most of the theories we have examined. In this case, we shall combine our comments and the apparent theoretical implications.

PSYCHOLOGICAL THEORIES First, in terms of the psychoanalytic model, Richard was the opposite of the presocial or psychopathic criminal who lacked sufficient ego or superego development. Thus, Richard would be viewed as one of the "unusual cases" of "acting-out neurotics" whose murder derives from exceptional situational factors. However, the fact that Richard is exceptional to the psychoanalytic framework calls it into question, both in terms of its predictive capacities and in its utility for understanding the phenomenon at hand. The criminal personality also does not apply to Richard.

SOCIAL-PSYCHOLOGICAL THEORIES   External restraint theory is somewhat difficult to apply, although it presents possibilities. External restraint was indicated, not in terms of occupational demands (which would be demands of a middle class occupation in this case), as the theory seems to postulate, but interpersonally in reference to Richard's relationship with his mother. Also, there was a strong relational system with his mother. However, the aggression was directed not toward his mother but toward his wife and children. And at the time of the murder, Richard was estranged from his wife rather than intimately involved with her. Thus, extending Henry and Short's analysis to Richard's case, there was a characteristic interpersonal malaise. His mother was primary in his life, though he at one time was very intimate with his wife and children. Intimacy with his mother was the basis of his need for perfection. He had internalized her requirements that he be "right and good and perfect." In adolescence, he had been the "all-American boy," competent as a scholar, athlete, school, and campus leader. He was even an overconformist in terms of violations of law. The demands and expectations of his mother were not the source of his frustration. The source was, instead, the deprivation and rejection of him by his wife. His strong conditioned need for love and his strong need for perfection were both contradicted by this rejection, and he chose the alternative of rejecting his rejector, rather than rejecting the internalized expectations of his mother.

Looking at containment theory, we find in this case both external and internal containment. Certainly in terms of his mother's expectations and his own self-expectations, the act of murder was not in line with being "right and good and perfect." This is a person with an exemplary history of inner containment, a "good boy," and a childhood of exterior containment. There is no basis for containment theory in this case.

SOCIOLOGICAL THEORIES   The subcultural approach is not apparent in this case, since Richard apparently had no exposure to the "subculture of violence" prior to his offense. In fact, the guilt Richard felt about his offense indicated his estrangement from the subculture of violence.

There appears to be little explanatory power in labeling, differental association, alienation, or anomie theories for Richard's murders.

Why, in the final analysis, did Richard commit the act of murder? It seems in this case that the murder involved an attempt to conform to perceived expectations of one's primary group. Paradoxically, though Richard's mother would not have approved of aggressive behavior, she instilled a value that in a particular situation made that aggressive behavior highly probable, and in fact, having carried out the act, it seems possible that Richard was emotionally rewarded by his mother for having removed the obstruction in his life acting as a barrier to the pursuit of her values—"Even after my offense she treated me as though I were a god." If there is any generality in this case, it may be that peer group or family norms figure into many or most murders in this way such that homicide is not an act set down by any subcultural norm, or an act always inhibited by the presence of strong norms against aggression, but is an act that occurs pursuant to primary group goals in situations where those goals are threatened. If this is true, then we should shift our focus in homicide theory to discovering what "incidents" occurring in specific situations come to be seen by prospective offenders as jeopardizing those primary group goals.

Richard's case calls into question the use of the death penalty as a deterrent in homicides. Richard was willing to take his own life following his murders. The threat of the state doing so, therefore, would not have deterred him. Likewise, with the support of his mother and others, Richard is now living a productive life. His death would have deprived society of his services. Given the spontaneity of Richard's actions in commission of his murders, there appears to be a valid argument for less availability of guns and other weapons.

QUESTIONS FOR DISCUSSION

1. Do you believe we have a "culture of violence" in the United States? Does the death penalty contribute to this atmosphere? Gun ownership? Abortion?
2. Discuss the impact of war on civilian behavior.
3. A number of students in the class at which he spoke felt that Richard should have spent the rest of his natural life in prison and should not now be free. Do you agree or disagree?
4. Do you think Richard will ever be able to live without suffering remorse?
5. Richard views himself as "obsessive-compulsive," a psychological disorder. What place would there be for such a disorder in the "culture of violence" perspective?
6. What changes in the *situation* of the murders would have prevented them from occurring, in your opinion?

RELATED READINGS

Bensing, Robert, and Schroeder, Oliver, Jr., *Homicide in an Urban Community* (Springfield, Ill.: Charles C. Thomas, 1960).

Bullock, Henry, "Urban Homicide in Theory and Fact," *Journal of Criminal Law, Criminology and Police Science*, 45 (1955), pp. 565–575.

Clark, Ramsey, *Crime in America* (New York: Simon and Schuster, 1970).

Curtis, Lynn A., *Violence, Race and Culture* (Lexington, Mass.: D. C. Heath, 1975).

Frankel, E., "One Thousand Murderers," *Journal of Criminal Law, Criminology and Police Science,* 29 (1938–1939), pp. 687–688.

Gibbs, Jack P., *Crime, Punishment and Deterrence* (New York: Elsevier, 1975).

Gold, Martin, "Suicide, Homicide, and the Socialization of Aggression," *American Journal of Sociology,* 63 (1958), pp. 651–661.

Henry, Andrew, and Short, James, Jr., *Suicide and Homicide* (New York: The Free Press, 1954).

Kleck, Gary, "Capital Punishment, Gun Ownership, and Homicide," *American Journal of Sociology,* 84 (January, 1979), pp. 882–910.

McClintock, F. H., *Crimes of Violence* (New York: St. Martin's Press, 1963).

Quinney, Richard, "Suicide, Homicide, and Economic Development," *Social Forces,* 43 (1965), pp. 401–406.

Reid, Sue Titus, "Punishment," in *Crime and Criminology,* 2nd ed. (New York: Holt, Rinehart and Winston, 1979), pp. 556–604.

Sellin, Thorsten, ed., *Capital Punishment* (New York: Harper and Row, 1967).

Waldo, Gordon, "The 'Criminality Level' of Incarcerated Murderers and Non-Murderers," *Journal of Criminal Law, Criminology and Police Science,* 61 (1970), pp. 60–70.

Wilson, James Q., *Thinking About Crime* (New York: Vintage Books, 1975).

Wolfgang, Marvin, *Patterns in Criminal Homicide* (Philadelphia: University of Pennsylvania Press, 1958).

Wolfgang, Marvin, and Ferracuti, Franco, *The Subculture of Violence* (London: Social Science Paperbacks, Tavistock Publications, 1967).

≡ NOTES

1. Herbert Bloch and Gilbert Geis, *Man, Crime, and Society* (New York: Random House, 1970), p. 225.

2. Erich Goode, *Deviant Behavior: An Interactionist Approach* (Englewood Cliffs, N.J.: Prentice-Hall, Inc., 1978), pp. 404–405.

3. Marvin Wolfgang, *Studies in Homicide* (New York: Harper and Row, 1967), pp. 274–275.

4. Robert Winslow, *Crime in the Free Society* (Encino, Calif.: Dickenson Publishing Co., 1968), pp. 58–59.

5. Andrew Henry and James Short, Jr., *Suicide and Homicide* (New York: The Free Press, 1954), p. 15.

6. Block and Geis, *Man, Crime, and Society,* p. 229.

7. Goode, *Deviant Behavior,* pp. 406–411.

8. Ibid., pp. 411–412.

9. Ibid., p. 412.

10. Ibid., pp. 407–411; Sue Titus Reid, *Crime and Criminology,* 2nd ed. (New York: Holt, Rinehart and Winston, 1979), pp. 291–292.

11. Reid, *Crime and Criminology,* pp. 566–591.

12. Ramsey Clark, *Crime in America* (New York: Simon and Schuster, 1970), p. 337.

13. James Q. Wilson, *Thinking About Crime* (New York: Vintage Books, 1975), p. 221.

14. Thorsten Sellin, *Capital Punishment* (New York: Harper and Row, 1967), pp. 135–160.

15. Jack P. Gibbs, *Crime, Punishment and Deterrence* (New York: Elsevier, 1975).

16. *Furman* v. *Georgia*, 408 U.S. 238, 371 (1972).

17. President's Commission on Law Enforcement and Administration of Justice, *Task Force Report: The Courts* (Washington, D.C.: U.S. Government Printing Office, 1967), p. 28.

18. Gary Kleck, "Capital Punishment, Gun Ownership and Homicide," *American Journal of Sociology*, 84 (January, 1979), p. 908.

19. Robert Winslow, *Society in Transition: A Social Approach to Deviancy* (New York: The Free Press, 1970), p. 133.

20. Samuel Yochelson and Stanton E. Samenow, *The Criminal Personality, Vol. I: A Profile for Change* (New York: Jason Aronson, 1976).

21. Henry and Short, *Suicide and Homicide*.

22. Ibid., p. 16.

23. Ibid., p. 17.

24. Ibid., p. 16.

25. Ibid., p. 17.

26. Ibid., p. 91.

27. Ibid., p. 95.

28. Walter Reckless, *The Crime Problem* (New York: Appleton-Century-Crofts, 1967).

29. Ibid., p. 473.

30. Marvin Wolfgang and Franco Ferracuti, *The Subculture of Violence* (London: Tavistock Publications, 1967), p. 146.

31. Reckless, *The Crime Problem*, p. 475.

32. Ibid., p. 479.

33. Wolfgang and Ferracuti, *The Subculture of Violence*, p. 275.

34. Wolfgang, *Studies in Homicide*, p. 274.

35. Ibid.

36. Wolfgang and Ferracuti, *The Subculture of Violence*, p. 315.

37. Ibid., p. 314.

The Victim

12

Victimology, the study of victims of crime and deviance, has developed rapidly in recent years. Previously, such investigation was confined mainly to the statistical analysis of rates of victimization by various demographic characteristics and by relationship to the offender. The feminist movement has sparked an interest in the role of the victim during the interactive situation in which rape occurs. In turn, this discussion has been reflected in the study of other crimes as well. While theoretical frameworks are somewhat rudimentary at this stage, there is an increasing volume of knowledge available. It is most appropriate that we consider the victim at this point in our format, which first viewed victimless deviant acts, then activities involving victims. In the course of our analysis, we will learn why the victim is often considered a "deviant." Because the greatest volume of literature and research has been geared to the specific study of rape victims, we will examine these victims, in particular, in our general study of victimology.

WHO ARE THE VICTIMS?

Potentially, all of us are victims of crime and deviance. In fact, the legal viewpoint is that the total public is the victim of crime.[1] Thus, we have the terms "the people versus . . . ," and "the state versus. . . ." This basic concept of the victim within law is responsible to a considerable degree for the manner in which victims are treated within the justice system. In addition to the legal sense, large numbers of us are victims of such white collar crimes as price-fixing, deceptive advertising, fraud, and so on. However, some individuals are more likely to be specific victims of certain crimes than are others. Rates of victimization give us an idea of what types of persons these are likely to be. The characteristics of victims and the circumstances in which they place themselves are what Amir terms "risk factors." [2]

The President's Commission on Law Enforcement and the Administration of Justice authorized a nationwide survey of victimization. The commission, in 1967, summarized some of the factors in victimization as follows:

Thus, the findings from the national survey show the risk of victimization is highest among the lower income groups for all Index offenses except homicide, larceny, and vehicle theft; it weighs most heavily on the non-whites for all Index offenses except larceny; it is borne by men more often than women, except, of course, for forcible rape; and the risk is greatest for the age category 20–29, except for larceny against women, and burglary, larceny, and vehicle theft against men.[3]

The commission noted, and other studies have confirmed, that most violent crimes (homicide, assault, and rape) are committed against persons known to the offender and frequently against a close friend or relative. Studies indicate that, in these three categories of violent crime, the percentage of victims who were drinking prior to being victimized is comparable to that of offenders[4] (whose use was cited in earlier chapters). Typically, the victim was drinking with the offender prior to the commission of the act. Crimes against the person are usually committed by persons of the same race as the victim and near the home of the offender. Crimes against property, however, are more likely to be interracial and occur at or near the home of the victim.[5]

Thus, a "typical" victim of a violent act is likely to be a young, nonwhite male from a lower income group. He is likely to be victimized by someone close to him socially after drinking with the offender in his own home or neighborhood. The "typical" rape victim, naturally, differs by sex. She is less likely than the murder victim to be acquainted with and the same race as her attacker, but more likely than the robbery victim to be acquainted with and the same race as her attacker.[6]

These typical patterns of risk vary from the *perception of risk* of large numbers of individuals.[7] For instance, the elderly are the least likely to be victimized for most crimes. However, due to their physical vulnerability and isolation, the elderly tend to fear crime more than others.[8] Other findings indicate that the perceptions of potential victimization by the public leads to an increasing fear and changes in attitude and behavior.[9] Based on many discussions we have had with convicts and ex-offenders, it is likely that the more fear shown by a potential victim in a situation, the more likely the person is of being victimized and of being harmed more seriously. Thus, we may speculate that the increased fear of victimization may contribute to a "self-fulfilling prophecy" when some individuals are confronted with a provoking situation. A result could be a crime being committed that might not have been otherwise or more serious injury inflicted than might have been the case.

THE ROLE OF THE VICTIM: "Victim-Precipitation" or "Male-Intimidation"?

The closeness of victims to offenders, the alcohol involvement in the situation, and displays of fear are elements mentioned above that have combined with other factors to serve as a focus of debate concerning the role of the victim in crime provocation. The controversy has centered upon the role of the rape victim, but some aspects apply equally as well to many other crimes. Menachem Amir interprets the data as "victim precipitation."[10] Susan Brownmiller, in her book *Against Our Will*, views all rape as a part of the subjugation of women and "male intimidation."[11]

Amir states that the choice of victim in rape is "no accident."[12] He claims that the choice of victim is made by the offender but that only certain individuals are likely to be victims and that the choice depends upon certain "risk factors."[13] Amir cites the psychoanalytic literature to point to the psychology of some women who may "wish to be raped" as a feminine tendency toward passivity.[14] Some females may alleviate anxiety and guilt through rape, others may see it as a pleasurable event or a "liberating experience," and some young girls of "lower class origins" may be "if not actually seductive, at least unconscious participants in the rape event" in order to give themselves "false sense of protection, attention, and status."[15] Additionally, just as adolescent boys use sex to achieve status, adolescent girls use it to enhance their popularity and appeal and to liberate themselves from home.[16] Some also may have a "bad" reputation.[17] These individual characteristics then enter into the interrelationship between victim and offender behavior in the social situation surrounding the rape.

Amir has drawn a "typology of victim behavior" that "assumes interrelationships and graduated interaction before and during the initial encounter between victim and offender."[18] The typology includes victim behavior that is "unsoliciting" (or purely accidental), that which is "precipitative" (through exposure to vulnerable or risk situations), and that which is "seductive" (either through conscious participation or through unconscious "victim proneness.")[19] Amir does not attempt to detail all situations and behavior that may occur. However, he claims that the victim's behavior may be "acts of commission (e.g., she agrees to drink or ride with a stranger) and omission (e.g., she fails to react strongly enough to sexual suggestions and overtures)."[20] Whether the person acts passively or actively, the interpretation by and interplay with the offender may lead him to exploit her.[21]

Amir compared "victim-precipitated" rapes and "nonvictim-precipitated" rapes in Philadelphia in 1958 and 1960 by using statements from police files, witnesses, and offenders. He defined "victim-precipitation" as:

> ...those rape situations in which the victim actually, or so it was deemed, agreed to sexual relations but retracted before the actual act or did not react strongly enough when the suggestion was made by the offender(s). The term applies also to cases in risky situations marred with sexuality, especially when she uses what could be interpreted as indecency in language and gestures, or constitutes what could be taken as an invitation to sexual relations.[22]

Amir found that 19 percent (122) of the 646 forcible rapes officially reported could be verified as fitting the above definition.[23] Victim-precipitated rapes differed from nonvictim-precipitated rapes in that they tended to involve victims who were white, between the ages of fifteen nineteen, had had "bad" reputations, and were related to, close friends of, or neighbors of the offender.[24]

The legal system has traditionally taken into account "victim-precipitation" in rape cases to the extent that reputation and degree of consent of the victim have been admissible as a defense.[25]

While Susan Brownmiller agrees with many of Amir's findings and those of other sociologists,[26] she disagrees as to why women may behave in a situation in the manner in which they do and the degree to which rape is nonvictim-precipitated. She disagrees strongly with a Freudian-oriented criminology that would picture the rapist as a "psychopath" who has a "disease."[27] Brownmiller maintains that such statements as "All women want to be raped," "No woman can be raped against her will," and "She was asking for it" are "deadly male myths" that most men believe and have used to convince women that they are willing participants.[28] Two factors are perhaps crucial to the Brownmiller argument. First, there is her definition of rape, which differs from the legal definition:

If a woman chooses not to have intercourse with a specific man and the man chooses to proceed against her will, that is a criminal act of rape.[29]

Thus, Brownmiller excludes the defenses of initial consent, contributory provocation, degree of resistance, lack of penetration, and marital relationship.[30]

Secondly, the Brownmiller argument hinges upon her concept of "male power" and the manner in which it has been utilized throughout history. Initial social order began when males discovered their genital organs and the manner in which they could be used to subjugate women who *"could not retaliate in kind."* [31] Brownmiller states:

> Man's discovery that his genitalia could serve as a weapon to generate fear must rank as one of the most important discoveries of prehistoric times, along with the use of fire and the first crude stone axe. From prehistoric times to the present, I believe, rape has played a critical function. It is nothing more or less than a conscious process of intimidation by which *all men* keep *all women* in a state of fear.[32]

From this assumption, Brownmiller traces the manner in which women have been subjugated to the power and authority of men based upon their fear of rape. She cites numerous historical incidents across several cultures to demonstrate her point. For instance, she notes how women have been utilized as booty and "rewards of battle" during war and times of riot and revolution.[33] She states that rape was a weapon utilized in subjugating Indians and black slaves in the early days of America.[34] Male power, moreover, has been employed to further increase their authority through laws, institutions,[35] and, most importantly, in the consciousness of women who have become "trained" to be victims of rape.[36] Thus, according to Brownmiller, what is termed "victim-precipitation" by others, is the result of a conscious effort by males to socialize females into a role in which they desire to become sex objects, adopt "passive-masochistic" attitudes, and engage in "conscious" and "subconscious" rape fantasies.[37] Homosexual rape in prison is an exercise of power against those who appear or act feminine, while sexual abuse of children is an act by an authority figure expressing power over his victim.[38]

Brownmiller proposes legislation that would cover all sexual assaults, be "genderless," include rape in marriage, and vary penalties according to the severity of injury inflicted and threat employed. She advocates the certainty of prison as a deterrent to rape.[39] Some states have incorporated various aspects of such proposals within their laws before and since the publication of Brownmiller's book.[40]

Other forms of crime have also been identified as having elements of victim-precipitation. Criticism has been made but in a different tone than that of Brownmiller. The National Commission on the Causes and Prevention of Violence defined victim-precipitation separately for various crimes, as follows:

In criminal homicide: when the victim was the first to use physical force against the subsequent slayer.

In aggravated assault: when the victim was the first to use either physical force or insinuating language, gestures, etc., against the attacker.

In armed robbery and unarmed robbery: temptation-opportunity situations in which the victim clearly had not acted with reasonable self-protective behavior in handling money, jewelry, or other valuables . . . e.g., a robbery victim flashes a great deal of money at a bar and then walks home alone along a dark street late at night.[41]

Utilizing these definitions in a seventeen-city survey, the commission found evidence of victim-precipitation at the following rates:[42]

Homicide	22%
Assault	14.4%
Armed Robbery	10.7%
Unarmed Robbery	6.1%

Wolfgang hypothesizes that victim-precipitated homicide may be a form of suicide.[43] Curtis notes that the extent of victim-precipitation in violent crimes among certain groups may actually be what is viewed as "normal" behavior within a "violent contraculture," as when a young black carries a knife and gets into fights.[44] Other studies have pointed to a degree of victim-precipitation in data that indicate a high proportion of victims of violent crime had been arrested either prior to or concurrent with the crime in question.[45]

Ryan, in his book *Blaming the Victim*, takes exception to such viewpoints. He points to the misleading nature of official crime data, the fact that the definition of crime does not include white collar crime, and the lack of enforcement activity directed toward organized crime—considering each of these factors as part of an ideology of "victim blaming."[46] This ideology leads to the greater chance of arrest among lower income groups and their likelihood of conviction. According to Ryan, it ignores such law violations as that of the slum landlord who violates building codes and other expoitations of the poor.[47] Thus, the true victims of crime are blamed for what becomes defined as "crime" in an "ideological warfare against the poor in the interest of maintaining the *status quo.*"[48]

The issue of victim-precipitation thus allows us to better understand why the victim of crime may be considered a "deviant."

IS THE VICTIM A DEVIANT?

Most of us would not ordinarily list a victim of crime if asked to name types of individuals considered to be deviant. However, the above discussion suggests that some victims of crime may be labeled as deviants. The proximity of the victim to the criminal, the alcohol use involved in many crimes, and the degree of lack of resistance or presumption of precipitation, all contribute to interactions that may stigmatize the victim. Within a labeling perspective, the stigma may be effective given the relative lack of power of those most likely to become victims: the young, the nonwhite, the poor, and those from "high-crime" areas.

Indeed, there is evidence that victims of crime are frequently treated harshly within the process of criminal justice. This appears to be particularly true in the case of the rape victim. The treatment includes that rendered by the medical profession. The victim becomes a "witness," a piece of "evidence." [49] The basis appears to rest in the concept, of "victim" in common law. The victim in our judicial system is not an individual but the state.[50] Ziegenhagen has traced the development of this concept in Western tradition as commensurate with the trend away from traditional, kinship-oriented, *Gemeinschaft* society to the modern, industrialized, *Gesellschaft* society.[51] In earlier communities, justice was administered by the individual victim and/or the kinship network. The aims were retribution, vengeance, and punishment as a means of social control. As social differentiation increased, the role of social control gradually shifted from the individual to the larger group. The aim of social control became increasingly oriented toward rehabilitation and restoration of the social order, rather than individual restitution.[52] As a result, the individual victim's role became that of "reporter" of the crime to the state and "witness" within the judicial process. Except in these roles, the victim no longer has a say in the process of social control. Indeed, the individual is only a "presumptive" victim until a conviction is made. Although there are some data to indicate that the social class, demeanor, race, and sex of the victim do have an influence upon judges and juries, the victim is removed from direct participation in plea bargaining or determining the severity of sentence. Thus, victims are simply "resources" for the prosecution to draw upon and such "resources" are often of less value if they belong to the lower strata or minority groups. The prosecutor is not responsible to the individual victim, but to those who have power within the community or society. This further weakens the input of lower socioeconomic groups and minorities.[53]

Given this system, and the presumptions that the victim "brought it on" himself or herself, the victim of crime becomes an "object" or "thing" to be utilized as evidence. Complaints have arisen of maltreatment by police who are attempting to "get the facts," to push for the pressing of charges, and to initially determine the honesty of the victim as a witness.[54] Other reactions have arisen in response to treatment by physicians and hospital personnel. These professionals are required to play a dual role. On the one hand, they are to treat the victim for whatever physical (and psychological) injury may have been inflicted. On the other hand, usually with police officers waiting nearby, they are required to serve as "detectives" who must gather evidence about which they may be later required to testify in court.[55] In the case of the rape victim, they must obtain a medical and sex history, examine the vagina for evidence of sperm and pubic hair, and frequently gather the victim's clothing and hair samples for additional evidence. Furthermore, they may be required to determine the degree of intoxication and the mental state of the victim as well as prescribe medication and follow-up treatment of possible venereal disease, infections, and pregnancy.[56] All of this is usually accomplished in a busy emergency room by personnel previously unknown to the victim.

Finally, the victim is required to prepare for trial and to undergo a public court proceeding in which the defense attorney attempts to build a case of "reasonable doubt" by cross-examination concerning the degree of consent involved and one's behavior prior to the incident, including alcohol use and past sexual or other personal history.[57] Often the victim undergoes a severe psychological trauma during this time. This is known as the "rape trauma" in the case of rape victims.[58] As a result, work patterns and family relationships are disrupted. Frequently, those closest to a victim react negatively and suspiciously at a time when the victim is in strong need of primary group support.[59]

The evidence seems clear, then, that the reactions to victims within the totality of the existing social system are often negative and stigmatizing rather than positive and sympathetic. The labeling and interactionist perspective appears to apply. The "spoiled woman" image of the rape victim and the "you asked for it" attitude toward victims in general operate within this context. Let us now review the applicability of some other theories before reviewing the case history of one rape victim.

THEORIES

For the most part, what has been said above already places the victim within several theoretical frameworks. We will, therefore, only briefly point out the general explanations that apply. In several instances, we will refer to material previously mentioned.

Biological Theories

There have been attempts to explain the victim within the same physiological frameworks as used for criminals. Thus, some have offered explanations of body types, genes, and cranial cavities to describe the behavior of the victim as similar to that of the offender.[60] It appears to us that these theories are offered in the presumptive context of victim-precipitation within violent contracultures. Such speculation seems unverified. Perhaps a more simple set of explanations is in order. This would take into account the physical size, bearing, and attractiveness of the victim that might explain interactions with the offender who chooses a victim within a particular social situation.

Psychological Theories

The major psychological factors involved in victimization have been outlined above in the discussion of Amir's model. These include the passivity-masochism of females as derived from Freudian theory, the use of sex for popularity and freedom, as well as the alleviation of guilt. Passive-masochistic explanations have also been advanced to explain the personality of victims in general. Others state that victims are feebleminded, lonely, or lethargic.[61] Ball has designed a model that is built around "frustration-instigated" behavior, which does not take into account the consequences of one's actions. This behavior may take the form of "aggression," which provokes the reaction of victimization; "regression," which may result either in harm to oneself directly or in rendering oneself vulnerable to others; or "resignation," which relies upon fate so that members of groups (such as those in the lower economic strata) allow themselves to be exploited as victims rather than fighting back to change their situation.[62]

Sociological Theories

In addition to Amir's typology combining both social and psychological variables, there are other interactionist explanations of victimization in sociology. This is probably due to the nature of victim as a concept that necessarily implies an interacting "other," the offender. With little additional comment, we may refer to the process by which the potential victim is defined by the offender as one of "*labeling.*" Similarly, it is a *labeling* process described above by which the victim becomes defined or treated as a "deviant." In many ways, the "blaming the victim" perspective of Ryan is essentially that of *confict theory* or an *alienation* concept. The Brownmiller view employs the *alienation* approach in the manner in which women are treated as objects by male-dominated society as well as the *differential association* approach whereby females are socialized into specific sex roles and modes of behavior. Although such concepts are not stated explicitly by Ryan or Brownmiller, they seem to be implied, as is *differential association* in those explanations that emphasize the manner in which victims have "learned" to behave and react within various strata of society. Merton's *anomie* concept is embodied, to a degree, within some subcultural theories that will be mentioned shortly. The Durkheimian concept of *anomie* (a condition in which the usual norms do not fit the situation) is perhaps indicated in the change of the victim's role from *Gemeinschaft* to *Gesellschaft*. This concept may also be evident in the current call for revision of laws dealing with sexual assault and victim compensation. An *opportunity* concept is evident in the debate concerning victim-precipitation, in that the victim is seen as providing the opportunity for the crime to be committed.

Two sociological frameworks deserve more detailed attention and have been advanced specifically to explain the role of the victim. A subcultural approach has been offered by Wolfgang and expanded upon by Curtis. Social control has had considerable application as a framework for understanding the victim's role.

SUBCULTURE OF VIOLENCE THEORY   The *subculture of violence,* as set forth by Wolfgang,[63] has been described in earlier chapters, particularly Chapter 11. The interacting role of the victim in this subculture is one of precipitating an attack by acting in a learned, violent manner. Wolfgang has suggested that homicides in this context may actually be "provoked suicides," [64] as mentioned earlier, but Curtis suggests that what may be viewed as victim-precipitation to an "outsider" of black ghetto life may be considered "normal" behavior within that subculture.[65] In the case of rape, the black ghetto subculture sets up a different pattern of interaction between black females and black males than it does within black-white contexts. A black female attempts to keep sexual activity under control but miscommunications with the black male and his superior physical strength may lead to her exploitation. The initial interactions differ outside this subculture and are less likely to result in a misinterpretation of the victim's willingness to engage in intercourse.[66]

SOCIAL CONTROL THEORY   *Social control* approaches to victimization appear to include the interactionist perspective of victim-precipitation by Amir as well as the "changing role of the victim" explanation by Ziegenhagen. Both of these perspectives were addressed earlier. Brodsky examined the possible reactions of potential rape victims that might serve as a "deterrent" or agent of social control. Role-played videotaped sequences of potential rape situations were shown to convicted rapists. The responses of the victims in the sequences were rated by the rapists as to their deterrent effect. The results varied according to the type of potential assailant. In general, the most successful methods of resistance were verbal attacks and discouragements, establishment of an interpersonal liaison, and arousal of sympathy.[67]

Other studies have compared rape victims with victims in attempted rape cases. Those women who successfully resisted rape differed from those who had not in that they were more suspicious initially, panicked less, considered methods of resistance, employed stronger forms of verbal resistance, were more assertive physically, and were more likely to scream.[68] It would appear that the results of this more current research might be utilized to expand the Amir typology to a more extensive theoretical framework that would specify the types of interactions between various potential victims and offenders. If this were incorporated within Amir's "unsoliciting" category of victim, a model of social control might result that could more clearly separate this category from the "precipitative" and "seductive" types. The model might be further expanded to incorporate the macro level concepts of Ziegenhagen.

Our rape victim informant will allow us to examine further the issues of social control, victim-precipitation, and labeling. The interactions surrounding her rape and subsequent treatment are revealing and somewhat dramatic.

MOLLY:
A Rape Victim

Molly is 21, white, and middle class. She is presently a graduate student in Social Work at Virginia Commonwealth University in Richmond, Virginia. She was raped eighteen months prior to her appearance in our class. At the time of the rape, Molly was a student at the University of Virginia in Charlottesville. She was accompanied by Cindy, of ROAR (Richmond Organization Against Rape), an organization headquartered at the local YWCA. Molly appeared to be extremely nervous at the beginning of her presentation, but relaxed as the discussion ensued.

MOLLY: I'm kind of nervous, so I really want you to help me out. I just want to try to remind you that it's really informal. This is something that's really important to me and I'd like to share it with you, but I am nervous, so keep that in mind. Two years ago, I was a student at the University of Virginia. I was living in Charlottesville in an apartment complex that was surrounded by fraternities. We were feeling real close. I was living with my boyfriend at the time and he was working at an all-night grocery store that was just down the corner from where we were living. At five o'clock in the morning, he was to get off of work and I was to pick him up. When I went to the store, he wasn't there. I came back home and I had been gone somewhere between three and five minutes. When I walked back in the door, a light went off in the bathroom and I assumed it was him. I went over to the bathroom and said, "Hello, how're you doing?" And there wasn't any answer. Then I started thinking, "Maybe I didn't see a light. It was just a flash." I thought that maybe I was just not paying attention. So I stood there for a while and I looked into the bathroom. It was all dark and I still couldn't see anything. I started getting nervous and then I started panicking.

I'm sure everybody's been through that kind of experience where you think you see something and you're kind of afraid, but it's just your imagination playing tricks on you. So I just stood there for a while, and then I saw what I thought to be the outline of an arm and I just froze. I didn't know what to do. So, finally, I couldn't wait. I didn't know what to do! I thought that maybe it was a robe hanging on the door or something. I just went toward the door and I pushed on it and a man jumped out at me with a knife in his hand. I just froze! I was paralyzed! The only way I can describe it was that I was in complete shock! My body went numb! My head went numb! I was sort of convulsing. I was just going, "Oh, God! Oh, my God!", and I was just shaking! He came up behind me and put his hand over my mouth and the knife to my throat. We went around the apartment and he turned off all the lights. I don't think he was wanting to hurt me at that point, but he wasn't aware, first of all, that he was smothering me. I was having a hard time breathing. He was sticking a knife in my throat, kind of jabbing it. So I was shaking and I was panicking. I was doing all kinds of things and feeling like I was going to blackout. So then I tried to talk to him a little bit. You know, saying "What do you think? What are you doing? Why are you here?" And he asked me if I had any money and I felt like saying, "Take my stereo and get get out of here! I don't care! Take anything!" But I didn't have any money. I didn't have anything there. He was looking for drugs too. That's one of the reasons he was in the bathroom. So that didn't work.

I kept asking him to leave. I told him my boyfriend was coming home soon and he really needed to go. My knees, at that point, started really doing a dance of their own. He got mad and said, "What's wrong with you?" And I said, "My God, I'm afraid!" And he said, "I'm afraid too." Then he asked me to take my pants off. At that point, I was really afraid. I knew what was coming and I was just angry and I was so pissed off! I blurted out something I kind of regret later on, because you think about those kinds of things, but you really don't know how dangerous a situation you're in until afterwards. I was *so* mad! I said, "I can't believe you're doing this! I can't believe this!" I started yelling at him. Then, the next thing you know, he's poking a knife in my throat and he's saying, "Shut up! I know what you're doing. It doesn't work." So I started getting afraid again. That's when the rape took place.

The hardest thing for me was feeling like I was going to die. Because, like I said, my boyfriend was coming home any minute. He just worked down the street, and he was late, and my fear was that he was going to walk in the door, and here's this guy raping me, the guy was going to freakout, and just go "slash!" That was the hardest thing to cope with at that time. I was just going, "Oh, my God! I'm going to die! I am going to die!" After the rape was over, he told me to get in the bathroom. I walked into the bathroom and I came back out again in a couple of seconds. He was still there. He lunged at me with the knife. It freaked me out! So I closed the door and I locked it. I just stayed there for a couple of minutes and, when I came back out again, he was gone.

Not even a minute later, my boyfriend walked in the door. I just sort of held onto him and I started shaking. I was afraid to say exactly what had happened because I didn't want to say the word "rape." I just sort of fumbled around and I said, "I think, I think I've been raped." We decided to go immediately to the hospital. I think it's important to understand how victims are affected. This has a lot to do with it. First of all, the kind of person they are beforehand. Just, you know, their personality, what kind of strengths and weaknesses you have. Then, also, it really has to do with circumstances about the rape itself. I know many women that have been cut and slashed and strangled, and they have a lot more to deal with afterwards than I did. I was very, very lucky. I didn't go into the hospital with physical wounds. I really think that has a lot to do with the circumstances. So, for me, I had been lucky.

I guess maybe I'll talk about the short-term kinds of things first. When I went to the hospital, I got the feeling that most people there expect you to be kind of freaked-out. They're looking for a show. They're looking for something like crying and screaming, or carrying-on, some kind of catatonic state. That's not my personality. That's not the way I work. When I went into the hospital, I was trying so hard to forget what had happened that my way of dealing with that was to watch other people and how they were dealing with it. So I forgot myself and started looking at other people. It was very interesting. At one point, at the hospital, there were nine people in this private room with me: three nurses, one male nurse, a couple of interns, a doctor, a policeman—all kinds of people. It was like a zoo. All these people were just staring at me and watching me. There was one nurse that stood in the very corner and wouldn't do anything. She was completely freaked-out by what had happened. She just stood in the corner going, "Oh, you can't even be safe in your own home anymore!" She just stood there doing this the whole time and saying, "What are you doing?" The doctor was very pissed off that he had to deal with me, because he knew that he was going to have to go through court proceedings and all that stuff, so he was very rough. When they do the kit, they have to take hair samples and other kinds of specimens for prosecution. He was coming in and out. It took him about an hour and a half to do it. He'd do a little bit, and then he'd come back in and say, "Well, I have to do something else." And I'm suffering, you know. It's not my fault.

I guess you all know that rape is a crime against the state, so the state has to prosecute. In order for that to happen, you have to go to the hospital. If you don't, they won't even take it. It was necessary for me to be there. I felt pretty strongly that I wanted to carry it through and see something done. I kind of felt like I should have been treated a little bit better at the hospital by everybody around. Like I said, I wasn't crying. I wasn't carrying on. I was getting into other people. The one thing I was not understanding about was that the one person I brought with me for support and some companionship was not allowed to be in there with me. The policeman sent my boyfriend off to get coffee. They sent him off somewhere else. I said, "Wait a minute! He's the one that understands! He's the one that can help me out the most through all this." But I think that the worst thing that happened, especially with the doctor, had to do with prescriptions. He came in to me at the very end of the whole test they gave me and threw two prescriptions at me and said, "Here, take these." I said, "What are they?" He said, "Just take them. You need them." He walked out. There was a woman with me that was working as a volunteer, much the same as ROAR. She was working with some kind of crisis thing and she had been my friend. I called her to come with me. She said,

> You need to know some more about that stuff. First of all, it's some kind of "morning after" pill. You have to take it twice a day for five days and it makes you violently ill. If you don't want to get pregnant, that's one avenue to take, but it is dangerous. There's also some sort of linkage to incidents of uterine cancer to daughters of women who take this medication.

The doctor had just given me a prescription for this and said, "Take it." So we called him back in and I said, "Now, what's the story here? I'm not sure I want to. I have to go back to work. I have other things to do. I can't take five days out of my life to be violently ill. I'll have a lot to deal with anyway." He looked at me and said, "Do you want a black man's child? Take the pill!"

I went to the police station after that. They were pretty good. They were giving me coffee and all kinds of things. They had rounded up a whole bunch of guys to go through lineups. Lineups are hard to go through. You're looking at a whole bunch of men. Among other things they do, they have you behind a door and they crack the door a little bit and they have each one of the men come up to the door and whisper something to you about what was said during the rape. That freaked me out. That was hard to do. Each one of them would come up to the door and say, "Get into the bathroom." That was very hard to do. Other than that, I pretty much kept my cool. I was pretty reserved and together. People were questioning me, "Well, did you really get raped? She's not flipping out. What's the matter?"

After I went to the police station, they let me come home. Immediately, within the next couple of days, I was having problems. It's a hard thing to go through. I think victims of any kind of a violent crime, because rape isn't a sexual thing, but a very violent act of aggression, these victims have a hard time. I was having a hard time sleeping. I went for seventy-two hours without sleeping. I was afraid to go to sleep. I was afraid to wake up. I didn't want to lose contact. I just couldn't. I also couldn't take showers. I couldn't be in the apartment by myself. When my boyfriend would be at work and I needed to go into the apartment, I would go get somebody from down the hall and ask them to go into my apartment with me. They'd come and beat the curtains. I know they thought it was kind of silly, but I couldn't help it. My whole sense of independence and privacy had been violated. I was afraid, very afraid. That went on, actually, that kind of stuff still goes on for me a little bit. I have a hard time walking into empty apartments.

The man that raped me was convicted of two other rapes and one attempted rape. They took us to court all in one day. So I had an opportunity to talk to the other women that he attacked. We all sort of went through the same kind of things. One woman wouldn't be by herself at all. She had her sister stay with her all the time. It creates a lot of problems, because you're just so helpless with all the insecurities. You're kind of on the edge of crying all the time. I wasn't alone in that. Most of the other women he attacked, he came into their apartments while they were asleep. They woke up with him sitting on their chests. I am really glad that didn't happen to me, because I know that would have been a harder thing to deal with. The women that did have that problem. They were having a hard time going to sleep. That's a pretty freaky kind of thing. Anyway, I guess what I'm trying to get across is that it's a hard thing to deal with. I had to eventually go and find a doctor that would give me a prescription for some sleeping pills. When you're awake for seventy-two hours, you're acting weird and you're crazy. You need the sleep. Your body needs it. That was hard to get through. I also had a hard time talking to other people. It was always on my mind. People would ask me, "What's wrong with you?" I thought, "My God, I've been raped! I've been through this awful experience! Somebody feel sorry for me! Somebody help me!"

I hadn't told my parents about it. I didn't want them to know, because I was afraid something would happen with living with my boyfriend and I figured that they'd do something. I didn't have that kind of support. I felt kind of alone in that respect. The only one that was really helping me and consistently supporting me was my boyfriend. But he was having some problems of his own. I guess the guys and him think about someone that they really care for being attacked like that. It's a hard thing. You have a lot to go through. He didn't feel like I was "tainted" or something, that he didn't want me anymore. It was just that we were close together. My being raped was like his being raped. He was going through many of the same things that I was going through at the same time. I also found weird things happening. Like, I was afraid to get on empty elevators. I was afraid to go out into the real world and be a real person. I just wanted to close myself up, and yet, I didn't want to be alone. I did get over that. I think that one of the things that helped me get over a lot of those feelings was going to the trial and getting it through. It was like bringing completion to an experience in your life. I really think that women who don't prosecute probably have a harder time bringing the whole experience to some sort of resolution. They're never sure in their mind what could have happened if they were right, and that kind of stuff. I do think bringing it to trial was a way to sort of clear it out of your system as best you can.

QUESTION: *You said before that you were really worried about the way you were treated in the hospital. I was wondering about during the court trial. Was it harder for you then, or was it harder in the very beginning? I can envision you on the stand required to testify before a defense attorney. Was that difficult?*

MOLLY: Yes, I worked that up in my mind. Right about the time I was attacked, they were doing a lot of publicity. Susan Brownmiller had just come out with a book and *Time* magazine did a big thing. It was just everywhere. It was just like rape was *Jaws*. It was a big thing. I think the media served to do some damage to what rape is really about and what courtroom scenes are really about. I was afraid, walking into it, and that had a lot to do with it. When I got in there, what I found was that the defense attorney was not as concerned with making me look bad. Insofar as my reputation, like I was a loose woman or something, he was trying to discredit my testimony. He would ask me things, trying to get me flustered on small issues like, "How far away were you at this point?", "Where were his pants?", and "Where were your shoes?" I would answer, "I don't know." I was trying not to think about it. I was freaked-out and in shock most of time. If you're up there on the stand and you're trying to answer these questions, they're just trying to make you look like you don't know what happened. They make your testimony look like it's not sound.

At the end of the whole thing, I went into the bathroom. I got sick and I was crying and all that stuff. That had mainly to do with how I had worked myself up and expected a lot. It was a kind of purging kind of thing. Besides that, when I saw the man who attacked me, I knew that he was just as crazy as a loon. They had kind of an idea he was. He was convicted of three rapes and one attempted rape over a period of time. They think he did a lot more, somewhere near twenty.

When they figured out who he was, they sent someone out looking for him. He came into the police station high and said, "What do you want? I hear you're looking for me." He was in drugs. He made a whole confession. He had a whole bunch of little, nit-picking details about each one of the rapes that no one could know unless he were there. He really cooked his own goose. At the trial, they weren't as concerned about proving what happened as they were really looking for what kind of a sentence they were going to give. That was one of the reasons that they combined all of the trials into one instead of making one separate trial for each one of the rapes. They combined them all to give him a better chance of a lighter sentence. He was given 30 years for each one and then 10 years for the attempt, so that was 100 years. That's a lot better than what could have happened.

I was very lucky that I had the support of the other women. We weren't allowed to hear any of the testimony. We didn't know what was going on. The jury was very attentive. As a matter of fact, the Commonwealth's attorney, when he was priming me, was sort of giving me clues to, shall we say, put myself at the mercy of the jury's emotions. He was saying, "Look them in the eyes," "Wear this certain kind of dress," and, "Talk like this," and, "Do this kind of stuff." He was giving me very specific instructions. I couldn't do that. That's not something that I felt good about doing. It was hard enough to get up there and talk to a jury, and a hard, hard thing to put a man in jail, having the thought of having that kind of power for 100 years—well, that gave me a lot to think about. I knew that I had been wronged and that he couldn't keep on going. He was getting more and more sure of himself and getting more violent each time, so I knew I had to do something. I think it is hard to put someone in jail. That's freaky.

There's one other thing I wanted to say about the whole thing about women wanting it and enjoying it. During the actual rape, I was completely grossed out. I thought I was going to be sick. I couldn't believe that somebody would actually have the audacity to want to do that. At one point, we were standing up and he was talking, he was rubbing against me or something, and I was literally getting sick. I really did not want it. I just wanted to bug-out.

QUESTION: *Could you tell us more about his background, or if he had been convicted of anything before?*

MOLLY: He was a marine, a black marine, who was AWOL. He skipped the Marine Corps, essentially just at that point. He was originally from Charlottesville. He was living back home, sort of hiding from the Marine Corps. All the while, I understand, his best friend was really an accomplished rapist. At the time I was attacked, his best friend was in jail for the same thing. They sort of learned it from each other. I can't think of anything else.

QUESTION: *You didn't know him before, then?*

MOLLY: No. No, one of the women that was attacked by him lived across the street from him. He had watched her for a long time. There was some question about knowing her. She was questioned about it at the trial. She had no idea who he was. She didn't even know he lived behind her.

QUESTION: *Did you ever find out why he chose you?*

MOLLY: I think he was really watching the apartment for a while. He was looking for burglarizing. I don't think he had any idea that I was going to come back as soon as I did. It was another one of those "crimes of opportunity." He was in there looking for money and drugs and whatever he could find. I just happened to walk in and froze like a stupid "whatever."

QUESTION: *We talked in the office before we came over about some theories concerning victims. Some say you should fight back, and others say you shouldn't fight because that will make the attacker more aggressive. Another theory is that you should not allow your fear to show and act calmly, trying to talk him down. It sounds to me that you were, at various points, doing all three. It doesn't seem that any one of them fully worked. How do you feel about such advice? You mentioned that you had read some of the books.*

MOLLY: Yeah, oh, yeah, I'm not really "gung ho" on Susan Brownmiller. I agree with her to a certain extent, but I think she's a little bit radical. She essentially proposes that rape is a crime that men have forced upon women, sort of as a way to control them over the centuries. She proposes that woman need to be more aggressive and more certain. I agree with that to a certain extent. I think that maybe some self-defense and stuff is good, but she is very antimale, very, very much antimen.

QUESTION: *Doesn't she recommend certain penalties for rapists?*

MOLLY: Oh, yeah, castration or something.

QUESTION: *Has she ever been raped?*

MOLLY: No, she hasn't. She makes a big thing about that in the beginning of the book. She says that she has to help people, like she had to justify herself a lot. She kind of bothers me. She started out, essentially, on the other side of the whole spectrum when she first looked into rape. You know, thinking, "They deserve it," "Women ask for it," and that kind of thing. After studying it some, she changed her tune. I guess one of the things I had a hard time dealing with was also feeling like I need to justify myself to other people, as to why it

happened. I was living in a first floor apartment. I certainly don't recommend that to anyone, especially a female living by herself. I had left
the door to the balcony unlocked. He climbed in through the balcony.
I guess it was about five feet off the ground.

QUESTION: *How much time went by between the offense and the trial?*

MOLLY: Six months. We had a kind of certification trial, a pretrial, where they take the evidence to the judge and decide whether it
can go any further, whether they need to take it in front of a jury.
We went into a small chamber. The Commonwealth's attorney was not
very helpful during the whole thing. I was going through it thinking,
"What is going to happen to me?" He was very lacking in information.
As a matter of fact, they subpoenaed me at work. Two armed policemen came to the door and read my full name and subpoenaed me. They
went into the whole deal.

Oh! Another thing happened at this pretrial. I was sitting two
feet away from the man that attacked me. It is my understanding that,
at the pretrial, you are never even supposed to see him. He's not supposed to be there. Nobody told me that. The Commonwealth's attorney
certainly wasn't interested in what I was thinking or feeling, but here's
this guy who's raped me sitting two feet away from me, laughing the
entire time I'm talking in the microphone. There were policemen standing all around. You feel sort of boxed in, in this little bitty room. I
couldn't believe it all! He was sitting there laughing!

Another weird thing about it, and I think it is pretty common for
women to think about it, was that I had a hard time identifying him.
When they finally caught him, they put him in a lineup, and I had been
through about three or four before, and I'll tell you, after going through
the experience, I didn't want to know what he looked like. I was looking away. Most of the time, I was completely grossed-out, or frightened,
or in shock, or something. I had no idea. I didn't remember what he
looked like at all. And that's a problem, you know. Somehow or other,
you're supposed to be all well and remember if he had this kind of
hair and this kind of build. No way! I wasn't interested in identifying
him, so that was one thing that was kind of "sticky" in terms of trying to get over it and convict him. But, like I say, he made a confession.
I was lucky in that respect.

QUESTION: *Did they give you complete identity, and so on, to the press?*

MOLLY: Yes, they gave my exact address. I had people call me
at all hours of the day and night, and pointing, and looking in my
window.

QUESTION: *How did it get to the news media?*

MOLLY: I have no idea. I didn't know they were going to do it. It happened on a Sunday morning at five o'clock, and Monday's paper and the school paper had it. I think they just got the information from a police dispatch or something. While I was in the hospital, the police had come. I went directly to the hospital without phoning the police. While I was there, my boyfriend and I had no idea what they would do or anything. We gave them the keys to the apartment. They went over there with three trucks, gathering evidence and stuff. All these policemen were swarming around the apartment building. Students were around, wanting to know what the police were doing there. While the police were there, they smeared black stuff all over the walls. I couldn't get it off. They looked for fingerprints and they took somewhere between $75 to $100 worth of my stuff. It's ludicrous to me that they would go to my apartment without me there because they didn't know what happened. They didn't know where it took place. They just took themselves inside, took everything off my bed, took stuff off the floors. They took everything. I never got the stuff back. I never got a receipt. I never got anything. I was calling and saying, "Hey, I need that stuff back. It's really important to me. Where are my things?"

Like I said before, a lot of how the rape affects you has to do with what kind of person you are. I consider myself overly sensitive, overly sentimental, and I was raped on my birthday. The police took the only gift I got. I started dwelling on that and stewing on for months at a time. I didn't have anything to do with the case itself. So I called the police station and was talking with the Commonwealth's attorney. I was saying things to them like, "I've been a pretty damn good victim for you people and you owe me a few things." I had to put up a stink and cry and act crazy, because that is what they expect, I guess.

QUESTION: *You are the victim. How do you feel about the criminal and what the system is doing to him, or for him?*

MOLLY: Yeah, I definitely think guys with medical problems have real problems. I didn't hate him. People that were close to me really hated him and talked about going out and getting him. When my parents finally found out, they just hated him. I didn't feel that way. I felt real sorry for him and the fact that he needed to do this. I felt real sorry for him. I thought he needed help for some problems. I've been to the state institutions myself and I simply don't think they are doing much good. I don't know what needs to be done with them. I don't know what can be done or what is realistic. I don't think they should be castrated, or shot, or hung, or executed, or anything like that. I think, maybe, if there's a lot of violence involved and everything, like in murder, that is pretty heavy. From the time between when I first saw him at the pretrial and at the other trial, he had lost 100 pounds. My understanding was that he had a lot of problems with other prisoners. He was beaten up and had lost an incredible amount of weight. He was a thin guy. He was a lot thinner by the time the trial came. As a matter of fact, his attorney used that and dressed him up in clothes that made him look real thin and skinny, to play on the sympathy of the jury. There are a lot of little tricks they use.

QUESTION: *Was he trying for an acquittal?*

MOLLY: No, just trying to get a lighter sentence. He had had another lawyer and the lawyer dropped him because the case looked so bad and he was hard to work with.

QUESTION: *Did the attorneys ever try to have him declared temporarily insane or permanently insane? Did they try to say that he should not be incarcerated? Or that he should be treated for mental illness?*

MOLLY: No, that never really came up. They did have a hard time with a jury selection in the beginning. We had eighteen people come in. There were about five or six black people on trial. In the process of selecting the jury, each attorney is allowed to cancel out a certain number of them. The Commonwealth's attorney cancelled out just about all the black ones. They were trying to make something out of that, saying, "Hey, this is kind of a racial thing." But it was also my understanding that the black people who were up for the jury, a couple of them, were in some kind of black group around Charlottesville. The Commonwealth's attorney didn't have to justify it because in the law you can "x" off anybody in the list for no rhyme or reason. So they couldn't do anything, and that was only a little delay in the trial. We did have some people from a black group monitoring the trial. They were making sure things were going alright. A guy in the back took pages and pages of notes. I guess they were trying to be sure that he was treated fairly and that the racial question didn't come up too much. I don't really think it did.

QUESTION: *What was the sex makeup of the jury?*

MOLLY: There were, I guess, more men than women. I guess there weren't more than five women.

QUESTION: *How many blacks were on the jury?*

MOLLY: I think there were only one or two.

QUESTION: *Maybe we should go into your contacts with ROAR and the types of counseling they offer. What do you see as beneficial there?*

MOLLY: I got in touch with ROAR. They helped me. My understanding of ROAR is that it is more of an educational type of group. It is a volunteer group that speaks, does training, and works with lobbying groups to get certain laws passed in Virginia. The counseling itself is mainly done through Crisis Intervention, Hot Line, and things like that.

QUESTION: *Did you ever partake in any of those?*

MOLLY: There weren't any in Charlottesville. I think it is really necessary. I wish there had been. As a matter of fact, that's one of the things I was doing. I was calling up and trying to see anybody who would see me, because I was so freaked-out for so long. I was just having a hard time holding together. I would go to work and just fall apart and start crying. I couldn't do anything. I didn't want to go anywhere. I think it is very important to have, first, immediate kinds of crisis counseling and then long-term counseling.

QUESTION: *Did you ever get any kind of counseling help?*

MOLLY: No, the only kind of help I really got was from the volunteer RAPE group. They tried to make sure that I was treated as fairly as possible by the different systems. You know, like the one girl that helped me out with the doctor that was being so rude with those pills. She went with me to all the lineups and to the pretrial. In terms of counseling itself, I didn't get any because there was none available.

QUESTION: *Cindy, could you tell us about what ROAR does?*

CINDY: Basically, as Molly said, we are a volunteer group and our basic concern is trying to educate people. We have programs and we speak a lot about all kinds of different things involved in rape. Our main thing is to make the female aware. We hope that by making her aware we will prevent future occurrences. We don't advocate that we have a rape prevention law so that we can say, "This is what you should do." We feel we can offer a few options by educating more, telling things that will make people aware, and that possibly may keep them from getting in that position. We have gotten involved, not that we are counseling in effect, but we do try for voluntary counseling. We see that as a future goal, providing that we get a government grant to promote it.

Right now, we do work very closely with Crisis Intervention. We have developed a Hot Line for twenty-four–hour service in Richmond. You call in and they take over. They will notify the police. They'll call Crisis Intervention if you want. They will follow up and get companion service for you. So far, that's the best thing that has been established. We are trying to help change some of the laws and make hospital facilities better by teaching doctors and dealing with doctors like the one

Molly had. We don't want doctors like that around. The reason we get a lot of them that act like that is because they don't want to get involved. They don't want to have to go to court. At the Medical College of Virginia they have set up a special G.Y.N. clinic where, if a person is raped, they can give them counseling right there. A counselor is called immediately. They have some special gynecologists, not your regular emergency room doctor. They are able to relate more to what has happened and be able to deal with a person better than the regular emergency room doctor or intern on duty. Those are the changes that have come about in the last two years. We've had excellent response to them. We hope the other hospitals will follow suit.

We did a training session for the Richmond Police Department. For two weeks, we met with them at the academy. We went through all the things we thought were correct. We feel victims have rights. There are certain things that they should demand. They should be treated in a certain way. We got some very good feedback from the police department and we worked out a very good alliance with them. I think we are finding that operation as cooperative and we are getting very few complaints right now. The same with Crisis Intervention. If we hear complaints, we call them. They know we will. So, normally, we're not just a speaking group. We still have monitors watching because, as a group, we will be able to change things so that other people won't have to experience what Molly had to experience.

Basically, your trial situation is considered another rape. It's like a traumatic experience all over again. Just to show you a parallel between Richmond and Charlottesville, Charlottesville has a part-time Commonwealth's attorney, which might explain his lack of interest and knowledge. He runs his own private law firm on the side. In Richmond, we have a full-time Commonwealth's attorney. They have a special line you call up if you are raped or the victim of any other crime. You can call and they will give you pretrial information, tell you when you should be in court, and you can come in for coaching. There are three people who've been set up on a special payroll and that is all they do. They set up the pretrial information, what to do, how, and that's all they do. That is something that just happened in the last nine months.

As far as the cases that do go to trial, we find that it's very seldom that they are sure of conviction. The ones in which they feel there's not enough evidence, they never make it to trial. They usually plea bargain ahead of time and try to get some lesser sentences. So far, there's nothing we've been able to do about that.

We have been involved with a group called "Close Up," which is Virginia Coalition on Sexual Thought Change. We are in the process of rewriting the whole Virginia state law on rape. We're hoping the Crime Commission will present it to the General Assembly in the next session. Keep your eyes and ears open. If you see anything about the proposal, you can write your General Assemblyman and help support it. The basic thing that we are concerned with is that we feel the victim needs a lawyer. The rapist has his own attorney and that attorney is able to influence the deal by representing him. The Commonwealth's attorney is overworked and, in a lot of instances, he can't give a person assistance needed.

QUESTION: *You said that the victim ought to have an attorney. Isn't the law now that the state is the victim? Is your proposal for the state to pay the lawyer's fees, or the victim? Who pays the lawyer's fees now?*

CINDY: It is a crime against the State of Virginia, and the Commonwealth's attorney is paid by the state as your attorney. In other words, you are just a witness. Like in Molly's subpoena, it's "The State versus the criminal."

QUESTION: *Where is the lawyer for the victim supposed to come from? The public defender's office? Will one be supplied?*

CINDY: I would say the person should hire a lawyer if he wants to. If he can't afford a lawyer, one should be appointed, just like with the rapist.

══════════ COMMENTARY

Molly is atypical of most rape victims in that she is white, middleclass, and has no prior arrest record. In addition, her rape was interracial, committed in her home, by someone with whom she not only had no previous drinking or other interactions, but who was a complete stranger. Thus, several theories applying to the typical rape or other victim, such as subcultural explanations, are not applicable in her situation. On the other hand, Molly is typical of rape victims in that she is a female, within the twenty-to-twenty-nine age bracket. Many aspects of her interactions with the rapist and of her treatment by the police, medical personnel, and court authorities are most revealing. The most striking feature is the manner in which Molly was, in many ways, treated as a deviant by others and the manner in which she struggled for her own self-concept and psychological well-being.

There is very little information in Molly's case that would support Amir's model of victim-precipitation. There is no evidence that Molly *wished* to be raped. We have no indication of a prior "bad" or negative reputation. Perhaps the rape would be best categorized within Amir's "unsoliciting" classification. Some might say that Molly's lack of physical assertiveness during the interaction or her failure to lock her balcony window earlier would fit Amir's "omission" category of precipitation. We would tend to look upon these behaviors as normal lack of preventive techniques that may not have altered the situation.

Likewise, there is little support from Molly for Brownmiller's general contentions of male power and authority behind Molly's victimization. Attitudes displayed by medical and legal personnel may reflect a degree of "male chauvinism" or, at least, a lack of understanding of the female victim's psychological state. There is some indication of the stigmatizing, "spoiled woman" syndrome in these interactions. Molly herself disagrees with some of Brownmiller's statements as "a little bit radical" and "very, very much anti-men." Moreover, although Molly appears to be in error regarding Brownmiller's recommendation of castration as a penalty for rape,[69] she also disagrees as to the effectiveness of prison as a "treatment" for her attacker. She has visited penal institutions and is aware of the violence and brutality within them.

The incidents surrounding Molly's rape can be best understood in the context of Ziegenhagen's model of the "role of the victim" in contemporary society. The emergency room as a "zoo" and the concern of the physician that he would have to testify later, the gathering of hair samples, the extent to which the police gathered evidence, the manner in which they questioned whether or not she "really got raped," the "pretrial" situation, the cross-examination by the defense attorney as to her prior reputation and veracity, and the prosecution's instructions regarding her courtroom appearance and behavior may be comprehended within this framework. The reforms suggested by Cindy are among those advocated by Ziegenhagen as well.[70] (It might be well to point out here that the next session of the Virginia General Assembly defeated the "Sexual Assault Bill" supported by Cindy's organization.)

Molly also provides us with insights into the positive role of support played by her boyfriend and refers to the effect of her rape upon him ("some problems of his own," "a hard thing . . . like his being raped and going through the same things that I was going through at the same time"). Her discussion of her own "rape trauma," the psychological aftereffects, the degree of support from her primary group relationships, especially her boyfriend, and the finalizing of the event by "reliving" it in the trial, allow us to perceive the nature of the victim's problems and a pattern of possible alleviation. Significant to this is the mutually supportive role of Molly's fellow rape victims.

Finally, in addition to the value of Molly's case for medical sociologists, criminologists may benefit from knowledge of the manner in which the justice system reacted toward her black attacker. This may be contrasted with the case of Joan Little[71] or other incidents in which rape or attempted rape was perpetrated by a white attacker upon a black woman.

Let us now attempt to analyze Molly's case within some of the major theoretical frameworks.

THEORETICAL IMPLICATIONS

There is no basis to support the validity of biological explanations for Molly's behavior. The fact that she is attractive physically did not seem to play a major part in the interaction between her and her attacker. His initial reason for being in her apartment was for burglary. Likewise, psychological factors are of little assistance in interpreting her behavior other than what might be expected in such a situation. There is no evidence that she brought about her rape due to guilt, masochism, or loneliness. She is definitely not feebleminded or lethargic. She did not provoke the attack and would not meet Ball's criteria for "aggression" as a form "instigating" the rape; nor does she fit the category of those who submit in "resignation" to her exploitation, as indicated by her later conduct. Again, some might interpret her failure to lock the balcony door as an indication that Molly was subconsciously "regressing," as would fit Ball's form of behavior that leaves one "vulnerable" to others, but we find no other psychological or behavioral sign that would support this. It would appear, then, that the sociological and interactionist insights gained from Molly's case may have the strongest implications.

Sociological Theories

Subcultural explanations are not applicable to our white, middle class victim. Perhaps her reaction was different than that of a typical black woman in a similar situation as hypothesized by Curtis, but we would have no means of creating the exact situation and controlling it for race and social class. Similarly, the only apparent applications of *anomie* theories are in the "opportunity" sense (the unlocked door) and in the broader context of the societal condition in which present legislation regarding victims does not meet present-day needs. *Alienation* appears almost absent in Molly's case. She is sympathetic toward her attacker and is not alienated from men or "male-dominated" society. The only sense of alienation is in regard to the judicial system and the situations that it created. The application of a *differential association* approach may rest in the total learning and socialization pattern of Molly's sex roles throughout her life, but this does not appear particularly enlightening on an individual case basis. Thus, the most significant insights appear to lie within an interactionist approach to either labeling or social control perspectives.

LABELING THEORY   Molly was not labeled as "easy" or as having a "bad" reputation prior to her rape. Indeed, she appears to have resisted a stigma quite successfully in spite of several indications that the interactions of others were in that direction. Molly was forced to deal with the stigmatization problem almost immediately, namely, when she told her boyfriend. She describes how difficult it was merely to use the word "rape." Perhaps his support (he appears to have been the most significant other in her life at that time) is the key as to how Molly avoided a negative self-concept. This was in spite of the treatment she was accorded by the physician and others at the hospital, the apparent doubts of the police ("Did he really rape you?"), the press publicity, and the tribulations incurred prior to and during her trial, including the attempts by the defense to discredit her testimony. It is also possible that a part of Molly's positive self-concept is the result of her acceptance of the label of "rape victim" in a positive rather than negative sense. This may be similar to the situation in which a member of A.A. adopts the label "alcoholic" as a step in rehabilitation. Molly has "gone public" with her story, not only in speaking to our classes, but also in testifying before legislative committees that consider relevant legislation. The lack of acceptance of a negative self-concept in spite of stigmatizing interactions would seem to be a most significant area for further investigation.

SOCIAL CONTROL EXPLANATIONS   The application of a social control approach is enlightening in the support for the level suggested by Ziegenhagen, that of viewing the "role of the victim" as an agent of social control in a modern, *Gesellschaft* society. It is noteworthy, too, that there is little support for the social control approach of "victim-precipitation" as posited by Amir.

The Brodsky approach of considering the "deterrent" capabilities of the rape victim in a potential situation deserves special comment. While Molly was unable to deter her attacker even though she made some attempts at verbal resistance and established a degree of interpersonal liaison with him, it is possible that had she been able to think more clearly ("I froze"), she might have kept control of the situation. The clue may be in her description of one point in the interaction. Molly told the rapist that her boyfriend was coming, but afterward she showed her fear. The attacker admitted his fear to her as well. She continued to verbalize, then "started yelling at him." She states that, at this point, he placed the knife to her throat, exclaiming:

> Shut up! I know what you're doing. It doesn't work.

It may be that the rapist was referring to Molly's screams. Or it may be that he was referring to her attempts to establish a relationship with him and that she had begun to affect him with her statement:

> I can't believe *you're* doing this!

Whether or not this interaction, alone with continued resistance, would have avoided the rape is speculative. Still, one should not dismiss lightly the complete analysis of possibilities for deterrence. It would seem that greater specificity attained in this regard, when all possible interactions of victim-offender relationships are explored, could provide a basis for training individuals in resistance techniques.

Several authors have proposed reforms in court proceedings, medical treatment of victims, public educational programs, and compensation programs, as well as revised statutes regarding sexual assault.[72] Increased focus upon the victim in our consideration of crime and deviance may be able to serve such public policy. As Ziegenhagen states:

> The legitimization of victim interests in the process of law rather than its substantive nature may be the beginning of a new form of social control that is related to, but apart from, law as we have conceived of it for the past two centuries. Much as law was withdrawn from the general population in America as a personalized tool of social control, we may be witnessing its evolution to serve highly individualized social purposes better known in tribal Europe than in the contemporary American criminal justice system.[73]

QUESTIONS FOR DISCUSSION

1. Should the state be obligated to compensate victims for physical and psychological injuries? How does the issue of victim-precipitation affect your response?
2. Do you agree with Susan Brownmiller that rape is "a conscious intimidation by which all men keep all women in a state of fear"?
3. Could Molly have prevented her rape? How?
4. What reforms would you suggest to alleviate the role of the victim in our criminal justice system?
5. Will prison be of benefit to Molly's attacker? In what ways? What would be of help to him and society should he be released on parole?
6. Many sociologists contend that rapes frequently go unreported because of the manner in which the victim is treated by the police and the courts and by the effect on her feminine image. Others claim that the most frequently unreported crime is "husband-beating." Comment.

RELATED READINGS

Amir, Menachem, *Patterns in Forcible Rape* (Chicago: University of Chicago Press, 1971).

Bode, Janet, *Fighting Back: How to Cope with the Medical, Emotional and Legal Consequences of Rape* (New York: Macmillan, 1978).

Brooks, James, "How Well Are Criminal Injury Compensation Programs Performing?", *Crime and Delinquency* (January, 1975), pp. 50–56.

Brownmiller, Susan, *Against Our Will: Men, Women, and Rape* (New York: Bantam Books, 1975).

Cannavale, Frank J., Jr., and Falcon, William D., *Witness Cooperation* (Lexington, Mass.: D. C. Heath and Company, 1976).

Chappell, D., Geis, R., and Geis, G., eds., *Forcible Rape: The Crime, the Victim and the Offender* (New York: Columbia University Press, 1977).

Curtis, Lynn A., *Violence, Race and Culture* (Lexington, Mass.: D. C. Heath and Company, 1975).

Fooner, Michael, "Victim-Induced Criminality," in *Science*, 153 (September 2, 1966), pp. 1080–1083.

Holmstrom, Lynda Lytle, and Burgess, Ann Wolbert, *The Victim of Rape: Institutional Reactions* (New York: John Wiley and Sons, 1978).

President's Commission on Law Enforcement and Administration of Justice, "The Victims of Crime," in *Task Force Report: Crime and Its Impact—An Assessment* (Washington, D.C.: U.S. Government Printing Office, 1967), pp. 80–84.

Ryan, William, *Blaming the Victim* (New York: Vintage Books, 1976).

Schafer, Stephen, "The Proper Role of a Victim-Compensation System," in *Crime and Delinquency* (January, 1975), pp. 45–49.

Thornberry, Terence P., and Sagarin, Edward, eds., *Images of Crime: Offenders and Victims* (New York: Praeger, 1974).

Walker, Marcia J., and Brodsky, Stanley L., eds., *Sexual Assault: The Victim and the Rapist* (Lexington, Mass.: D. C. Heath and Company, 1976).

Ziegenhagen, Eduard A., *Victims, Crime, and Social Control* (New York: Praeger, 1977).

NOTES

1. Eduard A. Ziegenhagen, *Victims, Crime and Social Control* (New York: Praeger, 1977), p. 2.

2. Menachem Amir, *Patterns in Forcible Rape* (Chicago: University of Chicago Press, 1971), p. 253.

3. President's Commission on Law Enforcement and Administration of Justice, "The Victims of Crime," in *Task Force Report: Crime and Its Impact—An Assessment* (Washington, D.C.: U.S. Government Printing Office, 1967), p. 80.

4. Ibid., pp. 82–83; Marvin Wolfgang and Franco Ferracuti, *The Subculture of Violence* (London: Tavistock Publications, 1967), p. 190.

5. President's Commission on Law Enforcement and Administration of Justice, "The Victims of Crime," pp. 81–84.

6. Susan Brownmiller, *Against Our Will: Men, Women and Rape* (New York: Bantam Books, 1977), pp. 200–201.

7. L. C. Mullins, "Victimization of the Elderly and Fear of Crime: A Review," unpublished paper presented to The Southern Sociological Society, Annual Meeting, New Orleans, La., March 30–April 2, 1978.

8. Ibid.

9. Charles W. Thomas, "Perceptions of Crime, Punishment and Legal Sanctions," unpublished paper presented to The American Society of Criminology Convention, Tucson, Arizona, November, 1976.

10. Amir, *Patterns in Forcible Rape*, p. 266.

11. Brownmiller, *Against Our Will*.

12. Amir, *Patterns in Forcible Rape*, p. 249.

13. Ibid., p. 253.
14. Ibid., p. 254.
15. Ibid., pp. 254–255.
16. Ibid., p. 255.
17. Ibid., pp. 258 and 265.
18. Ibid., p. 260.
19. Ibid.
20. Ibid., p. 261.
21. Ibid.
22. Ibid., p. 266.
23. Ibid.
24. Ibid., pp. 267–276.
25. Ibid., pp. 265–266.
26. Brownmiller, *Against Our Will*, pp. 195–203.
27. Ibid., pp. 192–195.
28. Ibid., p. 346.
29. Ibid., p. 8.
30. Ibid., pp. 422–433.
31. Ibid., p. 5.
32. Ibid., p. 51.
33. Ibid., pp. 24–149.
34. Ibid., pp. 150–188.
35. Ibid., pp. 6–22, 283–312.
36. Ibid., pp. 343–386.
37. Ibid., pp. 353–367.
38. Ibid., pp. 283–312.
39. Ibid., pp. 425–426.
40. Kenneth A. Cobb and Nancy R. Schauer, "Michigan's Criminal Sexual Assault Law," in Duncan Chappell, Robley Geis, and Gilbert Geis, eds., *The Crime, the Victim, and the Offender* (New York: Columbia University Press, 1977), pp. 170–186; Marcia J. Walker and Stanley L. Brodsky, *Sexual Assault* (Lexington, Mass.: D. C. Heath and Company, 1976), pp. 149–160.
41. Donald J. Mulvihill et al., *Crimes of Violence, A Staff Report to the National Commission on the Causes and Prevention of Violence* (Washington, D.C.: U.S. Government Printing Office, 1969), II, pp. 224–229.
42. Ibid., p. 226.
43. Marvin Wolfgang, "Suicide by Means of Victim-Precipitated Homicide," *Quarterly Review of Psychiatry and Neurology*, 20 (1959), pp. 335–349.
44. Lynn A. Curtis, *Violence, Race and Culture* (Lexington, Mass.: 1975), pp. 128–129.
45. Michael W. Agoplan, Duncan Chappell, and Gilbert Geis, "Interracial Rape in a North American City: An Analysis of 63 Cases," in Terence P. Thornberry and Edward Sagarin, eds., *Images of Crime: Offenders and Victims* (New York: Praeger, 1974), p. 111.
46. William Ryan, *Blaming the Victim*, rev. ed. (New York: Vintage Books, 1976), pp. 197–204.
47. Ibid., pp. 205–211.
48. Ibid., pp. 211–212.

49. Janet Bode, *Fighting Back: How to Cope with the Medical, Emotional and Legal Consequences of Rape* (New York: Macmillan, 1978), p. 133.

50. Ziegenhagen, *Victims, Crime and Social Control*, p. 2.

51. Ibid., pp. 32–69.

52. Ibid.

53. Ibid., pp. 75–88.

54. Lynda Lytle Holmstrom and Ann Wolbert Burgess, *The Victim of Rape: Institutional Reactions* (New York: John Wiley and Sons, 1978), pp. 34–60.

55. Ibid., pp. 63–117.

56. Bode, *Fighting Back*, pp. 126–127.

57. Ann Wolbert Burgess and Lynda Lytle Holmstrom, "Rape: Its Effect on Task Performance at Varying Stages in the Life Cycle," in Marcia J. Walker and Stanley L. Brodsky, eds., *Sexual Assault: The Victim and the Rapist* (Lexington, Mass.: D. C. Heath and Company, 1976), p. 24.

58. Ibid., pp. 25–32.

59. Ziegenhagen, *Victims, Crime and Social Control*, pp. 11–14.

60. Ibid., pp. 13–14.

61. Richard A. Ball, "The Victimological Cycle," unpublished paper presented to The Second International Symposium on Victimology, Boston, 1976, pp. 8–13.

62. Ziegenhagen, *Victims, Crime and Social Control*, pp. 15–16.

63. Marvin Wolfgang, *Studies in Homicide* (New York: Harper and Row, 1967).

64. Wolfgang, "Suicide by Means of Victim-Precipitated Homicide," pp. 335–349.

65. Curtis, *Violence, Race and Culture*, pp. 128–129.

66. Ibid., pp. 73–81.

67. Stanley L. Brodsky, "Prevention of Rape: Deterrence by the Potential Victim," in Walker and Brodsky, *Sexual Assault*, pp. 75–90.

68. Martin R. Haskell and Lewis Yablonsky, *Criminology: Crime and Criminality*, 2nd ed. (Chicago: Rand McNally, 1978), pp. 344–345.

69. Brownmiller, *Against Our Will*, p. 426.

70. Ziegenhagen, *Victims, Crime and Social Control*, pp. 91–137.

71. James Reston, Jr., *The Innocence of Joan Little* (New York: Bantam Books, 1979).

72. Bode, *Fighting Back*, pp. 190–228; Brownmiller, *Against Our Will*, pp. 421–454; Holmstrom and Burgess, *The Victim of Rape*, pp. 260–289; Donal E. MacNamara and John J. Sullivan, "Making the Victim Whole: Composition, Restitution, Compensation," in Thornberry and Sagarin, *Images of Crime*, pp. 79–90; Walker and Brodsky, *Sexual Assault*, pp. 139–175; Ziegenhagen, *Victims, Crime and Social Control*, pp. 91–137.

73. Ziegenhagen, *Victims, Crime and Social Control*, p. 149.

Deviant Reality
and the Study
of Deviancy

13

    In keeping with the scientific study of deviancy, we have examined individual cases of deviancy with the intention of clarifying, correcting, or reformulating definitions, theories, and hypotheses that we have drawn from scientific literature on the subject. However, the study of deviant reality includes more than examination of definitions, theories, and hypotheses. In fact, such a focus might be questionable. Critics might maintain that by our emphasis on causation of deviancy, we commit ourselves to prediction and control of the phenomenon (sometimes said to be the goal of science), thus assuming that the phenomenon is "evil" and should be eradicated. However, we believe that science implies more than a desire for prediction and control. It also entails a search for *understanding*. Through understanding the phenomenon, we may come to feel we can "live with it" or that, indeed, a given deviant lifestyle might possess positive as well as negative aspects. This shift from an emphasis upon deviancy theory to a focus upon understanding everyday life in deviant subcultures is indicated by the recent rise of ethnomethodology, which stresses the understanding of meanings, categories, expectancies, sanctions, and techniques of resolving crises used by deviant actors in everyday life.

    In these final pages, we would like to state what contributions we think our case studies and analyses provide to the scientific literature, both on concepts and causes of deviancy and on the understanding of deviant reality.

CONCEPTS AND CAUSES OF DEVIANCY

In our review of scientific literature on deviancy, we note no scarcity of *general* conceptions and explanations of deviancy. In fact, the emphasis in the current study of deviancy seems to be upon deviancy-in-general. Many of the problems in the study of deviancy, may be traced to this excessive concern with the general without a sufficient foundation in the reality of particular cases of deviancy.

The Concept of Deviancy

What, after all, is the point of defining the term *deviancy*? Ostensibly, defining the general area is a way of mapping out territory for special focused attention. However, in most general definitions, such as those reviewed in Chapter 1, no precise demarcation is really made. For instance, the "statistical-tolerance limits view" holds any behaviors beyond certain statistical limits, in a negative or undesirable direction, as deviance. But there are many dimensions of social behavior along which we could spell out such limits. The format of this book is such that it may leave one wondering why such "victimless" acts as drug abuse, homosexuality, and prostitution are selected as instances of deviance, while adultery, child-battering, atmospheric pollution, and failure to comply with Federal Aviation or Nuclear Regulatory Commission requirements are not. The consideration of the victim as a deviant is, thus, even more surprising. In actuality, the author's selection of topics is done by fiat rather than through a scientific study of public opinion, though he probably feels safe in his selection of topics because they currently receive much attention in the courts and mass media. The historical context of an act may be as important as its cultural context.

The same may be said of those who accept the view that deviancy is "that which is labeled as such by society." Instances of deviancy such as marijuana use and prostitution; are selected by authors of this view without the presentation of any proof that these are indeed labeled deviancy in the society. Again, the general definition gives us no real help as to its operationalization, and it is highly presumptuous to jump to certain forms of behavior that "everybody knows" are deviancy.

To be valid and accurate, the definition of deviancy must be operationalized and operationalizable, and the operationalization must be done periodically to take into account current opinion. Data such as the Sellin and Wolfgang findings reviewed in Chapter 1 can help us to operationalize the term *deviancy*. However, in the concrete terms of this study, even these data fall short of providing us the answer to a primary question of our inquiry—"Whom shall we call deviant?" Outside of formal criteria of deviancy, we have noted that in real, face-to-face confrontation with admitted or convicted offenders, our thinking of them as deviant is dependent upon our feeling of "trust," a feeling that is only partly derived from a knowledge of their "rap sheets." If the individual is prompt, courteous, and cooperative, and acts in accord with our expectancies in interaction, we tend to think, regardless of the "rap sheet," that he or she is reformed, trustworthy, doing well, and "OK now." On the other hand, failure to show for a classroom interview, unexpected behavior during an interview (e.g., one informant entered the audience to hold a girl's hand), unexpected disappearances and reappearances, all behavior quite independent of past offenses, confirm in our minds the feeling that we are dealing with a deviant. (We note through the retrospective accounts of our informants that such disruptions of everyday interactions seemed to be characteristic of their early development.) We also know from self-report studies that serious offenses are committed by many who do not get caught and who are considered law-abiding citizens. The "coolness" versus "uncoolness" dimension of deviancy certainly merits a further inspection since it may help us to differentiate the official from the unofficial rule-breaker.

Theories of Deviancy

Theories of deviancy, like definitions, have also lacked specificity. Our analyses of individual cases have revealed that it is clearly unrealistic to try to explain all deviancy by one or another theoretical factor.

PSYCHOLOGICAL THEORY Psychological factors appear to have only limited power of explanation, particularly if isolated from sociological variables. In some cases, childhood factors, such as repression of sexuality, parental rejection, discipline practices, and the like, do not seem to have much bearing on adult behavior (as in the case of the embezzler).

SOCIOLOGICAL THEORY We also find severe limitations to the application of many sociological theories. Anomie theory and subcultural explanations seem to have the most limited applications. This is most evident when they are utilized in their more traditional and limited sense to apply to lower socioeconomic and minority groups. Many, if not most, of our informants came from middle class rather than "deprived" families. In one case, that of Steve, the armed robber, anomie theory seems to apply, but only after Steve's opportunities had been severely limited by long imprisonment and penal stigma and after his awareness of the socioeconomic system had been fostered by such experiences. Steve, incidentally, came from (in his words) a wealthy family background. Sandy's prostitution also somewhat complies with the anomie model, but again only after a long socialization via the juvenile justice system. Albert's embezzlement perhaps involves a limited application of anomie theory, but there were also other necessary conditions, as specified by Cressey, in Albert's case. It seems that anomie theory applies primarily to adult property offenders, and then only under specified conditions.

Subcultural theory Subcultural explanations appear to be limited not only by their "class bias," but by the fact that most deviants appear to join a subculture either *after* their initial deviant behavior or after they have been labeled by others. As in the case of organized crime, one must question the degree to which such subcultures, or the "reality" of their existence, are created by the dominant culture.

Alienation theory Alienation or conflict approaches are limited primarily as a critique of the system at the macro level and require far greater specificity to explain individual behavior. Perhaps they may best be utilized in assessing the relative importance given to street crimes as opposed to white collar crimes, and the inequities existing within the justice system. Alienation approaches appear to have strength where anomie and subcultural explanations are weakest, but they lack the power to explain specific forms of deviance.

Differential association theory The theory of differential association, on the other hand, seems more promising in explaining many of our cases. Rick, the addict, first used heroin in the company of peers. Tom, the homosexual, was initiated into homosexuality by a "significant other" friend in high school. However, Darrell was not taken to a nudist camp by a friend, Albert talked to no one about his embezzlement, Fred was not taught how to rape by anybody, and Richard associated neither with murderers nor with offenders of any kind.

Labeling and stigma seem to be part of the background of many of our informants. In the case of Hazel, unwillingness to accept the label alcoholic seems to be part of her progression in alcohol use, and acceptance of the label as a member of Alcoholics Anonymous seems associated with sobriety. Similarly, in the cases of the embezzler and the murderer, there was no stigmatic labeling that might have influenced the development of a deviant career. The law-abiding self-concept, in fact, was so strong that they continued to maintain a noncriminal concept of self even after imprisonment.

In other instances, where a degree of labeling and acceptance of a negative self-concept were present, the applicability of this perspective appears to be enhanced by a broader interactionist framework. A broader model frequently may involve factors or concepts emphasized by other theories.

Social control theory Social control theories, if taken in their usual form, are limited as well. In an expanded form, they take into account external controls such as the legal and mental health systems, as well as specific variation of internal control mechanisms. In most instances, external measures are ineffective or even counterproductive. Thus, social control theories appear to have their greatest potential in explaining alcohol, drug, and sexual deviancies.

Models of Deviancy

SEQUENTIAL ROLE MODEL One resolution to the problem of the limited applicability of one or another theory may be found in the concept of "sequential role model."[1] At different stages in the development of a deviant career, the "causes" may differ. Thus, in early childhood development, family and personality factors may be operable. Labeling, peer subculture, and differential association may come into play in adolescence, whereas in adulthood, when conscious awareness of the larger socioeconomic order is greatest, anomie, alienation, and adult subcultures may prove to be the important factors. Internal control may develop early in life, and the degree to which external mechanisms are absent in later years may allow the deviancy to flourish or become more apparent.

INTERACTIONIST MODEL Another resolution would involve the construction of an elaborate "interactionist" model that would combine various aspects of differing approaches and take into account conceptual overlap and possible interaction. Indeed, throughout this volume, our theoretical analyses of several deviancies have pointed in this direction. A basis for this type of consideration may be found in the research of Harwin Voss, in which he demonstrated the theoretical convergence of differential association and containment theory.[2] Voss employed measurements of Sutherland's theory and Reckless' concept of "internal containment" to test their overlap.

In an examination of delinquent boys and nondelinquent boys Voss found considerable convergence. Voss hypothesized that what Sutherland emphasized was the "*process*" of differential association as similar to what Reckless described as a "*product*," or self-concept, resulting from what is, essentially, the socialization process.[3] Thus, Voss essentially isolated concepts, specified the assumptions contained therein (socialization within primary groups), and enlarged upon our knowledge of both. A much more extensive conceptualization would be required in developing a complete model of deviancy. We will not attempt here to build or detail the specifics of such a framework. Rather, we would like to suggest possible concepts and their interrelationships that might be considered. These would need to be further specified, clarified, and elaborated upon in later theory construction. Such a model would necessitate:

1. An interdisciplinary approach, including aspects of biology, psychology, and sociology.
2. Isolation of some key concepts from their original theoretical frameworks; for example, "self-concept" from labeling and social control theories.
3. The modification, in some instances, of certain elements. Examples might include the "external containment" concept of Reckless to incorporate legal sanctions and the extension of subcultural theories to higher socioeconomic groups.
4. A specification of the convergence of concepts from separate theories, as Voss has done with differential association and internal containment.
5. Recognition of the interacting nature of life events (as noted in the "sequential role model") and the feedback effect inherent in human behavior. For example, a low or "poor" self-image may be more receptive to the stigmatizing effect of labeling, leading to an even poorer (deviant) self-concept.

From many of our informants' histories, we are able to note the consideration of several linkages and interactions. Physiological deficiency, body type, or attractiveness may result in both a labeling effect and psychological insecurity. The psychological aspects of personality and self-image may be affected by and affect the receptivity to labeling's product, "self-concept." In turn, the labeling "self-concept" is similar to the "self-image" of one's psychological makeup and the "self-concept" of Reckless' social control theory. One's personality is influenced by early childhood experiences, the beginning of the socialization process inherent in Sutherland's differential association concept. The convergence of differential association and social control theory has been noted above. The learning process of differential association takes place within primary groups frequently found within various subcultures. Subcultures and peer groups may themselves be a source of external containment in addition to influencing the process of internal containment. Such subcultures and the lack of external control may open "opportunities" for deviancy. Those for whom legitimate opportunities in the economic system are not provided may feel alienated and further driven to subcultural values.

Conflict or alienation theory, as well as labeling theory, may also provide an overall critique of the system whereby deviancy is defined and who is defined as a deviant. Indeed, once deviancy is arrived at, further interactions occur. Alcohol and drug abuse may result in physiological as well as psychological and social changes. The deviant may join or even help in forming a deviant subculture as a result of the deviant action, rather than merely as a "cause" of it. (An example would be the need to maintain a heroin supply.)

The model would require additional elaboration and specification to explain certain types of deviancy. For example, an emphasis upon "masculine self-image" may be required as a portion of the "self-concept" in psychological, labeling, and social control approaches in explaining male homosexuality. Nevertheless, both the "sequential role model" and our suggested, comprehensive "interactionist" model attempt to solve the problem of limited applicability of individual theories by combining aspects from several. Both deserve further consideration.

However, neither a sequential analysis nor an interactionist framework solves our problem in all cases. Both appear limited, for instance, in fully explaining sexual and drug deviancies. Differential association may explain Rick's initial use of heroin, but once addiction had taken place, the desire for the drug and avoidance of withdrawal pain became the motive or "cause" for further use.[4] The same was true in the cases of George and Hazel, the two alcoholics. Similar logic may be applied to the sexual deviancies—homosexuality and nudism. It seems that sexual and drug preferences develop like other human tastes. We would not attempt to find the underlying causes of a liking for asparagus and in fact would treat this as a purely personal idiosyncratic choice. We may discover that we cannot find common, universal, underlying causes in the sexual, drug, and other "expressive deviations." Chambliss argues that such deviations are "pleasure-in-themselves" rather than a means to some other end, purpose, or "cause."[5] They may in fact qualify as "compulsive deviations," which Cressey notes are difficult to explain by differential association theory since the motivation appears to come from "within."[6] Could it be that we insist upon finding ·underlying causes because of our belief that we are dealing with social evil and thus we are in a sense pursuing demons? We do not concern ourselves with the causes of heterosexuality but treat it as natural or given, and yet with homosexuality we look for causes.

Even if universal causes could not be found, these phenomena are still worthy of sociological inquiry since they are defined as deviancy, taboo, as illegal, and they are reacted to by society. The expressive deviate, in turn, may react through the development of subcultures that themselves are indeed social entities worthy of sociological explanation. Under these circumstances, fruitful inquiry entails a search for understanding deviant subcultures perhaps, as we have said before, with an eye to "living with" these alternate subcultures.

UNDERSTANDING DEVIANT REALITY

We can get a glimpse of the world views that arise from deviant subcultures through a study of the transcripts contained in this volume. Many of our respondents gave us brief synopses of their perspectives, particularly those pertaining to their own deviancies. It seems that the alternate world views are more likely to exist and be held as valid in the case of expressive deviancies, especially deviancies where there is no physically harmed victim. Thus, Darrell maintains that nudity isn't intrinsically sexual but is positively beneficial in the sense that it leads to equalitarian relationships and has physical heath benefits. Tom, the homosexual, asserts that homosexuality is "natural" and accepted as normal in other cultures and other times in history. Penny, the lesbian, contends that lesbians do not hate men but see them as pals or buddies, and that not all lesbians are masculine in appearance. Liz, the trans-sexual, tells us that male or female sexual organs are not what make one male or female, but that gender is a role to which one is socialized regardless of sexual apparatus. Rick, the heroin addict, states simply that "drugs are good." Sandy, the prostitute, considers herself not too much different from promiscuous girls or wives who trade sex for gifts from their husbands, except perhaps in her honesty.

Even the more serious offenders develop challenging alternatives to conventional perspectives. Albert, the embezzler, sees our society as plastic and most people in it as insincere, patronizing, and incompetent. He sees business as a game and money as a way of keeping score. Steve, the armed robber, holds that "if you're a bigger animal in the jungle, then you do well." Fred, the rapist, is convinced that women who get raped actually want to be raped and unwittingly communicate this to their rapist, while Molly, the victim of rape, strongly denies this. These perspectives do not entirely explain the deviancy of those who hold them, since many in society may hold these same perspectives without committing the deviances. However, knowing them helps one to become oriented toward the deviant or deviant subculture, whether one's desire be to tolerate deviants, join with them, or fend them off.

Knowing deviants and understanding their reality may be of considerable value, as well, in the formulation and implementation of social policy. The failure of many programs to aid, "rehabilitate," or even control deviants appears to stem from a lack of understanding of their values, desires, life-styles, and subcultures. As we have seen, the responses of both the legal system and the medical profession are frequently rejected by deviants. The failure to respond to the deviant from his or her perception of reality may, indeed, be counterproductive.

══════════ CONCLUDING NOTE

What is the final product of our efforts in this volume? We offer neither statistical generalization nor a blanket endorsement of any general theory. We certainly could not provide any factor common in the determination of all deviancy, and in fact that would be antithetical to our whole thesis—that we should attempt to understand particular forms of deviant behavior and particular cases of these particular forms as a step antecedent to theoretical generalization. Individual case examination, we feel, has not been done enough in sociology, and indeed in many instances has not been done at all. One result is rampant armchair or "ivory tower" theorizing about deviancy. We have subjected many of the theories that have been developed through such methods to the acid test of an actual authentic case of the phenomenon. We can certainly at least question a generalization if, having intensively examined a case, we find no evidence at all to support it.

What we have provided are *real cases* to contend with as a starting point for generalization. These cases differ from many abstracted from literary sources in the sense that they are living and not imaginary, hypothetical, or drawn from the forgotten past. In our classroom interviews, we and the students queried our informants until there was a general, genuine feeling of "knowing" the individuals who consented to share their experiences with us.

We hope that users of this volume will continue case study along the same lines, even more extensively and intensively. We suspect that the examination of many individual cases is a powerful way to go about building theory. *If* the single cases are indeed representative of social phenomena, generalizations from these cases conceivably could be applicable to the phenomena they represent. Potentially through such study, as Cressey suggested, we could derive universal generalizations in many areas of deviancy.

Even if we find through our study of deviant cases that universal generalizations are not forthcoming, we will surely find that we have enhanced our intuitive understanding of life in deviant subcultures. In the final analysis, we may find that this will be the most valuable outcome of scientific inquiry into deviancy.

═══════ NOTES

1. Howard S. Becker, *Outsiders: Studies in the Sociology of Deviance* (New York: The Free Press: 1963), p. 23.
2. Harwin L. Voss, "Differential Association and Containment Theory: A Theoretical Convergence," in Harwin L. Voss, ed., *Society, Delinquency and Delinquent Behavior* (Boston: Little, Brown and Company, 1970), pp. 196–206.
3. Ibid., p. 206.
4. Lindesmith and Gagnon debunk anomie theory in its conception that retreatism causes drug addiction on the same basis as we are debunking differential association. "As the drug is continued after the initial trial, it is used progressively less for its euphoric effect, which diminishes and virtually disappears, and more and more for the purpose of staving off withdrawal symptoms, or to avoid pain." Alfred Lindesmith and John Gagnon, "Anomie and Drug Addiction," in Marshall Clinard, ed., *Anomie and Deviant Behavior: A Discussion and Critique* (New York: The Free Press, 1964), pp. 158–188.